Programming with

JAVA

A Primer

Third Edition

About the Author

E Balagurusamy is Chairman, EBG Foundation. Earlier, he was the Vice Chancellor, Anna University, Chennai. He is a teacher, trainer, and consultant in the fields of Information Technology and Management. He holds an M.E. (Hons) in Electrical Engineering and Ph. D. in Systems Engineering from the Indian Institute of Technology, Roorkee. His areas of interest include Object-Oriented Software Engineering, Electronic Business, Technology Management, Business Process Re-engineering, and Total Quality Management.

A prolific writer, he has authored a large number of research papers and several books. His best selling books, among others include:

- Programming in BASIC, 3/e
- Programming in ANSI C, 3/e
- Object-Oriented Programming with C++, 3/e
- Programming in C#
- Numerical Methods, and
- Reliability Engineering

A recipient of numerous honours and awards, he has been listed in the Directory of Who's Who of Intellectuals and in the Directory of Distinguished Leaders in Education.

Programming with
JAVA
A Primer
Third Edition

E Balagurusamy
Chairman
EBG Foundation

Tata McGraw-Hill Publishing Company Limited
NEW DELHI

McGraw-Hill Offices

New Delhi New York St Louis San Francisco Auckland Bogotá Caracas
Kuala Lumpur Lisbon London Madrid Mexico City Milan Montreal
San Juan Santiago Singapore Sydney Tokyo Toronto

 **Tata McGraw-Hill**

Published by the Tata McGraw-Hill Publishing Company Limited,
7 West Patel Nagar, New Delhi 110 008

Programming with Java – A Primer, 3/e

Fourth reprint 2007
DQLCRRYYRCZYQ

This edition can be exported from India only by the publishers,
Tata McGraw-Hill Publishing Company Limited.

ISBN-13: 978-0-07-061713-1
ISBN-10: 0-07-061713-9

Head - Higher Education: *S. Raghothaman*
Executive Publisher: *Vibha Mahajan*
Editorial Executive: *Shalini Jha*
Editorial Services Manager: *Mini Narayanan*

Deputy General Manager - Marketing: *Michael J. Cruz*
Asst. Product Manager: *Biju Ganesan*

Asst. General Manager - Production: *B L Dogra*
Manager - Production: *P L Pandita*

Typeset at Script Makers, 19, A1-B, DDA Market, Paschim Vihar, New Delhi 110 063, and printed at Gopson Papers Ltd., Noida

The **McGraw·Hill** *Companies*

Dedicated to

Dr V Krishnamurthy
Chairman
National Manufacturing Competitiveness Council
New Delhi

Contents

16.   Managing Input/Output Files in Java   287

17.   Assertion and Design by Contract   329

Preface to the Third Edition

Sun Microsystems has added many improvements and enhancements to Java since its release in 1995. Java 2, released in 1999, incorporated a number of new features to improve its performance. The latest release of Java is J2SE 5.0 (Java 2 Standard Edition, Version 5.0). J2SE 5.0, released in 2004, enhances the power and scope of the language by incorporating several important features such as generics, enhanced for loop, variable arguments in functions, boxing/unboxing, enumerations and static import.

In this third edition, the book incorporates not only the major updates of J2SE 5.0 but also improves the content wherever necessary. Debugging is an important drill in enhancing the programming skill of a learner. A section titled "Debugging Exercises" has been included at the end of each chapter to provide an opportunity to test the understanding of language features. This edition also includes two new chapters on Assertion and Java Collections.

E BALAGURUSAMY

Preface to the First Edition

Java is yet another computer language but with a difference. It is the only language that is purely object-oriented. Java's designers have borrowed the best features of many existing languages such as C and C++ and added a few new features to form a simple, easy-to-learn and object-oriented language. It is the most complete programming language available today. It is also a secure language, making it well-suited for Internet programming. One of the important reasons for Java's success, apart from its object-orientation, is the amazing functionality it adds to the World Wide Web.

Java has two lives, one as a stand-alone computer language for general-purpose programming and the other as a supporting language for Internet programming. The general-purpose programs are known as applications and programs written for Internet are known as applets. Till recently, C++ has been considered as an industry standard language for object-oriented programming. Now the battle between Java and C++ has begun. We must get ready for an industry starving for Java programmers.

This book is for novice as well as experienced programmers. While the book assumes that the reader's ultimate goal is to develop Java programs, both applications and applets, it does not assume any significant knowledge of programming on the part of the reader. If the reader is a C or C++ programmer, he or she may probably be able to read through some of the initial chapters quickly. However, a novice reader will need to go through the whole book carefully.

This book comprehensively covers all aspects of Java language. Beginning with an introduction to the language and its relationship with the Internet and World Wide Web, it explores Java's object-oriented features, and then moves on to discuss advanced topics that are unique to Java.

The concept of learning by example has been stressed throughout the book. Each major feature of the language is treated in depth followed by a complete program example to illustrate its use. Wherever necessary, concepts are explained pictorially to facilitate better understanding.

The book contains a large number of example programs. All programs have been tested and, wherever possible, the nature of output has been discussed. These programs also demonstrate the general principles of a good programming style. This book has all that a reader needs to start programming in Java right away.

Finally, this book is for everyone who is either excited about Internet or interested in Java Programming.

E BALAGURUSAMY

Acknowledgements

No book is created entirely by an individual. Many people have helped to create this book and each of their contribution has been valuable. The timely completion of this book is mainly due to the interest and persuasion of late Prof. N K Venkatasubramanian who was not only my teacher and colleague but also a good friend and guide. His contribution will be remembered forever.

I would like to thank many other individuals at PSG Institute of Management who have contributed greatly to the success of this project. Thanks are due to G P Raja, S Lalitha, K Balakrishnan, S Saravanan, J R Pratibha, and G Nithya for their valuable assistance in preparing the manuscript.

The idea of this book was planted by my wife, Sushila, while reading an article on Java in *The Hindu newspaper*. My special thanks are due to her not only for the idea but also for the encouragement and unstinted support throughout the writing of this book.

Finally, I wish to thank the publishing professionals at Tata McGraw-Hill for bringing out the book in its present form in record time.

E BALAGURUSAMY

Chapter **1**

Fundamentals of Object-Oriented Programming

1.1 Introduction

One characteristic that is constant in the software industry today is the "change". Change is one of the most critical aspects of software development and management. New tools and new approaches are announced almost every day. The impact of these developments is often very extensive and raises a number of issues that must be addressed by the software engineers. Most important among them are maintainability, reusability, portability, security, integrity, and user friendliness of software products.

To build today's complex software it is just not enough to put together a sequence of programming statements and sets of procedures and modules. We need to use sound construction techniques and program structures that are easy to comprehend, implement and modify in a wide variety of situations.

Since the invention of the computer, many programming approaches have been tried. These include techniques such as *modular programming, top-down programming, bottom-up programming* and *structured programming*. The primary motivation in each case has been the concern to handle the increasing complexity of programs that are reliable and maintainable. These techniques became popular among programmers over the last two decades.

With the advent of languages such as C, structured programming became very popular and was the paradigm of the 1980s. Structured programming proved to be a powerful tool that enabled programmers to write moderately complex programs fairly easily. However, as the programs grew larger, even the structured approach failed to show the desired results in terms of bug-free, easy-to-maintain, and reusable programs.

Object-Oriented Programming (OOP) is an approach to program organization and development, which attempts to eliminate some of the pitfalls of conventional programming methods by incorporating the best of structured programming features with several new concepts. It is a new way of organizing and developing programs and has nothing to do with any particular language. However, not all languages are suitable to implement the OOP concepts easily. Languages that support OOP features include Smalltalk, Objective C, C++, Ada and Object Pascal. C++, an extension of C language, is the most popular OOP language today. C++ is basically a procedural language with object-oriented extension. Java, a pure object-oriented language, is one of the recent languages added to this list, the latest one being C#.

1.2   Object-Oriented Paradigm

The major objective of object-oriented approach is to eliminate some of the flaws encountered in the procedural approach. OOP treats data as a critical element in the program development and does not allow it to flow freely around the system. It ties data more closely to the functions that operate on it and protects it from unintentional modification by other functions. OOP allows us to decompose a problem into a number of entities called *Objects* and then build data and functions (known as methods in Java) around these entities. The combination of data and methods make up an object (see Fig. 1.1).

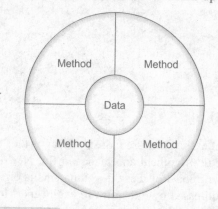

Fig. 1.1   *Object = Data + Methods*

The data of an object can be accessed only by the methods associated with that object. However, methods of one object can access the methods of other objects. Some of the features of object-oriented paradigm are:

- Emphasis is on data rather than procedure.
- Programs are divided into what are known as *Objects*.
- Data structures are designed such that they characterize the objects.
- Methods that operate on the data of an object are tied together in the data structure.
- Data is hidden and cannot be accessed by external functions.
- Objects may communicate with each other through methods.
- New data and methods can be easily added whenever necessary.
- Follows *bottom-up* approach in program design.

Object-oriented paradigm is the most recent concept among programming paradigms and still it means different things to different people. It is therefore important to have a working definition of object-oriented programming before we proceed further.

Our definition of object-oriented programming is: **Object-oriented programming is an approach that provides a way of modularizing programs by creating partitioned memory area for both data and functions that can be used as templates for creating copies of such modules on demand.** This means that an object is considered to be a partitioned area of computer memory that stores data and a set of operations that can access the data. Since the memory partitions are independent, the objects can be used in a variety of different programs without modifications.

1.3 Basic Concepts of Object-Oriented Programming

As mentioned earlier, *object-oriented* is a term, which is interpreted differently by different people. It is therefore necessary to understand some of the concepts used extensively in object-oriented programming. We shall now discuss the general concepts of OOP which form the heart of Java language.

Objects and Classes

Objects are the basic runtime entities in an object-oriented system. They may represent a person, a place, a bank account, a table of data or any item that the program may handle. They may also represent user-defined data types such as vectors and lists. Any programming problem is analyzed in terms of objects and the nature of communication between them. Program objects should be chosen such that they match closely with the real-world objects. As pointed out earlier, an object takes up space in the memory and has an associated address like a record in Pascal, or a structure in C.

When a program is executed, the objects interact by sending messages to one another. For example, 'customer' and 'account' are two objects in a banking program, then the customer object may send a message to the account object requesting for the balance. Each object contains data and code to manipulate the data. Objects can interact without having to know the details of each other's data or code. It is sufficient to know the type of message accepted and the type of response returned by the objects. Although different authors represent them differently, Fig. 1.2 shows a notation that is popularly used to represent an object in object-oriented analysis and design.

We just mentioned that objects contain data and code to manipulate that data. The entire set of data and code of an object can be made a user-defined data type using the concept of a *class*. A class may be thought of as a 'data type' and an object as a 'variable' of that data type. Once a class has been defined, we can create any number of objects belonging to that class. Each object is associated with the data of type class with which they are created. A class is thus a collection of objects of similar type. For example, mango, apple and orange are members of the class fruit. Classes are user-defined data types and behave like the built-in types of a programming language. For example, the syntax used to create an object is no different than the syntax used to create an integer object in C. If **fruit** has been defined as a class, then the statement

```
fruit mango*
```

will create an object **mango** belonging to the class **fruit**.

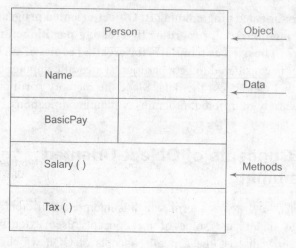

Fig. 1.2   *Representation of an object*

Data Abstraction and Encapsulation

The wrapping up of data and methods into a single unit (called class) is known as *encapsulation*. Data encapsulation is the most striking feature of a class. The data is not accessible to the outside world and only those methods, which are wrapped in the class, can access it. These methods provide the interface between the object's data and the program. This insulation of the data from direct access by the program is called *data hiding*. Encapsulation makes it possible for objects to be treated like 'black boxes', each performing a specific task without any concern for internal implementation (see Fig. 1.3).

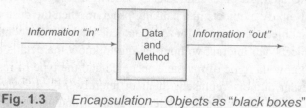

Fig. 1.3   *Encapsulation—Objects as "black boxes"*

Abstraction refers to the act of representing essential features without including the background details or explanations. Classes use the concept of abstraction and are defined as a list of abstract attributes such as size, weight and cost, and methods that operate on these attributes. They encapsulate all the essential properties of the objects that are to be created. Encapsulation is one of the three OOP principles, the other two being *inheritance* and *polymorphism*.

Inheritance

Inheritance is the process by which objects of one class acquire the properties of objects of another class. Inheritance supports the concept of hierarchical classification. For example, the bird robin is a part of the class flying bird, which is again a part of the class bird. As illustrated in Fig. 1.4, the principle behind this sort of division is that each derived class shares common characteristics with the class from which it is derived.

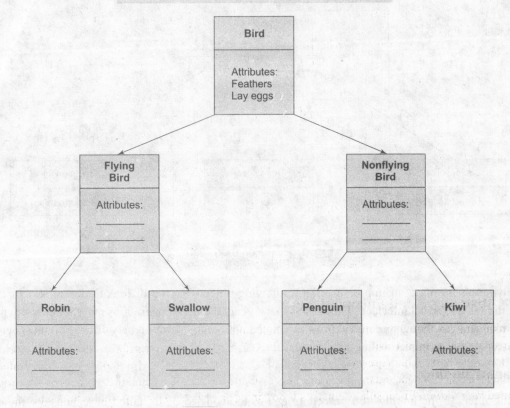

Fig. 1.4 *Property inheritance*

In OOP, the concept of inheritance provides the idea of *reusability*. This means that we can add additional features to an existing class without modifying it. This is possible by deriving a new class from the existing one. The new class will have the combined features of both the classes. Thus the real appeal and power of the inheritance mechanism is that it allows the programmer to reuse a class that is almost, but not exactly, what he wants, and to tailor the class in such a way that it does not introduce any undesirable side effects into the rest of the classes. In Java, the derived class is known as 'subclass'.

Note that each subclass defines only those features that are unique to it. Without the use of inheritance, each class would have to explicitly include all of its features.

Polymorphism

Polymorphism is another important OOP concept. Polymorphism means the ability to take more than one form. For example, an operation may exhibit different behaviour in different instances. The behaviour depends upon the types of data used in the operation. For example, consider the operation of addition. For two numbers, the operation will generate a sum. If the operands are strings, then the operation would produce a third string by concatenation. Figure 1.5 illustrates that a single function name can be used to handle different number and different types of arguments. This is something similar to a particular word having several different meanings depending on the context.

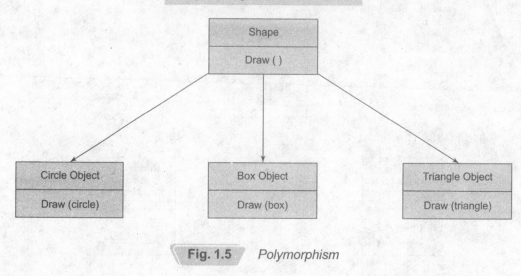

Fig. 1.5   *Polymorphism*

Polymorphism plays an important role in allowing objects having different internal structures to share the same external interface. This means that a general class of operations may be accessed in the same manner even though specific actions associated with each operation may differ. Polymorphism is extensively used in implementing inheritance.

Dynamic Binding

Binding refers to the linking of a procedure call to the code to be executed in response to the call. Dynamic binding means that the code associated with a given procedure call is not known until the time of the call at runtime. It is associated with polymorphism and inheritance. A procedure call associated with a polymorphic reference depends on the dynamic type of that reference.

Consider the procedure "draw" in Fig. 1.5. By inheritance, every object will have this procedure. Its algorithm is, however, unique to each object and so the draw procedure will be redefined in each class that defines the object. At run-time, the code matching the object under current reference will be called.

Message Communication

An object-oriented program consists of a set of objects that communicate with each other. The process of programming in an object-oriented language, therefore, involves the following basic steps:

1. Creating classes that define objects and their behaviour.
2. Creating objects from class definitions.
3. Establishing communication among objects.

Objects communicate with one another by sending and receiving information much the same way as people pass messages to one another as shown in Fig. 1.6. The concept of message passing makes it easier to talk about building systems that directly model or simulate their real-world counterparts.

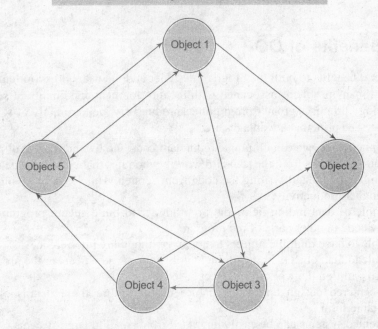

Fig. 1.6   *Network of objects communicating between them*

A message for an object is a request for execution of a procedure, and therefore will invoke a method (procedure) in the receiving object that generates the desired result, as shown in Fig. 1.7.

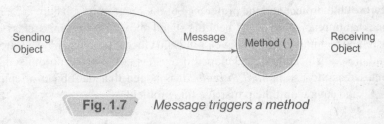

Fig. 1.7   *Message triggers a method*

Message passing involves specifying the name of the object, the name of the method (message) and the information to be sent. For example, consider the statement

```
Employee.salary (name);
```

Here, Employee is the object, salary is the message and name is the parameter that contains information.

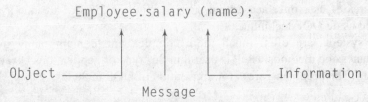

Objects have a life cycle. They can be created and destroyed. Communication with an object is feasible as long as it is alive.

1.4 Benefits of OOP

OOP offers several benefits to both the program designer and the user. Object-orientation contributes to the solution of many problems associated with the development and quality of software products. The new technology promises greater programmer productivity, better quality of software and lesser maintenance cost. The principal advantages are:

- Through inheritance, we can eliminate redundant code and extend the use of existing classes.
- We can build programs from the standard working modules that communicate with one another, rather than having to start writing the code from scratch. This leads to saving of development time and higher productivity.
- The principle of data hiding helps the programmer to build secure programs that cannot be invaded by code in other parts of the program.
- It is possible to have multiple objects to coexist without any interference.
- It is possible to map objects in the problem domain to those objects in the program.
- It is easy to partition the work in a project based on objects.
- The data-centered design approach enables us to capture more details of a model in an implementable form.
- Object-oriented systems can be easily upgraded from small to large systems.
- Message passing techniques for communication between objects make the interface descriptions with external systems much simpler.
- Software complexity can be easily managed.

While it is possible to incorporate all these features in an object-oriented system, their importance depends on the type of the project and the preference of the programmer. There are a number of issues that need to be tackled to reap some of the benefits stated above. For instance, class libraries must be available for reuse. The technology is still developing and current products may be superseded quickly. Strict controls and protocols need to be developed if reuse is not to be compromised.

A software that is easy to use is *hard to build*. It is hoped that the object-oriented programming languages like C++ and Java would help manage this problem.

1.5 Applications of OOP

OOP is one of the programming buzzwords today. There appears to be a great deal of excitement and interest among software engineers in using OOP. Applications of OOP are beginning to gain importance in many areas. The most popular application of object-oriented programming, up to now, has been in the area of user interface design such as windows. There are hundreds of windowing systems developed using OOP techniques.

Real-business systems are often much more complex and contain many more objects with complicated attributes and methods. OOP is useful in this type of applications because it can simplify a complex problem. The promising areas for application of OOP includes:

- Real-time systems
- Simulation and modelling
- Object-oriented databases

- Hypertext, hypermedia and expertext
- AI and expert systems
- Neural networks and parallel programming
- Decision support and office automation systems
- CIM/CAD/CAD system

It is believed that the richness of OOP environment will enable the software industry to improve not only the quality of software systems but also its productivity. Object-oriented technology is certainly changing the way software engineers think, analyze, design and implement systems today.

1.6 Summary

Java is an object-oriented language. It enables us not only to organize our program code into logical units called objects but also to take advantage of encapsulation, inheritance, and polymorphism. In this chapter, we have introduced the basic concepts of object-oriented programming which include

- Encapsulation,
- Inheritance, and
- Polymorphism

We also discussed briefly the benefits and applications of object-oriented programming approach.

Key Terms

Structured Programming, Object-Oriented Paradigm, Class, Object, Method, Abstraction, Encapsulation, Data Hiding, Inheritance, Reusability, Polymorphism, Dynamic Binding.

REVIEW QUESTIONS

1.1 What do you think are the major issues facing the software industry today?
1.2 Briefly discuss the software evolution during the period from 1950 to 1995.
1.3 What is object-oriented programming? How is it different from the procedure-oriented programming?
1.4 How are data and methods organized in an object-oriented program?
1.5 What are the unique advantages of an object-oriented programming paradigm?
1.6 Distinguish between the following terms:
   (a) Objects and classes
   (b) Data abstraction and data encapsulation
   (c) Inheritance and polymorphism
   (d) Dynamic binding and message passing
1.7 What kinds of things can become objects in OOP?
1.8 Describe inheritance as applied to OOP.
1.9 List a few areas of application of OOP technology.
1.10 State whether the following statements are TRUE or FALSE
   (a) In conventional, procedure-oriented programming, all data are shared by all functions.
   (b) The main emphasis of procedure-oriented programming is on algorithms rather than on data.

(c) One of the striking features of object-oriented programming is the division of programs into objects that represent real-world entities.

(d) Wrapping up of data of different types into a single unit is known as encapsulation.

(e) One problem with OOP is that once a class is created, it can never be changed.

(f) Inheritance means the ability to reuse the data values of one object by other objects.

(g) Polymorphism is extensively used in implementing inheritance.

(h) Object-oriented programs are executed much faster than conventional programs.

(i) Object-oriented systems can scale up better from small to large.

(j) Object-oriented approach cannot be used to create databases.

Chapter **2**

Java Evolution

2.1 Java History

Java is a general-purpose, object-oriented programming language developed by Sun Microsystems of USA in 1991. Originally called *Oak* by James Gosling, one of the inventors of the language, Java was designed for the development of software for consumer electronic devices like TVs, VCRs, toasters and such other electronic machines. The goal had a strong impact on the development team to make the language simple, portable and highly reliable. The Java team which included Patrick Naughton discovered that the existing languages like C and C++ had limitations in terms of both reliability and portability. However, they modelled their new language Java on C and C++ but removed a number of features of C and C++ that were considered as sources of problems and thus made Java a really simple, reliable, portable, and powerful language. Table 2.1 lists some important milestones in the development of Java.

Table 2.1 Java Milestones	
Year	Development
1990	Sun Microsystems decided to develop special software that could be used to manipulate consumer electronic devices. A team of Sun Microsystems programmers headed by James Gosling was formed to undertake this task.
1991	After exploring the possibility of using the most popular object-oriented language C++, the team announced a new language named "Oak".
1992	The team, known as Green Project team by Sun, demonstrated the application of their new language to control a list of home appliances using a hand-held device with a tiny touch-sensitive screen.

(Continued)

Table 2.1   (*Continued*)

Year	Development
1993	The World Wide Web (WWW) appeared on the Internet and transformed the text-based Internet into a graphical-rich environment. The Green Project team came up with the idea of developing Web applets (tiny programs) using the new language that could run on all types of computers connected to Internet.
1994	The team developed a Web browser called "HotJava" to locate and run applet programs on Internet. HotJava demonstrated the power of the new language, thus making it instantly popular among the Internet users.
1995	Oak was renamed "Java", due to some legal snags. Java is just a name and is not an acronym. Many popular companies including Netscape and Microsoft announced their support to Java.
1996	Java established itself not only as a leader for Internet programming but also as a general-purpose, object-oriented programming language. Sun releases Java Development Kit 1.0.
1997	Sun releases Java Development Kit 1.1 (JDK 1.1).
1998	Sun relases the Java 2 with version 1.2 of the Software Development Kit (SDK 1.2).
1999	Sun releases Java 2 Platform, Standard Edition (J2SE) and Enterprise Edition (J2EE).
2000	J2SE with SDK 1.3 was released.
2002	J2SE with SDK 1.4 was released.
2004	J2SE with JDK 5.0 (instead of JDK 1.5) was released. This is known as J2SE 5.0.

The most striking feature of the language is that it is a *platform-neutral* language. Java is the first programming language that is not tied to any particular hardware or operating system. Programs developed in Java can be executed anywhere on any system. We can call Java as a revolutionary technology because it has brought in a fundamental shift in how we develop and use programs. Nothing like this has happened to the software industry before.

 ## 2.2   Java Features

The inventors of Java wanted to design a language which could offer solutions to some of the problems encountered in modern programming. They wanted the language to be not only reliable, portable and distributed but also simple, compact and interactive. Sun Microsystems officially describes Java with the following attributes:

Java 2 Features	*Additional Features of J2SE 5.0*
• Compiled and Interpreted	• Ease of Development
• Platform-Independent and Portable	• Scalability and Performance
• Object-Oriented	• Monitoring and Manageability
• Robust and Secure	• Desktop Client
• Distributed	• Core XML Support
• Familiar, Simple and Small	• Supplementary character support
• Multithreaded and Interactive	• JDBC RowSet
• High Performance	
• Dynamic and Extensible	

Although the above appears to be a list of buzzwords, they aptly describe the full potential of the language. These features have made Java the first application language of the World Wide Web. Java will also become the premier language for general purpose stand-alone applications.

Compiled and Interpreted

Usually a computer language is either compiled or interpreted. Java combines both these approaches thus making Java a two-stage system. First, Java compiler translates source code into what is known as *bytecode* instructions. Bytecodes are not machine instructions and therefore, in the second stage, Java interpreter generates machine code that can be directly executed by the machine that is running the Java program. We can thus say that Java is both a compiled and an interpreted language.

Platform-Independent and Portable

The most significant contribution of Java over other languages is its portability. Java programs can be easily moved from one computer system to another, *anywhere* and *anytime*. Changes and upgrades in operating systems, processors and system resources will not force any changes in Java programs. This is the reason why Java has become a popular language for programming on Internet which interconnects different kinds of systems worldwide. We can download a Java applet from a remote computer onto our local system via Internet and execute it locally. This makes the Internet an extension of the user's basic system providing practically unlimited number of accessible applets and applications.

Java ensures portability in two ways. First, Java compiler generates bytecode instructions that can be implemented on any machine. Secondly, the size of the primitive data types are machine-independent.

Object-Oriented

Java is a true object-oriented language. Almost everything in Java is an *object*. All program code and data reside within objects and classes. Java comes with an extensive set of *classes,* arranged in *packages*, that we can use in our programs by inheritance. The object model in Java is simple and easy to extend.

Robust and Secure

Java is a robust language. It provides many safeguards to ensure reliable code. It has strict compile time and run time checking for data types. It is designed as a garbage-collected language relieving the programmers virtually all memory management problems. Java also incorporates the concept of exception handling which captures series errors and eliminates any risk of crashing the system.

Security becomes an important issue for a language that is used for programming on Internet. Threat of viruses and abuse of resources are everywhere. Java systems not only verify all memory access but also ensure that no viruses are communicated with an applet. The absence of pointers in Java ensures that programs cannot gain access to memory locations without proper authorization.

Distributed

Java is designed as a distributed language for creating applications on networks. It has the ability to share both data and programs. Java applications can open and access remote objects on Internet as easily as they can do in a local system. This enables multiple programmers at multiple remote locations to collaborate and work together on a single project.

Simple, Small and Familiar

Java is a small and simple language. Many features of C and C++ that are either redundant or sources of unreliable code are not part of Java. For example, Java does not use pointers, preprocessor header files, **goto** statement and many others. It also eliminates operator overloading and multiple inheritance. For more detailed comparison of Java with C and C++, refer to Section 2.3.

Familiarity is another striking feature of Java. To make the language look familiar to the existing programmers, it was modelled on C and C++ languages. Java uses many constructs of C and C++ and therefore, Java code "looks like a C++" code. In fact, Java is a simplified version of C++.

Multithreaded and Interactive

Multithreaded means handling multiple tasks simultaneously. Java supports multithreaded programs. This means that we need not wait for the application to finish one task before beginning another. For example, we can listen to an audio clip while scrolling a page and at the same time download an applet from a distant computer. This feature greatly improves the interactive performance of graphical applications.

The Java runtime comes with tools that support multiprocess synchronization and construct smoothly running interactive systems.

High Performance

Java performance is impressive for an interpreted language, mainly due to the use of intermediate bytecode. According to Sun, Java speed is comparable to the native C/C++. Java architecture is also designed to reduce overheads during runtime. Further, the incorporation of multireading enhances the overall execution speed of Java programs.

Dynamic and Extensible

Java is a dynamic language. Java is capable of dynamically linking in new class libraries, methods, and objects. Java can also determine the type of class through a query, making it possible to either dynamically link or abort the program, depending on the response.

Java programs support functions written in other languages such as C and C++. These functions are known as *native methods*. This facility enables the programmers to use the efficient functions available in these languages. Native methods are linked dynamically at runtime.

Ease of Development

Java 2 Standard Edition (J2SE) 5.0 supports features, such as Generics, Enhanced for Loop, Autoboxing or unboxing, Typesafe Enums, Varargs, Static import and Annotation. These features reduce the work of the programmer by shifting the responsibility of creating the reusable code to the compiler. The resulting source code is free from bugs because the errors made by the compiler are less when compared to those made by programmers. Thus, each of the linguistic features is designed to develop Java programs in an easier way.

Scalability and Performance

J2SE 5.0 assures a significant increase in scalability and performance by improving the startup time and reducing the amount of memory used in Java 2 runtime environment. For example, the introduction of the class, data sharing in the Hotspot Java Virtual Machine (JVM) improves the startup time by loading the core classes from the jar files into a shared archive. Memory utilization is reduced by sharing data in the shared archive among multiple JVM processes. In the earlier versions, the data was replicated in each JVM instance.

Monitoring and Manageability

Java supports a number of APIs, such as JVM Monitoring and Management API, Sun Management Platform Extension, Logging, Monitoring and Management Interface, and Java Management Extension (JMX) to monitor and manage Java applications. For example, Java provides JVM Monitoring and Management API to track the information at the application level and JVM level when deploying a large application. Java provides tools, such as jconsole, jps, jstat, and jstatd to make use of monitoring and management facilities. For example, GUI based tool called jconsole is used to monitor the JVM.

Desktop Client

J2SE 5.0 provides enhanced features to meet the requirements and challenges of the Java desktop users. It provides an improved Swing look and feel called Ocean. This feature is mainly used for developing graphics applications that require OpenGL hardware acceleration.

Miscellaneous Features

In addition to the above features, J2SE 5.0 supports the features such as:

Core XML Support   J2SE 5.0 adds a powerful XML feature to the Java platform. Java contains some special packages for interface, to instantiate Simple API for XML (SAX) and Document Object Model (DOM) parsers to parse an XML document, transform the content of an XML document, and validate an XML document against the schema.

Supplementary Character Support   Java adds the 32-bit supplementary character support as part of the Unicode 4.0 support. The supplementary characters are encoded with UTF-16 values to generate a different character called, *surrogate codepoint*.

JDBC RowSet   Java supports JDBC RowSet to send data in a tabular format between the remote components of a distributed enterprise application. JDBC RowSet contains CachedRowSet and WebRowSet objects. The CachedRowSet object is a JavaBean component which acts like a container. This object contains a number of rows of data, which are retrieved from the database. The data stored in the CachedRowSet can be directly accessed without connecting to the database or any other data source. The rows of data that are retrieved from the database can be synchronized later. The WebRowSet object can operate without being connected to the database or data source. The WebRowSet object uses XML format to read and write the rowset.

2.3   How Java Differs from C and C++

Although Java was modelled after C and C++ languages, it differs from C and C++ in many ways. Java does not incorporate a number of features available in C and C++. For the benefit of C and C++ programmers, we point out here a few major differences between C/C++ and Java languages.

Java and C

Java is a lot like C but the major difference between Java and C is that Java is an object-oriented language and has mechanism to define classes and objects. In an effort to build a simple and safe language, the Java team did not include some of the C features in Java.

- Java does not include the C unique statement keywords **sizeof**, and **typedef**.
- Java does not contain the data types **struct** and **union**.
- Java does not define the type modifiers keywords **auto, extern, register, signed,** and **unsigned**.
- Java does not support an explicit pointer type.
- Java does not have a preprocessor and therefore we cannot use # **define**, # **include**, and # **ifdef** statements.
- Java requires that the functions with no arguments must be declared with empty parenthesis and not with the **void** keyword as done in C.
- Java adds new operators such as **instanceof** and >>>.
- Java adds labelled **break** and **continue** statements.
- Java adds many features required for object-oriented programming.

Java and C++

Java is a true object-oriented language while C++ is basically C with object-oriented extension. That is what exactly the increment operator ++ indicates. C++ has maintained backward compatibility with C. It is therefore possible to write an old style C program and run it successfully under C++. Java appears to be similar to C++ when we consider only the "extension" part of C++. However, some object-oriented features of C++ make the C++ code extremely difficult to follow and maintain.

Listed below are some major C++ features that were intentionally omitted from Java or significantly modified.

- Java does not support operator overloading.
- Java does not have template classes as in C++.
- Java does not support multiple inheritance of classes. This is accomplished using a new feature called "interface".
- Java does not support global variables. Every variable and method is declared within a class and forms part of that class.
- Java does not use pointers.
- Java has replaced the destructor function with a finalize( ) function.
- There are no header files in Java.

Java also adds some new features. While C++ is a superset of C, Java is neither a superset nor a subset of C or C++. Java may be considered as a first cousin of C++ and a second cousin of C as illustrated in Fig. 2.1. A more detailed discussion on the differences between C++ and Java is available in Appendix C.

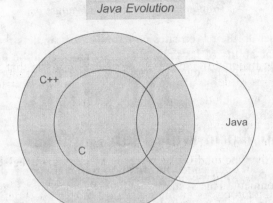

Fig. 2.1 *Overlapping of C, C++, and Java*

2.4 Java and Internet

Java is strongly associated with the Internet because of the fact that the first application program written in Java was HotJava, a Web browser to run applets on Internet. Internet users can use Java to create applet programs and run them locally using a "Java-enabled browser" such as HotJava. They can also use a Java-enabled browser to download an applet located on a computer anywhere in the Internet and run it on his local computer (see Fig. 2.2). In fact, Java applets have made the Internet a true extension of the storage system of the local computer.

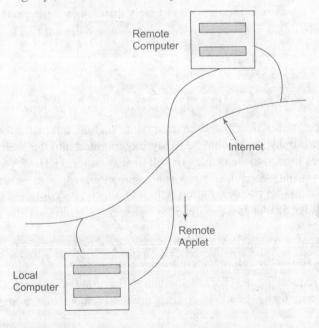

Fig. 2.2 *Downloading of applets via Internet*

Internet users can also set up their Web sites containing Java applets that could be used by other remote users of Internet. The ability of Java applets to hitch a ride on the Information Superhighway has made Java a unique programming language for the Internet. In fact, due to this, Java is popularly known as *Internet language*.

2.5   Java and World Wide Web

World Wide Web (WWW) is an open-ended information retrieval system designed to be used in the Internet's distributed environment. This system contains what are known as Web pages that provide both information and controls. Unlike a menu-driven system where we are guided through a particular direction using a decision tree structure, the Web system is open-ended and we can navigate to a new document in any direction as shown in Fig. 2.3. This is made possible with the help of a language called *Hypertext Markup Language* (HTML). Web pages contain HTML tags that enable us to find, retrieve, manipulate and display documents worldwide.

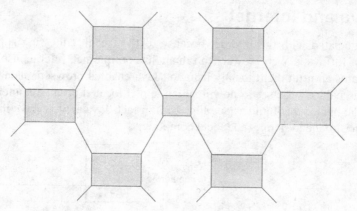

Fig. 2.3   *Web structure of information search*

Java was meant to be used in distributed environments such as Internet. Since, both the Web and Java share the same philosophy, Java could be easily incorporated into the Web system. Before Java, the World Wide Web was limited to the display of still images and texts. However, the incorporation of Java into Web pages has made it capable of supporting animation, graphics, games, and a wide range of special effects. With the support of Java, the Web has become more interactive and dynamic. On the other hand, with the support of Web, we can run a Java program on someone else's computer across the Internet.

Java communicates with a Web page through a special tag called <APPLET>. Figure 2.4 illustrates this process. The figure shows the following communication steps:

1. The user sends a request for an HTML document to the remote computer's Web server. The Web server is a program that accepts a request, processes the request, and sends the required document.

2. The HTML document is returned to the user's browser. The document contains the APPLET tag, which identifies the applet.

3. The corresponding applet bytecode is transferred to the user's computer. This bytecode had been previously created by the Java compiler using the Java source code file for that applet.
4. The Java-enabled browser on the user's computer interprets the bytecodes and provides output.
5. The user may have further interaction with the applet but with no further downloading from the provider's Web server. This is because the bytecode contains all the information necessary to interpret the applet.

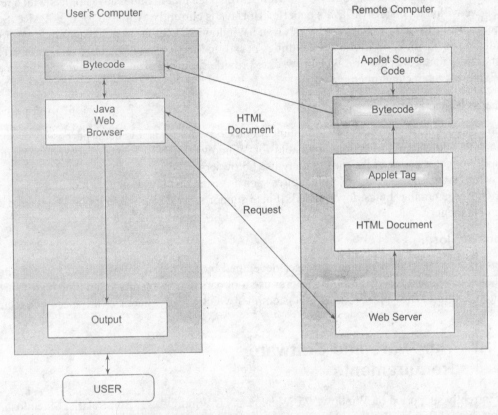

Fig. 2.4   *Java's interaction with the web*

2.6 **Web Browsers**

As pointed out earlier, the Internet is a vast sea of information represented in many formats and stored on many computers. A large portion of the Internet is organized as the World Wide Web which uses hypertext. Web browsers are used to navigate through the information found on the net. They allow us to retrieve the information spread across the Internet and display it using the hypertext markup language (HTML). Examples of Web browsers, among others, include:

- HotJava
- Netscape Navigator
- Internet Explorer

HTML documents and <APPLET> tags are discussed in detail in Chapter 14.

HotJava

HotJava is the Web browser from Sun Microsystems that enables the display of interactive content on the Web, using the Java language. HotJava is written entirely in Java and demonstrates the capabilities of the Java programming language.

When the Java language was first developed and ported to the Internet, no browsers were available that could run Java applets. Although we can view a Web page that includes Java applets with a regular browser, we will not gain any of Java's benefits. HotJava is currently available for the SPARC/Solaris platform as well as Windows 95, Windows NT and Windows XP. So far as being a Web browser goes, it is nothing special and does not offer anything special that most other Web browsers don't offer. Its biggest draw is that it was the first Web browser to provide support for the Java language, thus making the Web more dynamic and interactive.

Netscape Navigator

Netscape Navigator, from Netscape Communications Corporation, is a general-purpose browser that can run Java applets. With versions available for Windows 95, NT, Solaris and Apple Macintosh, Netscape Navigator is one of the most widely used browsers today.

Netscape Navigator has many useful features such as visual display about downloading process and indication of the number bytes downloaded. It also supports JavaScript, a scripting language used in HTML documents.

Internet Explorer

Internet Explorer is another popular browser developed by Microsoft for Windows 95, NT and XP Workstations. Both the Navigator and Explorer use tool bars, icons, menus and dialog boxes for easy navigation. Explorer uses a just-in-time (JIT) compiler which greatly increases the speed of execution.

2.7 Hardware and Software Requirements

Java is currently supported on Windows 95, Windows NT, Windows XP, Sun Solaris, Macintosh, and UNIX machines. Though, the programs and examples in this book were tested under Windows 95, the most popular operating system today, they can be implemented on any of the above systems.

The minimum hardware and software requirements for Windows 95 version of Java are as follows:

- IBM-compatible 486 system
- Minimum of 8 MB memory
- Windows 95 software
- A Windows-compatible sound card, if necessary
- A hard drive
- A CD-ROM drive
- A Microsoft-compatible mouse

2.8 Java Support Systems

It is clear from the discussion we had up to now that the operation of Java and Java-enabled browsers on the Internet requires a variety of support systems. Table 2.2 lists the systems necessary to support Java for delivering information on the Internet.

Table 2.2   Java Support Systems

Support System	Description
Internet Connection	Local computer should be connected to the Internet.
Web Server	A program that accepts requests for information and sends the required documents.
Web Browser	A program that provides access to WWW and runs Java applets.
HTML	A language for creating hypertext for the Web.
APPLET Tag	For placing Java applets in HTML document.
Java Code	Java code is used for defining Java applets.
Bytecode	Compiled Java code that is referred to in the APPLET tag and transferred to the user computer.

2.9   Java Environment

Java environment includes a large number of development tools and hundreds of classes and methods. The development tools are part of the system known as *Java Development Kit* (JDK) and the classes and methods are part of the *Java Standard Library* (JSL), also known as the *Application Programming Interface* (API).

Java Development Kit

The Java Development Kit comes with a collection of tools that are used for developing and running Java programs. They include:

- appletviewer (for viewing Java applets)
- javac (Java compiler)
- java (Java interpreter)
- javap (Java disassembler)
- javah (for C header files)
- javadoc (for creating HTML documents)
- jdb (Java debugger)

Table 2.3 lists these tools and their descriptions.

Table 2.3   Java Development Tools

Tool	Description
appletviewer	Enables us to run Java applets (without actually using a Java-compatible browser).
java	Java interpreter, which runs applets and applications by reading and interpreting bytecode files.
javac	The Java compiler, which translates Java sourcecode to bytecode files that the interpreter can understand.
javadoc	Creates HTML-format documentation from Java source code files.
javah	Produces header files for use with native methods.
javap	Java disassembler, which enables us to convert bytecode files into a program description.
jdb	Java debugger, which helps us to find errors in our programs.

The way these tools are applied to build and run application programs is illustrated in Fig. 2.5. To create a Java program, we need to create a source code file using a text editor. The source code is then compiled using the Java compiler **javac** and executed using the Java interpreter **java**. The Java debugger **jdb** is used to find errors, if any, in the source code. A compiled Java program can be converted into a source code with the help of Java disassembler **javap**. We learn more about these tools as we work through the book.

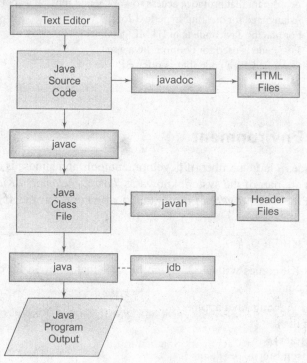

Fig. 2.5   *Process of building and running Java application programs*

Application Programming Interface

The Java Standard Library (or API) includes hundreds of classes and methods grouped into several functional packages (see Appendix G). Most commonly used packages are:

- **Language Support Package:** A collection of classes and methods required for implementing basic features of Java.
- **Utilities Package:** A collection of classes to provide utility functions such as date and time functions.
- **Input/Output Package:** A collection of classes required for input/output manipulation.
- **Networking Package:** A collection of classes for communicating with other computers via Internet.
- **AWT Package:** The Abstract Window Tool Kit package contains classes that implements platform-independent graphical user interface.
- **Applet Package:** This includes a set of classes that allows us to create Java applets.

The use of these library classes will become evident when we start developing Java programs.

2.10 Summary

In this chapter, we have introduced a brief history of Java and its salient features. Java is a pure object-oriented language introduced by Sun Microsystems of USA and has a number of characteristics that make it suitable for Internet programming. We have discussed briefly how Java can be incorporated into the World Wide Web system with the help of Web browsers.

We have also brought out some of the fundamental differences between Java and C/C++ languages. Finally, we discussed the environment required and various tools available for implementing Java programs.

Key Terms

Oak, Internet, World Wide Web, Applets, Package, Platform-neutral, Multithread, Bytecode, Dynamic linking, Native methods, HTML, Web browser, Applet tag, Web server, HotJava, Netscape Navigator, appletviewer, java, javac, javap, javah, javadoc, jdb.

REVIEW QUESTIONS

2.1   Why is Java known as platform-neutral language?
2.2   How is Java more secured than other languages?
2.3   What is multithreading? How does it improve the performance of Java?
2.4   List at least five major differences between C and Java.
2.5   List at least five major C++ features that were intentionally removed from Java.
2.6   How is Java strongly associated with the Internet?
2.7   What is World Wide Web? What is the contribution of Java to the World Wide Web?
2.8   What is Hypertext Markup Language? Describe its role in the implementation of Java applets.
2.9   Describe the various systems required for Internet programming?
2.10 Describe with a flowchart, how various Java tools are used in the application development.

Chapter **3**

Overview of Java Language

3.1   Introduction

Java is a general-purpose, object-oriented programming language. We can develop two types of Java programs:

- Stand-alone applications
- Web applets

They are implemented as shown in Fig. 3.1. Stand-alone applications are programs written in Java to carry out certain tasks on a stand-alone local computer. In fact, Java can be used to develop programs for all kinds of applications, which earlier, were developed using languages like C and C++. As pointed out earlier, HotJava itself is a Java application program. Executing a stand-alone Java program involves two steps:

1. Compiling source code into bytecode using **javac** compiler
2. Executing the bytecode program using **java** interpreter.

Applets are small Java programs developed for Internet applications. An applet located on a distant computer (Server) can be downloaded via Internet and executed on a local computer (Client) using a Java-capable browser. We can develop applets for doing everything from simple animated graphics to complex games and utilities. Since applets are embedded in an HTML (Hypertext Markup Language) document and run inside a Web page, creating and running applets are more complex than creating an application.

Stand-alone programs can read and write files and perform certain operations that applets cannot do. An applet can only run within a Web browser.

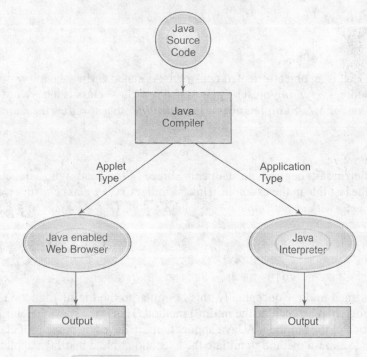

Fig. 3.1   *Two ways of using Java*

In this chapter, we shall consider some simple application programs, which would demonstrate the general structure of Java application programs. We shall also discuss here the basic elements of Java language and steps involved in executing a Java application program. Creation of applets will be discussed later in Chapter 14.

 ## 3.2   Simple Java Program

The best way to learn a new language is to write a few simple example programs and execute them. We begin with a very simple program that prints a line of text as output.

Program 3.1   *A simple Java program*

```
class SampleOne
{
  public static void main (String args[ ])
  {
     System.out.println("Java is better than C++.");
  }
}
```

Program 3.1 is perhaps the simplest of all Java programs. Nevertheless, it brings out some salient features of the language. Let us therefore discuss the program line by line and understand the unique features that constitute a Java program.

Class Declaration

The first line

```
class SampleOne
```

declares a class, which is an object-oriented construct. As stated earlier, Java is a true object-oriented language and therefore, *everything* must be placed inside a class. **class** is a keyword and declares that a new class definition follows. **SampleOne** is a Java *identifier* that specifies the name of the class to be defined.

Opening Brace

Every class definition in Java begins with an opening brace "{" and ends with a matching closing brace "}", appearing in the last line in the example. This is similar to C++ class construct. (*Note that a class definition in C++ ends with a semicolon.*)

The Main Line

The third line

```
public static void main (String args[ ])
```

defines a method named **main**. Conceptually, this is similar to the **main( )** function in C/C++. Every Java application program must include the **main( )** method. This is the starting point for the interpreter to begin the execution of the program. A Java application can have any number of classes but *only one* of them must include a **main** method to initiate the execution. (Note that Java applets will not use the **main** method at all.)

This line contains a number of keywords, **public, static** and **void**.

Public:	The keyword `public` is an access specifier that declares the `main` method as unprotected and therefore making it accessible to all other classes. This is similar to the C++ `public` modifier.
Static:	Next appears the keyword `static`, which declares this method as one that belongs to the entire class and not a part of any objects of the class. The `main` must always be declared as `static` since the interpreter uses this method before any objects are created. More about static methods and variables will be discussed later in Chapter 8.
Void:	The type modifier `void` states that the `main` method does not return any value (but simply prints some text to the screen.)

All parameters to a method are declared inside a pair of parentheses. Here, **String args[ ]** declares a parameter named **args**, which contains an array of objects of the class type **String**.

The Output Line

The only executable statement in the program is

```
System.out.println("Java is better than C++.");
```

This is similar to the **printf( )** statement of C or **cout** << construct of C++. Since Java is a true object oriented language, every method must be part of an object. The **println** method is a member of the **out** object, which is a static data member of **System** class. This line prints the string

```
Java is better than C++.
```

to the screen. The method **println** always appends a newline character to the end of the string. This means that any subsequent output will start on a new line. Note the semicolon at the end of the statement. *Every Java statement must end with a semicolon.* (Saving, compiling, and executing a Java program are discussed in Section 3.8)

3.3 More of Java

Assume that we would like to compute and print the square root of a number. A Java program to accomplish this is shown in Program 3.2. This is a slightly complex program. This program when compiled and run produces the output

        y = 2.23607

Program 3.2   *A Java program with multiple statements*

```
/*
 * More Java statements
 * This code computes square root
 */
import java.lang.Math;
class SquareRoot
{
    public static void main(String args[ ])
    {
        double x = 5 ;  // Declaration and initialization
        double y;       // Simple declaration
        y = Math.sqrt(x) ;
        System.out.println("y = " + y);
    }
}
```

The structure of the program is similar to the previous one except that it has more number of statements. The statement

        double x = 5;

declares a variable **x** and initializes it to the value 5 and the statement

        double y;

merely declares a variable **y**. Note that both of them have been declared as **double** type variables. (**double** is a data type used to represent a floating point number. Data types are discussed in the next chapter).
The statement

        y = Math.sqrt(x);

invokes the method **sqrt** of the **Math** class, computes square root of x and then assigns the result to the variable **y**. The output statement

        System.out.println("y =" + y);

displays the result on the screen as

        y = 2.23607

Note the use of + symbol. Here, the + acts as the concatenation operator of two strings. The value of **y** is converted into a string representation before concatenation.

Use of Math Functions

Note that the first statement in the program is

```
import java.lang.Math;
```

The purpose of this statement is to instruct the interpreter to load the **Math** class from the package **lang**. (This statement is similar to **#include** statement in C.) Remember, **Math** class contains the **sqrt** method required in the program.

Comments

Java permits both the single-line comments and multi-line comments available in C++. The single-line comments begin with // and end at the end of the line as shown on the lines declaring **x** and **y**. For longer comments, we can create long multi-line comments by starting with a /* and ending with a */ as shown at the beginning of the program.

 ## 3.4   An Application with Two Classes

Both the examples discussed above use only one class that contains the main method. A real-life application will generally require multiple classes. Program 3.3 illustrates a Java application with two classes.

Program 3.3   *A program with multiple classes*

```
class Room
{
     float length;
     float breadth;

     void getdata(float a, float b)
     {
         length = a;
         breadth = b;
     }
}
class RoomArea
{
    public static void main (String args[ ])
    {
        float area;
        Room room1 = new Room( ); // Creates an object room1
        room1.getdata(14, 10);    // Assigns values to length and breadth
        area = room1.length * room1. breadth;
        System.out.println ("Area =" + area);
    }
}
```

Program 3.3 defines two classes **Room** and **RoomArea**. The **Room** class defines two variables and one method to assign values to these variables. The class **RoomArea** contains the **main** method that initiates the execution.

The **main** method declares a local variable **area** and a **Room** type object **room1** and then assigns values to the data members of **Room** class by using the **getdata** method. Finally, it calculates the area and prints the results. Note the use of dot operator to access the variables and methods of **Room** class. Classes and methods are discussed in Chapter 8. The use of the keyword **new** is explained later in this Chapter.

3.5 Java Program Structure

As we have seen in the previous examples, a Java program may contain many classes of which only one class defines a main method. Classes contain data members and methods that operate on the data members of the class. Methods may contain data type declarations and executable statements. To write a Java program, we first define classes and then put them together. A Java program may contain one or more sections as shown in Fig. 3.2.

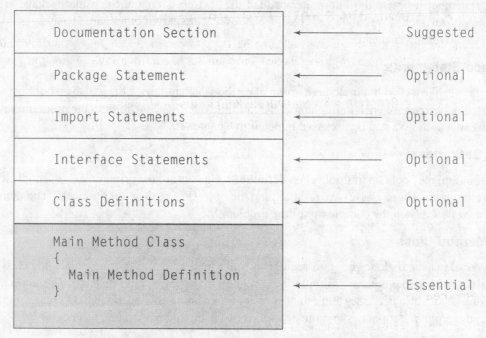

Documentation Section	←	Suggested
Package Statement	←	Optional
Import Statements	←	Optional
Interface Statements	←	Optional
Class Definitions	←	Optional

Main Method Class
{
  Main Method Definition
}
	←	Essential

Fig. 3.2 *General structure of a Java program*

Documentation Section

The documentation section comprises a set of comment lines giving the name of the program, the author and other details, which the programmer would like to refer to at a later stage. Comments must explain *why* and *what* of classes and *how* of algorithms. This would greatly help in maintaining the program. In addition to the two styles of comments discussed earlier, Java also uses a third style of comment /**....*/ known as *documentation comment*. This form of comment is used for generating documentation automatically.

Package Statement

The first statement allowed in a Java file is a **package** statement. This statement declares a **package** name and informs the compiler that the classes defined here belong to this package. Example:

```
package student;
```

The package statement is optional. That is, our classes do not have to be part of package. More about packages will be discussed in Chapter 11.

Import Statements

The next thing after a package statement (but before any class definitions) may be a number of **import** statements. This is similar to the **#include** statement in C. Example:

```
import student.test;
```

This statement instructs the interpreter to load the **test** class contained in the package **student**. Using import statements, we can have access to classes that are part of other named packages. More on import statements in Chapter 11.

Interface Statements

An interface is like a class but includes a group of method declarations. This is also an optional section and is used only when we wish to implement the multiple inheritance feature in the program. Interface is a new concept in Java and is discussed in detail in Chapter 10.

Class Definitions

A Java program may contain multiple class definitions. Classes are the primary and essential elements of a Java program. These classes are used to map the objects of real-world problems. The number of classes used depends on the complexity of the problem.

Main Method Class

Since every Java stand-alone program requires a **main** method as its starting point, this class is the essential part of a Java program. A simple Java program may contain only this part. The **main** method creates objects of various classes and establishes communications between them. On reaching the end of **main**, the program terminates and the control passes back to the operating system.

 ## 3.6 Java Tokens

A Java program is basically a collection of classes. A class is defined by a set of declaration statements and methods containing executable statements (see Fig. 3.3). Most statements contain expressions, which describe the actions carried out on data. Smallest individual units in a program are known as *tokens*. The compiler recognizes them for building up expressions and statements.

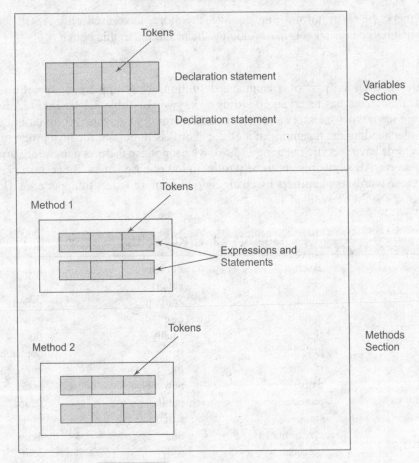

Fig. 3.3   *Elements of Java class*

In simple terms, a Java program is a collection of tokens, comments and white spaces. Java language includes five types of tokens. They are:

- Reserved Keywords
- Identifiers
- Literals
- Operators
- Separators

Java Character Set

The smallest units of Java language are the characters used to write Java tokens. These characters are defined by the *Unicode* character set, an emerging standard that tries to create characters for a large number of scripts worldwide.

The Unicode is a 16-bit character coding system and currently supports more than 34,000 defined characters derived from 24 languages from America, Europe, Middle East, Africa and Asia (including India). However, most of us use only the basic ASCII characters, which include letters, digits and punctuation marks, used in normal English. We, therefore, have used only ASCII character set (a subset of UNICODE character set) in developing the programs in this book.

Keywords

Keywords are an essential part of a language definition. They implement specific features of the language. Java language has reserved 50 words as keywords. Table 3.1 lists these keywords. These keywords, combined with operators and separators according to a syntax, form definition of the Java language. Understanding the meanings of all these words is important for Java programmers.

Since keywords have specific meaning in Java, we cannot use them as names for variables, classes, methods and so on. All keywords are to be written in lower-case letters. Since Java is case-sensitive, one can use these words as identifiers by changing one or more letters to upper case. However, it is a bad practice and should be avoided.

Table 3.1　Java Keywords

abstract	assert	boolean	break
byte	case	catch	char
class	const	continue	default
do	double	else	enum
extends	final	finally	float
for	goto	if	implements
import	instanceof	int	interface
long	native	new	package
private	protected	public	return
short	static	strictfp	super
switch	synchronized	this	throw
throws	transient	try	void
volatile	while		

Note:　We should also not attempt to use the `boolean` values `true` and `false` or `null` as names in our programs.

Identifiers

Identifiers are programmer-designed tokens. They are used for naming classes, methods, variables, objects, labels, packages and interfaces in a program. Java identifiers follow the following rules:

1. They can have alphabets, digits, and the underscore and dollar sign characters.
2. They must not begin with a digit.
3. Uppercase and lowercase letters are distinct.
4. They can be of any length.

Identifier must be meaningful, short enough to be quickly and easily typed and long enough to be descriptive and easily read. Java developers have followed some naming conventions.

- Names of all public methods and instance variables start with a leading lowercase letter.
  Examples:

```
average
sum
```

- When more than one words are used in a name, the second and subsequent words are marked with a leading uppercase letters. Examples:

```
dayTemperature
firstDayOfMonth
totalMarks
```

- All private and local variables use only lowercase letters combined with underscores. Examples:

```
length
batch_strength
```

- All classes and interfaces start with a leading uppercase letter (and each subsequent word with a leading uppercase letter). Examples:

```
Student
HelloJava
Vehicle
MotorCycle
```

- Variables that represent constant values use all uppercase letters and underscores between words. Examples:

```
TOTAL
F_MAX
PRINCIPAL_AMOUNT
```

They are like symbolic constants in C.

It should be remembered that all these are conventions and not rules. We may follow our own conventions as long as we do not break the basic rules of naming identifiers.

Literals

Literals in Java are a sequence of characters (digits, letters, and other characters) that represent constant values to be stored in variables. Java language specifies five major types of literals. They are:

- Integer literals
- Floating_point literals
- Character literals
- String literals
- Boolean literals

Each of them has a type associated with it. The type describes how the values behave and how they are stored. We will discuss these in detail when we deal with data types and constants in the next chapter.

Operators

An operator is a symbol that takes one or more arguments and *operates* on them to produce a result. Operators are of many types and are considered in detail in Chapter 5.

Separators

Separators are symbols used to indicate where groups of code are divided and arranged. They basically define the shape and function of our code. Table 3.2 lists separators and their functions.

Table 3.2 Java Separators	
Name	*What it is used for*
parentheses ( )	Used to enclose parameters in method definition and invocation, also used for defining precedence in expressions, containing expressions for flow control, and surrounding cast types.
braces { }	Used to contain the values of automatically initialized arrays and to define a block of code for classes, methods and local scopes
brackets [ ]	Used to declare array types and for dereferencing array values
semicolon ;	Used to separate statements
comma ,	Used to separate consecutive identifiers in a variable declaration, also used to chain statements together inside a 'for' statement
period .	Used to separate package names from sub-packages and classes; also used to separate a variable or method from a reference variable.

3.7 Java Statements

The statements in Java are like sentences in natural languages. A statement is an executable combination of tokens ending with a semicolon (;) mark. Statements are usually executed in sequence in the order in which they appear. However, it is possible to control the flow of execution, if necessary, using special statements. Java implements several types of statements as illustrated in Fig. 3.4 and described in Table 3.3. They are considered in depth as and when they are encountered.

Table 3.3 Summary of Java Statements		
Statement	*Description*	*Remarks*
Empty Statement	These do nothing and are used during program development as a place holder.	Same as C and C++
Labelled Statement	Any Statement may begin with a label. Such labels must not be keywords, already declared local variables or previously used labels in this module. Labels in Java are used as the arguments of Jump statements, which are described later in this list.	Identical to C and C++ except their use with jump statements
Expression Statement	Most statements are expression statements. Java has seven types of Expression statements: **Assignment, Pre-Increment, Pre-Decrement, Post-Increment, Post-Decrement, Method Call and Allocation Expression.**	Same as C++
Selection Statement	These select one of several control flows. There are Three types of selection statements in Java: **if, if-else,** and **switch**.	Same as C and C++

(Continued)

Table 3.3 *(Continued)*

Statement	Description	Remarks
Iteration Statement	These specify how and when looping will take place. There are three types of iteration statements; **while, do** and **for**.	Same as C and C++ except for jumps and labels
Jump Statement	Jump Statements pass control to the beginning or end of the current block, or to a labeled statement. Such labels must be in the same block, and **continue** labels must be on an iteration statement. The four types of Jump statement are **break, continue, return** and **throw**.	C and C++ do not use labels with jump statements
Synchronization Statement	These are used for handling issues with multithreading.	Now available in C and C++
Guarding Statement	Guarding statements are used for safe handling of code that may cause exceptions (such as division by zero). These statements use the keywords **try, catch,** and **finally**.	Same as in C++ except finally statement.

3.8   Implementing a Java Program

Implementation of a Java application program involves a series of steps. They include:

- Creating the program
- Compiling the program
- Running the program

Remember that, before we begin creating the program, the Java Development Kit (JDK) must be properly installed on our system.

Creating the Program

We can create a program using any text editor. Assume that we have entered the following program:

Program 3.4   *Another simple program for testing*

```
class Test
{
    public static void main (String args[ ])
    {
        System.out.println("Hellow!");
        System.out.println("Welcome to the world of Java.");
        System.out.println("Let us learn Java.");
    }
}
```

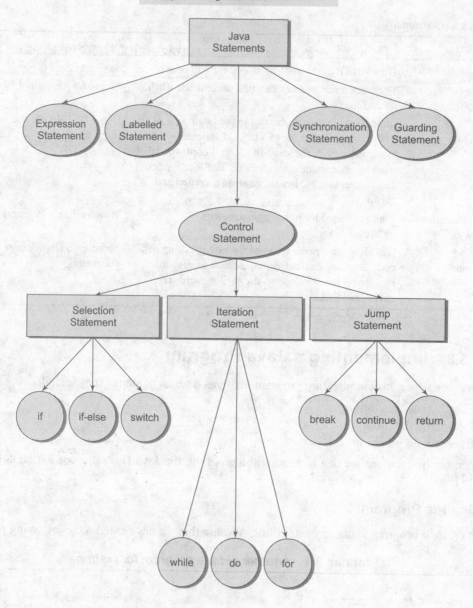

Fig. 3.4   *Classification of Java statements*

We must save this program in a file called **Test.java** ensuring that the filename contains the class name properly. This file is called the *source file*. Note that all Java source files will have the extension **java**. Note also that if a program contains multiple classes, the file name must be the classname of the class containing the **main** method.

Compiling the Program

To compile the program, we must run the Java Compiler **javac,** with the name of the source file on the command line as shown below:

```
javac Test.java
```

If everything is OK, the **javac** compiler creates a file called **Test.class** containing the bytecodes of the program. Note that the compiler automatically names the bytecode file as

```
<classname> .class
```

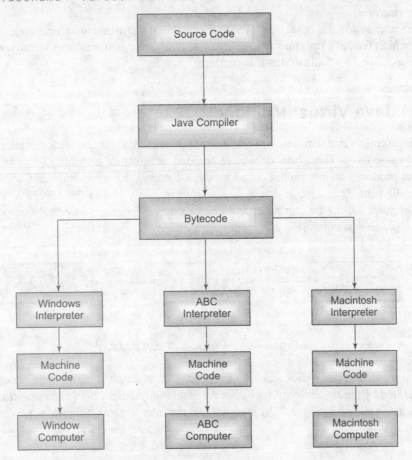

Fig. 3.5 *Implementation of Java programs*

Running the Program

We need to use the Java interpreter to run a stand-alone program. At the command prompt, type

```
java Test
```

Now, the interpreter looks for the main method in the program and begins execution from there. When executed, our program displays the following:

```
Hello!
Welcome to the world of Java.
Let us learn Java.
```

Note that we simply type "Test" at the command line and not "Test.class" or "Test.java".

Machine Neutral

The compiler converts the source code files into bytecode files. These codes are machine-independent and therefore can be run on any machine. That is, a program compiled on an IBM machine will run on a Macintosh machine.

Java interpreter reads the bytecode files and translates them into machine code for the specific machine on which the Java program is running. The interpreter is therefore specially written for each type of machine. Figure 3.5 illustrates this concept.

3.9   Java Virtual Machine

All language compilers translate source code into *machine code* for a specific computer. Java compiler also does the same thing. Then, how does Java achieve architecture neutrality? The answer is that the Java compiler produces an intermedia code known as *bytecode* for a machine that does not exist. This machine is called the *Java Virtual Machine* and it exists only inside the computer memory. It is a simulated computer within the computer and does all major functions of a real computer. Figure 3.6 illustrates the process of compiling a Java program into bytecode which is also referred to as *virtual machine code*.

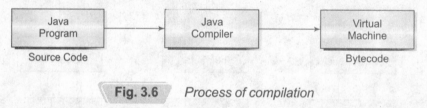

Fig. 3.6   *Process of compilation*

The virtual machine code is not machine specific. The machine specific code (known as machine code) is generated by the Java interpreter by acting as an intermediary between the virtual machine and the real machine as shown in Fig. 3.7. Remember that the interpreter is different for different machines.

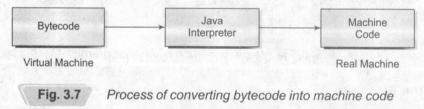

Fig. 3.7   *Process of converting bytecode into machine code*

Figure 3.8 illustrates how Java works on a typical computer. The Java object framework (Java API) acts as the intermediary between the user programs and the virtual machine which in turn acts as the intermediary between the operating system and the Java object framework.

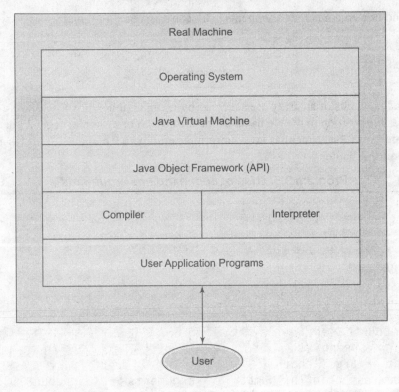

Fig. 3.8   *Layers of interactions for Java programs*

3.10   Command Line Arguments

There may be occasions when we may like our program to act in a particular way depending on the input provided at the time of execution. This is achieved in Java programs by using what are known as command line arguments. Command line arguments are parameters that are supplied to the application program at the time of invoking it for execution. It may be recalled that Program 3.4 was invoked for execution of the command line as follows:

```
java Test
```

Here, we have not supplied any command line arguments. Even if we supply arguments, the program does not know what to do with them.

We can write Java programs that can receive and use the arguments provided in the command line. Recall the signature of the **main( )** method used in our earlier example programs:

```
public static void main (String args[ ])
```

As pointed out earlier, **args** is declared as an array of strings (known as string objects). Any arguments provided in the command line (at the time of execution) are passed to the array **args** as its elements. We can simply access the array elements and use them in the program as we wish. For example, consider the command line

```
java Test BASIC FORTRAN C++ Java
```

This command line contains four arguments. These are assigned to **the** array **args** as follows:

```
BASIC       ──────→   args [0]
FORTRAN     ──────→   args [1]
C++         ──────→   args [2]
Java        ──────→   args [3]
```

The individual elements of an array are accessed by using an index or subscript like **args[i]**. The value of i denotes the position of the elements inside the array. For example, **args[2]** denotes the third element and represents C++. Note that Java subscripts begin with 0 and not 1. (Arrays and strings are discussed in detail in Chapter 9.)

Program 3.5　*Use of command line arguments*

```
/*
 * This program uses command line
 * arguments as input.
 */
Class ComLineTest
{
    public static void main (String args[ ])
    {
        int count, i=0;
        String string;
        count = args.length;
        System.out.println("Number of arguments = " + count);
        while (i < count)
        {
            string = args[i];
            i = i + 1;
            System.out.println(i+ "  :  " + "Java is" + string+ "!");
        }
    }
}
```

Program 3.5 illustrates the use of command line arguments. Compile and run the program with the command line as follows:

```
java ComLineTest Simple Object_Oriented Distributed Robust
Secure Portable Multithreaded Dynamic
```

Upon execution, the command line arguments Simple, Object_Oriented, etc. are passed to the program through the array **args** as discussed earlier. That is the element **args[0]** contains Simple, **args[1]** contains Object_Oriented, and so on. These elements are accessed using the loop variable i as an index like

```
name = args[i]
```

The index **i** is incremented using a **while** loop until all the arguments are accessed. The number of arguments is obtained by statement

```
count = args.length;
```

The output of the program would be as follows:

```
Number of arguments = 8
    1  :  Java is Simple!
    2  :  Java is Object_Oriented!
    3  :  Java is Distributed!
    4  :  Java is Robust!
    5  :  Java is Secure!
    6  :  Java is Portable!
    7  :  Java is Multithreaded!
    8  :  Java is Dynamic!
```

Note how the output statement concatenates the strings while printing.

3.11 Programming Style

Java is a *freeform* language. We need not have to indent any lines to make the program work properly. Java system does not care where on the line we begin typing. While this may be a license for bad programming, we should try to use this fact to our advantage for producing readable programs. Although several alternate styles are possible, we should select one and try to use it with total consistency.

For example, the statement

```
System.out.println("Java is Wonderful!")
```

can be written as

```
System.out.println
("Java is Wonderful!");
```

or, even as

```
System
.
out
println
(
"Java is Wonderful!"
);
```

In this book, we follow the format used in the example programs of this chapter.

3.12 Summary

Java is a general-purpose, object-oriented language. In this chapter, we have discussed some simple application programs to familiarize the readers with basic Java structure and syntax. We have also discussed the basic elements of the Java language and steps involved in creating and executing a Java application program.

Key Terms

class, Identifier, main, public, static, void, string, args, println, double, Math, sqrt, package, import, Interface, Tokens, Literals, Operators, Separators, Unicode, Keyword, Statement, Virtual Machine, Command Line Arguments, Freeform.

REVIEW QUESTIONS

3.1　Describe the structure of a typical Java program.

3.2　Why do we need the import statement?

3.3　What is the task of the **main** method in a Java program?

3.4　What is a token? List the various types of tokens supported by Java.

3.5　Why can't we use a keyword as a variable name?

3.6　Enumerate the rules for creating identifiers in Java.

3.7　What are the conventions followed in Java for naming identifiers? Give examples.

3.8　What are separators? Describe the various separators used in Java.

3.9　What is a statement? How do the Java statements differ from those of C and C++?

3.10　Describe in detail the steps involved in implementing a stand-alone program.

3.11　What are command line arguments? How are they useful?

3.12　Java is freeform language. Comment.

Chapter **4**

Constants, Variables, and Data Types

4.1 Introduction

A programming language is designed to process certain kinds of *data* consisting of numbers, characters and strings and to provide useful output known as *information*. The task of processing data is accomplished by executing a sequence of instructions constituting a *program*. These instructions are formed using certain symbols and words according to some rigid rules known as *syntax rules* (or *grammar*). Every program instruction must conform precisely to the syntax rules of the language.

Like any other language, Java has its own vocabulary and grammar. In this chapter, we will discuss the concepts of constants and variables and their types as they relate to Java language.

4.2 Constants

Constants in Java refer to fixed values that do not change during the execution of a program. Java supports several types of constants as illustrated in Fig. 4.1.

Integer Constants

An *integer* constant refers to a sequence of digits. There are three types of integers, namely, *decimal* integer, *octal* integer and *hexadecimal* integer.

Decimal integers consist of a set of digits, 0 through 9, preceded by an optional minus sign. Valid examples of decimal integer constants are:

```
123 -321  0     654321
```

Embedded spaces, commas, and non-digit characters are not permitted between digits. For example,

```
     15 750      20,000      $1000
```

are illegal numbers.

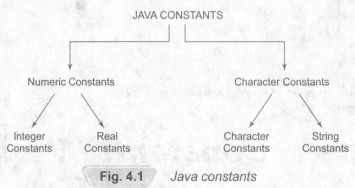

Fig. 4.1   *Java constants*

An *octal* integer constant consists of any combination of digits from the set 0 through 7, with a leading 0. Some examples of octal integer are:

```
     037      0      0435      0551
```

A sequence of digits preceded by 0x or 0X is considered as *hexadecimal* integer (hex integer). They may also include alphabets A through F or a through f. A letter A through F represents the numbers 10 through 15. Following are the examples of valid hex integers.

```
     0X2      0X9F   0xbcd    0x
```

We rarely use octal and hexadecimal numbers in programming.

Real Constants

Integer numbers are inadequate to represent quantities that vary continuously, such as distances, heights, temperatures, prices, and so on. These quantities are represented by numbers containing fractional parts like 17.548. Such numbers are called *real* (or *floating point*) constants. Further examples of real constants are:

```
          0.0083      –0.75      435.36
```

These numbers are shown in *decimal notation*, having a whole number followed by a decimal point and the fractional part, which is an integer. It is possible that the number may not have digits before the decimal point or digits after the decimal point. That is,

```
     215.      .95      –.71
```

are all valid real numbers.

A real number may also be expressed in *exponential* (or *scientific*) *notation*. For example, the value 215.65 may be written as 2.1565e2 in exponential notation. e2 means multiply by 10^2. The general form is:

```
     mantissa e exponent
```

The *mantissa* is either a real number expressed in *decimal notation* or an integer. The *exponent* is an integer with an optional *plus* or *minus* sign. The letter e separating the mantissa and the exponent can be written in either lowercase or uppercase. Since the exponent causes the decimal point to "float", this notation is said to represent a real number in *floating point form*. Examples of legal floating point constants are:

    0.65e4   12e-2   1.5e+5   3.18E3   −1.2E-1

Embedded white (blank) space is not allowed, in any numeric constant.

Exponential notation is useful for representing numbers that are either very large or very small in magnitude. For example, 7500000000 may be written as 7.5E9 or 75E8. Similarly, −0.000000368 is equivalent to −3.68E-7.

A floating point constant may thus comprise four parts:

- a whole number
- a decimal point
- a fractional part
- an exponent

Single Character Constants

A single character constant (or simply character constant) contains a single character enclosed within a pair of single quote marks. Examples of character constants are:

    '5'   'X'   ';'   ' '

Note that the character constant '5' is not the same as the *number* 5. The last constant is a blank space.

String Constants

A string constant is a sequence of characters enclosed between double quotes. The characters may be alphabets, digits, special characters and blank spaces. Examples are:

    "Hello Java"   "1997"   "WELL DONE"   "?...!"   "5+3"   "X"

Backslash Character Constants

Java supports some special backslash character constants that are used in output methods. For example, the symbol '\n' stands for newline character. A list of such backslash character constants is given in Table 4.1. Note that each one of them represents one character, although they consist of two characters. These characters combinations are known as *escape sequences*.

Table 4.1   Backslash Character Constants

Constant	Meaning
'\b'	back space
'\f'	form feed
'\n'	new line
'\r'	carriage return
'\t'	horizontal tab
'\''	single quote
'\"'	double quote
'\\'	backslash

4.3 Variables

A *variable* is an identifier that denotes a storage location used to store a data value. Unlike constants that remain unchanged during the execution of a program, a variable may take different values at different times during the execution of the program. In Chapter 3, we had used several variables. For instance, we used variables **length** and **breadth** to store the values of length and breadth of a room.

A variable name can be chosen by the programmer in a meaningful way so as to reflect what it represents in the program. Some examples of variable names are:

- average
- height
- total_height
- classStrength

As mentioned earlier, variable names may consist of alphabets, digits, the underscore(_) and dollar characters, subject to the following conditions:

1. They must not begin with a digit.
2. Uppercase and lowercase are distinct. This means that the variable **Total** is not the same as **total** or **TOTAL**.
3. It should not be a keyword.
4. White space is not allowed.
5. Variable names can be of any length.

4.4 Data Types

Every variable in Java has a data type. Data types specify the size and type of values that can be stored. Java language is rich in its *data types*. The variety of data types available allow the programmer to select the type appropriate to the needs of the application. Data types in Java under various categories are shown in Fig. 4.2. Primitive types (also called *intrinsic* or *built-in* types) are discussed in detail in

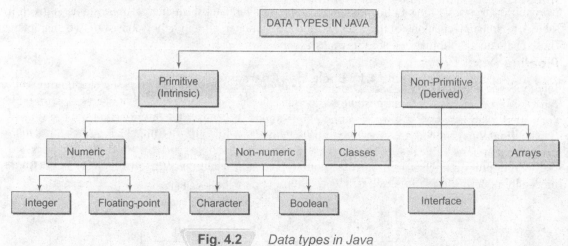

Fig. 4.2 *Data types in Java*

this chapter. Derived types (also known as *reference* types) are discussed later as and when they are encountered.

Integer Types

Integer types can hold whole numbers such as 123, -96, and 5639. The size of the values that can be stored depends on the integer data type we choose. Java supports four types of integers as shown in Fig. 4.3. They are **byte, short, int**, and **long**. Java does not support the concept of *unsigned* types and therefore all Java values are signed meaning they can be positive or negative. Table 4.3 shows the memory size and range of all the four integer data types.

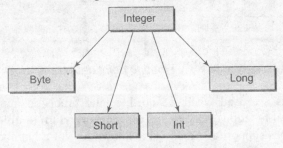

Fig. 4.3   *Integer data types*

Table 4.3   Size and Range of Integer Types

Type	Size	Minimum value	Maximum value
byte	One byte	−128	127
short	Two bytes	−32, 768	32, 767
int	Four bytes	−2, 147, 483, 648	2, 147, 483, 647
long	Eight bytes	−9, 223, 372, 036, 854, 775, 808	9, 223, 372, 036, 854, 775, 807

It should be remembered that wider data types require more time for manipulation and therefore it is advisable to use smaller data types, wherever possible. For example, instead of storing a number like 50 in an **int** type variable, we must use a **byte** variable to handle this number. This will improve the speed of execution of the program.

We can make integers **long** by appending the letter L or l at the end of the number. Example:

```
123L    or    123l
```

Floating Point Types

Integer types can hold only whole numbers and therefore we use another type known as *floating point* type to hold numbers containing fractional parts such as 27.59 and −1.375 (known as floating point constants). There are two kinds of floating point storage in Java as shown in Fig. 4.4.

The **float** type values are *single-precision* numbers while the **double** types represent *double-precision* numbers. Table 4.4 gives the size and range of these two types.

Floating point numbers are treated as double-precision quantities. To force them to be in single-precision mode, we must append f or F to the numbers. Example:

```
1.23f
7.56923e5F
```

Table 4.4 Size and Range of Floating Point Types

Type	Size	Minimum value	Maximum value
float	4 bytes	3.4e-038	3.4e+038
double	8 bytes	1.7e-308	1.7e+308

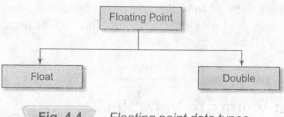

Fig. 4.4　*Floating point data types*

Double-precision types are used when we need greater precision in storage of floating point numbers. All mathematical functions, such as sin, cos and sqrt return **double** type values.

Floating point data types support a special value known as Not-a-Number (NaN). NaN is used to represent the result of operations such as dividing zero by zero, where an actual number is not produced. Most operations that have NaN as an operand will produce NaN as a result.

Character Type

In order to store character constants in memory, Java provides a character data type called **char**. The char type assumes a size of 2 bytes but, basically, it can hold only a single character.

Boolean Type

Boolean type is used when we want to test a particular condition during the execution of the program. There are only two values that a boolean type can take: **true** or **false**. Boolean type is denoted by the keyword **boolean** and uses only one bit of storage.

All comparison operators (see Chapter 5) return boolean type values. Boolean values are often used in selection and iteration statements. The words **true** and **false** cannot be used as identifiers.

4.5 Declaration of Variables

In Java, variables are the names of storage locations. After designing suitable variable names, we must declare them to the compiler. Declaration does three things:

1. It tells the compiler what the variable name is.
2. It specifies what type of data the variable will hold.
3. The place of declaration (in the program) decides the scope of the variable.

A variable must be declared before it is used in the program.

A variable can be used to store a value of any data type. That is, the name has nothing to do with the type. Java allows any properly formed variable to have any declared data type. The declaration statement defines the type of variable. The general form of declaration of a variable is:

```
type variable1, variable2, ......... variableN;
```

Variables are separated by commas. A declaration statement must end with a semicolon. Some valid declarations are:

```
int      count;
float    x, y;
double   pi;
byte     b;
char     c1, c2, c3;
```

 ## 4.6   Giving Values to Variables

A variable must be given a value after it has been declared but before it is used in an expression. This can be achieved in two ways:

1. By using an assignment statement
2. By using a read statement

Assignment Statement

A simple method of giving value to a variable is through the assignment statement as follows:

```
variableName = value;
```

For example:

```
initialValue  = 0;
finalValue    = 100;
yes           = 'x';
```

We can also string assignment expressions as shown below:

```
x = y = z = 0;
```

It is also possible to assign a value to a variable at the time of its declaration. This takes the form:

```
type variableName = value;
```

Examples:

```
int      finalValue  =   100;
char     yes         =   'x';
double   total       =   75.36;
```

The process of giving initial values to variables is known as the *initialization*. The ones that are not initialized are automatically set to zero.

The following are valid Java statements:

```
float  x, y, z;          // declares three float variables
int    m = 5, n = 10;    // declares and initialises two int variables
int    m, n = 10;        // declares m and n and initialises n
```

Read Statement

We may also give values to variables interactively through the keyboard using the **readLine( )** method as illustrated in Program 4.1.

Program 4.1   *Reading data from keyboard*

```java
import java.io.DataInputStream;

class Reading
{
  public static void main(String args[])
  {
    DataInputStream in = new DataInputStream(System.in);
    int intNumber = 0;
    float floatNumber = 0.0f;

    try
    {
      System.out.println("Enter an Integer: ");
      intNumber = Integer.parseInt(in.readLine());
      System.out.println("Enter a float number: ");
      floatNumber =
              Float.valueOf(in.readLine()) .floatValue();
    }

    catch (Exception e) { }

    System.out.println("intNumber = " + intNumber);
    System.out.println("floatNumber = " + floatNumber);
  }
}
```

The interactive input and output of Program 4.1 are shown below:

```
Enter an integer:
123
Enter a float number:
123.45
intNumber = 123
floatNumber = 123.45
```

The **readLine( )** method (which is invoked using an object of the class **DataInputStream**) reads the input from the keyboard as a string which is then converted to the corresponding data type using the data type wrapper classes. See Chapter 9 for more about wrapper classes.

Note that we have used the keywords **try** and **catch** to handle any errors that might occur during the reading process. Java requires this. See Chapter 13 for more details on error handling.

4.7   Scope of Variables

Java variables are actually classified into three kinds:

- *instance* variables,
- *class* variables, and
- *local* variables.

Instance and class variables are declared inside a class. Instance variables are created when the objects are instantiated and therefore they are associated with the objects. They take different *values* for each object. On the other hand, class variables are global to a class and belong to the entire set of objects that class creates. Only one memory location is created for each class variable. Instance and class variables will be considered in detail in Chapter 8.

Variables declared and used inside methods are called *local variables*. They are called so because they are not available for use outside the method definition. Local variables can also be declared inside program blocks that are defined between an opening brace { and a closing brace }. These variables are visible to the program only from the beginning of its program block to the end of the program block. When the program control leaves a block, all the variables in the block will cease to exist. The area of the program where the variable is accessible (i.e., usable) is called its *scope*.

We can have program blocks within other program blocks (called *nesting*) as shown in Fig. 4.5.

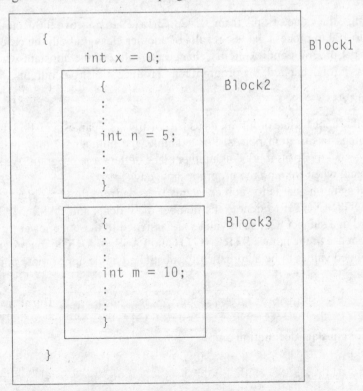

Fig. 4.5   *Nested program blocks*

Each block can contain its own set of local variable declarations. We cannot, however, *declare* a variable to have the same name as one in an outer block. In Fig. 4.5, the variable **x** declared in Block1 is available in all the three blocks. However, the variable **n** declared in Block2 is available only in Block2, because it goes out of the scope at the end of Block2. Similarly, **m** is accessible only in Block3.

Note that we cannot declare the variable **x** again in Block2 or Block3 (This is perfectly legal in C and C++).

4.8   Symbolic Constants

We often use certain unique constants in a program. These constants may appear repeatedly in a number of places in the program. One example of such a constants is 3.142, representing the value of the mathematical constant "pi". Another example is the total number of students whose mark-sheets are analysed by a 'test analysis program'. The number of students, say 50, may be used for calculating the class total, class average, standard deviation, etc. We face two problems in the subsequent use of such programs. They are:

1. Problem in modification of the program.
2. Problem in understanding the program.

Modifiability

We may like to change the value of "pi" from 3.142 to 3.14159 to improve the accuracy of calculations or the number 50 to 100 to process the test results of another class. In both the cases, we will have to search throughout the program and explicitly change the value of the constant wherever it has been used. If any value is left unchanged, the program may produce disastrous outputs.

Understandability

When a numeric value appears in a program, its use is not always clear, especially when the same value means different things in different places. For example, the number 50 may mean the number of students at one place and the 'pass marks' at another place of the same program. We may forget what a certain number meant, when we read the program some days later.

Assignment of a symbolic name to such constants frees us from these problems. For example, we may use the name **STRENGTH** to denote the number of students and **PASS_MARK** to denote the pass marks required in a subject. Constant values are assigned to these names at the beginning of the program. Subsequent use of the names **STRENGTH** and **PASS_MARK** in the program has the effect of causing their defined values to be automatically substituted at the appropriate points. A constant is declared as follows:

```
final type symbolic-name = value;
```

Valid examples of constant declaration are:

```
final int    STRENGTH = 100;
final int    PASS_MARK = 50;
final float  PI = 3.14159;
```

Note that:

1. Symbolic names take the same form as variable names. But, they are written in CAPITALS to visually distinguish them from normal variable names. This is only a convention, not a rule.
2. After declaration of symbolic constants, they should not be assigned any other value within the program by using an assignment statement. For example, STRENGTH = 200; is illegal.
3. Symbolic constants are declared for types. This is not done in C and C++ where symbolic constants are defined using the # define statement.
4. They can NOT be declared inside a method. They should be used only as class data members in the beginning of the class.

4.9 Type Casting

We often encounter situations where there is a need to store a value of one type into a variable of another type. In such situations, we must cast the value to be stored by proceeding it with the type name in parentheses. The syntax is:

```
type variable1 = (type) variable2;
```

The process of converting one data type to another is called *casting*.

Examples:

```
int    m     = 50;
byte   n     = (byte)m;
long   count = (long)m;
```

Casting is often necessary when a method returns a type different than the one we require.

Four integer types can be cast to any other type except boolean. Casting into a smaller type may result in a loss of data. Similarly, the **float** and **double** can be cast to any other type except boolean. Again, casting to smaller type can result in a loss of data. Casting a floating point value to an integer will result in a loss of the fractional part. Table 4.5 lists those casts, which are guaranteed to result in no loss of information.

Table 4.5   Casts that Results in No Loss of Information

From	To
byte	short, char, int, long, float, double
short	int, long, float, double
char	int, long, float, double
int	long, float, double
long	float, double
float	double

Automatic Conversion

For some types, it is possible to assign a value of one type to a variable of a different type without a cast. Java does the conversion of the assigned value automatically. This is known as *automatic* type conversion. Automatic type conversion is possible only if the destination type has enough precession to store the source value. For example, **int** is large enough to hold a **byte** value. Therefore,

```
byte   b = 75;
int    a = b;
```

are valid statements.

The process of assigning a smaller type to a larger one is known as *widening* or *promotion* and that of assigning a larger type to a smaller one is known as *narrowing*. Note that narrowing may result in loss of information.

Program 4.2 illustrates the creation of variables of basic types and also shows the effect of type conversions.

Program 4.2   *Creation and casting of variables*

```
class TypeWrap
{
  public static void main(String args[])
  {
    System.out.println("Variables created");
    chart c = 'x';
    byte b = 50;
    short s = 1996;
    int i = 123456789;
    long l = 1234567654321L;
    float f1 = 3.142F;
    float f2 = 1.2e-5F;
    double d2 = 0.000000987;

    System.out.println(" c = " + c);
    System.out.println(" b = " + b);
    System.out.println(" s = " + s);
    System.out.println(" i = " + i);
    System.out.println(" l = " + l);
    System.out.println(" f1 = " + f1);
    System.out.println(" f2 = " + f2);
    System.out.println(" d2 = " + d2);

    System.out.println(" ");
    System.out.println("Types converted");
    short s1 = (short)b;
    short s2 = (short)i;   // Produces incorrect result
    float n1 = (float)l;
    int m1 = (int)f1;      // Fractional part is lost

    System.out.println(" (short)b = " + s1);
    System.out.println(" (short)i = " + s2);
    System.out.println(" (float)l = " + n1);
    System.out.println(" (int) f1 = " + m1);
  }
}
```

Output of Program 4.2 is as follows:

```
Variables created
c = x
b = 50
s = 1996
i = 123456789
l = 1234567654321
f1 = 3.142
f2 = 1.2e-005
d2 = 9.87e-007
Types converted
(short)b = 50
(short)i = -13035
(float)l = 1.23457e+012
(int)f1 = 3
```

Note that floating point constants have a default type of **double**. What happens when we want to declare a **float** variable and initialize it using a constant? Example:

```
float x = 7.56;
```

This will cause the following compiler error;

```
"Incompatible type for declaration. Explicit cast needed to convert
double to float."
```

This should be written as:

```
float x = 7.56F;
```

4.10 Getting Values of Variables

A computer program is written to manipulate a given set of data and to display or print the results. Java supports two output methods that can be used to send the results to the screen.

- `print( ) method`   // print and wait
- `println( ) method`   // print a line and move to next line

The **print( )** method sends information into a buffer. This buffer is not flushed until a newline (or end-of-line) character is sent. As a result, the **print( )** method prints output on one line until a newline character is encountered. For example, the statements

```
System.out.print ("Hello ");
System.out.print("Java!");
```

will display the words **Hello Java!** on one line and waits for displaying further information on the same line. We may force the display to be brought to the next line by printing a newline character as shown below:

```
System.out.print ('\n');
```

For example, the statements

```
System.out.print("Hello");
System.out.print("\n");
System.out.print("Java!");
```

will display the output in two lines as follows:

```
Hello
Java!
```

The **println( )** method, by contrast, takes the information provided and displays it on a line followed by a line feed(carriage-return). This means that the statements

```
System.out.println("Hello");
System.out.println("Java!");
```

will produce the following output:

```
Hello
Java!
```

The statement

```
System.out.println( );
```

will print a blank line. Program 4.3 illustrates the behaviour of **print( )** and **println( )** methods.

Program 4.3 *Getting the result to the screen*

```
class Displaying
{
  public static void main(String args[])
  {
    System.out.println("Screen Display");
    for(int i = 1; i <= 9; i++)
    {
      for (int j = 1; j <= i; j++)
      {
        System.out.print(" ");
        System.out.print(i);
      }
      System.out.print("\n");
    }
    System.out.println("Screen Display Done");
  }
}
```

Program 4.3 displays the following on the screen:

```
Screen Display
1
2  2
3  3  3
4  4  4  4
5  5  5  5  5
6  6  6  6  6  6
7  7  7  7  7  7  7
8  8  8  8  8  8  8  8
9  9  9  9  9  9  9  9  9
Screen Display Done
```

4.11   Standard Default Values

In Java, every variable has a default value. If we don't initialize a variable when it is first created, Java provides default value to that variable type automatically as shown in Table 4.6.

Table 4.6 Default Values for Various Types	
Type of variable	*Default value*
byte	Zero : (byte) 0
Short	Zero : (short) 0
int	Zero : 0
long	Zero : 0L
float	0.0f
double	0.0d
char	null character
boolean	false
reference	null

4.12   Summary

This chapter has provided us with a brief description of Java constants and variables and how they are represented inside the computer. We have also seen how the variables are declared and initialized in Java.

Converting one type of data to another is often necessary during implementation of a program. We have discussed how data type conversion is achieved in Java without loss of accuracy.

All programs must read, manipulate and display data. We discussed briefly how values are assigned to variables and how the results are displayed on the screen. These concepts will be applied for developing larger programs in the forthcoming chapters.

 Key Terms

Data, Information, Syntax, Constants, Variables, Integer, Decimal, Octal, Hexadecimal, Real constants, Floating point constants, Character constants, Backslash characters, Reference types, Boolean, NaN, Initialization, Scope, Instance variables, Class variables, Local variables, Nesting, Casting, Widening, Narrowing.

Review Questions

4.1   What is a constant?
4.2   What is a variable?
4.3   How are constants and variables important in developing programs?
4.4   List the eight basic data types used in Java. Give examples.

4.5   What is scope of a variable?

4.6   What is type casting? Why is it required in programming?

4.7   What is initialization? Why is it important?

4.8   When dealing with very small or very large numbers, what steps would you take to improve the accuracy of the calculations?

4.9   What are symbolic constants? How are they useful in developing programs?

4.10 Which of the following are invalid constants and why?

0.0001	5 * 1.5	RS 75.50
+100	75.45E-2	"15.75"
−45.6	−1.45e(+4)	0.000001234

4.11 Which of the following are invalid variable names and why?

Minimum	first.Name	n1+n2
doubles	3rd-row	N$
float	Sum Total	Total-Marks

4.12 Find errors, if any, in the following declaration statements:

```
Int x;
float length, HEIGHT;
double = p,q;
character C1;
final int TOTAL;
final pi = 3.142;
long int m;
```

4.13 Write a program to determine the sum of the following harmonic series for a given value of n:

$$1 + 1/2 + 1/3 + \ldots + 1/n$$

The value of n should be given interactively through the keyboard.

4.14 Write a program to read the price of an item in decimal form (like 75.95) and print the output in paise (like 7595 paise).

4.15 Write a program to convert the given temperature in fahrenheit to celsius using the following conversion formula

$$C = \frac{F - 32}{1.8}$$

and display the values in a tabular form.

DEBUGGING EXERCISES

4.1   The following code results in compile time error. Identify the error.

```
public static void display()
{
    int x = 123456;
    float f = 100.12;
    System.out.println("Float Value = " + f);
}
```

4.2   The following code results in compile time error. Identify the error.

```
public static void display(x)
{
    int y;
    if (x > 10)
    {
        y = x;
    }
    System.out.println("Value of Y =" + y);
}
```

4.3   What modification should be done to the following code so that the value of the variable pie is not modifiable?

```
public static void calculate()
{
    float pie = 3.14f;
    System.out.println("Value of Pie = " + pie);
}
```

4.4   The following code results in compile time error while storing the values of int variable to a byte variable. Identify the problem with the code and provide the solution.

```
public static void convert()
{
    int i = 1245;
    byte b = i;
    System.out.println("Value of Byte Variable b = " + b);
}
```

4.5   Identify the error in the following code.

```
Class Scope
{
    public static void main (string args[ ])
    {
        int m = 10;
        {
            int m = 20;
        }
    }
}
```

Chapter 5

Operators and Expressions

5.1 Introduction

Java supports a rich set of operators. We have already used several of them, such as =, +, −, and *. An operator is a symbol that tells the computer to perform certain mathematical or logical manipulations. Operators are used in programs to manipulate data and variables. They usually form a part of mathematical or logical expressions.

Java operators can be classified into a number of related categories as below:

1. Arithmetic operators
2. Relational operators
3. Logical operators
4. Assignment operators
5. Increment and decrement operators
6. Conditional operators
7. Bitwise operators
8. Special operators

In this chapter, we discuss each one of these categories with illustrations.

5.2 Arithmetic Operators

Arithmetic operators are used to construct mathematical expressions as in algebra. Java provides all the basic arithmetic operators. They are listed in Table 5.1. The operators +, −, *, and / all work the same way as they do in other languages. These can operate on any built-in numeric data type of Java. We cannot use these operators on boolean type. The unary minus operator, in effect, multiplies its single operand by − 1. Therefore, a number preceded by a minus sign changes its sign.

Table 5.1   Arithmetic Operators

Operator	Meaning
+	Addition or unary plus
−	Subtraction or unary minus
*	Multiplication
/	Division
%	Modulo division (Remainder)

Arithmetic operators are used as shown below:

a − b	a + b
a * b	a / b
a % b	− a * b

Here **a** and **b** may be variables or constants and are known as operands.

Integer Arithmetic

When both the operands in a single arithmetic expression such as a + b are integers, the expression is called an *integer expression*, and the operation is called *integer arithmetic*. Integer arithmetic always yields an integer value. In the above examples, if a and b are integers, then for a = 14 and b = 4 we have the following results:

$$a - b = 10$$
$$a + b = 18$$
$$a * b = 56$$
$$a / b = 3 \text{ (decimal part truncated)}$$
$$a \% b = 2 \text{ (remainder of integer division)}$$

a/b, when **a** and **b** are integer types, gives the result of division of **a** by **b** after truncating the divisor. This operation is called the *integer division*.

For modulo division, the sign of the result is always the sign of the first operand (the dividend). That is

$$- 14 \% \quad 3 \ = \ - 2$$
$$- 14 \% \ - 3 \ = \ - 2$$
$$14 \% \ - 3 \ = \quad 2$$

(*Note that module division is defined as: a%b = a − (a/b)*b, where a/b is the integer division.*)

Real Arithmetic

An arithmetic operation involving only real operands is called *real arithmetic*. A real operand may assume values either in decimal or exponential notation. Since floating point values are rounded to the number of significant digits permissible, the final value is an approximation of the correct result.

Unlike **C** and **C++**, modulus operator % can be applied to the floating point data as well. The floating point modulus operator returns the floating point equivalent of an integer division. What this means is that the division is carried out with both floating point operands, but the resulting divisor is treated as an integer, resulting in a floating point remainder. Program 5.1 shows how arithmetic operators work on floating point values.

Program 5.1 *Floating point arithmetic*

```
class FloatPoint
{
    public static void main(String args[])
    {
        float a = 20.5F, b = 6.4F;
        System.out.println(" a = " + a);
        System.out.println(" b = " + b);
        System.out.println(" a+b = " + (a+b));
        System.out.println(" a-b = " + (a-b));
        System.out.println(" a*b = " + (a*b));
        System.out.println(" a/b = " + (a/b));
        System.out.println(" a%b = " + (a%b));
    }
}
```

The output of Program 5.1 is as follows:

```
a = 20.5
b = 6.4
a+b = 26.9
a-b = 14.1
a*b = 131.2
a/b = 3.20313
a%b = 1.3
```

Mixed-mode Arithmetic

When one of the operands is real and the other is integer, the expression is called a *mixed-mode arithmetic* expression. If either operand is of the real type, then the other operand is converted to real and the real arithmetic is performed. The result will be a real. Thus

    15/10.0 produces the result   1.5

whereas

    15/10 produces the result   1

More about mixed operations will be discussed later when we deal with the evaluation of expressions.

5.3 Relational Operators

We often compare two quantities, and depending on their relation, take certain decisions. For example, we may compare the age of two persons, or the price of two items, and so on. These comparisons can be done with the help of *relational operators*. We have already used the symbol '<' meaning 'less than'. An expression such as

    a < b or x < 20

containing a relational operator is termed as a *relational expression*. The value of relational expression is either true or false. For example, if x = 10, then

    x < 20 is true

while

    20 < x is false.

Java supports six relational operators in all. These operators and their meanings are shown in Table 5.2.

Table 5.2   Relational Operators

Operator	Meaning
<	is less than
<=	is less than or equal to
>	is greater than
>=	is greater than or equal to
==	is equal to
!=	is not equal to

A simple relational expression contains only one relational operator and is of the following form:

    ae-1 relational operator ae-2

ae–1 and *ae–2* are arithmetic expressions, which may be simple constants, variables or combination of them. Table 5.3 shows some examples of simple relational expressions and their values.

Table 5.3   Relational Expressions

Expression	Value
4.5 <= 10	TRUE
4.5 < –10	FALSE
–35 >= 0	FALSE
10 < 7+5	TRUE
a + b == c + d	TRUE*

* Only if the sum of values of a and b is equal to the sum of values of c and d.

When arithmetic expressions are used on either side of a relational operator, the arithmetic expressions will be evaluated first and then the results compared. That is, *arithmetic operators have a higher priority over relational operators*. Program 5.2 shows the implementation of relational operators.

Program 5.2 *Implementation of relational operators*

```
class RelationalOperators
{
    public static void main(String args[])
    {
        float a = 15.0F, b = 20.75F, c = 15.0F;
        System.out.println(" a = " + a);
        System.out.println(" b = " + b);
        System.out.println(" c = " + c);
        System.out.println(" a < b is " + (a<b));
        System.out.println(" a > b is " + (a>b));
        System.out.println(" a == c is " + (a==c));
        System.out.println(" a <= c is " + (a<=c));
        System.out.println(" a >= b is " + (a>=b));
        System.out.println(" b != c is " + (b!=c));
        System.out.println(" b == a+c is " + (b==a+c));
    }
}
```

The output of Program 5.2 would be:

```
a = 15
b = 20.75
c = 15
a < b is true
a > b is false
a == c is true
a <= c is true
a >= b is false
a != c is true
b == a+c is false
```

Relational expressions are used in *decision statements* such as, **if** and **while** to decide the course of action of a running program. Decision statements are discussed in detail in Chapters 6 and 7.

5.4 Logical Operators

In addition to the relational operators, Java has three logical operators, which are given in Table 5.4.

Table 5.4	Logical Operators	
Operator	*Meaning*	
&&	logical	AND
||	logical	OR
!	logical	NOT

The logical operators && and || are used when we want to form compound conditions by combining two or more relations. An example is:

```
a > b && x == 10
```

An expression of this kind which combines two or more relational expressions is termed as a *logical expression* or a *compound relational expression*. Like the simple relational expressions, a logical expression also yields a value of true or false, according to the *truth table* shown in Table 5.5. The logical expression given above is true only if both **a > b** and **x == 10** are true. If either (or both) of them are false the expression is false.

Table 5.5   Truth Table

| | | Value of the expression ||
op−1	op−2	op−1 && op−2	op−1 || op−2
true	true	true	true
true	false	false	true
false	true	false	true
false	false	false	false

Note:
- *op−1 && op−2 is true if both op−1 and op−2 are true and false otherwise.*
- *op−1 || op−2 is false if both op−1 and op−2 are false and true otherwise.*

Some examples of the usage of logical expressions are:

```
1. if (age>55 && salary<1000)
2. if (number<0 || number>100)
```

5.5 Assignment Operators

Assignment operators are used to assign the value of an expression to a variable. We have seen the usual assignment operator, '='. In addition, Java has a set of 'shorthand' assignment operators which are used in the form

```
v op= exp;
```

where v is a variable, *exp* is an expression and *op* is a Java binary operator. The operator **op** = is known as the shorthand assignment operator.
The assignment statement

```
v op= exp;
```

is equivalent to

```
v = v op(exp);
```

with v accessed only once. Consider an example

```
x += y+1;
```

This is same as the statement

```
x = x+(y+1);
```

The shorthand operator += means 'add y+1 to x' or 'increment x by y+1'. For y = 2, the above statement becomes

    x += 3;

and when this statement is executed, 3 is added to x. If the old value of x is, say 5, then the new value of x is 8. Some of the commonly used shorthand assignment operators are illustrated in Table 5.6.

Table 5.6   Shorthand Assignment Operators

Statement with simple assignment operator	Statement with shorthand operator
a = a+1	a += 1
a = a−1	a −= 1
a = a*(n+1)	a *= n+1
a = a/(n+1)	a /= n+1
a = a%b	a %= b

The use of shorthand assignment operators has three advantages:

1. What appears on the left-hand side need not be repeated and therefore it becomes easier to write.
2. The statement is more concise and easier to read.
3. Use of shorthand operator results in a more efficient code.

5.6   Increment and Decrement Operators

Java has two very useful operators not generally found in many other languages. These are the increment and decrement operators:

    ++ and −

The operator ++ adds 1 to the operand while −− subtracts 1. Both are unary operators and are used in the following form:

    ++m;   or   m++;
    −−m;   or   m−−;
    ++m; is equivalent to m = m + 1; (or m += 1;)
    −−m; is equivalent to m = m − 1; (or m −= 1;)

We use the increment and decrement operators extensively in **for** and **while** loops. (See Chapter 7.)

While ++m and m++ mean the same thing when they form statements independently, they behave differently when they are used in expressions on the right-hand side of an assignment statement. Consider the following:

    m = 5;
    y = ++m;

In this case, the value of y and m would be 6. Suppose, if we rewrite the above statement as

    m = 5;
    y = m++;

then, the value of y would be 5 and m would be 6. A prefix operator first adds 1 to the operand and then the result is assigned to the variable on left. On the other hand, a postfix operator first assigns the value to the variable on left and then increments the operand. Program 5.3 illustrates this.

Program 5.3 *Increment Operator Illustrated*

```
class IncrementOperator
{
  public static void main(String args[])
  {
    int m = 10, n = 20;
    System.out.println(" m = " + m);
    System.out.println(" n = " + n);
    System.out.println(" ++m = " + ++m);
    System.out.println(" n++ = " + n++);
    System.out.println(" m = " + m);
    System.out.println(" n = " + n);
  }
}
```

Output of Program 5.3 is as follows:

```
m = 10
n = 20
++m = 11
n++ = 20
m = 11
n = 21
```

Similar is the case, when we use ++ (or − −) in subscripted variables. That is, the statement

```
a[i++] = 10
```

is equivalent to

```
a[i]  =  10
i     =  i+1
```

5.7 Conditional Operator

The character pair ? : is a ternary operator available in Java. This operator is used to construct conditional expressions of the form

$$exp1 \ ? \ exp2 \ : \ exp3$$

where *exp1*, *exp2*, and *exp3* are expressions.

The operator ? : works as follows: *exp1* is evaluated first. If it is nonzero (true), then the expression *exp2* is evaluated and becomes the value of the conditional expression. If *exp1* is false, *exp3* is evaluated and its value becomes the value of the conditional expression. Note that only one of the expressions (either *exp2* or *exp3*) is evaluated. For example, consider the following statements:

```
a = 10;
b = 15;
x = (a > b) ? a : b;
```

In this example, x will be assigned the value of b. This can be achieved using the **if...else** statement as follows:

```
if(a > b)
    x = a;
else
    x = b;
```

5.8   Bitwise Operators

Java has a distinction of supporting special operators known as bitwise operators for manipulation of data at values of bit level. These operators are used for testing the bits, or shifting them to the right or left. Bitwise operators may not be applied to **float** or **double**. Table 5.7 lists the bitwise operators. They are discussed in detail in Appendix D.

Table 5.7   Bitwise Operators

Operator	Meaning
&	bitwise AND
!	bitwise OR
^	bitwise exclusive OR
~	one's complement
<<	shift left
>>	shift right
>>>	shift right with zero fill

5.9   Special Operators

Java supports some special operators of interest such as **instanceof** operator and member selection operator (.).

Instanceof Operator

The **instanceof** is an object reference operator and returns *true* if the object on the left-hand side is an instance of the class given on the right-hand side. This operator allows us to determine whether the object belongs to a particular class or not.

Example:

```
person        instanceof        student
```

is *true* if the object **person** belongs to the class **student**; otherwise it is *false*.

Dot Operator

The dot operator (.) is used to access the instance variables and methods of class objects. Examples:

```
person1.age        //    Reference to the variable age
person1.salary( )  //    Reference to the method salary()
```

It is also used to access classes and sub-packages from a package.

5.10 Arithmetic Expressions

An arithmetic expression is a combination of variables, constants, and operators arranged as per the syntax of the language. We have used a number of simple expressions in the examples discussed so far. Java can handle any complex mathematical expressions. Some of the examples of Java expressions are shown in Table 5.8. Remember that Java does not have an operator for exponentiation.

Table 5.8   Expressions

Algebraic expression	Java expression
a b−c	a*b−c
(m+n) (x+y)	(m+n)*(x+y)
$\dfrac{ab}{c}$	a*b/c
$3x^2+2x+1$	3*x*x+2*x+1
$\dfrac{x}{y} + c$	x/y+c

5.11 Evaluation of Expressions

Expressions are evaluated using an assignment statement of the form

```
variable = expression;
```

variable is any valid Java variable name. When the statement is encountered, the *expression* is evaluated first and the result then replaces the previous value of the variable on the left-hand side. All variables used in the expression must be assigned values before evaluation is attempted. Examples of evaluation statements are

```
x = a*b−c;
y = b/c*a;
z = a−b/c+d;
```

The blank space around an operator is optional and is added only to improve readability. When these statements are used in program, the variables **a,b,c** and **d** must be defined before they are used in the expressions.

5.12 Precedence of Arithmetic Operators

An arithmetic expression without any parentheses will be evaluated from left to right using the rules of precedence of operators. There are two distinct priority levels of arithmetic operators in Java:

```
High priority      * / %
Low priority       + −
```

The basic evaluation procedure includes two left-to-right passes through the expression. During the first pass, the high priority operators (if any) are applied as they are encountered.

During the second pass, the low priority operators (if any) are applied as they are encountered. Consider the following evaluation statement:

```
x = a−b/3 + c*2−1
```

When a = 9, b = 12, and c = 3, the statement becomes

```
x = 9−12/3+3*2−1
```

and is evaluated as follows:

First pass

```
Step1: x = 9−4+3*2−1        (12/3 evaluated)
Step2: x = 9−4+6−1          (3*2 evaluated)
```

Second pass

```
Step3: x = 5+6−1            (9−4 evaluated)
Step4: x = 11−1             (5+6 evaluated)
Step5: x = 10               (11−1 evaluated)
```

However, the order of evaluation can be changed by introducing parentheses into an expression. Consider the same expression with parentheses as shown below:

```
9−12/(3+3)*(2−1)
```

Whenever the parentheses are used, the expressions within parentheses assume highest priority. If two or more sets of parentheses appear one after another as shown above, the expression contained in the left-most set is evaluated first and the right-most in the last. Given below are the new steps.

First pass

```
Step1: 9−12/6*(2−1)
Step2: 9−12/6*1
```

Second pass

```
Step3: 9−2*1
Step4: 9−2
```

Third pass

```
Step5: 7
```

This time, the procedure consists of three left-to-right passes. However, the number of evaluation steps remain the same as 5 (i.e., equal to the number of arithmetic operators).

Parentheses may be nested, and in such cases, evaluation of the expression will proceed outward from the innermost set of parentheses. Just make sure that every opening parentheses has a matching closing one. For example

$$9-(12/(3+3)*2)-1 = 4$$

whereas

$$9-((12/3)+3*2)-1 = -2$$

While parentheses allow us to change the order of priority, we may also use them to improve understandability of the program. When in doubt, we can always add an extra pair just to make sure that the priority assumed is the one we require.

5.13 Type Conversions in Expressions

Automatic Type Conversion

Java permits mixing of constants and variables of different types in an expression, but during evaluation it adheres to very strict rules of type conversion. We know that the computer, considers one operator at a time, involving two operands. If the operands are of different types, the 'lower' type is automatically converted to the 'higher' type before the operation proceeds. The result is of the higher type.

If **byte, short** and **int** variables are used in an expression, the result is always promoted to **int**, to avoid overflow. If a single **long** is used in the expression, the whole expression is promoted to **long**. Remember that all integer values are considered to be **int** unless they have the 1 or L appended to them. If an expression contains a **float** operand, the entire expression is promoted to **float**. If any operand is **double,** result is **double**. Table 5.9 provides a reference chart for type conversion.

Table 5.9   Automatic Type Conversion Chart

	char	byte	short	int	long	float	double
char	int	int	int	int	long	float	double
byte	int	int	int	int	long	float	double
short	int	int	int	int	long	float	double
int	int	int	int	int	long	float	double
long	long	long	long	long	long	float	double
float	float	float	float	float	float	float	double
double	double	double	double	double	double	double	double

The final result of an expression is converted to the type of the variable on the left of the assignment sign before assigning the value to it. However, the following changes are introduced during the final assignment.

1. **float** to **int** causes truncation of the fractional part.
2. **double** to **float** causes rounding of digits.
3. **long** to **int** causes dropping of the excess higher order bits.

Casting a Value

We have already discussed how Java performs type conversion automatically. However, there are instances when we want to force a type conversion in a way that is different from the automatic conversion. Consider, for example, the calculation of ratio of females to males in a town.

```
ratio = female_number/male_number
```

Since **female_number and male_number** are declared as integers in the program, the decimal part of the result of the division would be lost and **ratio** would not represent a correct figure. This problem can be solved by converting locally one of the variables to the floating point as shown below:

```
ratio = (float)female_number/male_number
```

The operator **(float)** converts the **female_number** to floating point for the purpose of evaluation of the expression. Then using the rule of automatic conversion, the division is performed in floating point mode, thus retaining the fractional part of result.

Note that in no way does the operator **(float)** affect the value of the variable **female_number**. And also, the type of **female_number** remains as **int** in the other parts of the program.

The process of such a local conversion is known as *casting a value*. The general form of a cast is:

```
(type_name) expression
```

where type-name is one of the standard data types. The *expression* may be a constant, variable or an expression. Some examples of casts and their actions are shown in Table 5.10.

Table 5.10   Use of Casts

Examples	Action
x = (int) 7.5	7.5 is converted to integer by truncation
a = (int)21.3/(int)4.5	Evaluated as 21/4 and the result would be 5
b = (double) sum/n	Division is done in floating point mode.
y = (int) (a+b)	The result of a + b is converted to integer.
z = (int) a+b	a is converted to integer and then added to b.
p = cost ((double)x)	Converts x to double before using it as parameter.

Casting can be used to round-off a given value to an integer. Consider the following statement:

```
x = (int) (y+0.5);
```

If y is 27.6, y + 0.5 is 28.1 and on casting, the result becomes 28, the value that is assigned to **x**. Of course, the expression being cast is not changed.

When combining two different types of variables in an expression, never assume the rules of automatic conversion. It is always a good practice to explicitly force the conversion. It is more safer.

For example, when **y** and **p** are **double** and **m** is **int**, the following two statements are equivalent.

```
y = p+m;
y = p+(double)m;
```

However, the second statement is preferable.

Program 5.4 illustrates the use of casting in evaluating the equation

$$sum = \sum_{i=1}^{n} \frac{1}{i}$$

Program 5.4 *Illustration of use of casting operation*

```
class Casting
{
  public static void main(String args[])
  {
    float sum;
    int i;
    sum = 0.0F;
    for(i = 1; i <= 10; i++)
    {
      sum = sum + 1/(float)i;
      System.out.print(" i = " + i);
      System.out.print(" sum = " + sum);
    }
  }
}
```

Program 5.4 produces the following output:

```
i = 1     sum  = 1
i = 2     sum  = 1.5
i = 3     sum  = 1.83333
i = 4     sum  = 2.08333
i = 5     sum  = 2.28333
i = 6     sum  = 2.45
i = 7     sum  = 2.59286
i = 8     sum  = 2.71786
i = 9     sum  = 2.82897
i = 10    sum  = 2.92897
```

Generic Type Casting

Generics is one of the significant enhancements to Java by J2SE 5.0 programming language. Generics eliminates the need of explicit type casting in collections. A collection is a set of interfaces and classes that sort and manipulate a group of data into a single unit. For further information on collections, refer to Chapter 18.

To retrieve elements from a collection, we need to typecast the elements, because each element in a collection is considered to be an object. Also, typecasting is an unsafe operation because the compiler cannot check the wrong casts. The compiler throws an exception if the casts fail at runtime. When using generics, the compiler inserts type casts at appropriate places to implement type casting. Therefore, the typecast becomes implicit rather than explicit. Generics also determines the typecast errors at compile time rather than run time. Now, collections can contain objects of only one type. Using Generics, we can specify the type information of data using a parameter. The type information specifies the class and hierarchy of classes and interfaces to which the object belongs. The syntax to declare a generic class is:

```
class SampleGenericClass <T>
{
}
```

Here, <T> indicates that the SampleGenericClass class is of generic type. Program 5.5 illustrates the use of generic type in the ArrayList collection.

Program 5.5 *Illustration of use of generic type in collections.*

```
import java.util.*;
public class Arraylistcollection
{
  ArrayList<Integer> list = new ArrayList<Integer>();
  Numberinglist(list);
  int total = 0;
  Iterator<Integer> iter=list.iterator();
    while (iter.hasNext())
    {
      Integer val=iter.next();
      total = total + val;
    }
  System.out.println("The Total Amount is "+total);
  private static void Numberinglist(ArrayList<Integer> list)
  {
    list.add(new Integer(1));
    list.add(new Integer(2));
  }
}
```

Program 5.5 produces the following output:

    The Total Amount is 3

5.14 Operator Precedence and Associativity

Each operator in Java has a precedence associated with it. This precedence is used to determine how an expression involving more than one operator is evaluated. There are distinct levels of precedence and an operator may belong to one of the levels. The operators at the higher level of precedence are evaluated first. The operators of the same precedence are evaluated either from left to right or from right to left, depending on the level. This is known as the associativity property of an operator. Table 5.11 provides a complete lists of operators, their precedence levels, and their rules of association. The groups are listed in the order of decreasing precedence (rank 1 indicates the highest precedence level and 14 the lowest). The list also includes those operators which we have not yet discussed.

Table 5.11 Summary of Java Operators

Operator	Description	Associativity	Rank
.	Member selection	Left to right	1
( )	Function call		
[ ]	Array element reference		
−	Unary minus	Right to left	2
++	Increment		
−−	Decrement		
!	Logical negation		
~	Ones complement		
(type)	Casting		
*	Multiplication	Left to right	3
/	Division		
%	Modulus		
+	Addition	Left to right	4
−	Subtraction		
<<	Left shift	Left to right	5
>>	Right shift		
>>>	Right shift with zero fill		
<	Less than	Left to right	6
<=	Less than or equal to		
>	Greater than		
>=	Greater than or equal to		
instanceof	Type comparison		
==	Equality	Left to right	7
!=	Inequality		
&	Bitwise AND	Left to right	8
^	Bitwise XOR	Left to right	9
|	Bitwise OR	Left to right	10
&&	Logical AND	Left to right	11
||	Logical OR	Left to right	12
?:	Conditional operator	Right to left	13
=	Assignment operators	Right to left	14
op=	Shorthand assignment		

It is very important to note carefully, the order of precedence and associativity of operators. Consider the following conditional statement:

```
if(x == 10+15 && y<10)
```

The precedence rules say that the addition operator has a higher priority than the logical operator (&&)

and the relational operators (== and <). Therefore, the addition of 10 and 15 is executed first. This is equivalent to:

```
if(x == 25 && y<10)
```

The next step is to determine whether **x** is equal to 25 and **y** is less than 10. If we assume a value of 20 for x and 5 for y, then

```
x == 25 is FALSE
y < 10 is TRUE
```

Note that since the operator < enjoys a higher priority compared to ==, y < 10 is tested first and then x = = 25 is tested.

Finally we get:

```
if(FALSE && TRUE)
```

Because one of the conditions is **FALSE**, the compound condition is **FALSE.**

5.15   Mathematical Functions

Mathematical functions such as cos, sqrt, log, etc. are frequently used in analysis of real-life problems. Java supports these basic math functions through **Math** class defined in the **java.lang** package. Table 5.12 lists the math functions defined in the **Math** class. These functions should be used as follows:

```
Math.function_name( )
```

Example:

```
double y = Math.sqrt(x);
```

Table 5.12   Math Functions

Functions	Action
sin(x)	Returns the sine of the angle x in radians
cos(x)	Returns the cosine of the angle x in radians
tan(x)	Returns the tangent of the angle x in radians
asin(y)	Returns the angle whose sine is y
acos(y)	Returns the angle whose cosine is y
atan(y)	Returns the angle whose tangent is y
atan2(x,y)	Returns the angle whose tangent is x/y
pow(x,y)	Returns x raised to y (x^y)
exp(x)	Returns e raised to x (e^x)
log(x)	Returns the natural logarithm of x
sqrt(x)	Returns the square root of x
ceil(x)	Returns the smallest whole number greater than or equal to x. (Rounding up)
floor(x)	Returns the largest whole number less than or equal to x (Rounded down)
rint(x)	Returns the truncated value of x.
round(x)	Returns the integer closest to the argument
abs(a)	Returns the absolute value of a
max(a,b)	Returns the maximum of a and b
min(a,b)	Returns the minimum of a and b

Note: *x and y are double type parameters. a and b may be ints, longs, floats and doubles.*

5.16   Summary

We have discussed all the basic data types and operators available in Java and also seen their use in expressions. Type conversions and order of precedence of operators during the evaluation of expressions have been highlighted. Program 5.6 winds up our discussions by demonstrating the use of different types of expressions.

Finally, it is important to note that all Java types have fixed sizes. There is no ambiguity and all Java types are machine-independent.

Program 5.6   *Demonstration of Java expressions*

```
class ExpressWrap
{
   public static void main(String args[])
   {
      // Declaration and Initialization
      int a = 10, b = 5, c = 8, d = 2;
      float x = 6.4F, y = 3.0F;

      // Order of Evaluation
      int answer1 = a * b + c / d;
      int answer2 = a * (b + c) / d;

      // Type Conversions
      float answer3 = a / c;
      float answer4 = (float) a / c;
      float answer5 = a / y;

      // Modulo Operations
      int answer6 = a % c;
      float answer7 = x % y;

      // Logic Operations
      boolean bool1 = a > b && c > d;
      boolean bool2 = a < b && c > d;
      boolean bool3 = a < b || c > d;
      boolean bool4 = ! (a - b == c);

      System.out.println("Order of Evaluation');
      System.out.println(" a * b + c / d = " + answer1);
      System.out.println(" a * (b + c) / d = " + answer2);

      System.out.println("Type Conversion");
      System.out.println(" a / c = " + answer3);
      System.out.println(" (float) a / c = " + answer4);
      System.out.println(" a / y = " + answer5);
```

(Continued)

Program 5.6 (*Continued*)

```
System.out.println("Modulo Operations");
System.out.println(" a % c = " + answer6);
System.out.println(" x % y = " + answer7);

System.out.println("Logical Operations");
System.out.println(" a > b && c > d = " + bool1);
System.out.println(" a < b && c > d = " + bool2);
System.out.println(" a < b || c > d = " + bool3);
System.out.println(" ! (a – b == c) = " + bool4);
    }
}
```

Program 5.6 outputs the following:

```
Order of Evaluation
    a * b + c / d = 54
    a * (b + c) / d = 65
Type Conversions
    a / c = 1
    (float) a / c = 1.25
    a / y = 3.33333
Modulo Operations
    a % c = 2
    x % y = 0.4
Logical Operations
    a > b && c > d = true
    a < b && c > d = false
    a < b || c > d = true
    ! (a–b == c) = true
```

 ## Key Terms

Operands, Integer arithmetic, Real arithmetic, Mixed-mode arithmetic, Relational expression, Logical expression, Truth table, Ternary operator, Conditional operator, Increment operator, Decrement operator, Dot operator, **instanceof** operator, Casting, Operator precedence, Associativity

REVIEW QUESTIONS

5.1   Which of the following arithmetic expressions are valid?

(a) 25/3 % 2   (b) +9/4 + 5
(c) 7.5 % 3   (d) 14 % 3 + 7 % 2
(e) –14 % 3   (f) 15.25 + –5.0
(g) (5/3) * 3 + 5 % 3   (h) 21 % (int)4.5

5.2 Write Java assignment statements to evaluate the following equations:

(a) Area $= \pi r^2 + 2\pi r h$

(b) Torque $= \dfrac{2m_1 m_2}{m_1 + m_2} * g$

(c) Side $= \sqrt{a^2 + b^2 - 2ab \cos(x)}$

(d) Energy $= mass \left(acceleration * height + \dfrac{velocity^2}{2} \right)$

5.3 Identify unnecessary parentheses in the following arithmetic expressions.

(a) (x–(y/5)+z) % 8) + 25
(b) ((x–y) * p) + q
(c) (m*n) + (–x/y)
(d) x/(3*y)

5.4 Find errors, if any, in the following assignment statements and rectify them.

(a) x = y = z = 0.5, 2.0 – 5.75;
(b) m = ++a * 5;
(c) y = sqrt(100);
(d) p* = x/y;
(e) s = /5;
(f) a = b++ – c * 2

5.5 Determine the value of each of the following logical expressions if a = 5, b = 10 and c = –6

(a) a > b && a < c
(b) a < b && a > c
(c) a == c || b > a
(d) b > 15 && c < 0 || a > 0
(e) (a/2.0 == 0.0 && b/2.0! = 0.0) || c < 0.0

5.6 The straight-line method of computing the yearly depreciation of the value of an item is given by

$$Depreciation = \frac{Purchase\ price - Salvage\ value}{Years\ of\ service}$$

Write a program to determine the salvage value of an item when the purchase price, years of service, and the annual depreciation are given.

5.7 Write a program that will read a real number from the keyboard and print the following output in one line:

Smallest integer	The given number	Largest integer
not less than		not greater than
the number		the number

5.8 The total distance travelled by a vehicle in t seconds is given by

$$distance = ut + (at^2)/2$$

where u is the initial velocity (metres per second), *a* is the acceleration (metres per second^2). Write a program to evaluate the distance travelled at regular intervals of time, given the values of *u* and *a*. The program should provide the flexibility to the user to select his own time intervals and repeat the calculations for different values of *u* and *a*.

5.9 In inventory management, the Economic Order Quantity for a single item is given by

$$EOQ = \sqrt{\frac{2 * demand\ rate * setup\ costs}{holding\ cost\ per\ item\ per\ unit\ time}}$$

and the optimal Time Between Orders

$$TBO = \sqrt{\frac{2 * \text{setup costs}}{\text{demand rate} * \text{holding cost per item per unit time}}}$$

Write a program to computer EOQ and TBO, given demand rate (items per unit time), setup costs (per order), and the holding cost (per item per unit time).

5.10 For a certain electrical circuit with an inductance **L** and resistance **R**, the damped natural frequency is given by

$$\text{Frequency} = \sqrt{\frac{1}{LC} - \frac{R^2}{4C^2}}$$

It is desired to study the variation of this frequency with **C** (capacitance). Write a program to calculate the frequency for different values of **C** starting from 0.01 to 0.1 in steps of 0.01.

DEBUGGING EXERCISES

1. In the following code the expected value is 8, but it prints the value 2. What would you modify in the code to obtain the expected value?

```
public static void calculate()
{
    int i = 42 + 45 - 48 - 5;
    int j = 5 + 5 - 8 + 2;
    int ans = i % j;

    System.out.println("Value of Ans = " + ans);
}
```

2. In the following code the expected value is 78 but it returns the value 59. What would you modify in the code to obtain the expected value?

```
public static void calculate()
{
    int ans = 42 + 45 - 48 - 5 - 15 + 20 * 2;
    System.out.println("Value of Ans = " + ans);
}
```

3. The following code results in compilation error. Debug the code and rectify the problem.

```
public static void calculate()
{
    int ans = (2 (+5 - 8) (+ 5 - 5) + 10) * 2;
    System.out.println("Value of Ans = " + ans);
}
```

4. In the code given below, what should be changed to obtain the value of 40.0 for X?

```
public static void calculate()
{
    double x = Math.rint(40.6);
    double y = Math.abs(40.6);
    System.out.println("Value of X is = " +x + " and Y is =" + y);
}
```

Chapter **6**

Decision Making and Branching

6.1 Introduction

A Java program is a set of statements, which are normally executed sequentially in the order in which they appear. This happens when options or repetitions of certain calculations are not necessary. However, in practice, we have a number of situations, where we may have to change the order of execution of statements based on certain conditions, or repeat a group of statements until certain specified conditions are met. This involves a kind of decision making to see whether a particular condition has occurred or not and then direct the computer to execute certain statements accordingly.

When a program breaks the sequential flow and jumps to another part of the code, it is called *branching*. When the branching is based on a particular condition, it is known as *conditional branching*. If branching takes place without any decision, it is known as *unconditional branching*.

Java language possesses such decision making capabilities and supports the following statements known as *control* or *decision making* statements.

1. **if** statement
2. **switch** statement
3. Conditional operator statement

In this Chapter, we shall discuss the features, capabilities and applications of these statements which are classified as *selection* statements.

6.2 Decision Making with If Statement

The **if** statement is a powerful decision making statement and is used to control the flow of execution of statements. It is basically a *two-way* decision statement and is used in conjunction with an expression. It takes the following form:

if (*test expression*)

It allows the computer to evaluate the *expression* first and then, depending on whether the value of the *expression* (relation or condition) is 'true' or 'false', it transfers the control to a particular statement. This point of program has two paths to follow, one for the ***true*** condition and the other for the ***false*** condition as shown in Fig. 6.1.

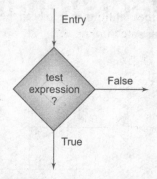

Fig. 6.1   *Two-way branching*

Some examples of decision making, using **if** statement are:

```
1. if (bank balance is zero)
   borrow money
2. if (room is dark)
   put on lights
3. if (code is 1)
   person is male
4. if (age is more than 55)
   person is retired
```

The **if** statement may be implemented in different forms depending on the complexity of conditions to be tested.

1. Simple if statement
2. if..else statement
3. Nested if..else statement
4. else if ladder

6.3 Simple If Statement

The general form of a simple **if** statement is

```
if(test expression)
{
    statement-block;
}
statement-x;
```

The 'statement-block' may be a single statement or a group of statements. If the *test expression* is true, the *statement-block* will be executed; otherwise the statement-block will be skipped and the execution will jump to the *statement-x*.

It should be remembered that when the condition is true both the statement-block and the statement-x are executed in sequence. This is illustrated in Fig. 6.2.

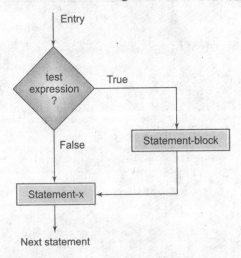

Fig. 6.2 *Flowchart of simple if control*

Consider the following segment of a program that is written for processing of marks obtained in an entrance examination.

```
..........
..........
if(category == SPORTS)
{
   marks = marks + bonus_marks;
}
System.out.println(marks);
..........
..........
```

The program tests the type of category of the student. If the student belongs to the SPORTS category, then additional bonus_marks are added to his marks before they are printed. For others, bonus_marks are not added.

Consider a case having two test conditions, one for weight and another for height. This is done using the compound relation

```
if (weight < 50 && height > 170) count = count +1;
```

This would have been equivalently done using two **if** statements as follows:

```
if(weight<50)
        if(height>170)
                count = count+1;
```

If the value of **weight** is less than **50**, then the following statement is executed, which in turn is another **if** statement. This if statement tests **height** and if the **height** is greater than **170**, then the **count** is incremented by 1. Program 6.1 illustrates the implementation of the above statement.

Program 6.1 *Counting with if statement*

```
class IfTest
{
  public static void main(String arg[])
  {
    int i, count, count1, count2;
    float[] weight = { 45.0F, 55.0F, 47.0F, 51.0F, 54.0F };
    float[] height = { 176.5F, 174.2F, 168.0F, 170.7F, 169.0F };
    count  = 0;
    count1 = 0;
    count2 = 0;
    for (i = 0; i <= 4; i++)
    {
      if(weight[i] < 50.0 && height[i] > 170.0)
      {
        count1 = count1 + 1;
      }
      count = count + 1; // Total persons
    }
    count2 = count - count1;
    System.out.println("Number of persons with ...");
    System.out.println("Weight<50 and height>170 = " +count1);
    System.out.println("Others = " + count2);
  }
}
```

The output of Program 6.1 will be:

```
Number of persons with ...
Weight < 50 and height > 170 = 1
Others = 4
```

6.4 The If...Else Statement

The **if...else** statement is an extension of the simple **if** statement. The general form is

```
if(test expression)
{
    True-block statement(s)
}
else
{
    False-block statement(s)
}
statement-x
```

If the *test expression* is true, then *the true-block statement(s)* immediately following the **if** statement, are executed; otherwise, the *false-block statement(s)* are executed. In either case, either *true-block* or *false-block* will be executed, not both. This is illustrated in Fig. 6.3. In both the cases, the control is transferred subsequently to the *statement-x*.

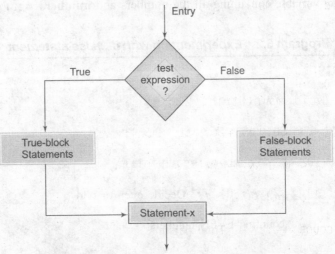

Fig. 6.3   *Flowchart of if....else control*

Let us consider an example of counting the number of boys and girls in a class. We use code 1 for a boy and 2 for a girl. The program statements to do this may be written as follows:

```
..........
..........
if(code == 1)
    boy = boy + 1;
if(code == 2)
    girl = girl + 1;
..........
..........
```

The first test determines whether or not the student is a boy. If yes, the number of boys is increased by 1 and the program continues to the second test. The second test again determines whether the student is a girl. This is unnecessary. Once a student is identified as a boy, there is no need to test again for a girl. A student can be either a boy or girl, not both. The above program segment can be modified using the **else** clause as follows:

```
. . . . . . . . . .
. . . . . . . . . .
if(code == 1)
   boy = boy + 1;
else
   girl = girl + 1;
xxx;
. . . . . . . . . .
```

Here, if the code is equal to 1, the statement **boy = boy + 1;** is executed and the control is transferred to the statement **xxx**, after skipping the **else** part. If the code is not equal to 1, the statement **boy = boy + 1;** is skipped and the statement in the **else** part **girl = girl + 1;** is executed before the control reaches the statement **xxx**.

Program 6.2 counts the even and odd numbers in a list of numbers using the **if....else** statement. **number[ ]** is an array variable containing all the numbers and **number.length** gives the number of elements in the array.

Program 6.2   *Experimenting with if....else statement*

```
class IfElseTest
{
   public static void main(String args[])
   {
      int number[] = { 50, 65, 56, 71, 81 };
      int even = 0, odd = 0;
      for (int i = 0; i < number.length; i++)
      {
         if ((number[i] % 2) == 0) // Decide even or odd
         {
            even += 1; // counting EVEN numbers
         }
         else
         {
            odd += 1; // counting ODD numbers
         }
      }
      System.out.println("Even Numbers : " + even +
              " Odd Numbers : " + odd);
   }
}
```

Output of Program 6.2:

```
      Even Numbers : 2    Odd Numbers : 3
```

6.5 Nesting of If....Else Statements

When a series of decisions are involved, we may have to use more than one **if....else** statement in *nested* form as follows:

```
if (test condition1)
{
    if (test condition2)
    {
        statement-1;
    }
    else
    {
        statement-2;
    }
}
else
{
    statement-3;
}
statement-x;
```

The logic of execution is illustrated in Fig. 6.4. If the *condition-1* is false, the statement-3 will be executed; otherwise it continues to perform the second test. If the *condition-2* true, the statement-1 will be evaluated; otherwise the statement-2 will be evaluated and then the control is transferred to the statement-x.

A commercial bank has introduced an incentive policy of giving bonus to all its deposit holders. The policy is as follows: A bonus of 2 per cent of the *balance* held on 31st December is given to every one, irrespective of their balances, and 5 per cent is given to female account holders if their balance is more than Rs 5000. This logic can be coded as follows:

```
. . . . . . . . . .
if(sex is female)
{
    if (balance > 5000)
        bonus = 0.05 * balance;
    else
        bonus = 0.02 * balance;
}
else
{
    bonus = 0.02 * balance;
}
```

```
balance = balance + bonus;
..........
..........
```

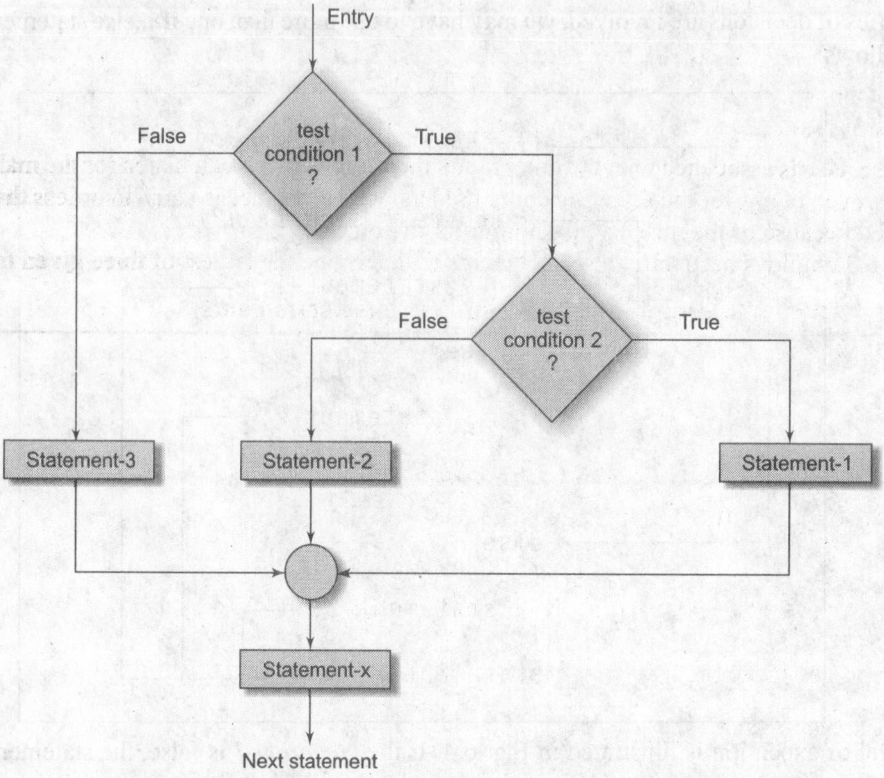

Fig. 6.4   *Flowchart of nested if....else statements*

When nesting, care should be exercised to match every **if** with an **else**. Consider the following alternative to the above program (which looks right at the first sight):

```
if(sex is female)
   if(balance > 5000)
      bonus = 0.05 * balance;
else
   bonus = 0.02 * balance;
   balance = balance + bonus;
```

There is an ambiguity as to over which **if** the **else** belongs to. In Java an **else** is linked to the closest non-terminated if. Therefore, the **else** is associated with the inner **if** and there is no **else** option for the outer **if**. This means that the computer is trying to execute the statement

```
balance = balance + bonus;
```

without really calculating the bonus for the male account holders.

Consider another alternative, which also looks correct:

```
     if(sex is female)
     {
        if (balance > 5000)
             bonus = 0.05 * balance;
     }
     else
        bonus = 0.02 * balance;
        balance = balance + bonus;
```

In this case, **else** is associated with the outer **if** and therefore bonus is calculated for the male account holders. However, bonus for the female account holders, whose balance is equal to or less than 5000 is not calculated because of the missing **else** option for the inner **if**.

Program 6.3 employs nested **if....else** statements to determine the largest of three given numbers.

Program 6.3   *Nesting if...else statements*

```
class IfElseNesting
{
   public static void main(String args[])
   {
     int a = 325, b = 712, c = 478;
     System.out.print("Largest value is : ");
     if (a > b)
     {
        if (a > c)
        {
        System.out.println(a);
        }
        else
        {
        System.out.println(c);
        }
     }
     else
     {
        if (c > b)
        {
        System.out.println(c);
        }
        else
        {
        System.out.println(b);
        }
     }
   }
}
```

Output of Program 6.3:

```
     Largest value is : 712
```

6.6 The Else If Ladder

There is another way of putting ifs together when multipath decisions are involved. A multipath decision is a chain of ifs in which the statement associated with each **else** is an **if**. It takes the following general form:

```
if (condition1)
    statement-1;

else if (condition2)
    statement-2;

    else if (condition3)
        statement-3;
        ........................

        else if (condition n)
            statement-n;

            else
                default-statement;

statement-x;
```

This construct is known as the **else if** ladder. The conditions are evaluated from the top (of the ladder), downwards. As soon as the true condition is found, the statement associated with it is executed and the control is transferred to the *statement-x* (skipping the rest of the ladder). When all the n conditions become false, then the final **else** containing the *default-statement* will be executed. Figure 6.5 shows the logic of execution of **else if** ladder statements.

Let us consider an example of grading the students in an academic institution. The grading is done according to the following rules:

Average marks	Grade
80 to 100	Honours
60 to 79	First Division
50 to 59	Second Division
40 to 49	Third Division
0 to 39	Fail

This grading can be done using the **else if** ladder as follows:

```
if(marks > 79)
    grade = "Honours";
```

```
else if(marks > 59)
      grade = "First Division";

    else if(marks > 49)
          grade = "Second Division";

          else if(marks > 39)
          grade = "Third Division";

          else
          grade = "Fail";
System.out.println("Grade: " + grade);
```

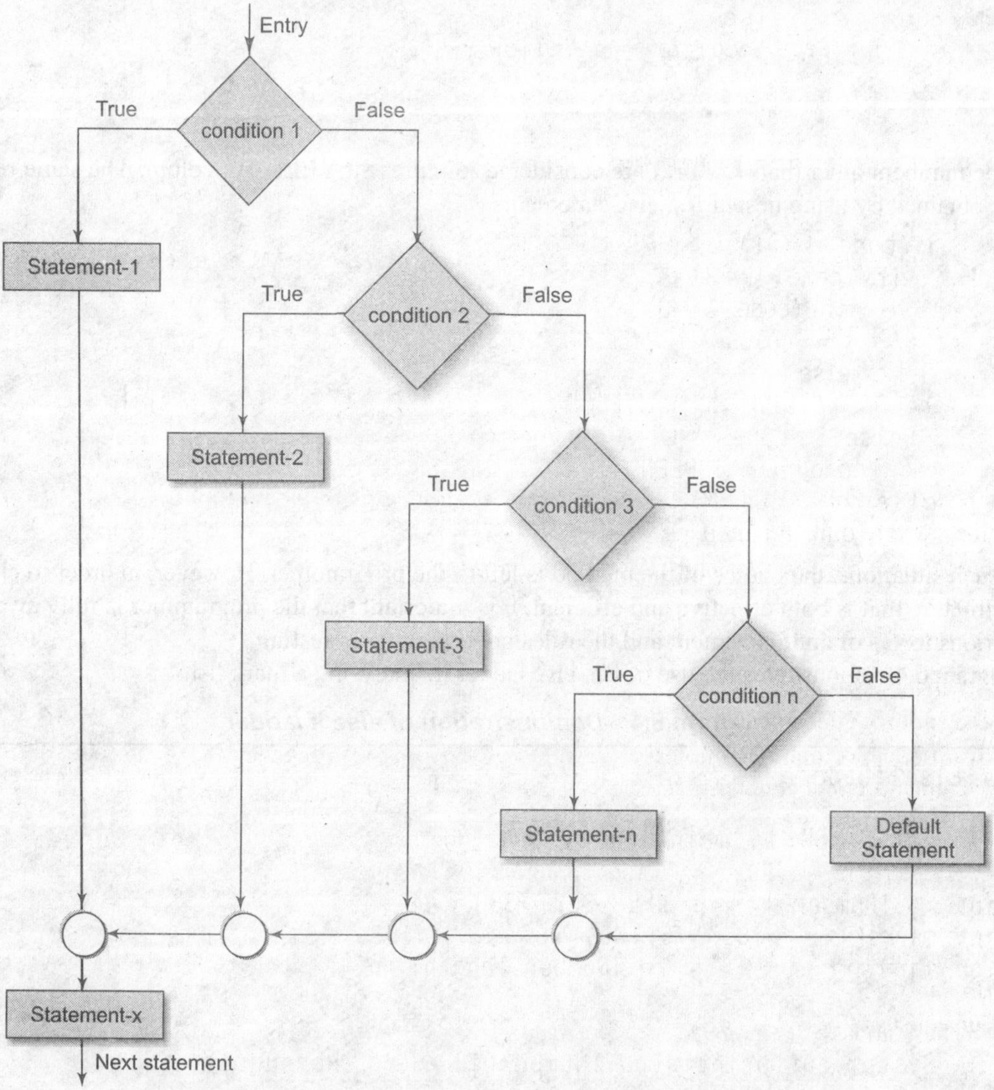

Fig. 6.5　*Flowchart of else...if ladder*

Consider another example given below:

```
. . . . . . . . .
. . . . . . . . .
if (code == 1)
    colour = "RED";

else if (code == 2)
    colour = "GREEN";

    else if (code == 3)
        code = "WHITE";

        else
            colour = "Yellow";
. . . . . . . . .
. . . . . . . . .
```

Code numbers other than 1, 2 or 3 are considered to represent YELLOW colour. The same results can be obtained by using nested **if....else** statements.

```
if(code != 1)
    if (code != 2)
        if (code != 3)
            colour = "YELLOW";
        else
            colour = "WHITE";
    else
        colour = "GREEN";
else
    colour = "RED";
```

In such situations, the choice of the method is left to the programmer. However, in order to choose an **if** structure that is both effective and efficient, it is important that the programmer is fully aware of the various forms of an **if** statement and the rules governing their nesting.

Program 6.4 demonstrates the use of **if....else** ladder in analysing a mark list.

Program 6.4　*Demonstration of else if ladder*

```
class ElseIfLadder
{
  public static void main(String args[])
  {
    int rollNumber[] = { 111, 222, 333, 444 };
    int marks[] = { 81, 75, 43, 58 };
    for (int i = 0; i < rollNumber.length; i++)
    {
      if (marks[i] > 79)
        System.out.println(rollNumber[i] + " Honours");
      else if (marks[i] > 59)
```

Program 6.4 (*Continued*)

```
            System.out.println(rollNumber[i] + " I Division");
        else if (marks[i] > 49)
            System.out.println(rollNumber[i] + " II Division");
        else
            System.out.println(rollNumber[i] + " FAIL");
    }
  }
}
```

Program 6.4 produces the following output:

```
111 Honours
222 I Division
333 FAIL
444 II Division
```

6.7   The Switch Statement

We have seen that when one of the many alternatives is to be selected, we can design a program using **if** statements to control the selection. However, the complexity of such a program increases dramatically when the number of alternatives increases. The program becomes difficult to read and follow. At times, it may confuse even the designer of the program. Fortunately, Java has a built-in multiway decision statement known as **switch**. The **switch** statement tests the value of a given variable (or expression) against a list of **case** values and when a match is found, a block of statements associated with that **case** is executed. The general form of the **switch** statement is as shown below:

```
switch (expression)
{
        case value-1:
                block-1
                break;
        case value-2:
                block-2
                break;
        ......

        ......
        default:
                default-block
                break;
}
statement-x;
```

The *expression* is an integer expression or characters. *value-1*, *value-2* .... are constants or constant expressions (evaluable to an integral constant) and are known as *case labels*. Each of these values should be unique within a **switch** statement. *block-1*, *block-2* .... are statement lists and may contain zero or more statements. There is no need to put braces around these blocks but it is important to note that case labels end with a colon (:).

When the **switch** is executed, the value of the expression is successively compared against the values *value-1*, *value-2*, ... If a **case** is found whose value matches with the value of the expression, then the block of statements that follows the case are executed.

The **break** statement at the end of each block signals the end of a particular case and causes an exit from the **switch** statement, transferring the control to the *statement-x* following the **switch**.

The **default** is an optional case. When present, it will be executed if the value of the expression does not match with any of the case values. If not present, no action takes place when all matches fail and the control goes to the *statement-x*.

The selection process of **switch** statement is illustrated in the flowchart shown in Fig. 6.6.

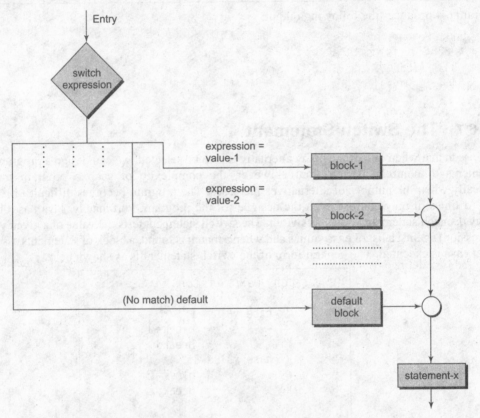

Fig. 6.6　*Selection process of the switch statement*

The **switch** statement can be used to grade the students as discussed in the last section. This is illustrated below:

```
        . . . . . . . . . .
        . . . . . . . . . .
        index = marks/10;
        switch(index)
        {
```

(Continued)

Program   (*Continued*)

```
            case 10:
            case 9:
            case 8:
                    grade = "Honours";
                    break;
            case 7:
            case 6:
                    grade = "First Division";
                    break;
            case 5:
                    grade = "Second Division";
                    break;
            case 4:
                    grade = "Third Division";
                    break;
            default:
                    grade = "Fail";
                    break;
        }
        System.out.println(grade);
        ..........
        ..........
```

Note that we have used a conversion statement

```
index = marks/10;
```

where, index is defined as an integer. The variable index takes the following integer values.

Marks	Index
100	10
90 – 99	9
80 – 89	8
70 – 79	7
60 – 69	6
50 – 59	5
40 – 49	4
30 – 39	3
20 – 29	2
10 – 19	1
0 – 9	0

The segment of the program illustrates two important features. First, it uses empty cases. The first three cases will execute the same statements

```
grade = "Honours";
break;
```

Same is the case with case 7 and case 6. Second, default condition is used for all other cases where marks is less than 40.

Program 6.5 illustrates the use of **switch** for designing a menudriven interactive program.

Program 6.5   *Testing the switch ( )*

```java
class CityGuide
{
  public static void main(String args[])
  {
    char choice;
    System.out.println("Select your choice");
    System.out.println(" M -> Madras");
    System.out.println(" B -> Bombay");
    System.out.println(" C -> Calcutta");
    System.out.print("Choice --->");
    System.out.flush();
    try
    {
      switch (choice = (char) System.in.read())
      {
        case 'M':
        case 'm': System.out.println("Madras : Booklet 5");
                  break;
        case 'B':
        case 'b': System.out.println("Bombay : Booklet 9");
                  break;
        case 'C':
        case 'c': System.out.println("Calcutta: Booklet15");
                  break;
        default: System.out.println("Invalid Choice (IC)");
      }
    }
    catch (Exception e)
    {
      System.out.println("I/O Error");
    }
  }
}
```

Output of the Program 6.5:

```
Run1
Select your choice
    M ---> Madras
    B ---> Bombay
    C ---> Calcutta
Choice ---> m
Madras : Booklet 5
```

```
Run2
Select your choice
     M ---> Madras
     B ---> Bombay
     C ---> Calcutta
Choice ---> M
Madras : Booklet 5
Run3
Select your choice
     M ---> Madras
     B ---> Bombay
     C ---> Calcutta
Choice ---> c
Calcutta : Booklet15
```

 ## 6.8   The ? : Operator

The Java language has an unusual operator, useful for making two-way decisions. This operator is a combination of ? and :, and takes three operands. This operator is popularly known as the conditional operator. The general form of use of the *conditional operator* is as follows:

> *conditional expression* **?** *expression1* **:** *expression2*

The *conditional expression* is evaluated first. If the result is true, *expression1* is evaluated and is returned as the value of the conditional expression. Otherwise, *expression2* is evaluated and its value is returned. For example, the segment

```
if (x < 0)
    flag = 0;
else
    flag = 1;
```

can be written as

```
flag = (x<0) ? 0 : 1;
```

Consider the evaluation of the following function:

```
y = 1.5x + 3   for x <= 2
y = 2x + 5            for x > 2
```

This can be evaluated using the conditional operator as follows:

```
y = (x>2) ? (2*x+5) : (1.5*x+3);
```

The conditional operator may be nested for evaluating more complex assignment decisions. For example, consider the weekly salary of a salesgirl who is selling some domestic products. If x is the number of products sold in a week, her weekly salary is given by

```
              {      4x + 100      for x < 40
salary  =     {      300           for  x = 40
              {      4.5x + 150  for x > 40
```

This complex equation can be written as

```
salary = (x!= 40) ? ((x<40) ? (4*x+100) : (4.5*x+150)) : 300;
```

The same can be evaluated using **if....else** statements as follows:

```
if (x <= 40)
    if (x<40)
        salary = 4*x+100;
    else
        salary = 300;
else
    salary = 4.5*x + 150;
```

When the conditional operator is used, the code becomes more concise and perhaps, more efficient. However, the readability is poor. It is better to use **if** statements when more than a single nesting of conditional operator is required.

6.9   Summary

We have discussed in this chapter the features of the following selection statements supported by Java:

- if statement
- switch statement
- ?: operator statement

We have seen the various forms of application of these statements and discussed how they can be used to solve real-life problems. Control execution is an extremely important tool in programming. The concepts discussed here will be certainly useful in developing complex systems.

 Key Terms

Decision Making, Branching, Control, Conditional Branching, Ladder, Selection, Switch, Conditional Operator.

REVIEW QUESTIONS

6.1   Determine whether the following are true or false:

(a)   When **if** statements are nested, the last **else** gets associated with the nearest **if** without an **else**.
(b)   One **if** can have more than one **else** clause.
(c)   A **switch** statement can always be replaced by a series of **if...else** statements.
(d)   A **switch** expression can be of any type.
(e)   A program stops its execution when a **break** statement in encountered.

6.2   In what ways does a **switch** statement differ from an **if** statement?

6.3   Find errors, if any, in each of the following segments:

(a) ```if (x+y = z && y>0)```

(b) `if(code>1);`
    `a = b+c`
  `else`
    `a = 0`

(c) `if (p<0) || (q<0)`

6.4 The following is a segment of a program:

```
X = 1;
y = 1;
if(n>0)
    X = x+1;
    Y = y-1;
```

What will be the values of **x** and **y** if **n** assumes a value of (a) **1** and (b) **0**.

6.5 Rewrite each of the following without using compound relations:

(a) `if(grade<=59 && grade>=50)`
      `second = second + 1`

(b) `if(number>100 || number<0)`
      `System.out.print("Out of range");`
  `else`
      `sum = sum + number;`

(c) `if((M1>60 && M2>60 || T>200)`
      `y=1;`
  `else`
      `y=0;`

6.6 Write a program to find the number of and sum of all integers greater than 100 and less than 200 that are divisible by 7.

6.7 A set of two linear equations with two unknowns x_1 and x_2 is given below:

$$ax_1 + bx_2 = m$$
$$cx_1 + dx_2 = n$$

The set has a unique solution

$$x_1 = \frac{md - bn}{ad - cb}$$

$$x_2 = \frac{na - mc}{ad - cb}$$

provided the denominator $ad - cd$ is not equal to zero.

Write a program that will read the values of constants a,b,c,d, m and n and compute the values of x_1 and x_2. An appropriate message should be printed if $ad - cb = 0.$

6.8 Given a list of marks ranging from **0** to **100**, write a program to compute and print the number of students who have obtained marks

(a) in the range 81 to 100,
(b) in the range 61 to 80,
(c) in the range 41 to 60, and
(d) in the range 0 to 40.

The program should use a minimum number of **if** statements.

6.9   Admission to a professional course is subject to the following conditions:

   (a) Marks in mathematics $>= 60$
   (b) Marks in physics $>= 50$
   (c) Marks in chemistry $>= 40$
   (d) Total in all three subjects $>= 200$
                          (or)
       Total in mathematics and physics $>= 150$

   Given the marks in the three subjects, write a program to process the applications to list the eligible candidates.

6.10 Write a program to print a two-dimensional Square Root Table as shown below, to provide the square root of any number from 0 to 9.9. For example, the value x will give the square root of 3.2 and y the square root of 3.9.

Square Root Table

Number	0.0	0.1	0.2	......	0.9
0.0 1.0 2.0					
3.0			x		y
. . 9.0					

6.11 Shown below is a Floyd's triangle.

          1
          2 3
          4 5 6
          7 8 9 10
          11 15
          .

          .
          79 91

   (a) Write a program to print this triangle.
   (b) Modify the program to produce the following form of Floyd's triangle.

          1
          0 1
          1 0 1
          0 1 0 1
          1 0 1 0 1

6.12 A cloth showroom has announced the following seasonal discounts on purchase of items:

Purchase amount	Discount	
	Mill cloth	Handloom items
0–100	—	5.0%
101–200	5.0%	7.5%
201–300	7.5%	10.0%
Above 300	10.0%	15.0%

Write a program using **switch** and **if** statements to compute the net amount to be paid by a customer.

6.13 Write a program that will read the value of x and evaluate the following function

$$y \quad = \begin{cases} 1 & \text{for } x > 0 \\ 0 & \text{for } x = 0 \\ -1 & \text{for } x < 0 \end{cases}$$

using

(a) nested **if** statements,
(b) **else if** statements, and
(c) conditional operator?:.

DEBUGGING EXERCISES

6.1 In the following code the student grade is declared based on the result achieved. The student must be declared 'Failed' if the grade is 'F'. Correct the code to declare the correct grade of the student?

```
class IfElse
{
    public static void main(String[] args)
    {
        int result = 55;
        char grade;

        if (result >= 90)
        {
                grade = 'A';
        }
        else if (result >= 80)
        {
                grade = 'B';
        }
        else if (result >= 70)
        {
        grade = 'C';
```

(Continued)

Program (*Continued*)

```
            }
            else if (result >= 60)
            {
                    grade = 'D';
            }
            else
            {
                    grade = 'F';
            }
            else
            {
                    grade = 'G';
            }
            System.out.println("Grade of the Student is " + grade);
        }
    }
```

6.2 Following code should compare the value of a variable with the expected value and print appropriate message. What would you modify in the code to obtain the expected message?

```
class CheckValue
{
    public static void main(String[] args)
    {
        inti=2;
        if(i=2) {
        System.out.println("Correct Value");
        }
        else
        {
                System.out.println("Incorrect Value");
        }
    }
}
```

6.3 The following code results in compilation errors. Debug the code and correct the problem.

```
class NumberValue
{
    public static void main(String[] args)
    {
        int number = 3;
        switch (number)
        {
            case 0;
                    System.out.println("Number is 0");
                    break;
```

Program (*Continued*)

```
                case 1:
                        System.out.println("Number is 1");
                        break;
                case 2:
                case 3:
                case 3:
                        System.out.println("Number is 2, 3 or 4");
                        break;
                default:
                        System.out.println("Number is less than 0 or
                        greater than 4");
            }
        }
    }
```

6.4 Provide the missing statement in the following code which derives the month name given the month number?

```
class MonthName
{
    public static void main(String[] args)
    {
        int month = 8;
        switch (month)
        {
        case 1:
                System.out.println("January");
                break;
        case 2:
                System.out.println("February");
                break;
        case 3:
                System.out.println("March");
                break;
        case 4:
                System.out.println("April");
                break;
        case 5:
                System.out.println("May");
                break;
        case 6:
                System.out.println("June");
                break;
        case 7:
                System.out.println("July");
                break;
        case 8:
```

Program   (*Continued*)

```java
                        System.out.println("August");
            case 9:
                    System.out.println("September");
                    break;
            case 10:
                    System.out.println("October");
                    break;
            case 11:
                    System.out.println("November");
                    break;
            case 12:
                    System.out.println("December");
                    break;
            default:
                    System.out.println("not a month!");
                    break;
        }
    }
}
```

6.5   Correct the code for comparison between three numbers?

```java
class NestedIf
{
    public static void main(String[] args)
    {
        int x = 3, y = 1, z = 5;
        if(x > y)
        {
            if(z <= y)
            {
                System.out.println("y is greater than z");
            }
            else if
            {
                System.out.println("z is greater than y");
            }
            System.out.println("x is greater than y");
        }
        else
        {
            if (y > z)
            {
                System.out.println("y is greater than z");
            }
        }
    }
}
```

Chapter **7**

Decision Making and Looping

7.1 Introduction

A computer is well suited to perform repetitive operations. It can do it tirelessly for 10, 100 or even 10,000 times. Every computer language must have features that instruct a computer to perform such repetitive tasks. The process of repeatedly executing a block of statements is known as *looping*. The statements in the block may be executed any number of times, from zero to *infinite* number. If a loop continues forever, it is called an *infinite loop*.

Java supports such looping features which enable us to develop concise programs containing repetitive processes without using unconditional branching statements like **goto** statement.

In looping, a sequence of statements are executed until some conditions for the termination of the loop are satisfied. A *program loop* therefore consists of two segments, one known as the *body of the loop* and the other known as the control statement. The *control statement* tests certain conditions and then directs the repeated execution of the statements contained in the body of the loop.

Depending on the position of the control statement in the loop, a control structure may be classified either as the *entry-controlled* loop or as *exit-controlled* loop. The flowcharts in Fig. 7.1 illustrate these structures. In the entry-controlled loop, the control conditions are tested before the start of the loop execution. If the conditions are not satisfied, then the body of the loop will not be executed. In the case of an exit-controlled loop, the test is performed at the end of the body of the loop and therefore the body is executed unconditionally for the first time.

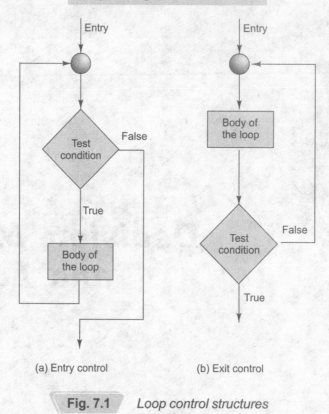

Fig. 7.1 *Loop control structures*

The test conditions should be carefully stated in order to perform the desired number of loop executions. It is assumed that the test condition will eventually transfer the control out of the loop. In case, due to some reason it does not do so, the control sets up an *infinite* loop and the body is executed over and over again.

A looping process, in general, would include the following four steps:

1. Setting and initialization of a counter.
2. Execution of the statements in the loop.
3. Test for a specified condition for execution of the loop.
4. Incrementing the counter.

The test may be either to determine whether the loop has been repeated the specified number of times or to determine whether a particular condition has been met with.

The Java language provides for three constructs for performing loop operations. They are:

1. **while** construct
2. **do** construct
3. **for** construct

We shall discuss the features and applications of each of these constructs in this chapter.

7.2 The While Statement

The simplest of all the looping structures in Java is the **while** statement. The basic format of the **while** statement is

```
Initialization;
While (test condition)
{
        Body of the loop
}
```

The **while** is an *entry-controlled* loop statement. The *test condition* is evaluated and if the condition is true, then the body of the loop is executed. After execution of the body, the test condition is once again evaluated and if it is true, the body is executed once again. This process of repeated execution of the body continues until the test condition finally becomes false and the control is transferred out of the loop. On exit, the program continues with the statement immediately after the body of the loop.

The body of the loop may have one or more statements. The braces are needed only if the body contains two or more statements. However, it is a good practice to use braces even if the body has only one statement.

Consider the following code segment:

```
. . . . . . . . .
. . . . . . . . .
sum = 0;
n = 1;

while(n <= 10)
{
        sum = sum + n * n;
        n = n+1;
}
System.out.println("Sum = "+ sum);
. . . . . . . . .
. . . . . . . . .
```

The body of the loop is executed 10 times for n = 1, 2, ..., 10 each time adding the square of the value of n, which is incremented inside the loop. The test condition may also be written as n < 11; the result would be the same. Program 7.1 illustrates the use of the **while** for reading a string of characters from the keyboard. The loop terminates when c = '\ n', the newline character.

Program 7.1 *Using while loop*

```
class WhileTest
{
    public static void main(String args[ ])
    {
```

(Continued)

Program 7.1 (*Continued*)

```
StringBuffer string = new StringBuffer();
char c;
System.out.println("Enter a string ");

try
{
    while ( (c = (char)System.in.read()) != '\n')
    {
        string.append(c); // Append character
    }
}
catch (Exception e)
{
    System.out.println("Error in input");
}
System.out.println(" You have entered ...");
system.out.println(string);
}
}
```

Given below is the output of Program 7.1:

```
Enter a string
Java is a true Object-Oriented Language
      You have entered ...
Java is a true Object-Oriented Language
```

7.3 The do Statement

The **while** loop construct that we have discussed in the previous section makes a test condition *before* the loop is executed. Therefore, the body of the loop may not be executed at all if the condition is not satisfied at the very first attempt. On some occasions it might be necessary to execute the body of the loop before the test is performed. Such situations can be handled with the help of the **do** statement. This takes the form:

```
Initialization;
do
{
        Body of the loop
}
while (test condition);
```

On reaching the **do** statement, the program proceeds to evaluate the body of the loop first. At the end of the loop, the *test condition* in the **while** statement is evaluated. If the condition is true, the program continues to evaluate the body hf the *loop* once again. This process continues as long as the *condition* is true. When the condition becomes false, the loop will be terminated and the control goes to the statement that appears immediately after the **while** statement.

Since the *test condition* is evaluated at the bottom of the loop, the **do....while** construct provides an *exit-controlled* loop and therefore the body of the lop is always executed at least once.

Consider an example:

```
. . . . . . . . .
. . . . . . . . .
i = 1;
sum = 0;

do
{
 sum = sum + i;
 i = i+2;
}
while(sum < 40 || i < 10);
. . . . . . . . .
. . . . . . . . .
```

The loop will be executed as long as one of the two relations is true. Program 7.2 illustrates the use of **do....while** loops for printing a multiplication table.

Program 7.2   *Printing multiplication table using do....while loop*

```
class DoWhileTest
{
  public static void main(String args[])
  {
    int row, column, y;
    System.out.println("Multiplication Table \n");
    row = 1;

    do
    {
    column = 1;
    do
    {
      y = row * column;
      System.out.print("   " + y);
      column = column + 1;
    }
    while (column <= 3);

    Sysem.out.println("\n");
    row = row + 1;
    }
  while (row <= 3);
  }
}
```

Program 7.2 uses two **do-while** loops in nested form and produces the following output:

Multiplication Table

1	2	3
2	4	6
3	6	9

7.4   The for Statement

The **for** loop is another *entry-controlled* loop that provides a more concise loop control structure. The general form of the **for** loop is

```
for (initialization ; test condition ; increment)
{
        Body of the loop
}
```

The execution of the **for** statement is as follows:

1. *Initialization* of the *control variables* is done first, using assignment statements such as i = 1 and count = 0. The variables **i** and **count** are known as loop-control variables.
2. The value of the control variable is tested using the *test condition*. The test condition is a relational expression, such as i < 10 that determines when the loop will exit. If the condition is *true*, the body of the loop is executed; otherwise the loop is terminated and the execution continues with the statement that immediately follows the loop.
3. When the body of the loop is executed, the control is transferred back to the **for** statement after evaluating the last statement in the loop. Now, the control variable is *incremented* using an assignment stement such as i = i + 1 and the new value of the control variable is again tested to see whether it satisfies the loop condition. If the condition is satisfied, the body of the loop is again executed. This process continues till the value of the control variable fails to satisfy the test condition.

Consider the following segment of a program

```
for (x = 0 ; x < = 9; x = x+1)
{
        System.out.println(x);
}
```

This **for** loop is executed 10 times and prints the digits 0 to 9 in one line. The three sections enclosed within parentheses must be separated by semicolons. Note that there is no semicolon at the end of the *increment* section, **x = x + 1.**

The **for** statement allows for negative *increments*. For example, the loop discussed above can be written as follows:

```
for (x = 9; x >| = 0; x = x-1)
        System.out.println(x);
```

This loop is also executed 10 times, but the output would be from 9 to 0 instead of 0 to 9. Note that braces are optional when the body of the loop contains only one statement.

Since the conditional test is always performed at the beginning of the loop, the body of the loop may not be executed at all, if the condition fails at the start. For example,

```
for (x = 9; x < 9; x = x-1)
{
. . . . . . . . . .
. . . . . . . . . .
}
```

will never be executed beause the test condition fails at the very beginning itself.

Let us consider the problem of sum of squares of integers discussed in Section 7.2. This problem can be coded using the **for** statement as follows:

```
. . . . . . . . . .
. . . . . . . . . .
sum = 0;
for (n = 1; n <= 10; n = n+1)
{
     sum = sum + n*n;
}
. . . . . . . . . .
. . . . . . . . . .
```

The body of the loop

```
sum = sum + n*n;
```

is executed 10 times for n = 1, 2, ..., 10 each time incrementing the **sum** by the square of the value of **n**.

One of the important points about the **for** loop is that all the three actions, namely *initialization*, *testing* and *incrementing*, are placed in the **for** statement itself, thus making them visible to the programmes and users, in one place. The **for** statement and its equivalent of **while** and **do** statements are shown in Table 7.1.

Table 7.1 Comparison of the Three Loops		
for	*while*	*do*
`for (n=1;n<=10;++n)`	`n = 1`	`n = 1`
`{`	`while (n<=10)`	`do`
`. . . . . . . . .`	`{`	`{`
`. . . . . . . . .`	`. . . . . . . . .`	`. . . . . . . . .`
`}`	`. . . . . . . . .`	`. . . . . . . . .`
	`n = n+1;`	`n = n+1`
	`}`	`}`
		`while (n<=10);`

Program 7.3 illustrates the use of **for** loop for computing and printing the "power of 2" table.

Program 7.3   *Computing the 'power of 2' using for loop*

```
Class ForTest
{
  public static void main(String args[ ])
  {
    long p;
    int n;
    double q;
    System.out.println("2 to power -n    n    2 to power n");

    p = 1;
    for (n = 0; n < 10; ++n)
    {
      if (n == 0)
        p = 1;
      else
        p = p * 2;
      q = 1.0 / (double)p;
      System.out.println("  " + q + "  " + n + "  " + p);
    }
  }
}
```

Output of Program 7.3 would be:

2 to power –n	n	2 to power n
1	0	1
0.5	1	2
0.25	2	4
0.125	3	8
0.0625	4	16
0.03125	5	32
0.015625	6	64
0.00390625	7	128
0.00195313	8	256
0.00195313	9	512

Additional Features of for Loop

The **for** loop has several capabilities that are not found in other loop construts. For example, more than one variable can be initialized at a time in the **for** statement. The statements

```
      p = 1;
      for (n=0; n<17; ++n)
```

can be rewritten as

```
      for (p=1, n=0; n<17; ++n)"
```

Notice that the initialization section has two parts p = 1 and n = 1 separated by a *comma*.

Like the initialization section, the increment section may also have more than one part. For example, the loop

```
for (n=1, m=50; n<=m; n=n+1, m=m-1)
{
    .........
    .........
}
```

is perfectly valid. The multiple arguments in the increment section are separated by *commas*.

The third feature is that the test condition may have any compound relation and the testing need not be limited only to the loop control variable. Consider the example that follows:

```
sum = 0;
for (i = 1, i < 20 && sum < 100; ++i)
{
    .........
    .........
}
```

The loop uses a compound test condition with the control variable i and external variable **sum**. The loop is executed as long as both the conditions i < 20 and sum < 100 are true. The sum is evaluated inside the loop.

It is also permissible to use expressions in the assignment statements of initialization and increment sections. For example, a statement of the type

```
for (x = (m+n)/2; x > 0; x = x/2)
```

is perfectly valid.

Another unique aspect of **for** loop is that one or more sections can be omitted, if necessary. Consider the following statements:

```
.........
.........
m = 5;
for ( ;m != 100 ; )
{
    System.out.println(m);
    m = m+5;
}
.........
.........
```

Both the initialization and increment sections are omitted in the **for** statement. The initialization has been done before the **for** statement and the control variable is incremented inside the loop. In such cases, the sections are left blank. However, the semicolons separating the sections must remain. If the test condition is not present, the **for** statement sets up an infinite loop.

We can set up time delay loops using the null statement as follows:

```
for (j = 1000; j > 0; j = j-1)
    ;
```

This loop is executed 1000 times without producing any output; it simply causes a time delay. Notice that the body of the loop contains only a semicolon, known as a *empty* statement. This can also be written as

```
for (j=1000; j > 0; j = j-1);
```

This implies that the compiler will not give an error message if we place a semicolon by mistake at the end of a **for** statement. The semicolon will be considered as an *empty* statement and the program may produce some nonsense.

Nesting of for Loops

Nesting of loops, that is, one **for** statement within another **for** statement, is allowed in Java. We have used this concept in Program 7.2. Similarly, **for** loops can be nested as follows:

```
. . . . . . . . . .
. . . . . . . . . .
for (i = 1; i < 10; ++i)
{

        . . . . . . . . . .
        . . . . . . . . . .
    for (j = 1; j < ! = 5; ++j)
    {

            . . . . . . . . . .
            . . . . . . . . . .    Inner loop        Outer
    }                                                Loop
        . . . . . . . . . .
        . . . . . . . . . .
}
. . . . . . . . . .
. . . . . . . . . .
```

The loops should be properly indented so as to enable the reader to easily determine which statements are contained within each **for** statement.

A program segment to print a multiplication table using **for** loops is shown below:

```
. . . . . . . . . .
. . . . . . . . . .
for (row = 1; row <= ROWMAX: ++row)
{
    for (column = 1; column <= COLMAX: ++column)
    {
            Y = row * column
            System.out.print(" " + Y);
    }
    System.out.println(" " );
}
. . . . . . . . . .
. . . . . . . . . .
```

The outer loop controls the rows while the inner one controls the columns.

The Enhanced for Loop

The enhanced **for** loop, also called *for each loop*, is an extended language feature introduced with the J2SE 5.0 release. This feature helps us to retrieve the array of elements efficiently rather than using array indexes. We can also use this feature to eliminate the iterators in a for loop and to retrieve the elements from a collection. The enhanced for loop takes the following form:

```
for (Type Identifier : Expression)
{
    //statements;
}
```

where, *Type* represents the data type or object used; *Identifier* refers to the name of a variable; and *Expression* is an instance of the java.lang.Iterable interface or an array.

For example, consider the following statements:

```
int numarry[3] = {56, 48, 79};
for (int k=0; k<=3; k++)
{
    if (numarray[k]>50 && numarray[k]<100)
    {
        System.out.println("The selected value is "+numarray[k]);
    }
}
```

which is equivalent to the following code:

```
int numarray[3] = [56, 48, 79};
for (int k:nummary)
{
    if (k>50 && k<100)
    {
        System.out.println("The selected value is "+k);
    }
}
```

Thus, we can use the enhanced for loop to track the elements of an array efficiently. In the same manner, we can track the collection elements using the enhanced for loop as follows:

```
Stack samplestack = new Stack();
samplestack.push(new Integer(56));
samplestack.push(new Integer(48));
samplestack.push(new Integer(79));
for(Object obj : samplestack)
{
    System.out.println(obj);
}
```

Program 7.4 *Use of enhanced for loop to retrieve the elements of arrays*

```
import java.util.*;
class EnhanceForLoop
{
    public static void main(String args[])
    {
        System.out.println();
        String
        states[] = {"TamilNadu", "AndhraPradesh", "UttarPradesh",
                    "Rajasthan"};
        for(int i=0;i<states.length;i++)
        {
            System.out.println("Standard for-loop : state name : "+states[i]);
        }
        System.out.println();
        for(String i:states)                    // enhanced for loop
        {
            System.out.println("Enhanced for-loop : state name : " + i);
        }
        System.out.println();
        ArrayList<String> cities = new ArrayList<String>();
            cities.add("Delhi");
            cities.add("Mumbai");
            cities.add("Calcutta");
            cities.add("Chennai");
            System.out.println();
        for(int i=0;i<cities.size();i++)
        {
            System.out.println("Standard for-loop : city name : "+cities.get(i));
        }
        System.out.println();
            for(String city : cities)    // enhanced for loop
                System.out.println("Enhanced for-loop : city name : "+city);
        System.out.println();
        System.out.println("In Collections");
        System.out.println();
            printcollection(cities);
    }
    public static<AnyType> void printcollection(Collection<AnyType> c)
    {
        for (AnyType val : c)
        System.out.println(val);
    }
}
```

The output of the above program is as follows:

```
Standard for-loop : state name : TamilNadu
Standard for-loop : state name : AndhraPradesh
Standard for-loop : state name : UttarPradesh
Standard for-loop : state name : Rajasthan

Enhanced for-loop : state name : TamileNadu
Enhanced for-loop : state name : AndhraPradesh
Enhanced for-loop : state name : UttarRradesh
Enhanced for-loop : state name : Rajasthan

Standard for-loop : city name : Delhi
Standard for-loop : city name : Mumbai
Standard for-loop : city name : Calcutta
Standard for-loop : city name : Chennai

Enhanced for-loop : city name : Delhi
Enhanced for-loop : city name : Mumbai
Enhanced for-loop : city name : Calcutta
Enhanced for-loop : city name : Chennai

In Collections:

Delhi
Mumbai
Calcutta
Chennai
```

7.5 Jumps in Loops

Loops perform a set of operations repeatedly until the control variable fails to satisfy the test condition. The number of times a loop is repeated is decided in advance and the test condition is written to achieve this. Sometimes, when executing a loop it becomes desirable to skip a part of the loop or to leave the loop as soon as a certain condition occurs. For example, consider the case of searching for a particular name in a list containing, say, 100 names. A program loop written for reading and testing the names a 100 times must be terminated as soon as the desired name is found. Java permits a jump from one statement to the *end* or *beginning* of a loop as well as a *jump out of a loop*.

Jumping Out of a Loop

An early exit from a loop can be accomplished by using the **break** statement. We have already seen the use of the **break** in the **switch** statement. This statement can also be used within **while**, **do** or **for** loops as illustrated in Fig. 7.2.

When the **break** statement is encountered inside a loop, the loop is immediately exited and the program continues with the statement immediately following the loop. When the loops are nested, the break would only exit from the loop containing it. That is, the break will exit only a single loop.

```
      While (..........)                        do
      {                                         {
          ..........                                ..........
          ..........                                ..........
          if (condition)                            if (condition)
            ┌──── break;                             ┌──── break;
Exit      │   ..........              Exit         │   ..........
from      │   ..........              from         │   ..........
loop  }   │                           loop         } while (..........)
      └──→ ..........                              └──→ ..........

            (a)                                       (b)


      for(..........)                           for(..........)
      {                                         {
          ..........                                ..........
          ..........                                ..........
          if (error)                                for(..........)
            ┌──── break;                            {
Exit      │   ..........                                ..........
from      │   ..........            Exit                if (condition)
loop  }   │                         from                  ┌──── break;
      └──→ ..........               Inner               │   ..........
                                    loop    }           │
                                            └──→ ..........
                                                }

            (c)                                       (d)
```

Fig. 7.2   *Exiting a loop with break statement*

Skipping a Part of a Loop

During the loop operations, it may be necessary to skip a part of the body of the loop under certain conditions. For example, in processing of applications for some job, we might like to exclude the processing of data of applicants belonging to a certain category. On reading the category code of an applicant, a test is made to see whether his application should be considered or not. If it is not to be considered, the part of the program loop that processes the application details is skipped and the execution continues with the next loop operation.

Like the **break** statement, Java supports another similar statement called the **continue** statement. However, unlike the **break** which causes the loop to be terminated, the **continue**, as the name implies, causes the loop to be continued with the next iteration after skipping any statements in between. The continue statement tells the compiler. "SKIP THE FOLLOWING STATEMENTS AND CONTINUE WITH THE NEXT ITERATION". The format of the **continue** statement is simply

```
Continue;
```

The use of the **continue** statement in loops is illustrated in Fig. 7.3. In **while** and **do** loops, **continue** causes the control to go directly to the *test condition* and then to continue the iteration process. In the case of **for** loop, the *increment* section of the loop is executed before the *test condition* is evaluated.

```
    ┌─► while (test condition)          do
    │   {                               {
    │     ..........                      ..........
    │     if(..........)                  if(..........)
    └───── continue;                ┌───── continue;
          ..........                │     ..........
          ..........                │     ..........
    }                               └──► } while (test condition);
         (a)                                    (b)
  ┌─► for (initialization; test condition; increment)
  │   {
  │     ..........
  │     if(..........)
  └───── continue;
        ..........
        ..........
  }
                          (c)
```

Fig. 7.3   *Bypassing and continuing in loops*

7.6 Labelled Loops

In Java, we can give a label to a block of statements. A label is any valid Java variable name. To give a label to a loop, place it before the loop with a colon at the end. Example:

```
loop1:      for (..........)
            {
                  ..........
                  ..........
            }
            ..........
```

A block of statements can be labelled as shown below:

```
block1:          {   ..........
                     ..........
block2:          {   ..........
                     ..........
                 }
                 ..........
                 ..........
            }
```

We have seen that a simple **break** staement causes the control to jump outside the nearest loop and a simple **continue** statement restarts the current loop. If we want to jump outside a nested loops or to continue a loop that is outside the current one, then we may have to use the labelled **break** and labelled **continue** statements. Example:

```
outer: for (int m = 1; m<11; m++)
        {
            for (int n = 1; n<11; n++)
            {
                System. out. print (" " + m*n);
                if (n == m)
                    continue outer;
            }
        }
```

Here, the **continue** statement terminates the inner loop when n = m and continues with the next iteration of the outer loop (counting m).

Another example:

```
loop1:    for (int  i = 0; i < 10; i++)
          {
loop2:        while (x < 100)
              {
                  Y = i * x;
                  if (Y > 500)
                  break loop1;
                  ..........
                  ..........
              }
              ..........
          }
          ..........
```

Jumping out of both loops

Here, the label **loop1** labels the outer loop and therefore the statement

```
break loop1;
```

causes the execution to break out of both the loops. Program 7.4 illustrates the use of **break** and **continue** statements.

Program 7.5   *Use of continue and break statements*

```
class ContinueBreak
{
    public static void main(String args[])
    {
        LOOP1 : for (int i = 1; i < 100; i++)
                {
                    System.out.println (" ");
                    if (i >= 10) break;
                    for (int j = 1; j < 100; j++)
                    {
                        System.out.print (" * ");
```

(Continued)

Program 7.5 (*Continued*)

```
                        if (j == i)
                            continue LOOP1;
                    }
                }
                System.out.println("Termination by BREAK");
    }
}
```

Program 7.5 produces the following output:

```
        *
        *    *
        *    *    *
        *    *    *    *
        *    *    *    *    *
        *    *    *    *    *    *
        *    *    *    *    *    *    *
        *    *    *    *    *    *    *    *
        *    *    *    *    *    *    *    *    *

        Termination by BREAK
```

7.7 Summary

The loops and conditional statements covered here and in Chapter 6 are the backbone of any programming language. We dicussed in this chapter the following loop constructs:

- **while** structure
- **do** structure
- **for** structure

They would be extremely useful in developing concise, compact and structured programs. We have also seen how to use the **break** and **continue** statements to skip or jump out of a loop, if need be.

 Key Terms

Looping, Infinite Loop, Entry-control, Exit-control, Nesting, Empty Statement, Enhanced for loop, Labelled Loops, Continue, Break.

REVIEW QUESTIONS

7.1   Compare in terms of their functions, the following pairs of statements:

   (a) while and do....while

   (b) while and for

   (c) break and continue

7.2 Analyze each of the program segments that follow and determine how many times the body of each loop will be executed.

(a)
```
x = 5;
y = 50;
while(x <= y)
{
  x = y/x;
  ..........
  ..........
}
```

(b)
```
m = 1;
do
{
  ..........
  ..........
  m = m+2;
}
while (m < 10)
```

(c)
```
int i;
for (i=0; i<=5; i = i+2/3)
{
  ..........
  ..........
}
```

(d)
```
int m = 10;
int n = 7
while (m % n >= 0)
{
  ..........
  m = m+1;
  n = n+2;
  ..........
}
```

7.3 Find errors, if any, in each of the following looping segments. Assume that all the variables have been declared and assigned values.

(a)
```
while (count != 10);
{
  count = 1;
  sum = sum + x;
  count = count + 1;
}
```

(b)
```
name = 0;
do { name = name + 1;
System.out.println("My name is
John \n";}
while (name = 1)
```

(c)
```
for (x=1, x>10; x = x+1)
{
  ..........
  ..........
}
```

(d)
```
m = 1;
n = 0;
for (; m+n < 19; ++n)
System.out.println("Hello \n");
m = m+10;
```

7.4 What is an empty statement? Explain its usefulness.

7.5 Given a number, write a program using **while** loop to reverse the digits of the number. For example, the number

   12345

should be written as

   54321

(Hint: Use modulus operator to extract the last digit and the integer division by 10 to get the n–1 digit number from the *n* digit number).

7.6 The factorial of an integer *m* is the product of consecutive integers from 1 to *m*. That is factorial m = m! = m * (m–1)* .... * 1.

Write a program that computes and prints a table of factorials for any given *m*.

7.7 Write a program to compute the sum of the digits of a given integer number.

7.8 The numbers in the sequence

     1 1 2 3 5 8 13 21 ....

are called Fibonacci numbers. Write a program using a **do....while** loop to calculate and print the first *m* Fibonacci numbers.

(Hint: After the first two numbers in the series, each number is the sum of the two preceding numbers).

7.9 Write a program to evaluate the following investment equation

    $V = P(1+r)^n$

and print the tables which would give the value of V for various combination of the following values of P, r and n.

    P: 1000, 2000, 3000, ..., 10,000
    r: 0.10, 0.11, 0.12, ..., 0.20
    n: 1, 2, 3, ..., 10

(Hint: P is the principal amount and V is the value of money at the end of n years. This equation can be recursively written as

    $V = P(1+r)$
    $P = V$

That is, the value of money at the end of first year becomes the principal amount for the next year and so on).

7.10 Write a program to print the following outputs using **for** loops.

(a)   1
     2 2
     3 3 3
     4 4 4 4
     5 5 5 5 5

(b) $ $ $ $ $
     $ $ $ $
     $ $ $
     $ $
     $

(c)   1
       2 2
     3 3 3
    4 4 4 4
   5 5 5 5 5

DEBUGGING EXERCISES

7.1 Following is the code for printing a list of number using while loop. Modify the code to achieve the result.

```java
class numberlist
{
    public static void main(String[] args)
    {
        int i=1;
        while(i>=10)
        {
            System.out.println(i);
            i++;
        }
    }
}
```

7.2   Debug the given code for displaying the numbers 1 to 10 using do-while loop.

```java
class doWhile
{
    public static void main(String[] args)
    {
        int num=1;
        do
        {
            System.out.println(num);
            num++;
        } while(num>=10);
    }
}
```

7.3   Correct the code to rectify the compile time error thrown.

```java
class ForLoop
{
    public static void main(String[] args)
    {
        int num=10;
        for(num>=1)
        {
            num=num-1;
            System.out.println(num);
        }
    }
}
```

7.4   Program for calculating factorial of a number has been written using For loop. Correct the code.

```java
class factorial
{
    public static void main(String[] args)
    {
        int num=0,fact=1;
        for(int num=5;num>=1;num--)
        {
            fact*=num;
        }
        System.out.println("Factorial of 5 is "+fact);
    }
}
```

7.5   For finding a value in an array, following code is available. Does the program generate correct output? If not, why? Modify the code.

```java
class FindValue
{
    public static void main(String[ ] args)
```

```
    {
        int[] array = {32, 87, 3, 589, 12, 1076, 2000, 8, 622, 127};
        int searchVal = 12;
        int i = 0;
        boolean found = false;
        for(;i<array.length;i++)
        {
            if(array[i] == searchVal)
            {
                found = true;
            }
        }
        if (found)
        {
            System.out.println("Found" + searchVal + " at index " + i);
        }
        else
        {
            System.out.println(searchVal + " not in the array");
        }
    }
}
```

Chapter **8**

Classes, Objects and Methods

8.1 Introduction

Java is a true object-oriented language and therefore the underlying structure of all Java programs is classes. Anything we wish to represent in a Java program must be encapsulated in a class that defines the *state* and *behaviour* of the basic program components known as *objects*. Classes create objects and objects use methods to communicate between them. That is all about object-oriented programming.

Classes provide a convenient method for packing together a group of logically related data items and functions that work on them. In Java, the data items are called *fields* and the functions are called *methods*. Calling a specific method in an object is described as sending the object a message.

A class is essentially a description of how to make an object that contains fields and methods. It provides a sort of *template* for an object and behaves like a basic data type such as **int**. It is therefore important to understand how the fields and methods are defined in a class and how they are used to build a Java program that incorporates the basic OOP concepts such as *encapsulation, inheritance* and *polymorphism*.

8.2 Defining a Class

As stated earlier, a class is a user-defined data type with a template that serves to define its properties. Once the class type has been defined, we can create "variables" of that type using declarations that are similar to the basic type declarations. In Java, these variables are termed as *instances* of classes, which are the actual *objects*. The basic form of a class definition is:

```
class classname [extends superclassname]
{
        [ fields declaration; ]
        [ methods declaration; ]
}
```

Everything inside the square brackets is optional. This means that the following would be a valid class definition:

```
class Empty
{
}
```

Because the body is empty, this class does not contain any properties and therefore cannot do anything. We can, however, compile it and even create objects using it. *C++ programmers may note that there is no semicolon after closing brace.*

classname and *superclassname* are any valid Java identifiers. The keyword **extends** indicates that the properties of the *superclassname* class are extended to the *classname* class. This concept is known as *inheritance* and is discussed in Section 8.11. Fields and methods are declared inside the body.

8.3 Fields Declaration

Data is encapsulated in a class by placing data fields inside the body of the class definition. These variables are called *instance variables* because they are created whenever an object of the class is instantiated. We can declare the instance variables exactly the same way as we declare local variables. Example:

```
class Rectangle
{
        int length;
        int width;
}
```

The class **Rectangle** contains two integer type instance variables. It is allowed to declare them in one line as

```
int length, width;
```

Remember these variables are only declared and therefore no storage space has been created in the memory. Instance variables are also known as *member variables*.

8.4 Methods Declaration

A class with only data fields (and without methods that operate on that data) has no life. The objects created by such a class cannot respond to any messages. We must therefore add methods that are necessary for manipulating the data contained in the class. Methods are declared inside the body of the class but immediately after the declaration of instance variables. The general form of a method declaration is

```
type methodname (parameter-list)
{
    method-body;
}
```

Method declarations have four basic parts:

- The name of the method (*methodname*)
- The type of the value the method returns (*type*)
- A list of parameters (*parameter-list*)
- The body of the method

The *type* specifies the type of value the method would return. This could be a simple data type such as **int** as well as any class type. It could even be **void** type, if the method does not return any value. The *methodname* is a valid identifier. The *parameter* list is always enclosed in parentheses. This list contains variable names and types of all the values we want to give to the method as input. The variables in the list are separated by commas. In the case where no input data are required, the declaration must retain the empty parentheses. Examples:

```
(int m, float x, float y)    // Three parameters
( )                          // Empty list
```

The *body* actually describes the operations to be performed on the data. Let us consider the **Rectangle** class again and add a method **getData ( )** to it.

```
class Rectangle
{
    int length;
    int width;
    void getData (int x, int y) // Method declaration
    {
        length = x;
        width  = y;
    }
}
```

Note that the method has a return type of **void** because it does not return any value. We pass two integer values to the method which are then assigned to the instance variables **length** and **width**. The **getData** method is basically added to provide values to the instance variables. Notice that we are able to use directly **length** and **width** inside the method.

Let us add some more properties to the class. Assume that we want to compute the area of the rectangle defined by the class. This can be done as follows:

```
class Rectangle
{
    int length, width;  // Combined declaration
    void getData(int x, int y)
```

```
        {
            length = x;
            width  = y;
        }
        int rectArea( ) // Declaration of another method
        {
            int area = length * width;
            return (area);
        }
    }
```

The new method **rectArea( )** computes area of the rectangle and returns the result. Since the result would be an integer, the return type of the method has been specified as **int**. Also note that the parameter list is empty.

Remember that while the declaration of instance variables (and also local variables) can be combined as

```
    int length, width;
```

the parameter list used in the method header should always be declared independently separated by commas. That is,

```
    void getData (int x, y) // Incorrect
```

is illegal.

Now, our class **Rectangle** contains two instance variables and two methods. We can add more variables and methods, if necessary.

Most of the times when we use classes, we will have many methods and variables within the class. Instance variables and methods in classes are accessible by all the methods in the class but a method cannot access the variables declared in other methods. Example:

```
    class Access
    {
        int x ;
        void method1( )
        {
            int y ;
            x = 10 ;        // legal
            y = x ;         // legal
        }
        void method2( )
        {
            int z ;
            x = 5 ;         // legal
            z = 10 ;        // legal
            y = 1 ;         // illegal
        }
    }
```

8.5 Creating Objects

As pointed out earlier, an object in Java is essentially a block of memory that contains space to store all the instance variables. Creating an object is also referred to as *instantiating* an object.

Objects in Java are created using the **new** operator. The **new** operator creates an object of the specified class and returns a reference to that object. Here is an example of creating an object of type **Rectangle**.

```
Rectangle rect1;            // declare the object
rect1 = new Rectangle( );   // instantiate the object
```

The first statement declares a variable to hold the object reference and the second one actually assigns the object reference to the variable. The variable **rect1** is now an object of the **Rectangle** class (see Fig. 8.1)

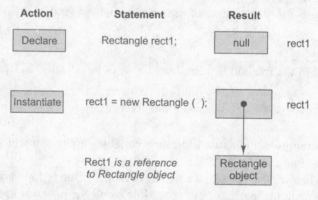

Fig. 8.1   *Creating object references*

Both statements can be combined into one as shown below:

```
Rectangle rect1 = new Rectangle( );
```

The method **Rectangle( )** is the default constructor of the class. We can create any number of objects of **Rectangle**. Example:

```
Rectangle rect1 = new Rectangle( );
Rectangle rect2 = new Rectangle( );
and so on.
```

It is important to understand that each object has its own copy of the instance variables of its class. This means that any changes to the variables of one object have no effect on the variables of another. It is also possible to create two or more references to the same object (see Fig. 8.2).

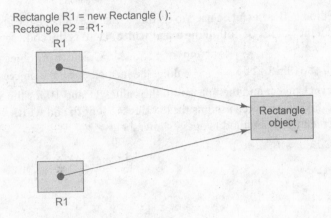

```
Rectangle R1 = new Rectangle ( );
Rectangle R2 = R1;
```

Both R1 and R2 refer to the same object.

Fig. 8.2   *Assigning one object reference variable to another*

8.6 Accessing Class Members

Now that we have created objects, each containing its own set of variables, we should assign values to these variables in order to use them in our program. Remember, all variables must be assigned values before they are used. Since we are outside the class, we cannot access the instance variables and the methods directly. To do this, we must use the concerned object and the *dot* operator as shown below:

```
objectname.variablename = value;
objectname.methodname(parameter-list);
```

Here *objectname* is the name of the object, *variablename* is the name of the instance variable inside the object that we wish to access, *methodname* is the method that we wish to call, and *parameter-list* is a comma separated list of "actual values" (or expressions) that must match in type and number with the parameter list of the methodname declared in the class. The instance variables of the **Rectangle** class may be accessed and assigned values as follows:

```
rect1.length   = 15;
rect1.width    = 10;
rect2.length   = 20;
rect2.width    = 12;
```

Note that the two objects **rect1** and **rect2** store different values as shown below:

	rec1		rec2
rect1.length	15	rec2.length	20
rect1.width	10	rec2.width	12

This is one way of assigning values to the variables in the objects. Another way and more convenient way of assigning values to the instance variables is to use a method that is declared inside the class.

In our case, the method **getData** can be used to do this work. We can call the **getData** method on any **Rectangle** object to set the values of both **length** and **width**. Here is the code segment to achieve this.

```
Rectangle rect1 = new Rectangle( ); // Creating an object
rect1.getData(15, 10);  // Calling the method using the object
```

This code creates **rect1** object and then passes in the values 15 and 10 for the **x** and **y** parameters of the method **getData**. This method then assigns these values to **length** and **width** variables respectively. For the sake of convenience, the method is again shown below:

```
void getData (int x, int y)
{
    length = x;
    width = y;
}
```

Now that the object **rect1** contains values for its variables, we can compute the area of the rectangle represented by **rect1**. This again can be done in two ways.

- The first approach is to access the instance variables using the dot operator and compute the area. That is,

```
int area1 = rect1.length * rect1.width;
```

- The second approach is to call the method **rectArea** declared inside the class. That is,

```
int area1 = rect1.rectArea( );    // Calling the method
```

Program 8.1 illustrates the concepts discussed so far.

Program 8.1 *Application of classes and objects*

```
class Rectangle
{
    int length, width;             //      Declaration of variables
    void getData(int x, int y)     //      Definition of method
    {
        length = x;
        width  = y;
    }
    int rectArea()                 //      Definition of another method
    {
        int area = length * width;
        return (area);
    }
}
class RectArea                     //      Class with main method
{
    public static void main (String args[ ])
    {
        int area1, area2;
        Rectangle rect1 = new Rectangle();         //    Creating objects
```

(Continued)

Program 8.1 (*Continued*)

```
    Rectangle rect2 = new Rectangle();
    Rect1.length = 15;                      //    Accessing variables
    rect1.width = 10;
    area1 = rect1.length * rect1.width;
    rect2.getData (20,12);                  //    Accessing methods
    area2 = rect2.rectArea();
    System.out.println("Area1 = " + area1);
    System.out.println("Area2 = " + area2);
  }
}
```

Program 8.1 would output the following:

```
    Area1 = 150
    Area2 = 240
```

8.7 **Constructors**

We know that all objects that are created must be given initial values. We have done this earlier using two approaches. The first approach uses the dot operator to access the instance variables and then assigns values to them individually. It can be a tedious approach to initialize all the variables of all the objects.

The second approach takes the help of a method like **getData** to initialize each object individually using statements like,

```
        rect1.getData(15,10);
```

It would be simpler and more concise to initialize an object when it is first created. Java supports a special type of method, called a *constructor*, that enables an object to initialize itself when it is created.

Constructors have the same name as the class itself. Secondly, they do not specify a return type, not even **void**. This is because they return the instance of the class itself.

Let us consider our **Rectangle** class again. We can now replace the **getData** method by a constructor method as shown below:

```
    class Rectangle
    {
        int length;
        int width;
        Rectangle(int x, int y) // Constructor method
        {
            length = x;
            width  = y;
        }
        int rectArea( )
        {
```

```
                 return (length * width);
        }
    }
```

Program 8.2 illustrates the use of a constructor method to initialize an object at the time of its creation.

Program 8.2 *Application of constructors*

```
class Rectangle
{
    int length, width;
    Rectangle (int x, int y)                    // Defining constructor
    {
        length = x;
        width  = y;
    }
    int rectArea( )
    {
        return (length * width);
    }
}
class RectangleArea
{
    public static void main (string args[ ])
    {
        Rectangle rect1 = new Rectangle(15, 10); // Calling constructor
        int area1 = rect1.rectArea( );
        System.out.println("Area1 = "+ area1);
    }
}
```

Output of Program 8.2:

```
        Area1 = 150
```

8.8 Methods Overloading

In Java, it is possible to create methods that have the same name, but different parameter lists and different definitions. This is called *method overloading*. Method overloading is used when objects are required to perform similar tasks but using different input parameters. When we call a method in an object, Java matches up the method name first and then the number and type of parameters to decide which one of the definitions to execute. This process is known as *polymorphism*.

To create an overloaded method, all we have to do is to provide several different method definitions in the class, all with the same name, but with different parameter lists. The difference may either be in the number or type of arguments. That is, each parameter list should be unique. Note that the method's return type does not play any role in this. Here is an example of creating an overloaded method.

```
class Room
{
    float length;
    float breadth;
    Room(float x, float y)                  // constructor1
    {
        length = x;
        breadth = y;
    }
    Room(float x)                           // constructor2
    {
        length = breadth = x;
    }
    int area( )
    {
        return (length * breadth);
    }
}
```

Here, we are overloading the constructor method **Room( )**. An object representing a rectangular room will be created as

```
Room room1 = new Room(25.0, 15.0);      // using constructor1
```

On the other hand, if the room is square, then we may create the corresponding object as

```
Room room2 = new Room (20.0);           // using constructor2
```

 ## 8.9 Static Members

We have seen that a class basically contains two sections. One declares variables and the other declares methods. These variables and methods are called *instance variables* and *instance methods*. This is because every time the class is instantiated, a new copy of each of them is created. They are accessed using the objects (with dot operator).

Let us assume that we want to define a member that is common to all the objects and accessed without using a particular object. That is, the member belongs to the class as a whole rather than the objects created from the class. Such members can be defined as follows:

```
static int count;
static int max(int x, int y);
```

The members that are declared **static** as shown above are called *static members*. Since these members are associated with the class itself rather than individual objects, the static variables and static methods are often referred to as *class variables* and *class methods* in order to distinguish them from their counterparts, instance variables and instance methods.

Static variables are used when we want to have a variable common to all instances of a class. One of the most common examples is to have a variable that could keep a count of how many objects of a class have been created. Remember, Java creates only one copy for a static variable which can be used even if the class is never actually instantiated.

Like static variables, static methods can be called without using the objects. They are also available for use by other classes. methods that are of general utility but do not directly affect an instance of that class are usually declared as class methods. Java class libraries contain a large number of class methods. For example, the **Math** class of Java library defines many static methods to perform math operations that can be used in any program. We have used earlier statements of the types.

```
float x = Math.sqrt(25.0);
```

The method **sqrt** is a class method (or static method) defined in **Math** class.

We can define our own static methods as shown in Program 8.3.

Program 8.3 *Defining and using static members*

```
class Mathoperation
{
    static float mul(float x, float y)
    {
        return x*y;
    }
    static float divide (float x, float y)
    {
        return x/y;
    }
}
class MathApplication
{
    public void static main(string args[ ])
    {
        float a = MathOperation.mul(4.0,5.0);
        float b = MathOperation.divide(a,2.0);
        System.out.println("b = "+ b);
    }
}
```

Output of Program 8.3:

```
b = 10.0
```

Note that the static methods are called using class names. In fact, no objects have been created for use. Static methods have several restrictions:

1. They can only call other **static** methods.
2. They can only access **static** data.
3. They cannot refer to **this** or **super** in any way.

8.10 Nesting of Methods

We discussed earlier that a method of a class can be called only by an object of that class (or class itself, in the case of static methods) using the dot operator. However, there is an exception to this. A method can be called by using only its name by another method of the same class. This is known as *nesting of methods*.

Program 8.4 illustrates the nesting of methods inside a class. The class **Nesting** defines one constructor and two methods, namely **largest( )** and **display( )**. The method **display( )** calls the method **largest( )** to determine the largest of the two numbers and then displays the result.

Program 8.4 *Nesting of methods*

```
class Nesting
{
    int m, n;
    Nesting (int x, int y)              // constructor method
    {
        m = x;
        n = y;
    }
    int largest( )
    {
        if (m >= n)
            return(m);
        else
            return(n);
    }
    void display( )
    {
        int large = largest( );        // calling a method
        System.out.println ("Largest value = " + large);
    }
}
class NestingTest
{
    public static void main(String args[ ])
    {
        Nesting nest = new Nesting(50, 40);
        nest.display( );
    }
}
```

Output of Program 8.4 would be:

```
    Largest value = 50
```

A method can call any number of methods. It is also possible for a called method to call another method. That is, **method1** may call **method2**, which in turn may call **method3**.

8.11 Inheritance: Extending a Class

Reusability is yet another aspect of OOP paradigm. It is always nice if we could reuse something that already exists rather than creating the same all over again. Java supports this concept. Java classes can be reused in several ways. This is basically done by creating new classes, reusing the properties of existing ones. The mechanism of deriving a new class from an old one is called *inheritance*. The old class is known as the *base class* or *super class* or *parent class* and the new one is called the *subclass* or *derived class* or *child class*.

The inheritance allows subclasses to inherit all the variables and methods of their parent classes. Inheritance may take different forms:

- Single inheritance (only one super class)
- Multiple inheritance (several super classes)
- Hierarchical inheritance (one super class, many subclasses)
- Multilevel inheritance (Derived from a derived class)

These forms of inheritance are shown in Fig. 8.3. Java does not directly implement multiple inheritance. However, this concept is implemented using a secondary inheritance path in the form of *interfaces*. Interfaces are discussed in Chapter 10.

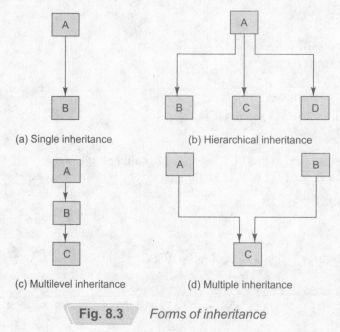

(a) Single inheritance   (b) Hierarchical inheritance

(c) Multilevel inheritance   (d) Multiple inheritance

Fig. 8.3   *Forms of inheritance*

Defining a Subclass

A subclass is defined as follows:

```
class subclassname extends superclassname
{
      variables declaration;
      methods declaration;
}
```

The keyword **extends** signifies that the properties of the *superclassname* are extended to the *subclassname*. The subclass will now contain its own variables and methods as well those of the superclass. This kind of situation occurs when we want to add some more properties to an existing class without actually modifying it. Program 8.5 illustrates the concept of single inheritance.

Program 8.5   *Application of single inheritance*

```
class Room
{
      int length;
      int breadth;
      Room(int x, int y)
      {
            length  = x;
            breadth = y;
      }
      int area( )
      {
            return (length * breadth);
      }
}
class BedRoom extends Room                          // Inheriting Room
{
      int height;
      BedRoom(int x, int y, int z)
      {
            super(x, y)                    //  pass values to superclass
            height = z;
      }
      int volume( )
      {
            return (length * breadth * height);
      }
}
class InherTest
{
      public static void main(String args[ ])
      {
            BedRoom room1 = new BedRoom(14,12,10);
            int area1 = room1.area( );              // superclass method
            int volume1 = room1.volume( );       // baseclass method
            System.out.println("Area1 = "+ area1);
            System.out.println("Volume = "+ volume);
      }
}
```

The output of Program 8.5 is:

```
      Area1  = 168
      Volume1 = 1680
```

The program defines a class **Room** and extends it to another class **BedRoom**. Note that the class **BedRoom** defines its own data members and methods. The subclass BedRoom now includes three instance variables, namely, **length, breadth** and **height** and two methods, **area** and **volume**.

The constructor in the derived class uses the **super** keyword to pass values that are required by the base constructor. The statement

```
BedRoom room1 = new BedRoom(14,12,10);
```

calls first the **BedRoom** constructor method, which in turn calls the **Room** constructor method by using the **super** keyword.

Finally, the object **room1** of the subclass **BedRoom** calls the method **area** defined in the super class as well as the method volume defined in the subclass itself.

Subclass Constructor

A subclass constructor is used to construct the instance variables of both the subclass and the superclass. The subclass constructor uses the keyword **super** to invoke the constructor method of the superclass. The keyword **super** is used subject to the following conditions.

- **super** may only be used within a subclass constructor method
- The call to superclass constructor must appear as the first statement within the subclass constructor
- The parameters in the **super** call must match the order and type of the instance variable declared in the superclass.

Program 8.5 illustrated the use of **super( )** method for passing parameters to a superclass.

Multilevel Inheritance

A common requirement in object-oriented programming is the use of a derived class as a super class. Java supports this concept and uses it extensively in building its class library. This concept allows us to build a chain of classes as shown in Fig. 8.4.

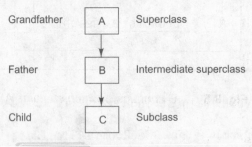

Fig. 8.4 *Multilevel inheritance*

The class **A** serves as a base class for the derived class **B** which in turn serves as a base class for the derived class **C**. The chain ABC is known as *inheritance path*.

A derived class with multilevel base classes is declared as follows.

```
class A
{
      ..........
      ..........
}
```

```
class B extends A  // First level
{
    ..........
    ..........
}
class C extends B  // Second level
{
    ..........
    ..........
}
```

This process may be extended to any number of levels. The class **C** can inherit the members of both **A** and **B** as shown in Fig. 8.5.

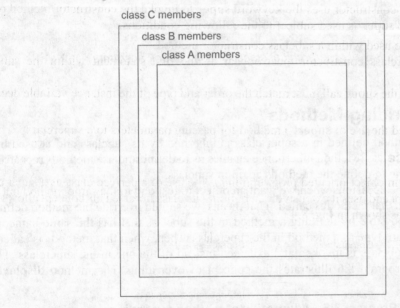

class C members

class B members

class A members

Fig. 8.5   *C contains B which contains A*

Hierarchical Inheritance

Another interesting application of inheritance is to use it as a support to the hierarchical design of a program. Many programming problems can be cast into a hierarchy where certain features of one level are shared by many others below the level. As an example, Fig. 8.6 shows a hierarchical classification of accounts in a commercial bank. This is possible because all the accounts possess certain common features.

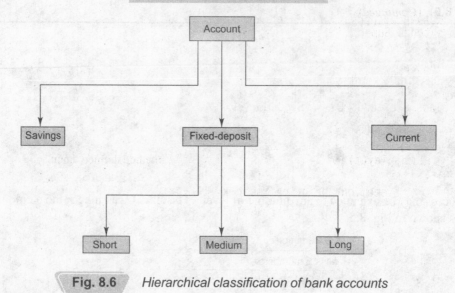

Fig. 8.6   *Hierarchical classification of bank accounts*

8.12 Overriding Methods

We have seen that a method defined in a super class is inherited by its subclass and is used by the objects created by the subclass. Method inheritance enables us to define and use methods repeatedly in subclasses without having to define the methods again in subclass.

However, there may be occasions when we want an object to respond to the same method but have different behaviour when that method is called. That means, we should override the method defined in the superclass. This is possible by defining a method in the subclass that has the same name, same arguments and same return type as a method in the superclass. Then, when that methods is called, the method defined in the subclass is invoked and executed instead of the one in the superclass. This is known as overriding. Program 8.6 illustrates the concept of overriding. The method **display( )** is overriden.

Program 8.6   *Illustration of method overriding*

```
class Super
{
     int x;
     Super(int x)
     {
          this.x = x;
     }
     void display( )                          // method defined
     {
          System.out.println("Super x = " + x);
     }
}
```

(Continued)

Program 8.6 *(Continued)*

```
Class Sub extends Super
{
        int y ;
        sub (int x, int y)
        {
                super(x);
                this.y = y;
        }
        void display( )                          // method defined again
        {
                System.out.printin("Super x = " + x);
                System.out.println("Sub y = " + y);
        }
}
class OverrideTest
{
        public static void main(String args[ ])
        {
                Sub sl = new Sub(100,200);
                sl.display( );
        }
}
```

Output of Program 8.6:
```
        Super x = 100
        Sub y    = 200
```
Note that the method display ( ) defined in the subclass is invoked.

8.13 Final Variables and Methods

All methods and variables can be overridden by default in subclasses. If we wish to prevent the subclasses from overriding the members of the superclass, we can declare them as final using the keyword **final** as a modifier. Example:

```
final int SIZE = 100;
final void showstatus( ) {...........}
```

Making a method final ensures that the functionality defined in this method will never be altered in any way. Similarly, the value of a final variable can never be changed. Final variables, behave like class variables and they do not take any space on individual objects of the class.

8.14 Final Classes

Sometimes we may like to prevent a class being further subclasses for security re~~~~
cannot be subclassed is called a *final class*. This is achieved in Java using the keywor~~~~

```
final class Aclass {.........}
final class Bclass extends Someclass {..........}
```

Any attempt to inherit these classes will cause an error and the compiler will not allow it.

Declaring a class **final** prevents any unwanted extensions to the class. It also allows the compiler to perform some optimisations when a method of a final class is invoked.

8.15 Finalizer Methods

We have seen that a constructor method is used to initialize an object when it is declared. This process is known as *initialization*. Similarly, Java supports a concept called *finalization*, which is just opposite to initialization. We know that Java run-time is an automatic garbage collecting system. It automatically frees up the memory resources used by the objects. But objects may hold other non-object resources such as file descriptors or window system fonts. The garbage collector cannot free these resources. In order to free these resources we must use a *finalizer method*. This is similar to *destructors* in C++.

The finalizer method is simply **finalize( )** and can be added to any class. Java calls that method whenever it is about to reclaim the space for that object. The **finalize** method should explicitly define the tasks to be performed.

8.16 Abstract Methods and Classes

We have seen that by making a method *final* we ensure that the method is not redefined in a subclass. That is, the method can never be subclassed. Java allows us to do something that is exactly opposite to this. That is, we can indicate that a method must always be redefined in a subclass, thus making overriding compulsory. This is done using the modifier keyword **abstract** in the method definition. Example:

```
abstract class Shape
{
        ..........
        ..........
        abstract void draw( );
        ..........
        ..........
}
```

When a class contains one or more abstract methods, it should also be declared **abstract** as shown in the example above.

While using abstract classes, we must satisfy the following conditions:

- We cannot use abstract classes to instantiate objects directly. For example,

```
Shape s = new Shape( )
```

is illegal because **shape** is an abstract class.
- The abstract methods of an abstract class must be defined in its subclass.
- We cannot declare abstract constructors or abstract static methods.

8.17   Methods with Varargs

Varargs represents variable length arguments in methods, which is one of the features introduced by J2SE 5.0. It makes the Java code simple and flexible. Varargs takes the following form:

```
<access specifier> <static> void method-name(Object...arguments)
{
}
```

In the above syntax, the method contains an argument called *varargs* in which Object is the type of an argument, ellipsis (...) is the key to varargs and *arguments* is the name of the variable.

Thus, varargs allows us to declare a method with the unspecified number of parameters for a given argument. The varargs must be the final argument in the argument list of a method. Varargs is identified by the type of an argument followed by the ellipsis (...) and the name of a variable.

For example, consider the following declaration of the method, **sample,** which contains the same type of arguments. String is used for more than one arguments.

```
public void sample (String username, String password, String mailid);
```

The above code is an example for simple method declaration. The above method declaration can be replaced by varargs, as shown below:

```
public void sample(String ... var_name);
```

Where **String ... var_name** specifies that we can pass any number of String arguments to the sample method. The following declarations invoke the constructor method of the class, which contains the method, sample:

```
public void method_name(String user, String pword);
public void method_name(String user, String pword, String mailid);
or
public void method_name(String user, String pword, String mailid,
Stringdesc);
```

It is possible to use the variable length argument as a final argument to other type of constructors. Hence, in the above declaration, the third line can be rewritten as:

```
public void method_name(String user, String ... var_arg);
```

Program 8.7   *Illustrates the use of varargs to print the String value passed as an argument to a method*

```
class Exampleprg
{
  Exampleprg(String... person)
  {
  for(String name: person)
  {
    System.out.println("Hello " + name);
  }
}
}
```

```
public static void main(String args[])
{
    Exampleprg("John", "David", "Suhel");
}
}
```

Program 8.7 produces the following output:

```
Hello John
Hello David
Hello Suhel
```

At compile time, String... var_arg is converted to String [ ] var_arg. We can also pass an array of strings to the method, as follows:

```
class Exampleprg
{
    String str1, str2;
    Exampleprg(String[] vargs)
    {
        for(int i=0; i<vargs.length; i++)
        {
            str1=vargs[i];
            System.out.println("Hello "+str1+".");
        }
    }
    public static void main(String[]args)
    {
        Exampleprg ex=new Exampleprg(args);
    }
}
```

Compile and run the above program as shown below:

```
Javac Exampleprg John David Suhel
```

This code yields the same output as the above program.

Note : Varargs does not generate any compile time errors even if an empty argument is passed as a parameter to a method.

 ## 8.18   Visibility Control

We stated earlier that it is possible to inherit all the members of a class by a subclass using the keyword **extends**. We have also seen that the variables and methods of a class are visible everywhere in the program. However, it may be necessary in some situations to restrict the access to certain variables and methods from outside the class. For example, we may not like the objects of a class directly alter the value of a variable or access a method. We can achieve this in Java by applying *visibility modifiers* to the instance variables and methods. The visibility modifiers are also known as *access modifiers*. Java provides three types of visibility modifiers: **public, private** and **protected**. They provide different levels of protection as described below.

public Access

Any variable or method is visible to the entire class in which it is defined. What if we want to make it visible to all the classes outside this class? This is possible by simply declaring the variable or method as **public**. Example:

```
public int number;
public void sum( ) {..........}
```

A variable or method declared as **public** has the widest possible visibility and accessible everywhere. In fact, this is what we would like to prevent in many programs. This takes us to the next levels of protection.

friendly Access

In many of our previous examples, we have not used **public** modifier, yet they were still accessible in other classes in the program. When no access modifier is specified, the member defaults to a limited version of public accessibility known as "friendly" level of access.

The difference between the "public" access and the "friendly" access is that the **public** modifier makes fields visible in all classes, regardless of their packages while the friendly access makes fields visible only in the same package, but not in other packages. (A package is a group of related classes stored separately. They are explored in detail in Chapter 11). A package in Java is similar to a source file in C.

protected Access

The visibility level of a "protected" field lies in between the public access and friendly access. That is, the **protected** modifier makes the fields visible not only to all classes and subclasses in the same package but also to subclasses in other packages. Note that non-subclasses in other packages cannot access the "protected" members.

private Access

private fields enjoy the highest degree of protection. They are accessible only with their own class. They cannot be inherited by subclasses and therefore not accessible in subclasses. A method declared as **private** behaves like a method declared as **final**. It prevents the method from being subclassed. Also note that we cannot override a non-private method in a subclass and then make it private.

private protected Access

A field can be declared with two keywords **private** and **protected** together like:

```
private protected int codeNumber;
```

This gives a visibility level in between the "protected" access and "private" access. This modifier makes the fields visible in all subclasses regardless of what package they are in. Remember, these fields are not accessible by other classes in the same package. Table 8.1 summarises the visibility provided by various access modifiers.

Table 8.1   Visibility of Field in a Class

Access modifier → / Access location ↓	public	protected	friendly (default)	private protected	private
Same class	Yes	Yes	Yes	Yes	Yes
Subclass in same package	Yes	Yes	Yes	Yes	No
Other classes in same package	Yes	Yes	Yes	No	No
Subclass in other packages	Yes	Yes	No	Yes	No
Non-subclasses in other packages	Yes	No	No	No	No

Rules of Thumb

The details discussed so far about field visibility may be quite confusing and seem complicated. Given below are some simple rules for applying appropriate access modifiers.

1. Use **public** if the field is to be visible everywhere.
2. Use **protected** if the field is to be visible everywhere in the current package and also subclasses in other packages.
3. Use "default" if the field is to be visible everywhere in the current package only.
4. Use **private protected** if the field is to be visible only in subclasses, regardless of packages.
5. Use **private** if the field is *not* to be visible anywhere except in its own class.

8.19   Summary

Classes, objects, and methods are the basic components used in Java programming. The concept of classes is at the root of Java's design. We have discussed in detail the following in this chapter:

- How to define a class
- How to create objects
- How to add methods to classes
- How to extend or reuse a class
- How to write application programs

We have also discussed various features that could be used to restrict the access to certain variables and methods from outside the class. The concepts discussed here provides the basics of writing not only standalone application programs but also applets for use on Internet.

Key Terms

Classes, Objects, Methods, Fields, Instance, Template, Inheritance, Subclass, Superclass, Instantiation, Dot operator, Constructor, Overloading, Overriding, Static, Final, Nesting, Visibility Control, Visibility Modifiers, Public Access, Friendly Access, Private Access, Protected Access, Package, Varargs.

REVIEW QUESTIONS

8.1 What is class? How does it accomplish data hiding?

8.2 How do classes help us to organise our programs?

8.3 What are the three parts of a simple, empty class?

8.4 What are objects? How are they created from a class?

8.5 How is a method defined?

8.6 When do we declare a member of a class **static**?

8.7 What is a constructor? What are its special properties?

8.8 How do we invoke a constructor?

8.9 What is inheritance and how does it help us create new classes quickly?

8.10 Describe different forms of inheritance with examples.

8.11 Describe the syntax of single inheritance in Java.

8.12 Compare and contrast overloading and overriding methods.

8.13 When do we declare a method or class **final**?

8.14 When do we declare a method or class **abstract**?

8.15 Discuss the different levels of access protection available in Java.

8.16 Design a class to represent a bank account. Include the following members:

Data members
- Name of the depositor
- Account number
- Type of account
- Balance amount in the account

Methods
- To assign initial values
- To deposit an amount
- To withdraw an amount after checking balance
- To display the name and balance

8.17 Modify the program of Question 8.16 to incorporate a constructor to provide initial values.

8.18 Assume that a bank maintains two kinds of account for its customers, one called savings account and the other current account. The savings account provides compound interest and withdrawal facilities but no cheque book facility. The current account provides cheque book facility but no interest. Current account holders should also maintain a minimum balance and if the balance falls below this level, a service charge is imposed.

Create a class **Account** that stores customer name, account number and type of account. From this derive the classes **Curr-acct** and **Sav-acct** to make them more specific to their requirements. Include the necessary methods in order to achieve the following tasks:

(a) Accept deposit from a customer and update the balance.

(b) Display the balance.

(c) Compute and deposit interest.

(d) Permit withdrawal and update the balance.

(e) Check for the minimum balance, impose penalty, if necessary, and update the balance.

Do not use any constructors. Use methods to initialize the class members.

8.19 Modify the program of Question 8.18 to include constructors for all the three classes.

8.20 An educational institution wishes to maintain a database of its employees. The database is divided into a number of classes whose hierarchical relationships are shown in Fig. 8.7. The figure also shows the minimum information required for each class. Specify all the classes and define methods to create the database and retrieve individual information as and when required.

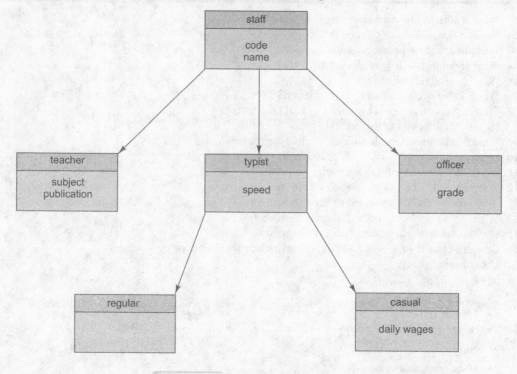

Fig. 8.7 *Class relationships*

DEBUGGING EXERCISES

8.1 Correct the error in the following code.

```
class VarName
{
    public static void main(String[] args)
    {
        System.out.println("Hellow World!");
    }
};
```

8.2 Following code should return the name when the method getName() is called. Modify the code to achieve the desired result.

```
class ReturnValue
{
    public String name="Tom";
    public String getName()
    {
        System.out.println("Name is: "+name);
    }
    public static void main(String[] args)
    {
        ReturnValue rv=new ReturnValue();
        rv.getName();
    }
}
```

8.3 Debug the code to rectify the compile time error thrown by the given code.

```
class NoDefConst
{
    NoDefConst(String s)
    {
        System.out.println("fsdf")
    }
}
class SubClass extends NoDefConst
{
}
```

8.4 Provide the missing statement in the following code which provides overriding of methods?

```
abstract class Figure
{
    int x, y;
    void changePosition(int newX, int newY) {}
    abstract void draw();
}
class CircleObject extends Figure
{
    void draw()
    {
        System.out.println("Draw Method Called");
    }
}
class RectangleObject extends Figure
{
    void changePosition(int newX, int newY)
    {
        System.out.println("Change Position Method Called");
```

```
        }
    }
```

8.5   Correct the code for overloading methods?

```
    public class Figure
    {
      public String draw(String s)
    {
                return "Figure Drawn";
    }
      public void draw(String s) {}
      public void draw(double f) {}
    }
```

Chapter **9**

Arrays, Strings and Vectors

9.1   Introduction

An array is a group of contiguous or related data items that share a common name. For instance, we can define an array name **salary** to represent a set of salaries of a group of employees. A particular value is indicated by writing a number called *index* number or *subscript* in brackets after the array name. For example,

```
salary[10]
```

represents the salary of the 10th employee. While the complete set of values is referred to as an *array*, the individual values are called *elements*. Arrays can be of any variable type.

The ability to use a single name to represent a collection of items and to refer to an item by specifying the item number enables us to develop concise and efficient programs. For example, a loop with the subscript as the control variable can be used to read the entire array, perform calculations and, print out the results.

In this chapter, we shall discuss in depth how arrays are created and used. We shall also discuss two related concepts, namely strings and vectors which are often used in Java programs.

9.2   One-dimensional Arrays

A list of items can be given one variable name using only one subscript and such a variable is called a *single-subscripted* variable or a *one-dimensional* array. In mathematics, we often deal with variables that are single-subscripted. For instance, we use the equation,

$$A = \frac{\sum_{i-1}^{n} X_i}{n}$$

to calculate the average of n values of x. The subscripted variable x_1 refers to the *i*th element of x. In Java, single-subscripted variable x_1 can be expressed as

```
x[1], x[2], x[3] ......... x[n]
```

The subscript can also begin with number 0. That is

```
x[0]
```

is allowed. For example, if we want to represent a set of five numbers, say (35, 40, 20, 57, 19), by an array variable number, then we may create the variable number as follows

```
int number [ ] = new int[5];
```

and the computer reserves five storage locations as shown below :

	number [0]
	number [1]
	number [2]
	number [3]
	number [4]

The values to the array elements can be assigned as follows:

```
number[0] = 35;
number[1] = 40;
number[2] = 20;
number[3] = 57;
number[4] = 19;
```

This would cause the array number to store the values shown as follows:

number [0]	35
number [1]	40
number [2]	20
number [3]	57
number [4]	19

Note: In Java, subscripts start with the value 0.

These elements may be used in programs just like any other Java variable. For example, the following are valid statements:

```
aNumber   = number[0] + 10;
number[4] = number[0] + number[2];
number[2] = x[5] + y[10];
value[6]  = number[i] * 3;
```

The subscript of an array can be integer constants, integer variables like **i**, or expressions that yield integers.

9.3 Creating an Array

Like any other variables, arrays must be declared and created in the computer memory before they are used. Creation of an array involves three steps:

1. Declaring the array
2. Creating memory locations
3. Putting values into the memory locations.

Declaration of Arrays

Arrays in Java may be declared in two forms :

Form 1

```
type arrayname[ ];
```

Form 2

```
type [ ] arrayname;
```

Examples:

```
int       number[ ];
float     average[ ];
int[ ]    counter;
float[ ]  marks;
```

Remember, we do not enter the size of the arrays in the declaration.

Creation of Arrays

After declaring an array, we need to create it in the memory. Java allows us to create arrays using **new** operator only, as shown below:

```
arrayname = new type[size];
```

Examples:

```
number  = new int[5];
average = new float[10];
```

These lines create necessary memory locations for the arrays **number** and **average** and designate them as **int** and **float** respectively. Now, the variable **number** refers to an array of 5 integers and **average** refers to an array of 10 floating point values.

It is also possible to combine the two steps—declaration and creation—into one as shown below:

```
int number[ ] = new int[5];
```

Figure 9.1 illustrates creation of an array in memory.

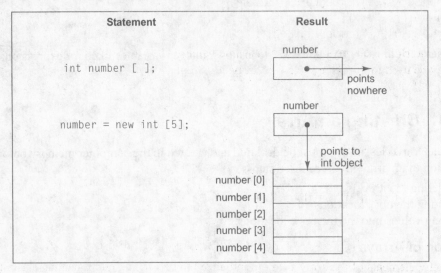

Statement	Result

Fig. 9.1 *Creation of an array in memory*

Initialization of Arrays

The final step is to put values into the array created. This process is known as *initialization*. This is done using the array subscripts as shown below.

```
arrayname[subscript] = value ;
```

Example:

```
number[0] = 35;
number[1] = 40;
..........
..........
number[4] = 19;
```

Note that Java creates arrays starting with the subscript of 0 and ends with a value one less than the *size* specified.

Unlike C, Java protects arrays from overruns and underruns. Trying to access an array bound its boundaries will generate an error message.

We can also initialize arrays automatically in the same way as the ordinary variables when they are declared, as shown below:

```
type arrayname[ ] = {list of values};
```

The array initializer is a list of values separated by commas and surrounded by curly braces. Note that no size is given. The compiler allocates enough space for all the elements specified in the list.

Example:
```
int number[ ] = {35, 40, 20, 57, 19};
```
It is possible to assign an array object o another. Example:
```
int a[ ] = {1, 2, 3};
int b[ ];
b = a;
```
are valid in Java. Both the arrays will have the same values.

Loops may be used to initialize large size arrays. Example:
```
..........
..........
for(int i = 0; i < 100; i++)
{
        if(i < 50)
           sum[i] = 0.0;
        else
           sum[i] = 1.0;
}
..........
..........
```

The first fifty elements of the array **sum** are initialized to zero while the remaining are initialized to 1.0.

Consider another example as shown below:
```
for(int x = 0; x < 10; x++)
average[x] = (float)x;
```
This loop initializes the array average to the values 0.0 to 9.0.

Array Length

In Java, all arrays store the allocated size in a variable named **length**. We can obtain the length of the array **a** using **a.length**. Example:
```
int aSize = a.length;
```
This information will be useful in the manipulation of arrays when their sizes are not known. Program 9.1 illustrates the use of an array for sorting a list of numbers.

Program 9.1 *Sorting a list of numbers*

```
class NumberSorting
{
  public static void main(String args[ ])
  {
    int number[] = { 55, 40, 80, 65, 71 };
    int n = number.length;                        // Array length
    System.out.print("Given list : ");
    for (int i= 0; i < n; i++)
```

(Continued)

Program 9.1 (*Continued*)

```
    {
        System.out.print(" " + number[i]);
    }
    System.out.println("/n");
    // Sorting begins
    for (int i = 0; i < n; i++)
    {
        for (int j = i+1; j < n; j++0
        {
            if (number[i] < number[j])
            {
                // Interchange values
                int temp = number[i];
                number[i] = number[j';
                number[j] = temp;
            }
        }
    }  // Sorting ends
    System.out.print("Sorted list : ");
    for (int i = 0; i < n; i++)
    {
        System.out.print(" " + number[i]);
    }
    System.out.println(" ");
    }
}
```

Program 9.1 displays the following output:

```
Given list    :    55    40    80    65    71
Sorted list   :    80    71    65    55    40
```

9.4 Two-dimensional Arrays

So far we have discussed the array variables that can store a list of values. There will be situations where a table of values will have to be stored. Consider the following data table, which shows the value of sales of three items by four salesgirls:

	Item1	Item2	Item3
Salesgirl #1	310	275	365
Salesgirl #2	210	190	325
Salesgirl #3	405	235	240
Salesgirl #4	260	300	380

The table contains a total of 12 values, three in each line. We can think of this table as a matrix consisting of four *rows* and three *columns*. Each row represents the values of sales by a particular salesgirl and each column represents the values of sales of a particular item.

In mathematics, we represent a particular value in a matrix by using two subscripts such as v_{ij}. Here v denotes the entire matrix and v_{ij} refers to the value in the *i*th row and *j*th column. For example, in the above table v_{23} refers to the value 325. Java allows us to define such tables of items by using *two-dimensional* arrays. The table discussed above can be represented in Java as

```
v[4][3]
```

Two dimensional arrays are stored in memory as shown in Fig. 9.2. As with the single dimensional arrays, each dimension of the array is indexed from zero to its maximum size minus one; the first index selects the row and the second index selects the column within that row.

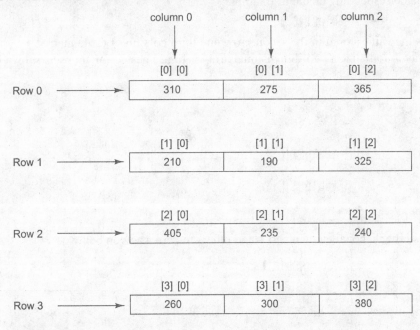

Fig. 9.2   *Representation of a two-dimensional array in memory*

For creating two-dimensional arrays, we must follow the same steps as that of simple arrays. We may create a two-dimensional array like this:

```
int myArray[ ][ ];
myArray = new int[3][4];
```

or

```
int myArray[ ][ ] = new int[3][4];
```

This creates a table that can store 12 integer values, four across and three down.

Like the one-dimensional arrays, two-dimensional arrays may be initialized by following their declaration with a list of initial values enclosed in braces. For example,

```
int table[2][3] = {0, 0, 0, 1, 1, 1};
```

initializes the elements of the first row to zero and the second row to one. The initialization is done row by row. The above statement can be equivalently written as

```
int table[ ][ ] = {{0, 0, 0}, {1, 1, 1}};
```

by surrounding the elements of each row by braces.

We can also initialize a two-dimensional array in the form of a matrix as shown below:

```
int table[ ][ ] = {
                    {0, 0, 0},
                    {1, 1, 1}
                   };
```

Note the syntax of the above statements. Commas are required after each brace that closes off a row, except in the case of the last row.

We can refer to a value stored in a two-dimensional array by using subscripts for both the column and row of the corresponding element. Example:

```
int value = table[1][2];
```

This retrieves the value stored in the second row and third column of **table** matrix.

A quick way to initialize a two-dimensional array is to use nested **for** loops as shown below:

```
for (i = 0; i < 5; i++)
{
    for (j = 0; j < 5; j++)
    {
        if (i == j)
            table[i][j] = 1;
        else
            table[i][j] = 0;
    }
}
```

This will set all the diagonal elements to 1 and others to zero as given below :

```
1   0   0   0   0
0   1   0   0   0
0   0   1   0   0
0   0   0   1   0
0   0   0   0   1
```

Program 9.2 illustrates the use of two-dimensional arrays in real-life situations.

Program 9.2   *Application of two-dimensional arrays*

```
class MulTable
{
  final static int ROWS = 20;
  final static int COLUMNS = 20;
  public static void main(String args[ ])
  {
    int product[][] = new int[ROWS][COLUMNS];
    int row, column;

    System.out.println("MULTIPLICATION TABLE");
    System.out.println("  ");
```

(Continued)

Program 9.2 (*Continued*)

```
int i,j;
for (i=10; i<ROWS; i++)
{
   for (j=10; j<CCOLUMNS; j++)
   {
      product[i][j] = i*j;
      System.out.print("  " +product[i][j]);
   }
   System.out.println("  ");
}
}
```

Program 9.2 produces the following output:

```
MULTIPLICATION TABLE
   100   110   120   130   140   150   160   170   180   190
   110   121   132   143   154   165   176   187   198   209
   120   132   144   156   168   180   192   204   216   228
   130   143   156   169   182   195   208   221   234   247
   140   154   168   182   196   210   224   238   252   266
   150   165   180   195   210   225   240   255   270   285
   160   176   192   208   224   240   256   272   288   304
   170   187   204   221   238   255   272   289   306   323
   180   198   216   234   252   270   288   306   324   342
   190   209   228   247   266   285   304   323   342   361
```

Variable Size Arrays

Java treats multidimensional array as "arrays of arrays". It is possible to declare a two-dimensional array as follows:

```
int x[][] = newint[3][];
x[0] = new int[2];
x[1] = new int[4];
x[2] = new int[3];
```

These statements create a two-dimensional array as having different lengths for each row as shown in Fig. 9.3.

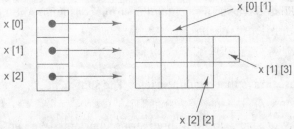

Fig. 9.3   *Variable size arrays*

9.5   Strings

String manipulation is the most common part of many Java programs. Strings represent a sequence of characters. The easiest way to represent a sequence of characters in Java is by using a character array. Example:

```
char charArray[ ] = new char[4];
charArray[0]      = 'J';
charArray[1]      = 'a';
charArray[2]      = 'v';
charArray[3]      = 'a';
```

Although character arrays have the advantage of being able to query their length, they themselves are not good enough to support the range of operations we may like to perform on strings. For example, copying one character array into another might require a lot of book keeping effort. Fortunately, Java is equipped to handle these situations more efficiently.

In Java, strings are class objects and implemented using two classes, namely, **String** and **StringBuffer.** A Java string is an instantiated object of the **String** class. Java strings, as compared to C strings, are more reliable and predictable. This is basically due to C's lack of bounds-checking. A Java string is not a character array and is not NULL terminated. Strings may be declared and created as follows:

```
String stringName;
StringName = new String ("string");
```

Example:

```
String firstName;
firstName = new String("Anil");
```

These two statements may be combined as follows:

```
String firstName = new String ("Anil");
```

Like arrays, it is possible to get the length of string using the **length** method of the **String** class.

```
int m = firstName.length(  );
```

Note the use of parentheses here. Java strings can be concatenated using the + operator. Examples:

```
String fullName = name1 + name2;
String city1    = "New" + "Delhi";
```

where **name1** and **name2** are Java strings containing string constants. Another example is:

```
System.out.println(firstName + "Kumar");
```

String Arrays

We can also create and use arrays that contain strings. The statement

```
String itemArray[ ] = new String[3];
```

will create an **itemArray** of size 3 to hold three string constants. We can assign the strings to the **itemArray** element by element using three different statements or more efficiently using a **for** loop.

String Methods

The **String** class defines a number of methods that allow us to accomplish a variety of string manipulation tasks. Table 9.1 lists some of the most commonly used string methods, and their tasks. Program 9.3 shows the use of the method **compareTo( )** to sort an array of strings in alphabetical order.

Table 9.1 Some Most Commonly Used String Methods

Method Call	Task performed
s2 = s1.toLowerCase;	Converts the string s1 to all lowercase
s2 = s1.toUppercCase;	Converts the string s1 to all Uppercase
s2 = s1.replace('x', 'y');	Replace all appearances of x with y
s2 = s1.trim();	Remove white spaces at the beginning and end of the string s1
s1.equals(s2)	Returns 'true'if s1 is equal to s2
s1.equalsIgnoreCase(s2)	Returns 'true'if s1 = s2, ignoring the case of characters
s1.length()	Gives the length of s1
s1.ChartAt(n)	Gives nth character of s1
s1.compareTo(s2)	Returns negative if s1 < s2, positive if s1 > s2, and zero if s1 is equal s2
s1.concat(s2)	Concatenates s1 and s2
s1.substring(n)	Gives substring starting from n^{th} character
s1.substring(n, m)	Gives substring starting from n^{th} character up to m^{th} (not including m^{th})
String.ValueOf(p)	Creates a string object of the parameter p (simple type or object)
p.toString()	Creates a string representation of the object p
s1.indexOf('x')	Gives the position of the first occurrence of 'x' in the string s1
s1.indexOf('x', n)	Gives the position of 'x' that occurs after nth position in the string s1
String.ValueOf(Variable)	Converts the parameter value to string representation

Program 9.3 *Alphabetical ordering of strings*

```
class StringOrdering
{
  static String name[] = {"Madras", "Delhi", "Ahmedabad", "Calcutta", "Bombay"};
  public static void main(String args[ ])
  {
    int size = name.length;
    String temp = null;
    for (int i = 0; i < size; i++)
    {
      for (int j = i+1; j < size; j++)
      {
        if (name[j].compareTo(name[i]) < 0)
        {
          // swap the strings
          temp = name[i];
          name[i] = name[j];
          name[j] = temp;
```

(Continued)

Program 9.3 (*Continued*)

```
            }
        }
    }
    for (int i = 0; i < size; i++)
    {
        System.out.println(name[i]);
    }
}
}
```

Program 9.3 produces the following sorted list:

```
    Ahmedabad
    Bombay
    Calcutta
    Delhi
    Madras
```

StringBuffer Class

StringBuffer is a peer class of **String**. While **String** creates strings of fixed_length, **StringBuffer** creates strings of flexible length that can be modified in terms of both length and content. We can insert characters and substrings in the middle of a string, or append another string to the end. Table 9.2 lists some of the methods that are frequently used in string manipulations.

Table 9.2   Commonly Used StringBuffer Methods

Method	Task
s1.setChartAt(n, 'x')	Modifies the nth character to x
s1.append(s2)	Appends the string s2 to s1 at the end
s1.insert(n, s2)	Inserts the string s2 at the position n of the string s1
s1.setLength(n)	Sets the length of the string s1 to n. If n<s1.length() s1 is truncated. If n>s1.length() zeros are added to s1

Program 9.4 shows how some of the string methods are used for manipulating strings.

Program 9.4   *Manipulation of strings*

```
class StringManipulation
{
    public static void main(String args[ ])
    {
        StringBuffer str = new StringBuffer("Object language");
        System.out.println("Original String :" + str);
        // obtaining string length
        System.out.println("Length of string :" + str.length());
```

(*Continued*)

Program 9.4 (*Continued*)

```
// Accessing characters in a string
for (int i = 0; i < str.length(); i++)
{
   int p = i + 1;
   System.out.println("Character at position : " + p + " is " + str.charAt(i));
}
// Inserting a string in the middle
String aString = new String(str.toString());
int pos = aString.indexOf(" language");
str.insert(process," Oriented ");
System.out.println("Modified string : " + str);
// Modifying characters
str.setCharAt(6, '-');
System.out.println("String now : " + str);
// Appending a string at the end
str.append(" improves security.");
System.out.println("Appended string : " + str);
}
}
```

Output of Program 9.4 would be:

```
Original String      : Object language
Length of string     : 15
Character at position : 1 is O
Character at position : 2 is b
Character at position : 3 is j
Character at position : 4 is e
Character at position : 5 is c
Character at position : 6 is t
Character at position : 7 is
Character at position : 8 is l
Character at position : 9 is a
Character at position : 10 is n
Character at position : 11 is g
Character at position : 12 is u
Character at position : 13 is a
Character at position : 14 is g
Character at position : 15 is e
Modified string : Object Oriented language
String now : Object-Oriented language
Appended string : Object-Oriented language improves security.
```

9.6 Vectors

We have seen that J2SE 5.0 version supports the concept of variable arguments to methods. This feature can also be achieved in Java through the use of the **Vector** class contained in the **java.util** package. This class can be used to create a generic dynamic array known as *vector* that can hold *objects of any type* and *any number*. The objects do not have to be homogeneous. Arrays can be easily implemented as vectors. Vectors are created like arrays as follows:

```
Vector intVect = new Vector( );  // declaring without size
Vector list   = new Vector(3);   // declaring with size
```

Note that a vector can be declared without specifying any size explicitly. A vector without size can accommodate an unknown number of items. Even, when a size is specified, this can be overlooked and a different number of items may be put into the vector. Remember, in contrast, an array must always have its size specified.

Vectors possess a number of advantages over arrays.

1. It is convenient to use vectors to store objects.
2. A vector can be used to store a list of objects that may vary in size.
3. We can add and delete objects from the list as and when required.

A major constraint in using vectors is that we cannot directly store simple data type in a vector; we can only store objects. Therefore, we need to convert simple types to objects. This can be done using the *wrapper classes* discussed in the next section. The **vector** class supports a number of methods that can be used to manipulate the vectors created. Important ones are listed in Table 9.3.

To learn more information about vector class, refer to the Chapter 18.

Table 9.3 Important Vector Methods

Method Call	Task performed
list.addElement(item)	Adds the item specified to the list at the end
list.elementAt(10)	Gives the name of the 10th object
list.size()	Gives the number of objects present
list.removeElement(item)	Removes the specified item from the list
list.removeElementAt(n)	Removes the item stored in the nth position of the list
list.removeAllElements( )	Removes all the elements in the list
list.copyInto(array)	Copies all items from list to array
list.insertElementAt (item, n)	Inserts the item at nth position

Program 9.5 illustrates the use of arrays, strings and vectors. This program converts a string vector into an array of strings and displays the strings.

Program 9.5 *Working with vectors and arrays*

```
import java.util.*;                // Importing Vector class
class LanguageVector
{
  public static void main(String args[ ])
  {
```

(Continued)

Program 9.5 (*Continued*)

```
Vector list = new Vector();
int length = args.length;
for (int i = 0; i <length; i++)
{
    list.addElement(args[i]);
}
list.insertElementAt("COBOL",2);
int size = list.size();
String listArray[] = new String[size];
list.copyInto(listArray);
System.out.println("List of Languages");
for (int i = 0; i < size; i++)
{
    System.out.println(listArray[i]);
}
}
}
```

Command line input and output are:

```
C:\JAVA\prog>java LanguageVector Ada BASIC C++ FORTRAN Java
List of Languages
Ada
BASIC
COBOL
C++
FORTRAN
Java
```

9.7 Wrapper Classes

As pointed out earlier, vectors cannot handle primitive data types like **int, float, long, char,** and **double.** Primitive data types may be converted into object types by using the wrapper classes contained in the **java.lang** package. Table 9.4 shows the simple data types and their corresponding wrapper class types.

Table 9.4   Wrapper Classes for Converting Simple Types

Simple Type	*Wrapper Class*
boolean	Boolean
char	Character
double	Double
float	Float
int	Integer
long	Long

The wrapper classes have a number of unique methods for handling primitive data types and objects. They are listed in the following tables.

Table 9.5   Converting Primitive Numbers to Object Numbers Using Constructor Methods

Constructor Calling	Conversion Action
`Integer IntVal = new Integer(i);`	Primitive integer to Integer object
`Float FloatVal = new Float(f);`	Primitive float to Float object
`Double DoubleVal = new Double(d);`	Primitive double to Double object
`Long LongVal = new Long(l);`	Primitive long to Long object

Note: *i, f, d and l are primitive data values denoting int, float, double and long data types. They may be constants or variables.*

Table 9.6   Converting Object Numbers to Primitive Numbers Using typeValue( ) method

Method Calling	Conversion Action
`int i    = IntVal.intValue( );`	Object to primitive integer
`float f  = FloatVal.floatValue( );`	Object to primitive float
`long l   = LongVal.longValue( );`	Object to primitive long
`double d = DoubleVal.doubleValue( );`	Object to primitive double

Table 9.7   Converting Numbers to Strings Using to String( ) Method

Method Calling	Conversion Action
`str = Integer.toString(i)`	Primitive integer to string
`str = Float.toString(f);`	Primitive float to string
`str = Double.toString(d);`	Primitive double to string
`str = Long.toString(l);`	Primitive long to string

Table 9.8   Converting String Objects to Numeric Objects Using the Static Method ValueOf( )

Method Calling	Conversion Action
`DoubleVal = Double.Valueof(str);`	Converts string to Double object
`FloatVal = Float.ValueOf(str);`	Converts string to Float object
`IntVal = Integer.Valueof(str);`	Converts string to Integer object
`LongVal = Long.ValueOf(str);`	Converts string to Long object

Note: *These numeric objects may be converted to primitive numbers using the typeValue( ) method as shown in Table 9.6.*

Table 9.9 Converting Numeric Strings to Primitive Numbers Using Parsing Methods	
Method Calling	*Conversion Action*
`int i = Integer.parseInt(str);`	Converts string to primitive integer
`long i = Long.parseLong(str);`	Converts string to primitive long

Note: *parseInt( ) and parseLong( ) methods throw a NumberFormatException if the value of the str does not represent an integer.*

Program 9.6 illustrates the use of some most commonly used wrapper class methods.

Program 9.6 *Use of wrapper class methods*

```
import java.io.*;
class Invest
{
  public static void main(String args[ ])
  {
    Float principalAmount = new Float(0);   // Converting number to object
    Float interestRate = new Float(0);
    int numYears = 0;
    try
    {
      DataInputStream in = new DataInputStream(System.in);
      System.out.print("Enter Principal Amount : ");
      System.out.flush();
      String principalString = in.readLine();
      principalAmount = Float.valueOf(principalString);   // String object to number object
      System.out.print("Enter Interest Rate : ");
      System.out.flush();
      String interestString = in.readLine();
      interestRate = Float.valueOf(interestString);
      System.out.print("Enter Number of Years : ");
      System.out.flush();
      String yearsString = in.readLine();
      numYears = Integer.parseInt(yearsString);   // Numeric strings to numbers
    }
    catch (IOException e)
    {
      System.out.println("I/O Error");
      System.exit(1);
    }
    float value =loan(principalAmount.flaotValue(),
                      interetRate.floatValue(), numYears);
```

Program 9.6　　(*Continued*)

```
    printline();
    System.out.println("Final Value = " + value);
    printline();
}
    // Method to compute Final Value
static float loan (float p, float r, int n)
{
    int year = 1;
    float sum = p;
    While (year <= n)
    {
        sum = sum * (1+r);
        year = year + 1;
    }
    return sum;
}
    // Method to draw a line
static void printline()
{
    for (int i = 1; i <= 30; i++)
    {
        System.out.print("=");
    }
    System.out.println("  ");
}
}
```

The output of Program 9.6 would be:

```
    Enter Principal Amount : 5000
    Enter Interest Rate : 0.15
    Enter Number of Years : 4
    ──────────────────────────
    Final Value = 8745.03
```

Autoboxing and Unboxing

The autoboxing and unboxing feature, introduced in J2SE 5.0, facilitates the process of handling primitive data types in collections. We can use this feature to convert primitive data types to wrapper class types automatically. The compiler generates a code implicitly to convert primitive type to the corresponding wrapper class type and vice-versa. For example, consider the following statements:

```
    Double d_object = 98.42;
    double d_primitive = d_object.doubleValue( );
```

Using the autoboxing and unboxing feature, we can rewrite the above code as:

```
    Double d_object = 98.42;
    double d_primitive = d_object;
```

How, the Java compiler provides restrictions to perform the following conversions:

- Convert from null type to any primitive type.
- Convert to the null type other than the identify conversion.
- Convert from any class type C to any array type if C is not object.

Program 9.7 illustrates how to add two elements from the collections, Stack without using autoboxing and unboxing:

Program 9.7 . *Adding two elements from stack*

```java
import java.util.Stack;
public class autounboxex
{
  public static void main(String args[])
  {
    Stack mystack = new Stack();
    mystack.push(new Integer(10));
    mystack.push(new Integer(20));
    Integer stksum1 = (Integer) mystack.pop();
    Integer stksum2 = (Integer) mystack.pop();
    int stksum = stksum1.intValue()+stksum2.intValue();
    System.out.println(stksum);
  }
}
```

The above code can be rewritten using autoboxing and unboxing feature, as shown below:

```java
import java.util.Stack;
public class autounboxex
{
  public static void main(String args[])
  {
    Stack<Integer> MyStack = new Stack<Integer>();
    myStack.push(10);   //autobox
    myStack.push(20);   //autobox
    int stackSum = myStack.pop() + myStack.pop();   //unboxing
    System.out.println("The topmost element from the stack is:
    "+mystack.pop());
    System.out.println("The next to topmost element .from the stack is:
    "+mystack.pop());
    System.out.println("The sum of two elements from the Stack"+stackSum);
  }
}
```

The output for the above program is

```
The topmost element from the stack is: 10
The next topmost element from the stack is: 20
The sum of two elements from the stack is: 30
```

9.8 Enumerated Types

J2SE 5.0 allows us to use the enumerated type in Java using the **enum** keyword. This keyword can be used similar to the static final constants in the earlier version of Java. For example, consider the following code:

```
public class Days
{
  public static final int DAY_SUNDAY=0;
  public static final int DAY_MONDAY=1;
  public static final int DAY_TUESDAY=2;
  public static final int DAY_WEDNESDAY=3;
  public static final int DAY_THURSDAY=4;
  public static final int DAY_FRIDAY=5;
  public static final int DAY_SATURDAY=6;
}
```

Using the enumerated type feature provided by J2SE 5.0, the above code can be rewritten as:

```
public enum Day{SUNDAY, MONDAY, TUESDAY, WEDNESDAY, THURSDAY, FRIDAY,
    SATURDAY}
```

The advantages of using the enumerated type are:

- Compile-time type safety
- We can use the enum keyword in switch statements

Program 9.8 illustrates the use of enum type:

Program 9.8 *Use of enum type data*

```
public class Workingdays
{
  enum Days
  {
    Sunday,
    Monday,
    Tuesday,
    Wednesday,
    Thursday,
    Friday,
    Saturday
  }
  public static void main(String args[])
  {
    for (Days d : Days.values())
    {
      weekend(d);
```

(Continued)

Program 9.8 (*Continued*)

```
    }
  }
  private static void weekend(Days d)
  {
  if(d.equals(Days.sunday)
    System.out.println("value = " + d +" is a Holiday");
  else
    System.out.println("value = "+ d+" is a working day"):
  }
}
```

The output of the above program is:

```
value = Sunday is a Holiday
value = Monday is a Working Day
value = Tuesday is a Working Day
value = Wednesday is a Working Day
value = Thursday is a Working Day
value = Friday is a Working Day
value = Saturday is a Working Day
```

 ## 9.9 Annotations

The annotations feature, introduced by J2SE 5.0, is also known as metadata. We can use this feature to merge additional Java elements with the programming elements, such as classes, methods, parameters, local variables, packages, and fields.

Metadata is stored in Java class files by the compiler and these class files are used by the JVM or by the program to find the metadata for interacting with the programming elements. Java contains the following standard annotations:

Annotation	Purpose
@Deprecated	Compiler warns when deprecated java elements are used in non-deprecated program.
@Overrides	Compiler generated error when the method uses this annotation type does not override the methods present in the super-class.

In addition to the above standard annotations, Java also contains some meta-annotations available in the java.lang.annotation package. The following table provides the meta-annotations:

Meta-annotation	Purpose
@Documented	Indicates annotation of this type to be documented by Javadoc.
@Inherited	Indicates that this type is automatically inherited.
@Retention	Indicates the extended period using annotation type.
@Target	Indicates to which program element the annotation is applicable.

The declaration of annotation is similar to that of an interface. We use the symbol '@' before keyword interface. For example, consider the following code that contains the declaration of an annotation:

```
package njunit.annotation;
Import java.lang.annotation.*;
@Retention(Retentionpolicy.RUNTIME)
@Target((ElementType.METHOD))
public @interface UnitTest
{
   String value() ;
}
```

where, @Retention is a meta-annotation, which declares that the @UnitTest annotation must be stored in a class file. The @Target meta-annotation is used to declare the @UnitTest annotation, which annotates the methods in the Java class files. The @interface meta-annotation is used to declare the @UnitTest annotation with the member called value, which returns String as an object.

While using annotations, we need to follow some guidelines:

- Do not use extends clause. It automatically extends the marker interface java.lang.annotation.Annotation
- Do not use any parameter for a method
- Do not use generic methods
- Do not use throws clause

An annotation can also be applied to programming elements. For example, consider the code in which an annotation is applied to the methods, positive() and negative() of a class, Checking:

```
import njunit.annotation.*;
public class Checking
{
   @UnitTest(value="Test 1. This test will positive")
   public void positive(int no)
   {
      assert no > 0;
   }
   @UnitTest("Test 2. This test will negative.");
   public void negative(int no)
   {
      assert no < 0;
   }
}
```

After merging the annotation with the programming element, we can use the methods available in the interface, Java.lang.reflect. Annotated Element to query about the existence of programming element and get their values. The methods of the AnnotatedElement interface are:

- IsAnnotationPresent()
- getAnnotations()
- getAnnotation()
- getDeclaredAnnotations()

The classes that implement the AnnotatedElement interface are:

- java.lang.reflect.accessibleobject
- java.lang.class
- java.lang.reflect.constructor
- java.lang.reflect.field
- java.lang.reflect.method
- java.lang.package

Program 9.9 illustrates the use of annotations:

Program 9.9 *Use of annotations*

```
import java.lang.annotation.*;
import java.lang.reflect.*;
@Retention(RetentionPolicy.RUNTIME)
@interface MySingle
{
   int value(); // this variable name must be value
}
public class Single
{
   // Annotate a method using a marker.
   @MySingle(100)
   public static void myMeth()
   {
      Single ob = new Single();
      try
      {
         Method m = ob.getClass().getMethod("myMeth");
         MySingle anno = m.getAnnotation(MySingle.class);
         System.out.println("The value is : "anno.value());
            // displays 100
      }
      catch (NoSuchMethodException exc)
      {
         System.out.println("Method Not Found.");
      }
   }
   public static void main(String args[])
   {
      myMeth();
   }
}
```

The output of the above program is
```
   The value is: 100
```

9.10   Summary

In this chapter, we have discussed three important Java data structures namely arrays, strings and vectors. We learned the following:

- What is an array in Java
- How are arrays used
- How does Java handle strings
- How to use the **String** and **StringBuffer** classes
- What is a vector in Java
- How to use vectors to store a list of objects that may vary in size
- How are wrapper classes useful

We have also discussed the features enumerated types and annotations introduced by J2SE 5.0 version.

 Key Terms

Array, Index, Subscript, Elements, String, StringBuffer, Substring, Concatenation, Vector, Wrapper class, Enumerated type, Annotations

REVIEW QUESTIONS

9.1   What is an array?

9.2   Why are arrays easier to use compared to a bunch of related variables?

9.3   Write a statement to declare and instantiate an array to hold marks obtained by students in different subjects in a class. Assume that there are up to 60 students in a class and there 8 subjects.

9.4   Find errors, if any, in the following code segment:

```
int m;
int x[ ] = int[10];
int[.] y = int[11];
for(m=1; m<=10; ++m)
    x[m] = y[m] = m;
x = y = new int[20];
for (m=0; m<10; ++m)
    System.out.println(x[m])
```

9.5   Write a program for fitting a straight line through a set of points(x_i, y_i), i = 1, ..., n. The straight line equation is

```
y = mx + c
```

and the values of m and c are given by

$$m = \frac{n\sum(x_i y_i) - (\sum x_i)(\sum y_i)}{n(\sum x_i^2) - (\sum y_i)^2}$$

$$c = \frac{1}{n}\left(\sum y_i - m\sum x_i\right)$$

·All summations are from 1 to n.

9.6   The daily maximum temperatures recorded in 10 cities during the month of January (for all 31 days) have been tabulated as follows:

Day	1	2	City	10
1				
2				
3				
·				
·				
·				
31				

Write a program to read the table elements into a two-dimensional array **temperature**, and to find the city and day corresponding to (a) the highest temperature and (b) the lowest temperature.

9.7   An election is contested by 5 candidates. The candidates are numbered 1 to 5 and the voting is done by marking the candidate number on the ballot paper. Write a program to read the ballots and count the votes cast for each candidate using an array variable **count**. In case, a number read is outside the range 1 to 5, the ballot should be considered as a 'spoilt ballot' and the program should also count the number of spoilt ballots.

9.8   The annual examination results of 100 students are tabulated as follows:

Roll No.	Subject 1	Subject 2	Subject 3
·			
·			
·			
·			

Write a program to read the data and determine the following:

(a) Total marks obtained by each student.
(b) The highest marks in each subject and the Roll No. of the student who secured it.
(c) The student who obtained the highest total marks.

9.9   Given are two one-dimensional arrays **A** and **B** which are sorted in ascending order. Write a program to merge them into a single sorted array **C** that contains every item from arrays **A** and **B**, in ascending order.

9.10 Two matrices that have the same number of rows and columns can be multiplied to produce a third matrix. Consider the following two matrices.

$$A = \begin{bmatrix} a_{11} & a_{12} & .... & a_{1n} \\ a_{21} & a_{22} & .... & a_{2n} \\ \vdots & & & \\ a_{n1} & .... & .... & a_{nn} \end{bmatrix}; \quad B = \begin{bmatrix} b_{11} & b_{12} & .... & b_{1n} \\ b_{21} & b_{22} & .... & b_{2n} \\ \vdots & & & \\ b_{n1} & .... & .... & b_{nn} \end{bmatrix}$$

The product of **A** and **B** is a third matrix **C** to size n by n where each element of **C** is given by the following equation.

$$C_{ij} = \sum_{k=1}^{n} a_{ik} \, b_{kj}$$

Write a program that will read the values of elements of **A** and **B** and produce the product matrix **C**.

9.11 How does **String** class differ from the **StringBuffer** class?

9.12 Write a method called

```
delete(String str, int m)
```

that returns the input string with the mth element removed.

9.13 Write a program to do the following:

(a) To output the question "Who is the inventor of C++"?
(b) To accept an answer.
(c) To print out "Good" and then stop, if the answer is correct.
(d) To output the message "try again", if the answer is wrong.
(e) To display the correct answer when the answer is wrong even at the third attempt and stop.

9.14 Write a program to extract a portion of a character string and print the extracted string. Assume that m characters are extracted, starting with the nth character.

9.15 Write a program, which will read a text and count all occurrences of a particular word.

9.16 Write a program, which will read a string and rewrite it in the alphabetical order. For example, the word STRING should be written as GINRST.

9.17 What is a vector? How is it different from an array?

9.18 What are the applications of wrapper classes?

9.19 Write a program that accepts a shopping list of five items from the command line and stores them in a vector.

9.20 Modify the program of Question 9.19 to accomplish the following:

- To delete an item in the list.
- To add an item at a specified location in the list.
- To add an item at the end of the list.
- To print the contents of the vector.

DEBUGGING EXERCISES

9.1 Following code for creating an int array has a missing statement. Add the statement to successfully create the array.

```
class IntArray
{
    public static void(String[] args)
    {
        // declare an array of integers
        int[] anArray;
        // assign a value to each array element and print
        for (int i = 0; i < anArray.length; i++)
        {
            anArray[i] = i;
            System.out.print(anArray[i] + " ");
        }
```

```
      System.out.println();
   }
}
```

9.2 Debug the given code for displaying the contents of an array containing language names.

```
class ArrayData
{
  public static void main(String[] args)
  {
    // declare an array containing language names
    String[] stringArray={"Java", "Visual Basic", "VC++", "C"};
    // print value of each array element
    for (int i = 0; i < stringArray.length(); i++)
      System.out.print(stringArray[i] + ", ");
  }
}
```

9.3 Correct the code to eliminate the compile time error thrown.

```
class Palindrome {
  public static void main(String[] args) {
    String palindrome = new String("Rod saw I was Dor");
    int len = palindrome.length();
    String dest = new String();
    for (int i = (len - 1); i >= 0; i-) {
      dest.append(palindrome.charAt(i));
    }
    System.out.format("%s%n", dest.toString());
  }
}
```

9.4 The code checks for duplicate values in a vector and removes them. Identify errors, if any.

```
import java.util.*;
class DupValue
{
  public static void main(String[] args)
  {
    Vector v =new Vector();
    v.add("Delhi");
    v.add("Mumbai");
    v.add("Calcutta");
    v.add("Chennai");
    v.add("Delhi");
    Vector tmpVector=new Vector();
    String tmpValue;
    for (int j = 0; j <= v.size(); j++)
    {
      tmpValue = (String)v.elementAt(j);
```

```
            if (tmpValue!=null)
            {
               if ( tmpVector.isEmpty() )
               tmpVector.addElement(tmpValue);
               if (tmpVector.indexOf(tmpValue)==-1)
               {
                    tmpVector.addElement(tmpValue);
               }
            }
         };
         for (int j = 0; j < tmpVector.size(); j++)
         System.out.print(tmpVcr.elementAt(j));
      }
   }
```

9.5   The code given below converts a given string to Hexadecimal value. Identify error(s), if any.

```
import java.io.*;
import java.util.*;

class ConvertInt
{
   public static void main(String[] args)
   {
   String s = "";
   int i = Integer.parseInt(s,27);
   System.out.print("Hex Value of: "+ s +" = " + i);
   }
}
```

10
Interfaces: Multiple Inheritance

10.1 Introduction

In Chapter 8, we discussed about classes and how they can be inherited by other classes. We also learned about various forms of inheritance and pointed out that Java does not support multiple inheritance. That is, classes in Java cannot have more than one superclass. For instance, a definition like

```
class A extends B extends C
{
    ..........
    ..........
}
```

is not permitted in Java. However, the designers of Java could not overlook the importance of multiple inheritance. A large number of real-life applications require the use of multiple inheritance whereby we inherit methods and properties from several, distinct classes. Since C++ like implementation of multiple inheritance proves difficult and adds complexity to the language, Java provides an alternate approach known as *interfaces* to support the concept of multiple inheritance. Although a Java class cannot be a subclass of more than one superclass, it can *implement* more than one interface, thereby enabling us to create classes that build upon other classes without the problems created by multiple inheritance.

10.2 Defining Interfaces

An interface is basically a kind of class. Like classes, interfaces contain methods and variables but with a major difference. The difference is that interfaces define only abstract methods and final fields. This means that interfaces do not specify any code to implement these methods and data fields contain only constants. Therefore, it is the responsibility of the class that implements an interface to define the code for implementation of these methods.

The syntax for defining an interface is very similar to that for defining a class. The general form of an interface definition is:

```
interface InterfaceName
{
        variables declaration;
        methods declaration;
}
```

Here, **interface** is the key word and *InterfaceName* is any valid Java variable (just like class names). Variables are declared as follows:

```
static final type VariableName = Value;
```

Note that all variables are declared as constants. Methods declaration will contain only a list of methods without any body statements. Example:

```
return-type methodName1 (parameter_list);
```

Here is an example of an interface definition that contains two variables and one method:

```
interface Item
{
    static final int code = 1001;
    static final String name = "Fan";
    void display ( ) ;
}
```

Note that the code for the method is not included in the interface and the method declaration simply ends with a semicolon. The class that implements this interface must define the code for the method.

Another example of an interface is:

```
interface Area
{
    final static float pi = 3.142F;
    float compute (float x, float y);
    void show ( );
}
```

10.3   Extending Interfaces

Like classes, interfaces can also be extended. That is, an interface can be subinterfaced from other interfaces. The new subinterface will inherit all the members of the superinterface in the manner similar to subclasses. This is achieved using the keyword **extends** as shown below:

```
interface name2 extends name1
{
      body of name2
}
```

For example, we can put all the constants in one interface and the methods in the other. This will enable us to use the constants in classes where the methods are not required. Example:

```
interface ItemConstants
{
      int code = 1001;
      string name = "Fan";
}
interface Item extends ItemConstants
{
      void display ( );
}
```

The interface **Item** would inherit both the constants **code** and **name** into it. Note that the variables **name** and **code** are declared like simple variables. It is allowed because all the variables in an interface are treated as constants although the keywords **final** and **static** are not present.

We can also combine several interfaces together into a single interface. Following declarations are valid:

```
interface ItemConstants
{
      int code = 1001;
      String name = "Fan";
}
interface ItemMethods
{
      void display( );
}
interface Item extends ItemConstants, ItemMethods
{
      ..........
      ..........
}
```

While interfaces are allowed to extend to other interfaces, subinterfaces cannot define the methods declared in the superinterfaces. After all, subinterfaces are still interfaces, not classes. Instead, it is the responsibility of any class that implements the derived interface to define all the methods. Note that when an interface extends two or more interfaces, they are separated by commas.

It is important two remember that an interface cannot extend classes. This would violate the rule that an interface can have only abstract methods and constants.

10.4 Implementing Interfaces

Interfaces are used as "superclasses" whose properties are inherited by classes. It is therefore necessary to create a class that inherits the given interface. This is done as follows:

```
class classname implements interfacename
{
        body of classname
}
```

Here the class *classname* "implements" the interface *interfacename*. A more general form of implementation may look like this:

```
class classname extends superclass
        implements interface1, interface2, ......
{
        body of classname
}
```

This shows that a class can extend another class while implementing interfaces.

When a class implements more than one interface, they are .separated by a comma. The implementation of interfaces can take various forms as illustrated in Fig. 10.1.

Implementation of interfaces as class types is illustrated by Program 10.1. In this program, first we create an interface **Area** and implement the same in two different classes, **Rectangle** and **Circle**. We create an instance of each class using the **new** operator. Then we declare an object of type **Area**, the interface class. Now, we assign the reference to the Rectangle object **rect** to **area**. When we call the **compute** method of **area**, the **compute** method of **Rectangle** class is invoked. We repeat the same thing with the **Circle** object.

Program 10.1 Implementing interfaces

```
// InterfaceTest.java
interface Area// Interface defined
{
  .final static float pi = 3.14F;
   float compute (float x, float y);
}
class Rectangle implements Area                    // Interface implemented
{
    public float compute (float x, float y)
    {
```

(Continued)

Program 10.1 (*Continued*)

```
        return (x*y);
    }
}
class Circle implements Area                    // Another implementation
{
    public float compute (float x, float y)
    {
        return (pi*x*x);
    }
}
class InterfaceTest
{
    public static void main(String args[ ])
    {
        Rectangle rect = new Rectangle( );
        Circle cir = new Circle( );
        Area area;                              // Interface object
        area = rect;                            //  area refers to rect object
        System.out.println("Area of Rectangle = "
                                    + area.compute(10, 20));
        area = cir;                                // area refers to cir object
        System.out.println("Area of Circle = "
                                    + area.compute(10, 0));
    }
}
```

The Output is as follows:

```
        Area of Rectangle = 200
        Area of Circle = 314
```

Any number of dissimilar classes can implement an interface. However, to implement the methods, we need to refer to the class objects as types of the interface rather than types of their respective classes. Note that if a class that implements an interface does not implement all the methods of the interface, then the class becomes an ***abstract*** class and cannot be instantiated.

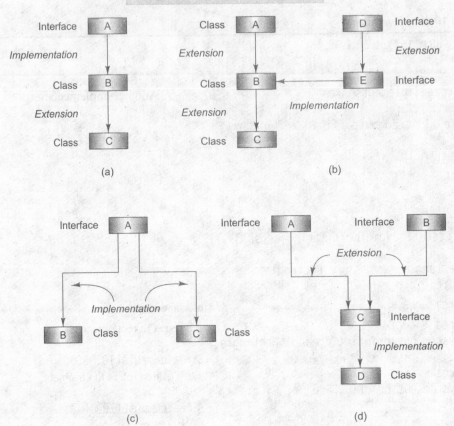

Fig. 10.1   *Various forms of interface implementation*

 ## 10.5 Accessing Interface Variables

Interfaces can be used to declare a set of constants that can be used in different classes. This is similar to creating header files in C++ to contain a large number of constants. Since such interfaces do not contain methods, there is no need to worry about implementing any methods. The constant values will be available to any class that implements the interface. The values can be used in any method, as part of any variable declaration, or anywhere where we can use a final value. Example:

```
interface A
{
        int m = 10;
        int n = 50;
}
class B implements A
{
        int x = m ;
```

```
        void methodB(int size)
        {
        ..........
        ..........
        if (size < n)
        ..........
        }
    }
```

Program 10.2 illustrates the implementation of the concept of multiple inheritance using interfaces.

Program 10.2   *Implementing multiple inheritance*

```
class Student
{
    int rollNumber;
    void getNumber(int n)
    {
        rollNumber = n;
    }
    void putNumber( )
    {
        System.out.println(" Roll No :  " + rollNumber);
    }
}
class Test extends Student
{
    float part1, part2;
    void getMarks(float m1, float m2)
    {
        part1 = m1;
        part2 = m2;
    }
    void putMarks( )
    {
        System.out.println("Marks obtained ");
        System.out.println("part 1 = " + part1);
        System.out.println("Part2 = " + part2);
    }
}
interface Sports
{
    float sportWt = 6.0F;
    void putwt( );
}
class Results extends Test implements Sports
```

(Continued)

Program 10.2   *(Continued)*

```
{
    float total;
    public void putWt( )
    {
        System.out.println("Sports Wt = " + sportWt);
    }
    void display( )
    {
        total = part1 + part2 + sportWt;
        putNumber( );
        putMarks( );
        putWt( );
        System.out.println("Total score = " + total);
    }
}
class Hybrid
{
    public static void main(String args[ ])
    {
        Results student1 = new Results( );
        student1.getNumber(1234);
        student1.getMarks(27.5F, 33.0F);
        student1.display( );
    }
}
```

Output of the Program 10.2:

```
    Roll No : 1234
Marks obtained
Part1 = 27.5
Part2 = 33
Sports Wt = 6
Total score = 66.5
```

10.6 Summary

Java does not support multiple inheritance. Since multiple inheritance is an important concept in OOP paradigm, Java provides an alternate way of implementing this concept. We have discussed in this chapter

- How to design an interface
- How to extend one interface by the other
- How to inherit an interface and
- How to implement the concept of multiple inheritance using interfaces

The concepts discussed in this chapter will enable us to build classes using other classes available already.

 Key Terms

Interface, Implementation, Multiple inheritance.

REVIEW QUESTIONS

10.1 What is an interface?
10.2 How do we tell Java that the class we are creating implements a particular interface?
10.3 What is the major difference between an interface and a class?
10.4 What are the similarities between interfaces and classes?
10.5 Describe the various forms of implementing interfaces. Give examples of Java code for each case.
10.6 Given an example where interface can be used to support multiple inheritance. Develop a standalone Java program for the example.

DEBUGGING EXERCISES

10.1 Following code creates an interface. Will this code compile successfully?

```java
public interface FamousLine
{
    void ShowLine()
    {
        System.out.println("Show Line");
    };
}
```

10.2 Debug the given code for implementing interfaces.

```java
interface FamousLine
{
    void ShowLine();
}
class Novel1 implements FamousLine
{
    public void ShowLine()
    {
        System.out.println("To be, or not to be");
    }
}
class Novel2 implements FamousLine
{
    public void AuthorName()
    {
        System.out.println("Shakespeare");
```

```
          }
        }
      public class UseInterface
      {
        public static void main(String args[])
        {
          Novel1 hamlet = new Novel1();
          Novel2 juliet = new Novel2();
          hamlet.ShowLine();
          juliet.AuthorName();
        }
      }
```

10.3 Correct the code to rectify the compile time error thrown.

```
      interface NewShape
      {
              void draw();
      }
      interface Circle extends NewShape
      {
        void getRadius();
        int radius=10;
      }
      class NewCircle implements Circle
      {
              public void getRadius()
              {
                  System.out.println(radius);
              }
      }
      class ExtendInterface extends NewCircle
      {
              public static void main(String[] args)
              {
                  Circle nc = new NewCircle();
                  nc.getRadius();
              }
      }
```

10.4 In this code, the interface acts as a type. Will this code compile successfully?, If not, correct the code.

```
      interface NewShape
      {
              void draw();
      }
      class NewCircle1 implements NewShape
      {
```

```
            public void draw()
            {
                  System.out.println("New Circle 1 Drawn");
            }
      }
class NewCircle2
{
            public void draw()
            {
                  System.out.println("New Circle 2 Drawn");
            }
}
class CastInterface
{
            public static void main(String[] args)
            {
                  NewShape nc1= new NewCircle1();
                  NewShape nc2= new NewCircle2();
                  nc1.draw();
                  nc2.draw();
            }
}
```

10.5 Check if the code will compile successfully. If not, correct the code.

```
      interface NewShape
      {
            void draw();
            int radius = 10;
      }
      class NewCircle1 implements NewShape
      {
            public void draw()
            {
                  radius=12;
                  System.out.println("Radius is: " + radius);
            }
      }
      class InterfaceVar
      {
            public static void main(String[] args)
            {
                  NewShape nc1 = new NewCircle1();
                  nc1.draw();
            }
      }
```

Chapter **11**

Packages: *Putting Classes Together*

11.1   Introduction

We have repeatedly stated that one of the main features of OOP is its ability to reuse the code already created. One way of achieving this is by extending the classes and implementing the interfaces we had created as discussed in Chapters 8 and 10. This is limited to reusing the classes within a program. What if we need to use classes from other programs without physically copying them into the program under development? This can be accomplished in Java by using what is known as *packages*, a concept similar to "class libraries" in other languages. Another way of achieving the reusability in Java, therefore, is to use packages.

Packages are Java's way of grouping a variety of classes and/or interfaces together. The grouping is usually done according to functionality. In fact, packages act as "containers" for classes. By organizing our classes into packages we achieve the following benefits:

1. The classes contained in the packages of other programs can be easily reused.
2. In packages, classes can be unique compared with classes in other packages. That is, two classes in two different packages can have the same name. They may be referred by their fully qualified name, comprising the package name and the class name.
3. Packages provide a way to "hide" classes thus preventing other programs or packages from accessing classes that are meant for internal use only.
4. Packages also provide a way for separating "design" from "coding". First we can design classes and decide their relationships, and then we can implement the Java code needed for the methods. It is possible to change the implementation of any method without affecting the rest of the design.

For most applications, we will need to use to different sets of classes, one for the internal representation of our program's data, and the other for external presentation purposes. We may have to build our own classes for handling our data and use existing class libraries for designing user interfaces. Java packages are therefore classified into two types. The first category is known as *Java API packages* and the second is known as user *defined packages*.

We shall consider both the categories of packages in this chapter and illustrate how to use them in our programs.

11.2   Java API Packages

Java API provides a large number of classes grouped into different packages according to functionality. Most of the time we use the packages available with the Java API. Figure 11.1 shows the functional breakdown of packages that are frequently used in the programs. Table 11.1 shows the classes that belong to each package (see Appendix E).

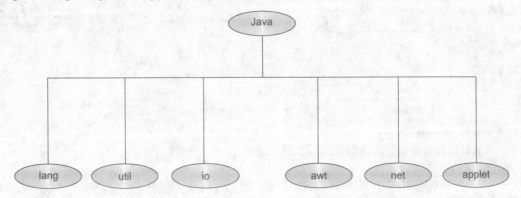

Fig. 11.1   *Frequently used API packages*

Table 11.1   Java System Packages and Their Classes

Package name	Contents
java.lang	Language support classes. These are classes that Java compiler itself uses and therefore they are automatically imported. They include classes for primitive types, strings, math functions, threads and exceptions.
java.util	Language utility classes such as vectors, hash tables, random numbers, date, etc.
java.io	Input/output support classes. They provide facilities for the input and output of data.
java.awt	Set of classes for implementing graphical user interface. They include classes for windows, buttons, lists, menus and so on.
java.net	Classes for networking. They include classes for communicating with local computers as well as with internet servers.
java.applet	Classes for creating and implementing applets.

11.3 Using System Packages

The packages are organised in a hierarchical structure as illustrated in Fig. 11.2. This shows that the package named **java** contains the package **awt**, which in turn contains various classes required for implementing graphical user interface.

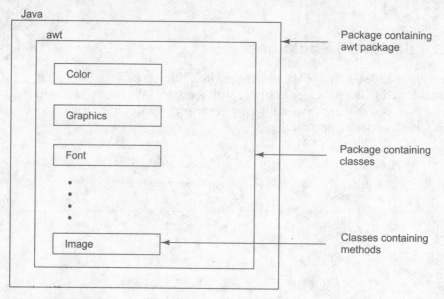

Fig. 11.2   *Hierarchical representation of java.awt package*

There are two ways of accessing the classes stored in a package. The first approach is to use the *fully qualified class name* of the class that we want to use. This is done by using the package name containing the class and then appending the class name to it using the dot operator. For example, if we want to refer to the class **Color** in the **awt** package, then we may do so as follows:

```
java.awt.Colour
```

Notice that **awt** is a package within the package **java** and the hierarchy is represented by separating the levels with dots. This approach is perhaps the best and easiest one if we need to access the class only once or when we need not have to access any other classes of the package.

But, in many situations, we might want to use a class in a number of places in the program or we may like to use many of the classes contained in a package. We may achieve this easily as follows:

```
import packagename.classname;
or
import packagename.*
```

These are known as *import statements* and must appear at the top of the file, before any class declarations, **import** is a keyword.

The first statement allows the specified class in the specified package to be imported. For example, the statement

```
import java.awt.Color;
```

imports the class **Colour** and therefore the class name can now be directly used in the program. There is no need to use the package name to qualify the class.

The second statement imports every class contained in the specified package. For example, the statement

```
import java.awt.*;
```

will bring all classes of **java.awt** package.

11.4 Naming Conventions

Packages can be named using the standard Java naming rules. By convention, however, packages begin with lowercase letters. This makes it easy for users to distinguish package names from class names when looking at an explicit reference to a class. We know that all class names, again by convention, begin with an uppercase letter. For example, look at the following statement:

```
double y = java.lang.Math.sqrt(x);
```

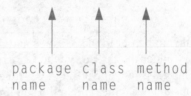

This statement uses a fully qualified class name **Math** to invoke the method **sqrt( )**. Note that methods begin with lowercase letters. Consider another example:

```
java.awt.Point pts[ ];
```

This statement declares an array of **Point** type objects using the fully qualified class name.

Every package name must be unique to make the best use of packages. Duplicate names will cause run-time errors. Since multiple users work on Internet, duplicate package names are unavoidable. Java designers have recognised this problem and therefore suggested a package naming convention that ensures uniqueness. This suggests the use of domain names as prefix to the preferred package names. For example:

```
cbe.psg.mypackage
```

Here **cbe** denotes city name and **psg** denotes organisation name. Remember that we can create a hierarchy of packages within packages by separating levels with dots.

11.5 Creating Packages

We have seen in detail how Java system packages are organised and used. Now, let us see how to create our own packages. We must first declare the name of the package using the **package** keyword followed by a package name. This must be the first statement in a Java source file (except for comments and white spaces). Then we define a class, just as we normally define a class. Here is an example:

```
package firstPackage;              // package declaration
public class FirstClass            // class definition
{
      ...........
      .......... (body of class)
      .........
}
```

Here the package name is **firstPackage**. The class **FirstClass** is now considered a part of this package. This listing would be saved as a file called **FirstClass.java**, and located in a directory named **firstPackage**. When the source file is compiled, Java will create a **.class** file and store it in the same directory.

Remember that the **.class** files must be located in a directory that has the same name as the package, and this directory should be a subdirectory of the directory where classes that will import the package are located.

To recap, creating our own package involves the following steps:

1. Declare the package at the beginning of a file using the form

```
package packagename;
```

2. Define the class that is to be put in the package and declare it **public**.
3. Create a subdirectory under the directory where the main source files are stored.
4. Store the listing as the classname.java file in the subdirectory created.
5. Compile the file. This creates **.class** file in the subdirectory.

Remember that case is significant and therefore the subdirectory name must match the package name exactly.

As pointed out earlier, Java also supports the concept of package hierarchy. This is done by specifying multiple names in a package statement, separated by dots. Example:

```
package firstPackage.secondPackage;
```

This approach allows us to group related classes into a package and then group related packages into a larger package. Remember to store this package in a subdirectory named **firstPackage/secondPackage.**

A java package file can have more than one class definitions. In such cases, only one of the classes may be declared **public** and that class name with **.java** extension is the source file name. When a source file with more than one class definition is compiled, Java creates independent **.class** files for those classes.

 ## 11.6 Accessing a Package

It may be recalled that we have discussed earlier that a Java system package can be accessed either using a fully qualified class name or using a shortcut approach through the **import** statement. We use the **import** statement when there are many references to a particular package or the package name is too long and unwieldy.

The same approaches can be used to access the user-defined packages as well. The **import** statement can be used to search a list of packages for a particular class. The general form of **import** statement for searching a class is as follows:

```
import package1 [.package2] [.packag3].classname;
```

Here *package1* is the name of the top level package, *package2* is the name of the package that is inside the *package1*, and so on. We can have any number of packages in a package hierarchy. Finally, the explicit *classname* is specified.

Note that the statement must end with a semicolon (;). The **import** statement should appear before any class definitions in a source file. Multiple import statements are allowed. The following is an example of importing a particular class:

```
import firstPackage.secondPackage.MyClass;
```

After defining this statement, all the members of the class **MyClass** can be directly accessed using the class name or its objects (as the case may be) directly without using the package name.

We can also use another approach as follows:

```
import packagename.*;
```

Here, *packagename* may denote a single package or a hierarchy of packages as mentioned earlier. The star (*) indicates that the compiler should search this entire package hierarchy when it encounters a class name. This implies that we can access all classes contained in the above package directly.

The major drawback of the shortcut approach is that it is difficult to determine from which package a particular member came. This is particularly true when a large number of packages are imported. But the advantage is that we need not have to use long package names repeatedly in the program.

11.7 Using a Package

Let us now consider some simple programs that will use classes from other packages. The listing below shows a package named **package1** containing a single class **ClassA**.

```
package package1;
public class ClassA
{
    public void displayA( )
    {
        System.out.println("Class A");
    }
}
```

This source file should be named **ClassA.java** and stored in the subdirectory **package1** as stated earlier. Now compile this java file. The resultant **ClassA.class** will be stored in the same subdirectory.

Now consider the listing shown below:

```
import package1. ClassA;
class PackageTest1
{
    public static void main(String args[ ] )
    {
        ClassA objectA = new ClassA( ) ;
        objectA.displayA( );
    }
}
```

This listing shows a simple program that imports the class **ClassA** from the package **package1**. The source file should be saved as **PackageTest1.java** and then compiled. The source file and the compiled file would be saved in the directory of which **package1** was a subdirectory. Now we can run the program and obtain the results.

During the compilation of **PackageTest1.java** the compiler checks for the file **ClassA.class** in the **package1** directory for information it needs, but it does not actually include the code from **ClassA.class** in the file **PackageTest1.class**. When the **PackageTest1** program is run, Java looks for the file **PackageTest1.class** and loads it using something called *class loader*. Now the interpreter knows that it also needs the code in the file **ClassA.class** and loads it as well.

Now let us consider another package named **package2** containing again a single class as shown below:

```
package package2;
public class ClassB
{
    protected int m = 10
    public void displayB( )
    {
        System.out.println("Class B");
        System.out.println("m = " + m);
    }
}
```

As usual, the source file and the compiled file of this package are located in the subdirectory **package2**.

Program 11.1 shown below uses classes contained in both the packages and therefore it imports **package1** and **package2**. Note that we have used star instead of explicit class name in importing **package2**.

Program 11.1 *Importing classes from other packages*

```
import package1.ClassA;
import package2.*;
class PackageTest2
{
    public static void main(String args[ ])
```

(Continued)

Program 11.1   (*Continued*)

```
      {
            ClassA objectA = new ClassA( );
            ClassB objectB = new ClassB( );
            objectA.displayA( );
            objectB.displayB( );
      }
}
```

This program may be saved as **PackageTest2.java**, compiled and run to obtain the results. The output will be as under

```
Class A
Class B
m = 10
```

When we import multiple packages it is likely that two or more packages contain classes with identical names. Example:

```
package pack1;
public class Teacher
{..........}
public class Student
{..........}
package pack2;
public class Courses
{..........}
public class Student
{..........}
```

We may import and use these packages like:

```
import pack1.*;
import pack2.*;
Student studetn1;            // create a student object
```

Since both the packages contain the class **Student,** compiler cannot understand which one to use and therefore generates an error. In such instance, we have to be more explicit about which one we intend to use.

Example:

```
import pack1.*;
import pack2.*;
pack1.Student student1;          // OK
pack2.Student student2;          // OK
Teacher teacher1;                // No problem
Courses course1;                 // No problem
```

It is also possible to subclass a class that has been imported from another package. This is illustrated by Program 11.2. The output will be:

```
Class B
m = 10
Class C
m = 10
n = 20
```

Note that the variable **m** has been declared as **protected**. A subclass in another package can inherit a **protected** member. It would not have been possible if it has been declared as either **private** or "default".

Program 11.2 *Subclassing an imported class*

```java
// PackageTest3.java
import package2.ClassB;
class ClassC extends ClassB
{
  int n = 20;
  void displayC( )
  {
    System.out.println("Class C");
    System.out.println("m = " + m);
    System.out.println("n = " + n);
  }
}
class PackageTest3
{
  public static void main(String args[ ])
  {
    ClassC objectC = new ClassC( );
    objectC.displayB( );
    objectC.displayC( );
  }
}
```

While using packages and inheritance in a program, we should be aware of the visibility restrictions imposed by various access protection modifiers. As pointed out earlier, packages act as containers for classes and other packages, and classes act as containers for data and methods. Data members and methods can be declared with the access protection modifiers such as **private, protected,** and **public** as well as "default". The effect of use of these modifiers was discussed in detail in Chapter 8. For the sake of easy reference, the access protection details given in Table 8.1 are reproduced Table 11.2.

Table 11.2   Access Protection

Access modifier → Access location ↓	public	protected	friendly (default)	private protected	private
Same class	Yes	Yes	Yes	Yes	Yes
Subclass in same package	Yes	Yes	Yes	Yes	No
Other classes in same package	Yes	Yes	Yes	No	No
Subclass in other packages	Yes	Yes	No	(Yes)	No
Non-subclasses in other packages	Yes	No	No	No	No

11.8   Adding a Class to a Package

It is simple to add a class to an existing package. Consider the following package:

```
package p1;
public ClassA
{
      // body of A
}
```

The package **p1** contains one public class by name **A**. Suppose we want to add another class **B** to this package. This can be done as follows:

1. Define the class and make it public.
2. Place the package statement

   ```
   package p1;
   ```

   before the class definition as follows:

   ```
   package p1;
   public class B
   {
         // body of B
   }
   ```

3. Store this as **B.java** file under the directory **p1**.
4. Compile **B.java** file. This will create a **B.class** file and place it in the directory **p1**.

Note that we can also add a non-public class to a package using the same procedure.

Now, the package **p1** will contain both the classes **A** and **B**. A statement like

```
import p1.*;
```

will import both of them.

Remember that, since a Java source file can have only one class declared as **public,** we cannot put two or more public classes together in a **.java** file. This is because of the restriction that the file name should be same as the name of the public class with **.java** extension.

If we want to create a package with multiple public classes in it, we may follow the following steps:

1. Decide the name of the package.
2. Create a subdirectory with this name under the directory where main source files are stored.
3. Create classes that are to be placed in the package in separate source files and declare the package statement

```
package packagename;
```

at the top of each source file.
4. Switch to the subdirectory created earlier and compile each source file. When completed, the package would contain **.class** files of all the source files.

 ## 11.9   Hiding Classes

When we import a package using asterisk (*), all public classes are imported. However, we may prefer to "not import" certain classes. That is, we may like to hide these classes from accessing from outside of the package. Such classes should be declared "not public". Example:

```
package p1;
public class X                 // public class, available outside
{
     // body of X
}
class Y                        // not public, hidden
{
     // body of Y
}
```

Here, the class **Y** which is not declared public is hidden from outside of the package **p1**. This class can be seen and used only by other classes in the same package. Note that a Java source file should contain only one public class and may include any number of non-public classes. We may also add a single non-public class using the procedure suggested in the previous section.

Now, consider the following code, which imports the package **p1** that contains classes X and Y:

```
import p1.*;
X   objectX;                   // OK; class X is available here
Y   objectY;                   // Not OK: Y is not available
```

Java compiler would generate an error message for this code because the class **Y**, which has not been declared **public**, is not imported and therefore not available for creating its objects.

11.10   Static Import

Static import is another language feature introduced with the J2SE 5.0 release. This feature eliminates the need of qualifying a static member with the class name. The static import declaration is similar to that of import. We can use the import statement to import classes from packages and use them without qualifying the package. Similarly, we can use the static import statement to import static members from classes and use them without qualifying the class name. The syntax for using the static import feature is:

```
import static package-name.subpackage-name.class-
name.staticmember-name;
(or)
import static package-name.subpackage-name.class-name.*;
```

Before introducing the static import feature, we had to use the static member with the qualifying class name. For example, consider the following code that contains the static member PI:

```
double area_of_circle = Math.PI * radius * radius;
```

In the above code, PI is the static member of the class, **Math**. So the static member PI is used in the above program with the qualified class name called **Math**.

Also, before implementing the static import feature, if we use static member in an interface and we need to use it in a class, then we have to implement that interface in the class. Now, we can use this feature to import the interface into the class. Consider the following code that provides an example of importing the interface, salary_increment into the class, salary_hike:

```
public interface Salary_increment
{
    public static final double Manager=0.5;
    public static final double Clerk=0.25;
}
```

Here, let us assume that the interface is available in the subpackage, employee_details of the employee package. If we need to access the interface, we can import the interface using the static import statement as follows:

```
import static employee.employee_details.Salary_increment;
    class Salary_hike
    {
        public static void main(String args[])
        {
            double manager_salary=Manager*Manager_current_salary;
            double clerk_salary=Clerk*Clerk_current_salary;
            ..........
            ..........
        }
    }
```

Thus, we can use the static member in the code without qualifying the class name or interface name. Also, the static import feature eliminates the redundancy of using the qualified class name with the static member name and increases the readability of the program. Program 11.3 illustrates the use of static import:

Program 11.3   *Use of Static import*

```
import static java.lang.Math.*:
public class mathop
{
     public void circle(double r)
        {
             double area=PI*r* r:
             System.out.println("The Area of Circle is :"+area):
        }

        public static void main(String args[])
        {
          mathop obj=new mathop():
          obj.circle(2.3):
        }
}
```

The output for the above programs is:
        The Area of Circle is 16.619025137490002

11.11   Summary

In this chapter we saw the building blocks of coding in Java and high-level requirements for designing applets and application programs. Java has several levels of hierarchy for code organisation, the highest of which is the package. We have seen here

- How to create a package,
- How to add more classes to a package,
- How to access the contents of a package,
- How to protect a class from accidental access, and
- How to use Java system packages.

This chapter essentially has shown us how to organise classes into packages to better keep track of them.

 Key Terms

Package, Import, public, protected, Friendly, static import

REVIEW QUESTIONS

11.1   What is a package?
11.2   How do we tell Java that we want to use a particular package in a file?
11.3   How do we design a package?
11.4   How do we add a class or an interface to a package?

11.5 Consider the example Program 10.2. Design a package to contain the class **student** and another package to contain the interface **sports**. Rewrite the Program 10.2 using these packages.

11.6 Discuss the various levels of access protection available for packages and their implications.

11.7 What is static import? How is it useful?

DEBUGGING EXERCISES

11.1 The following code finds out a duplicate value in a vector. Will this code work? If not , Why?

```
class DupValue
{
        public static void main(String[] args)
        {
                Vector v = new Vector();
                v.add("Delhi");
                v.add("Mumbai");
                v.add("Calcutta");
                v.add("Chennai");
                v.add("Delhi");

                Vector tempVector = new Vector();
                String tmpValue;

                for (int j = 0;j<= v.size(); j++)
                {
                        tmpValue = (String)v.elementAt(j);
                        if(tmpValue!=null) {
                                if( tmpVector.isEmpty() )
                                tmpVector.addElement(tmpValue);
                                if(tmpVector.indexOf(tmpValue)==-1){
                                tmpVector.addElement(tmpValue);}}
                }
                for(int j = 0; j < tmpVector.size(); j++) {
                        System.out.print(tmpVector.elementAt(j));
                }
        }
}
```

11.2 The class given below has been saved in the folder "circle". Will the program run?

```
package Circle;
class NewCircle
{
        public void draw(){}
        public void getRadius(){}
        public static void main(String args[])
        {
```

```
            System.out.println("Package Creation done");
        }
    }
```

11.3   The code uses the class defined above. Class ImportClass is not defined in circle folder. Will the code run without giving any errors?

```
    import circle.NewCircle;
    class ImportClass
    {
        public static void main(String[] args)
        {
            circle.NewCircle nc=new circle.NewCircle();
            System.out.println("Hello World!");
        }
    }
```

11.4   The method draw() in NewCircle has been set as private. Class SamePackage is in the same package as NewCircle. Will the class be able to use the method?

```
    package circle;
    import circle.NewCircle;
    class SamePackage
    {
        public static void main(String[] args)
        {
            NewCircle nc=new NewCircle();
            nc.draw();
        }
    }
```

11.5   Importing a complete package with all its classes has been demonstrated in the program. Will the class compile?

```
    import circle;
    class ImportClass
    {
        public static void main(String[] args)
        {
            circle.NewCircle nc=new circle.NewCircle();
            System.out.println("Hello World!");
        }
    }
```

12

Multithreaded Programming

12.1   Introduction

Those who are familiar with the modern operating systems such as Windows 95 and Windows XP may recognize that they can execute several programs simultaneously. This ability is known as *multitasking*. In system's terminology, it is called *multithreading*.

Multithreading is a conceptual programming paradigm where a program (process) is divided into two or more subprograms (processes), which can be implemented at the same time in parallel. For example, one subprogram can display an animation on the screen while another may build the next animation to be displayed. This is something similar to dividing a task into subtasks and assigning them to different people for execution independently and simultaneously.

In most of our computers, we have only a single processor and therefore, in reality, the processor is doing only one thing at a time. However, the processor switches between the processes so fast that it appears to human beings that all of them are being done simultaneously.

Java programs that we have seen and discussed so far contain only a single sequential flow of control. This is what happens when we execute a normal program. The program begins, runs through a sequence of executions, and finally ends. At any given point of time, there is only one statement under execution.

A *thread* is similar to a program that has a single flow of control. It has a beginning, a body, and an end, and executes commands sequentially. In fact, all main programs in our earlier examples can be called *single-threaded* programs. Every program will have at least one thread as shown in Fig. 12.1.

A unique property of Java is its support for multithreading. That is, Java enables us to use multiple flows of control in developing programs. Each flow of control may be thought of as a separate tiny program (or module) known as a *thread* that runs in parallel to others as shown in Fig. 12.2. A program that contains multiple flows of control is known as *multithreaded program*. Figure 12.2 illustrates a Java program with four threads, one main and three others. The main thread is actually the **main** method module, which is designed to create and start the other three threads, namely A, B and C.

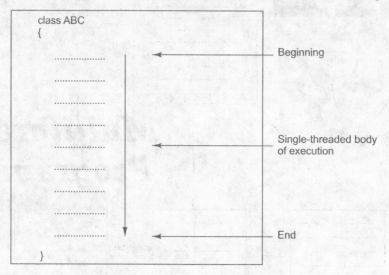

Fig. 12.1   *Single-threaded program*

Once initiated by the main thread, the threads A, B, and C run concurrently and share the resources jointly. It is like people living in joint families and sharing certain resources among all of them. The ability of a language to support multithreads is referred to as *concurrency*. Since threads in Java are subprograms of a main application program and share the same memory space, they are known as *lightweight threads* or *lightweight processes*.

It is important to remember that 'threads running in parallel' does not really mean that they actually run at the same time. Since all the threads are running on a single processor, the flow of execution is shared between the threads. The Java interpreter handles the switching of control between the threads in such a way that it appears they are running concurrently.

Multithreading is a powerful programming tool that makes Java distinctly different from its fellow programming languages. Multithreading is useful in a number of ways. It enables programmers to do multiple things at one time. They can divide a long program (containing operations that are conceptually concurrent) into threads and execute them in parallel. For example, we can send tasks such as printing into the background and continue to perform some other task in the foreground. This approach would considerably improve the speed of our programs.

Threads are extensively used in Java-enabled browsers such as HotJava. These browsers can download a file to the local computer, display a Web page in the window, output another Web page to a printer and so on.

Any application we are working on that requires two or more things to be done at the same time is probably a best one for use of threads.

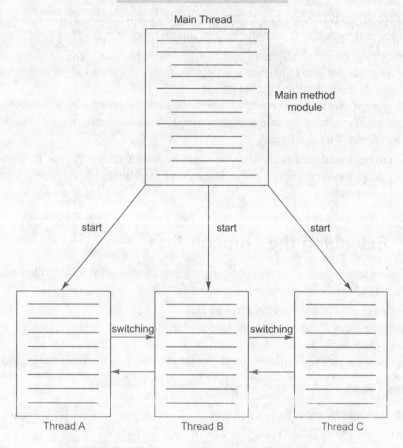

Fig. 12.2   *A Multithreaded program*

12.2 Creating Threads

Creating threads in Java is simple. Threads are implemented in the form of objects that contain a method called **run( )**. The **run( )** method is the heart and soul of any thread. It makes up the entire body of a thread and is the only method in which the thread's behaviour can be implemented. A typical **run( )** would appear as follows:

```
public void run( )
{
    . . . . . . . . . .
    . . . . . . . . . .    (statements for implementing thread)
    . . . . . . . . . .
}
```

The **run( )** method should be invoked by an object of the concerned thread. This can be achieved by creating the thread and initiating it with the help of another thread method called **start ( ).**

A new thread can be created in two ways.

1. *By creating a thread class:* Define a class that extends **Thread** class and override its **run( )** method with the code required by the thread.

2. *By converting a class to a thread:* Define a class that implements **Runnable** interface. The **Runnable** interface has only one method, **run( )**, that is to be defined in the method with the code to be executed by the thread.

The approach to be used depends on what the class we are creating requires. If it requires to extend another class, then we have no choice but to implement the **Runnable** interface, since Java classes cannot have two superclasses.

12.3 Extending the Thread Class

We can make our class runnable as thread by extending the class **java.lang.Thread.** This gives us access to all the thread methods directly. It includes the following steps:

1. Declare the class as extending the **Thread** class.
2. Implement the **run( )** method that is responsible for executing the sequence of code that the thread will execute.
3. Create a thread object and call the **start( )** method to initiate the thread execution.

Declaring the Class

The **Thread** class can be extended as follows:

```
class MyThread extends Thread
{
         . . . . . . . . . .
         . . . . . . . . . .
         . . . . . . . . . .
}
```

Now we have a new type of thread **MyThread.**

Implementing the *run()* Method

The **run( )** method has been inherited by the class **MyThread.** We have to override this method in order to implement the code to be executed by our thread. The basic implementation of **run( )** will look like this:

```
public void run( )
{
         . . . . . . . . . .
         . . . . . . . . . .    // Thread code here
         . . . . . . . . . .
}
```

When we start the new thread, Java calls the thread's **run( )** method, so it is the **run( )** where all the action takes place.

Starting New Thread

To actually create and run an instance of our thread class, we must write the following:

```
MyThread aThread = new MyThread( );

aThread.start( );                    // invokes run() method
```

The first line instantiates a new object of class **MyThread.** Note that this statement just creates the object. The thread that will run this object is not yet running. The thread is in a *newborn* state.

The second line calls the **start( )** method causing the thread to move into the *runnable* state. Then, the Java runtime will schedule the thread to run by invoking its **run( )** method. Now, the thread is said to be in the *running* state.

An Example of Using the Thread Class

Program 12.1 illustrates the use of **Thread** class for creating and running threads in an application. The program creates three threads A, B, and C for undertaking three different tasks. The **main** method in the **ThreadTest** class also constitutes another thread which we may call the "main thread".

The main thread dies at the end of its **main** method. However, before it dies, it creates and starts all the three threads A, B, and C. Note the statements like

```
new A( ).start( );
```

in the main thread. This is just a compact way of starting a thread. This is equivalent to:

```
A threadA = new A( );

threadA.start( );
```

Immediately after the thread A is started, there will be two threads running in the program: the main thread and the thread A. The **start( )** method returns back to the main thread immediately after invoking the **run( )** method, thus allowing the main thread to start the thread B.

Program 12.1 *Creating threads using the thread class*

```
class A extends Thread
{
    public void run( )
    {
        for (int i=1; i<=5; i++)
        {
                System.out.println("\tFrom ThreadA : i = " + i);
        }
        System.out.println("Exit form A ");
    }
}
class B extends Thread
{
```

(Continued)

Program 12.1   (*Continued*)

```
    public void run( )
    {
        for(int j=1; j<=5; j++)
        {
                System.out.println("\tFrom Thread B :j = " + j);
        }
        System.out.println("Exit from B ");
    }
}
class B extends Thread
{
    public void run( )
    {
        for(int k=1; k<=5; k++)
        {
            System.out.println("\tFrom Thread C : k = " + k);
        }
        System.out.println("Exit from C ");
    }
}
class ThreadTest
{
    public static void main(String args[ ])
    {
        new A( ).start( );
        new B( ).start( );
        new C( ).start( );
    }
}
```

Output of Program 12.1 would be:

First run

From	Thread	A	:	i	=	1
From	Thread	A	:	i	=	2
From	Thread	B	:	j	=	1
From	Thread	B	:	j	=	2
From	Thread	C	:	k	=	1
From	Thread	C	:	k	=	2
From	Thread	A	:	i	=	3
From	Thread	A	:	i	=	4
From	Thread	B	:	j	=	3
From	Thread	B	:	j	=	4
From	Thread	C	:	k	=	3
From	Thread	C	:	k	=	4

```
From    Thread    A    :    i    =    5
Exit from A
From    Thread    B    :    j    =    5
Exit from B
From    Thread    C    :    k    =    5
Exit from C

Second run
From    Thread    A    :    i    =    1
From    Thread    A    :    i    =    2
From    Thread    C    :    k    =    1
From    Thread    C    :    k    =    2
From    Thread    A    :    i    =    3
From    Thread    A    :    i    =    4
From    Thread    B    :    j    =    1
From    Thread    B    :    j    =    2
From    Thread    C    :    k    =    3
From    Thread    C    :    k    =    4
From    Thread    A    :    i    =    5
Exit from A
From    Thread    B    :    k    =    4
From    Thread    B    :    j    =    5
From    Thread    C    :    k    =    5
Exit from C
From    Thread    B    :    j    =    5
Exit from B
```

Similarly, it starts C thread. By the time the main thread has reached the end of its **main** method, there are a total of four separate threads running in parallel.

We have simply initiated three new threads and started them. We did not hold on to them any further. They are running concurrently on their own. Note that the output from the threads are not specially sequential. They do not follow any specific order. They are running independently of one another and each executes whenever it has a chance. Remember, once the threads are started, we cannot decide with certainty the order in which they may execute statements. Note that a second run has a different output sequence.

 ## 12.4 Stopping and Blocking a Thread

Stopping a Thread

Whenever we want to stop a thread from running further, we may do so by calling its **stop( )** method, like:

```
aThread.stop( );
```

This statement causes the thread to move to the *dead* state. A thread will also move to the dead state automatically when it reaches the end of its method. The **stop( )** method may be used when the *premature death* of a thread is desired.

Blocking a Thread

A thread can also be temporarily suspended or blocked from entering into the runnable and subsequently running state by using either of the following thread methods:

```
sleep( )              // blocked for a specified time
suspend( )            // blocked until further orders
wait( )               // blocked until certain condition occurs
```

These methods cause the thread to go into the *blocked* (or *not-runnable*) state. The thread will return to the runnable state when the specified time is elapsed in the case of **sleep( )**, the **resume( )** method is invoked in the case of **suspend( )**, and the **notify( )** method is called in the case of **wait( )**.

12.5   Life Cycle of a Thread

During the life time of a thread, there are many states it can enter. They include:

1. Newborn state
2. Runnable state
3. Running state
4. Blocked state
5. Dead state

A thread is always in one of these five states. It can move from one state to another via a variety of ways as shown in Fig. 12.3.

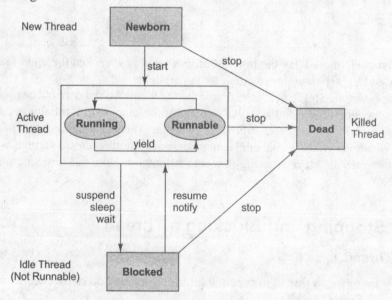

Fig. 12.3   *State transition diagram of a thread*

Newborn State

When we create a thread object, the thread is born and is said to be in *newborn* state. The thread is not yet scheduled for running. At this state, we can do only one of the following things with it:

- Schedule it for running using **start( )** method.
- Kill it using **stop( )** method.

If scheduled, it moves to the runnable state (Fig. 12.4). If we attempt to use any other method at this stage, an exception will be thrown.

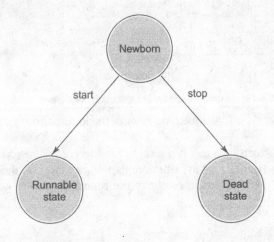

Fig. 12.4   *Scheduling a newborn thread*

Runnable State

The *runnable* state means that the thread is ready for execution and is waiting for the availability of the processor. That is, the thread has joined the queue of threads that are waiting for execution. If all threads have equal priority, then they are given time slots for execution in round robin fashion, i.e., first-come, first-serve manner. The thread that relinquishes control joins the queue at the end and again waits for its turn. This process of assigning time to threads is known as *time-slicing*.

However, if we want a thread to relinquish control to another thread to equal priority before its turn comes, we can do so by using the **yield( )** method (Fig. 12.5).

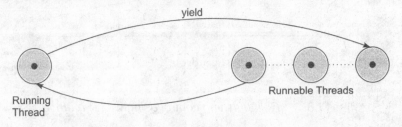

Fig. 12.5   *Relinquishing control using yield( ) method*

Running State

Running means that the processor has given its time to the thread for its execution. The thread runs until it relinquishes control on its own or it is preempted by a higher priority thread. A running thread may relinquish its control in one of the following situations.

1. It has been suspended using **suspend( )** method. A suspended thread can be revived by using the **resume( )** method. This approach is useful when we want to suspend a thread for some time due to certain reason, but do not want to kill it.

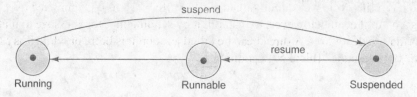

Fig. 12.6   *Relinquishing control using suspend( ) method*

2. It has been made to sleep. We can put a thread to sleep for a specified time period using the method **sleep**(*time*) where *time* is in milliseconds. This means that the thread is out of the queue during this time period. The thread re-enters the runnable state as soon as this time period is elapsed.

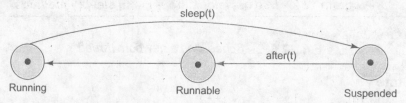

Fig. 12.7   *Relinquishing control using sleep( ) method*

3. It has been told to wait until some event occurs. This is done using the **wait( )** method. The thread can be scheduled to run again using the **notify( )** method.

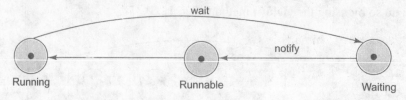

Fig. 12.8   *Relinquishing control using wait( ) method*

Blocked State

A thread is said to be *blocked* when it is prevented from entering into the runnable state and subsequently the running state. This happens when the thread is suspended, sleeping, or waiting in order to satisfy certain requirements. A blocked thread is considered "not runnable" but not dead and therefore fully qualified to run again.

Dead State

Every thread has a life cycle. A running thread ends its life when it has completed executing its **run( )** method. It is a natural death. However, we can kill it by sending the stop message to it at any state thus causing a premature death to it. A thread can be killed as soon it is born, or while it is running, or even when it is in "not runnable" (blocked) condition.

12.6   Using Thread Methods

We have discussed how **Thread** class methods can be used to control the behaviour of a thread. We have used the methods **start( )** and **run( )** in Program 12.1. There are also methods that can move a thread from one state to another. Program 12.2 illustrates the use of **yield( )**, **sleep( )** and **stop( )** methods. Compare the outputs of Programs 12.1 and 12.2.

Program 12.2   *Use of yield( ), stop( ), and sleep( ) methods*

```
class A extends Thread
{
    public void run( )
    {
        for(int i = 1; i<=5; i++)
        {
            if(i==1) yield( );
            System.out.println("\tFrom Thread A : i = " +i);
        }
        System.out.println("exit from A ");
    }
}

class B extends Thread
{
    public void run( )
    {
        for(int i=1; i<=5; j++)
        {
            System.out.println("\tFrom Thread B : j = " + j);
            if(j==3) stop( );
        }
```

(Continued)

Program 12.2 (*Continued*)

```java
            System.out.println("Exit from B ");
        }
    }
class C extends Thread
{
    public void run( )
    {
        for (int k=1; k<=5; k++)
        {
            System.out.println("\tFrom Thread C : k = " +k);
            if(k==1)
            try
                {
                    sleep(1000);
                }
            catch (Exception e)
                {
                }
        }
        System.out.println("Exit from C ");
    }
}
class ThreadMethods
{
    public static void main(String args[ ])
    {
        A threadA = new A( );
        B threadB = new B( );
        C threadC = new C( );

        System.out.println("Start thread A");
        threadA.start( );

        System.out.println("Start thread B");
        threadB.start( );

        System.out.println("Start thread C");
        threadC.start( );

        System.out.println("End of main thread");
    }
}
```

Here is the output of Program 12.2:

```
Start thread A
Start thread B
Start thread C
      From Thread B : j = 1
      From Thread B : j = 2
      From Thread A : i = 1
      From Thread A : i = 2
End of main thread
      From Thread C : k = 1
      From Thread B : j = 3
      From Thread A : i = 3
      From Thread A : i = 4
      From Thread A : i = 5
Exit from A
      From Thread C : k = 2
      From Thread C : k = 3
      From Thread C : k = 4
      From Thread C : k = 5
Exit from C
```

Program 12.2 uses the **yield( )** method in thread A at the iteration i = 1. Therefore, the thread A, although started first, has relinquished its control to the thread B. The **stop( )** method in thread B has killed it after implementing the **for** loop only three times. Note that it has not reached end of **run( )** method. The thread C started sleeping after executing the for loop only once. When it woke up (after 1000 milliseconds), the other two threads have already completed their runs and therefore was running alone. The main thread died much earlier than the other three threads.

 ## 12.7 Thread Exceptions

Note that the call to **sleep( )** method is enclosed in a **try** block and followed by a **catch** block. This is necessary because the **sleep( )** method throws an exception, which should be caught. If we fail to catch the exception, program will not compile.

Java run system will throw **IllegalThreadStateException** whenever we attempt to invoke a method that a thread cannot handle in the given state. For example, a sleeping thread cannot deal with the **resume( )** method because a sleeping thread cannot receive any instructions. The same is true with the **suspend( )** method when it is used on a blocked (Not Runnable) thread.

Whenever we call a thread method that is likely to throw an exception, we have to supply an appropriate exception handler to catch it. The **catch** statement may take one of the following forms:

```
catch (ThreadDeath e)
{
    ..........
    ..........          // Killed thread
}
```

```
catch (InterruptedException e)
{
    . . . . . . . . . .
    . . . . . . . . . .              // Cannot handle it in the current state
}
catch (IllegalArgumentException e)
{
    . . . . . . . . . .
    . . . . . . . . . .              // Illegal method argument
}
catch (Exception e)
{
    . . . . . . . . . .
    . . . . . . . . . .              // Any other
}
```

Exception handling is discussed in detail in Chapter 13.

12.8 Thread Priority

In Java, each thread is assigned a priority, which affects the order in which it is scheduled for running. The threads that we have discussed so far are of the same priority. The threads of the same priority are given equal treatment by the Java scheduler and, therefore, they share the processor on a first-come, first-serve basis.

Java permits us to set the priority of a thread using the **setPriority( )** method as follows:

```
ThreadName.setPriority(intNumber);
```

The **intNumber** is an integer value to which the thread's priority is set. The **Thread** class defines several priority constants:

```
MIN_PRIORITY    =              1
NORM_PRIORITY   =              5
MAX_PRIORITY    =             10
```

The **intNumber** may assume one of these constants or any value between 1 and 10. Note that the default setting is NORM_PRIORITY.

Most user-level processes should use NORM_PRIORITY, plus or minus 1. Back-ground tasks such as network I/O and screen repainting should use a value very near to the lower limit. We should be very cautious when trying to use very high priority values. This may defeat the very purpose of using multithreads.

By assigning priorities to threads, we can ensure that they are given the attention (or lack of it) they deserve. For example, we may need to answer an input as quickly as possible. Whenever multiple threads are ready for execution, the Java system chooses the highest priority thread and executes it. For a thread of lower priority to gain control, one of the following things should happen:

1. It stops running at the end of **run( )**.
2. It is made to sleep using **sleep( )**.
3. It is told to wait using **wait( )**.

However, if another thread of a higher priority comes along, the currently running thread will be *preempted* by the incoming thread thus forcing the current thread to move to the runnable state. Remember that the highest priority thread always preempts any lower priority threads.

Program 12.3 and its output illustrate the effect of assigning higher priority to a thread. Note that although the thread A started first, the higher priority thread B has preempted it and started printing the output first. Immediately, the thread C that has been assigned the highest priority takes control over the other two threads. The thread A is the last to complete.

Program 12.3 *Use of priority in threads*

```
class A extends Thread
{
    public void run( )
    {
        System.out.println("threadA started");
        for(int i=1; i<=4; i++)
        {
            System.out.println("\tFrom Thread A : i = " +i);
        }
        System.out.println("Exit from A ");
    }
}
class B extends Thread
{
    public void run( )
    {
        System.out.println("threadB started");
        for(int j=1; j<=4; j++)
        {
            System.out.println("\tFrom Thread B : j = " + j);
        }
        System.out.println("Exit from B ");
    }
}
class C extends Thread
{
    public void run( )
    {
        System.out.println("threadC started");
        for(int k=1; k<=4; k++)
        {
            System.out.println("\tFrom Thread C : k = " + k);
        }
```

(Continued)

Program 12.3 *(Continued)*

```
        System.out.println("Exit from C ");
        }
}
class ThreadPriority
{
    public static void main(String args[ ])
    {
        A threadA = new A( );
        B threadB = new B( );
        C threadC = new C( );

        threadC.setPriority(Thread.MAX_PRIORITY);
        threadB.setPriority(threadA.getPriority( )+1);
        threadA.setPrioirty(Thread.MIN_PRIORITY);

        System.out.println("Start thread A");
        threadA.start( );

        System.out.println("Start thread B");
        threadB.start( );

        System.out.println("Start thread C");
        threadC.start( );

        System.out.println("End of main thread");
    }
}
```

Output of Program 12.3:

```
        Start thread A
        Start thread B
        Start thread C
        threadB started
            From Thread B : j = 1
            From Thread B : j = 2
        threadC started
            From Thread C : k = 1
            From Thread C : k = 2
            From Thread C : k = 3
            From Thread C : k = 4
        Exit from C
        End of main thread
            From Thread B : j = 3
            From Thread B : j = 4
```

```
Exit from B
threadA started
    From Thread A : i = 1
    From Thread A : i = 2
    From Thread A : i = 3
    From Thread A : i = 4
Exit from A
```

 ## 12.9　Synchronization

So far, we have seen threads that use their own data and methods provided inside their **run( )** methods. What happens when they try to use data and methods outside themselves? On such occasions, they may compete for the same resources and may lead to serious problems. For example, one thread may try to read a record from a file while another is still writing to the same file. Depending on the situation, we may get strange results. Java enables us to overcome this problem using a technique known as *synchronization*.

In case of Java, the keyword **synchronised** helps to solve such problems by keeping a watch on such locations. For example, the method that will read information from a file and the method that will update the same file may be declared as **synchronized**. Example:

```
synchronized void update( )
{
    . . . . . . . . . .
    . . . . . . . . . .    // code here is synchronized
    . . . . . . . . . .
}
```

When we declare a method synchronized, Java creates a "monitor" and hands it over to the thread that calls the method first time. As long as the thread holds the monitor, no other thread can enter the synchronized section of code. A monitor is like a key and the thread that holds the key can only open the lock.

It is also possible to mark a block of code as synchronized as shown below:

```
synchronized (lock-object)
{
    . . . . . . . . . .    // code here is synchronized
    . . . . . . . . . .
}
```

Whenever a thread has completed its work of using synchronized method (or block of code), it will hand over the monitor to the next thread that is ready to use the same resource.

An interesting situation may occur when two or more threads are waiting to gain control of a resource. Due to some reasons, the condition on which the waiting threads rely on to gain control does not happen. This results in what is known as *deadlock*. For example, assume that the thread A must access Method1 before it can release Method2, but the thread B cannot release Method1 until it gets hold of Method2. Because these are mutually exclusive conditions, a deadlock occurs. The code below illustrates this:

Thread A

```
synchronized method2( )
{
    synchronized method1( )
    {
        .........
        .........
    }
}
```

Thread B

```
synchronized method1( )
{
    synchronized method2( )
    {
        .........
        .........
    }
}
```

12.10 Implementing the 'Runnable' Interface

We stated earlier that we can create threads in two ways: one by using the extended **Thread** class and another by implementing the **Runnable** interface. We have already discussed in detail how the **Thread** class is used for creating and running threads. In this section, we shall see how to make use of the **Runnable** interface to implement threads.

The **Runnable** interface declares the **run( )** method that is required for implementing threads in our programs. To do this, we must perform the steps listed below:

1. Declare the class as implementing the **Runnable** interface.
2. Implement the **run( )** method.
3. Create a thread by defining an object that is instantiated from this "runnable" class as the target of the thread.
4. Call the thread's **start( )** method to run the thread.

Program 12.4 illustrates the implementation of the above steps. In main method, we first create an instance of **X** and then pass this instance as the initial value of the object **threadX** (an object of **Thread** Class). Whenever, the new thread **threadX** starts up, its **run( )** method calls the **run( )** method of the target object supplied to it. Here, the target object is **runnable**. If the direct reference to the thread **threadX** is not required, then we may use a shortcut as shown below:

```
new Thread (new X( )).start( );
```

Program 12.4   *Using Runnable interface*

```
class X implements Runnable                              // Step 1
{
    public void run( )                                  // Step 2
    {
        for(int i = 1; i<=10; i++)
        {
            System.out.println("\tThreadX : " +i);
        }
        System.out.println("End of ThreadX");
    }
}
class RunnableTest
{
    public static void main(String args[ ])
    {
        X runnable = new X( );
        Thread threadX = new Thread(runnable);          // Step 3
        threadX.start( );                               // Step 4
        System.out.println("End of main Thread");
    }
}
```

Output of Program 12.4

```
        End of main Thread
            ThreadX : 1
            ThreadX : 2
            ThreadX : 3
            ThreadX : 4
            ThreadX : 5
            ThreadX : 6
            ThreadX : 7
            ThreadX : 8
            ThreadX : 9
            ThreadX : 10
        End of ThreadX
```

12.11 Summary

A thread is a single line of execution within a program. Multiple threads can run concurrently in a single program. A thread is created either by subclassing the **Thread** class or implementing the **Runnable** interface. We have discussed both the approaches in detail in this chapter. We have also learned the following in this chapter:

- How to synchronize threads,
- How to set priorities for threads, and
- How to control the execution of threads

Careful application of multithreading will considerably improve the execution speed of Java programs.

 Key Terms

Thread, Multithread, Multitask, Concurrency, Lightweight Processes, Time-slicing, Priority, Synchronization, Deadlock.

REVIEW QUESTIONS

12.1 What is a thread?

12.2 What is the difference between multiprocessing and multithreading? What is to be done to implement these in a program?

12.3 What Java interface must be implemented by all threads?

12.4 How do we start a thread?

12.5 What are the two methods by which we may stop threads?

12.6 What is the difference between suspending and stopping a thread?

12.7 How do we set priorities for threads?

12.8 Describe the complete life cycle of a thread.

12.9 What is synchronization? When do we use it?

12.10 Develop a simple real-life application program to illustrate the use of multithreads.

DEBUGGING EXERCISES

12.1 Sleep( ) method has been demonstrated in the following code. Will this code compile successfully?

```
class A extends Thread
{
    public void run()
    {
        for(int i=1; i<=5; i++)
        {
            System.out.println("\tFrom threadA. i = " +i);
            Thread.sleep(100);
        }
    }
}
class ThreadClass
{
    public static void main(String[] args)
    {
        A a = new A();
        a.start();
    }
}
```

12.2   Debug the given code which creates two different classes, one extending 'Thread' class and other, implementing 'Runnable' interface.

```
class multi1 extends Thread
{
    public void run()
        {
            for(int i=1; i<=5; i++)
            {
                System.out.println("\tFrom Thread 1 i = " +i);
            }
        }
};
class multi2 implements Runnable
{
    public void run()
        {
            for(int j=1; j<=5; j++)
            {
                System.out.println("\tFrom Thread 1 j = " +j);
            }
        }
};
class threadcheck
{
    public static void main(String[] args)
    {
        multi1 m1 = new multi1();
        m1.start();
        multi2 m2 = new multi2();
        m2.start();
    }
}
```

12.3   Will the code compile? If not, why?

```
class multi1 extends Thread
{
    public void start()
    {
        for(int i=1; i<=5; i++)
        {
            System.out.println("\tFrom Thread 1 i = " +i);
        }
    }
};
class multi2 implements Runnable
{
```

```
              public void start()
              {
                  for(int  j=1;  j<=5;  j++)
                  {
                      System.out.println("\tFrom Thread 1  j = " +j);
                  }
              }
          };
          class runthread
          {
              public static void main(String[] args)
              {
                  multil m1 = new multil();
                  m1.start();
              }
          }
```

12.4 The code given below calls the run( ) method of two threads while setting their priority. Will this code compile successfully? If not, correct the code.

```
          class t1 extends Thread
          {
              public void run()
              {
                  System.out.println("This is Thread1 class");
              }
          }
          class t2 extends Thread
          {
              public void run()
              {
                  System.out.println("This is Thread2 Class");
              }
          }
          public class ThreadP
          {
              public static void main(String s[])
              {
                  t1 t = new t1();
                  t2 tt = new t2();
                  t.setPriority(Thread.MIN_PRIORITY);
                  tt.setPriority(Thread.MIN_PRIORITY);
                  t1.run();
                  t2.run();
              }
          }
```

12.5   Priority of a thread is defined in the given code. Debug the code.

```
class thread1 extends Thread
{
    public void run()
    {
        System.out.println("This is Thread1 class");
    }
}
class thread2 extends Thread
{
    public void run()
    {
        System.out.println("This is Thread2 Class");
    }
}
public class ThreadPrior
{
    public static void main(String s[])
    {
        thread1 t1 = new thread1();
        thread2 t2 = new thread2();
        t1.setPriority(Thread.Max_Priority);
        t1.run();
        t2.run();
    }
}
```

13

Managing Errors and Exceptions

 ## 13.1 Introduction

Rarely does a program run successfully at its very first attempt. It is common to make mistakes while developing as well as typing a program. A mistake might lead to an error causing to program to produce unexpected results. *Errors* are the wrongs that can make a program go wrong.

An error may produce an incorrect output or may terminate the execution of the program abruptly or even may cause the system to crash. It is therefore important to detect and manage properly all the possible error conditions in the program so that the program will not terminate or crash during execution.

 ## 13.2 Types of Errors

Errors may broadly be classified into two categories:

* Compile-time errors
* Run-time errors

Compile-Time Errors

All syntax errors will be detected and displayed by the Java compiler and therefore these errors are known as compile-time errors. Whenever the compiler displays an error, it will not create the **.class** file. It is therefore necessary that we fix all the errors before we can successfully compile and run the program.

Program 13.1 *Illustration of compile-time errors*

```
/* This program contains an error */
class Error1
{
        public static void main(String args[])
        {
            System.out.println("Hello Java!") //  Missing;
        }
}
```

The Java compiler does a nice job of telling us where the errors are in the program. For example, if we have missed the semicolon at the end of print statement in Program 13.1, the following message will be displayed in the screen:

```
Error1.java :7: ';' expected
System.out.println ("Hello Java!")
^
1 error
```

We can now go to the appropriate line, correct the error, and recompile the program. Sometimes, a single error may be the source of multiple errors later in the compilation. For example, use of an undeclared variable in a number of places will cause a series of errors of type "undefined variable". We should generally consider the earliest errors as the major source of our problem. After we fix such an error, we should recompile the program and look for other errors.

Most of the compile-time errors are due to typing mistakes. Typographical errors are hard to find. We may have to check the code word by word, or even character by character. The most common problems are:

- Missing semicolons
- Missing (or mismatch of) brackets in classes and methods
- Misspelling of identifiers and keywords
- Missing double quotes in strings
- Use of undeclared variables
- Incompatible types in assignments / initialization
- Bad references to objects
- Use of = in place of = = operator
- And so on

Other errors we may encounter are related to directory paths. An error such as

```
javac : command not found
```

means that we have not set the path correctly. We must ensure that the path includes the directory where the Java executables are stored.

Run-Time Errors

Sometimes, a program may compile successfully creating the **.class** file but may not run properly. Such programs may produce wrong results due to wrong logic or may terminate due to errors such as stack overflow. Most common run-time errors are:

- Dividing an integer by zero
- Accessing an element that is out of the bounds of an array
- Trying to store a value into an array of an incompatible class or type
- Trying to cast an instance of a class to one of its subclasses
- Passing a parameter that is not in a valid range or value for a method
- Trying to illegally change the state of a thread
- Attempting to use a negative size for an array
- Using a null object reference as a legitimate object reference to access a method or a variable.
- Converting invalid string to a number
- Accessing a character that is out of bounds of a string
- And may more

When such errors are encountered, Java typically generates an error message and aborts the program. Program 13.2 illustrates how a run-time error causes termination of execution of the program.

Program 13.2   *Illustration of run-time errors*

```
class Error2
{
    public static void main(String args[ ])
    {
        int a = 10;
        int b = 5;
        int c = 5;

        int x = a/(b-c);         // Division by zero
        System.out.println("x = " + x);

        int y = a/(b+c);
        System.out.println("y = " + y);
    }
}
```

Program 13.2 is syntactically correct and therefore does not cause any problem during compilation. However, while executing, it displays the following message and stops without executing further statements.

```
java.lang.ArithmeticException: / by zero
        at Error2.main(Error2.java:10)
```

When Java run-time tries to execute a division by zero, it generates an error condition, which causes the program to stop after displaying an appropriate message.

 13.3   Exceptions

An *exception* is a condition that is caused by a run-time error in the program. When the Java interpreter encounters an error such as dividing an integer by zero, it creates an exception object and throws it (i.e. informs us that an error has occurred).

If the exception object is not caught and handled properly, the interpreter will display an error message as shown in the output of Program 13.2 and will terminate the program. If we want the program to continue with the execution of the remaining code, then we should try to catch the exception object thrown by the error condition and then display an appropriate message for taking corrective actions. This task is known as *exception handling*.

The purpose of exception handling mechanism is to provide a means to detect and report an "exceptional circumstance" so that appropriate action can be taken. The mechanism suggests incorporation of a separate error handling code that performs the following tasks:

1. Find the problem (*Hit* the exception).
2. Inform that an error has occurred (*Throw* the exception)
3. Receive the error information (*Catch* the exception)
4. Take corrective actions (*Handle* the exception)

The error handling code basically consists of two segments, one to detect errors and to throw exceptions and the other to catch exceptions and to take appropriate actions.

When writing programs, we must always be on the lookout for places in the program where an exception could be generated. Some common exceptions that we must watch out for catching are listed in Table 13.1.

Table 13.1 Common Java Exceptions

Exception Type	Cause of Exception
ArithmeticException	Caused by math errors such as division by zero
ArrayIndexOutOfBoundsException	Caused by bad array indexes
ArrayStoreException	Caused when a program tries to store the wrong type of data in an array
FileNotFoundException	Caused by an attempt to access a nonexistent file
IOException	Caused by general I/O failures, such as inability to read from a file
NullPointerException	Caused by referencing a null object
NumberFormatException	Caused when a conversion between strings and number fails
OutOfMemoryException	Caused when there's not enough memory to allocate a new object
SecurityException	Caused when an applet tries to perform an action not allowed by the browser's security setting
StackOverFlowException	Caused when the system runs out of stack space
StringIndexOutOfBoundsException	Caused when a program attempts to access a nonexistent character position in a string

13.4 Syntax of Exception Handling Code

The basic concepts of exception handling are throwing an exception and catching it. This is illustrated in Fig. 13.1.

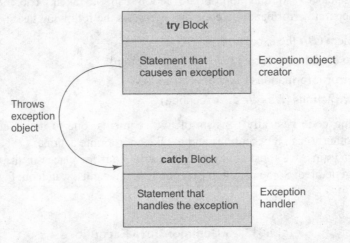

Fig. 13.1 *Exception handling mechanism*

Java uses a keyword **try** to preface a block of code that is likely to cause an error condition and "throw" an exception. A catch block defined by the keyword **catch** "catches" the exception "thrown" by thee try block and handles it appropriately. The catch block is added immediately after the try block. The following example illustrates the use of simple **try** and **catch** statements:

```
. . . . . . . . . .
. . . . . . . . . .
try
{
    statement;     // generates an exception
}
catch (Exception-type e)
{
    statement;     // processes the exception
}
. . . . . . . . . .
. . . . . . . . . .
```

The try block can have one or more statements that could generate an exception. If any one statement generates an exception, the remaining statements in the block are skipped and execution jumps to the catch block that is placed next to the try block.

The catch block too can have one or more statements that are necessary to process the exception. Remember that every **try** statement should be followed by *at least one* **catch** statement; otherwise compilation error will occur.

Note that the **catch** statement works like a method definition. The **catch** statement is passed a single parameter, which is reference to the exception object thrown (by the try block). If the catch parameter matches with the type of exception object, then the exception is caught and statements in the catch block will be executed. Otherwise, the exception is not caught and the default exception handler will cause the execution to terminate.

Program 13.3 illustrates the use of try and catch blocks to handle an arithmetic exception. Note that Program 13.3 is a modified version of Program 13.2.

Program 13.3 *Using try and catch for exception handling*

```
class Error3
{
        public static void main(String args[ ])
        {
                int a = 10;
                int b = 5;
                int c = 5;
                int x, y ;
                try
                {
                        x = a / (b-c);          // Exception here
                }
                catch (ArithmeticException e)
                {
                        System.out.println("Division by zero");
                }
                y = a / (b+c);
                System.out.println("y = " + y);
        }
}
```

Program 13.3 displays the following output:

```
        Division by zero
        y = 1
```

Note that the program did not stop at the point of exceptional condition. It catches the error condition, prints the error message, and then continues the execution, as if nothing has happened. Compare with the output of Program 13.2 which did not give the value of **y**.

Program 13.4 shows another example of using exception handling mechanism. Here, the try-catch block catches the invalid entries in the list of command line arguments.

Program 13.4 *Catching invalid command line arguments*

```
class CLineInput
{
    public static void main(String args[ ])
    {
        int invalid = 0;    // Number of invalid arguments
        int number, count = 0;
        for (int i = 0; i < args.length; i++)
        {
            try
            {
                number = Integer.parseInt(args[i]);
            }
            catch(NumberFormatException e)
            {
                invalid = invalid + 1;        // Caught an invalid number
                System.out.println("Invalid Number: "+args[i]);
                continue;                     // Skip the remaining part of the loop
            }
            count = count + 1;
        }
        System.out.println("Valid Numbers = " + count);
        System.out.println("Invalid Numbers = " + invalid);
    }
}
```

Note the use of the wrapper class **Integer** to obtain an **int** number from a string:

```
number = Integer.parseInt(args[i])
```

Remember that the numbers are supplied to the program through the command line and therefore they are stored as strings in the array **args[ ]**. Since the above statement is placed in the try block, an exception is thrown if the string is improperly formatted and the number is not included in the count.

When we run the program with the command line:

```
java CLineInput 15 25.75 40 Java 10.5 65
```

it produces the following output:

```
Invalid Number:    25.75
Invalid Number: Java
Invalid Number: 10.5
Valid Numbers    = 3
Invalid Numbers  = 3
```

 ## 13.5 Multiple Catch Statements

It is possible to have more than one catch statement in the catch block as illustrated below:

```
.........
.........
try
{
    statement ;              // generates an exception
}
catch (Exception-Type-1 e)
{
    statement;               // processes exception type 1
}
catch (Exception-Type-2 e)
{
    statement;               // processes exception type 2
}
    .
    .
    .
catch (Exception-Type-N e)
{
    statement ;              // processes exception type N
 }
.........
.........
```

When an exception in a **try** block is generated, the Java treats the multiple **catch** statements like cases in a **switch** statement. The first statement whose parameter matches with the exception object will be executed, and the remaining statements will skipped.

Note that Java does not require any processing of the exception at all. We can simply have a catch statement with an empty block to avoid program abortion.

Example:

```
        catch (Exception e);
```

The **catch** statement simply ends with a semicolon, which does nothing. This statement will catch an exception and then ignore it.

Program 13.5 *Using multiple catch blocks*

```
class Erro4
{
    public static void main(String args[ ])
    {
        int a[ ] = {5, 10};
        int b = 5;
        try
        {
            int x = a[2] / b - a[1];
        }
```

(*Continued*)

Program 13.5   (*Continued*)

```
catch(ArithmeticException e)
{
        System.out.println("Division by zero");
}
catch(ArrayIndexOutOfBoundsException e)
{
        System.out.println("Array index error");
}
catch(ArrayStoreException e)
{
        System.out.println("Wrong data type");
}
int y = a[1] / a[0];
System.out.println("y = " + y);
}
}
```

Program 13.5 uses a chain of catch blocks and, when run, produces the following output:

```
Array index error
y = 2
```

Note that the array element a[2] does not exist because array **a** is defined to have only two elements, a[0] and a[1]. Therefore, the index 2 is outside the array boundary thus causing the block

```
Catch(ArrayIndexOutOfBoundsException e)
```

to catch and handle the error. Remaining catch blocks are skipped.

 13.6   Using Finally Statement

Java supports another statement known as **finally** statement that can be used to handle an exception that is not caught by any of the previous catch statements. **finally** block can be used to handle any exception generated within a try block. It may be added immediately after the try block or after the last catch block shown as follows:

```
try                             try
{                               {
    ...........                     ..........
    ..........                      ..........
}                               }
finally                         catch  (....)
{                               {
    ...........                     ..........
    ..........                      ..........
}                               }
```

```
                                    catch     (.,...)
                                    {
                                        ..........
                                        ..........
                                    }
                                    .
                                    .
                                    .
                                    finally
                                    {
                                        ..........
                                        ..........
                                    }
```

When a **finally** block is defined, this is guaranteed to execute, regardless of whether or not in exception is thrown. As a result, we can use it to perform certain house-keeping operations such as closing files and releasing system resources.

In Program 13.5, we may include the last two statements inside a **finally** block as shown below:

```
finally
{
    int y = a[1]/a[0];
    System.out.println("y = " +y);
}
```

This will produce the same output.

 ## 13.7 **Throwing Our Own Exceptions**

There may be times when we would like to throw our own exceptions. We can do this by using the keyword **throw** as follows:

```
throw new Thorwable_subclass;
```

Examples:

```
throw new ArithmeticException( );
throw new NumberFormatException( );
```

Program 13.6 demonstrates the use of a user-defined subclass of Throwable class. Note that **Exception** is a subclass of **Throwable** and therefore **MyException** is a subclass of **Throwable** class. An object of a class that extends **Throwable** can be thrown and caught.

Program 13.6 *Throwing our own exception*

```
import java.lang.Exception;
class MyException extends Exception
```

(*Continued*)

Program 13.6   *(Continued)*

```
{
        MyException(String message)
        {
            super(message);
        }
}
class TestMyException
{
    public static void main(Strings args[ ])
    {
        int x = 5, y = 1000;
        try
        {
            float z = (float) x / (float) y ;
            if(z < 0.01)
            {
                throw new MyException("Number is too small");
            }
        }
        catch (MyException e)
        {
            System.out.println("Caught my exception");
            System.out.println(e.getMessage( ) );
        }
        finally
        {
            System.out.println("I am always here");
        }
    }
}
```

A run of program 13.6 produces:

```
Caught my exception
Number is too small
I am always here
```

The object e which contains the error message "Number is too small" is caught by the **catch** block which then displays the message using the getMessage( ) method.

Note that Program 13.6 also illustrates the use of **finally** block. The last line of output is produced by the **finally** block.

13.8   Using Exceptions for Debugging

As we have seen, the exception-handling mechanism can be used to hide errors from rest of the program. It is possible that the programmers may misuse this technique for hiding errors rather than debugging the code. Exception handling mechanism may be effectively used to locate the type and place of errors. Once we identify the errors, we must try to find out why these errors occur before we cover them up with exception handlers.

13.9 Summary

A good program does not produce unexpected results. We should incorporate features that could check for potential problem spots in programs and guard against program failures. The problem conditions known as exceptions in Java must be handled carefully to avoid any program failures.

In this chapter we have discussed the following:

- What exceptions are
- How to throw system exceptions
- How to define our own exceptions
- How to catch and handle different types of exceptions
- Where to use exception handling tools

We must ensure that common exceptions are handled where appropriate.

 Key Terms

Errors, Compile-time errors, Run-time errors, Exception, Exception handling, try, catch, throw, finally.

REVIEW QUESTIONS

13.1   What is an exception?

13.2   How do we define a **try** block?

13.3   How do we define a **catch** block?

13.4   List some of the most common types of exceptions that might occur in Java. Give examples.

13.5   Is it essential to catch all types of exceptions?

13.6   How many **catch** blocks can we use with one **try** block?

13.7   Create a **try** block that is likely to generate three types of exception and then incorporate necessary **catch** blocks to catch and handle them appropriately.

13.8   What is a **finally** block? When and how is it used? Give a suitable example.

13.9   Explain how exception handling mechanism can be used for debugging a program.

13.10 Define an exception called "NoMatchException" that is thrown when a string is not equal to "India". Write a program that uses this exception.

DEBUGGING EXERCISES

13.1   The following code catches Arithmetic Exception. Will this code work? If not, why?

```
class excep1
{
    public static void main(String args[])
    {
        try
```

```
                {
                    int n=Integer.parseInt(args[0]);
                    int n1=Integer.parseInt(args[1]);
                    int n2=n + n1;
                }
                catch(ArithmeticException ex)
                {
                    System.out.println("Arithmetic Exception block 1");
                }
                catch(ArithmeticException ex)
                {
                    System.out.println("Arithmetic Exception block 2");
                }
            }
        }
```

13.2   Which exception may be thrown if the given code is executed?

```
        class excep2
        {
            public static void main(String args[])
            {
                try
                {
                    int n = Integer.parseInt(args[0]);
                    int n1 = Integer.parseInt(args[1]);
                    int n2 = n+n1;
                    System.out.println("Sum is " + n2);
                }
                catch(ArithmeticException ex)
                {
                    System.out.println("Arithmetic Exception:"+ex.getMessage());
                }
                catch(NumberFormatException ex)
                {
                    System.out.println("Format Exception :"+ex.getMessage());
                }
                catch(Exception ex)
                {
                    System.out.println("Exception :"+ex);
                }
            }
        }
```

13.3   The code throws an exception in case the desired input is not received. Debug the code.

```
        class excep3
        {
            public static void main(String args[])
            {
                if(args[0]=="Hello")
```

```
            System.out.println("String is right");
        else
            throw new Exception("Invalid String");
    }
}
```

13.4 Custom exception has been created in the code given below. Correct the code.

```
class myexception extends Exception
{
    myexception(String s)
    {
        super(s);
    }
}
class excep4
{
    public static void main(String args[])
    {
        if(args[0]=="Hello")
            System.out.println("String is right");
        else
        try
        {
            throw new myexception("Invalid String");
        }catch(myexception ex)
        {
            System.out.println(ex.getmessage());
        }
    }
}
```

13.5 The program calculates sum of two numbers inputted as command-line arguments. When will it give an exception?

```
class excep
{
    public static void main(String []args)
    {
        Try {
            int n = Integer.parseInt(args[0]);
            int n1 = Integer.parseInt(args[1]);
            int n2 = n+n1;
            System.out.println("Sum is: " + n2);
        }
        catch(NumberFormatException ex)
        {
            System.out.println(ex);
        }
    }
}
```

Chapter 14

Applet Programming

14.1 Introduction

Applets are small Java programs that are primarily used in Internet computing. They can be transported over the Internet from one computer to another and run using the **Applet Viewer** or any Web browser that supports Java. An applet, like any application program, can do many things for us. It can perform arithmetic operations, display graphics, play sounds, accept user input, create animation, and play interactive games.

Java has revolutionized the way the Internet users retrieve and use documents on the world wide network. Java has enabled them to create and use fully interactive multimedia Web documents. A web page can now contain not only a simple text or a static image but also a Java applet which, when run, can produce graphics, sounds and moving images. Java applets therefore have begun to make a significant impact on the World Wide Web.

Local and Remote Applets

We can embed applets into Web pages in two ways. One, we can write our own applets and embed them into Web pages. Second, we can download an applet from a remote computer system and then embed it into a Web page.

An applet developed locally and stored in a local system is known as a *local applet*. When a Web page is trying to find a local applet, it does not need to use the Internet and therefore the local system does not require the Internet connection. It simply searches the directories in the local system and locates and loads the specified applet (see Fig. 14.1).

A *remote applet* is that which is developed by someone else and stored on a remote computer connected to the Internet. If our system is connected to the Internet, we can download the remote applet onto our system via at the Internet and run it (see Fig. 14.2).

In order to locate and load a remote applet, we must know the applet's address on the Web. This address is known as *Uniform Resource Locator (URL)* and must be specified in the applet's HTML document as the value of the CODEBASE attribute (see Section 14.11). Example:

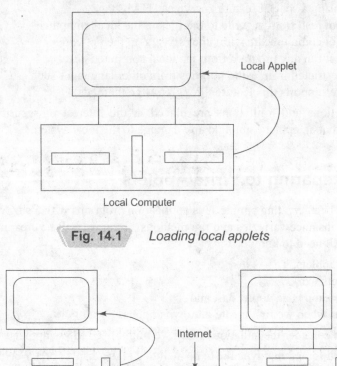

Local Applet

Local Computer

Fig. 14.1 *Loading local applets*

Internet

Local Computer
(Client)

Remote
Applet

Remote Computer
(Server)

Fig. 14.2 *Loading a remote applet*

```
CODEBASE = http : // www.netserve.com / applets
```

In the case of local applets, CODEBASE may be absent or may specify a local directory.

In this chapter we shall discuss how applets are created, how they are located in the Web documents and how they are loaded and run in the local computer.

14.2 How Applets Differ from Applications

Although both the applets and stand-alone applications are Java programs, there are significant differences between them. Applets are not full-featured application programs. They are usually written to accomplish a small task or a component of a task. Since they are usually designed for use on the Internet, they impose certain limitations and restrictions in their design.

- Applets do not use the **main( )** method for initiating the execution of the code. Applets, when loaded, automatically call certain methods of Applet class to start and execute the applet code.
- Unlike stand-alone applications, applets cannot be run independently. They are run from inside a Web page using a special feature known as HTML tag.
- Applets cannot read from or write to the files in the local computer.
- Applets cannot communicate with other servers on the network.
- Applets cannot run any program from the local computer.
- Applets are restricted from using libraries from other languages such as C or C++. (Remember, Java language supports this feature through **native** methods).

All these restrictions and limitations are placed in the interest of security of systems. These restrictions ensure that an applet cannot do any damage to the local system.

14.3   Preparing to Write Applets

Until now, we have been creating simple Java application programs with a single **main( )** method that created objects, set instance variables and ran methods. Here, we will be creating applets exclusively and therefore we will need to know

- When to use applets,
- How an applets works,
- What sort of features an applet has, and
- Where to start when we first create our own applets.

First of all, let us consider the situations when we might need to use applets.

1. When we need something dynamic to be included in the display of a Web page. For example, an applet that displays daily sensitivity index would be useful on a page that lists share prices of various companies or an applet that displays a bar chart would add value to a page that contains data tables.
2. When we require some "flash" outputs. For example, applets that produce sounds, animations or some special effects would be useful when displaying certain pages.
3. When we want to create a program and make it available on the Internet for us by others on their computers.

Before we try to write applets, we must make sure that Java is installed properly and also ensure that either the Java **appletviewer** or a Java-enabled browser is available. The steps involved in developing and testing in applet are:

1. Building an applet code (**.java** file)
2. Creating an executable applet (**.class** file)
3. Designing a Web page using HTML tags
4. Preparing <APPLET> tag
5. Incorporating <APPLET> tag into the Web page
6. Creating HTML file
7. Testing the applet code

Each of these steps is discussed in the following sections.

14.4 Building Applet Code

It is essential that our applet code uses the services of two classes, namely, **Applet** and **Graphics** from the Java class library. The **Applet** class which is contained in the **java.applet** package provides life and behaviour to the applet through its methods such as **init( )**, **start( )** and **point( )**. Unlike the applications, where Java calls the **main( )** method directly to initiate the execution of the program, when an applet is loaded, Java automatically calls a series of **Applet** class methods for starting, running, and stopping the applet code. The **Applet** class therefore maintains the *lifecycle* of an applet.

The **paint( )** method of the **Applet** class, when it is called, actually displays the result of the applet code on the screen. The output may be text, graphics, or sound. The **paint( )** method, which requires a **Graphics** object as an argument, is defined as follows:

```
public void paint (Graphics g)
```

This requires that the applet code imports the **java.awt** package that contains the **Graphics** class. All output operations of an applet are performed using the methods defined in the **Graphics** class. It is thus clear from the above discussions that an applet code will have a general format as shown below:

```
import java.awt.*;
import java.applet.*;
..........
..........
public class appletclassname extends Applet
{
     ..........
     ..........
     public void paint (Graphics g)
     {
          ..........
          ..........          / /  Applet operations code
          ..........
     }
     ..........
     ..........
}
```

The *appletclassname* is the main class for the applet. When the applet is loaded, Java creates an instance of this class, and then a series of **Applet** class methods are called on that instance to execute the code. Program 14.1 shows a simple HelloJava applet.

Program 14.1   *The HelloJava applet*

```
import java.awt.*;
import java.applet.*;
public class HelloJava extends Applet
{
     public void paint (Graphics g)
```

(Continued)

Program 14.1 (*Continued*)

```
    {
            g.drawString("Hello Java", 10, 100);
    }
}
```

The applet contains only one executable statement.

```
        g.drawString("Hello Java", 10, 100);
```

which, when executed, draws the string

```
        Hello Java
```

at the position 10, 100 (pixels) of the applet's reserved space as shown in Fig. 14.3.

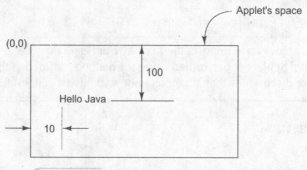

Fig. 14.3 *Output of Program 14.1*

Remember that the applet code in Program 14.1 should be saved with the file name **HelloJava.java**, in a java subdirectory. Note the **public** keyword for the class **HelloJava**. Java requires that the main applet class be declared public.

Remember that **Applet** class itself is a subclass of the **Panel** class, which is again a subclass of the **Container** class and so on as shown in Fig. 14.4. This shows that the main applet class inherits properties from a long chain of classes. An applet can, therefore, use variables and methods from all these classes.

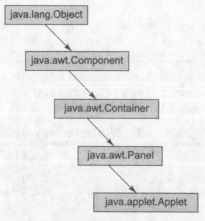

Fig. 14.4 *Chain of classes inherited by Applet class*

14.5 Applet Life Cycle

Every Java applet inherits a set of default behaviours from the **Applet** class. As a result, when an applet is loaded, it undergoes a series of changes in its state as shown in Fig. 14.5. The applet states include:

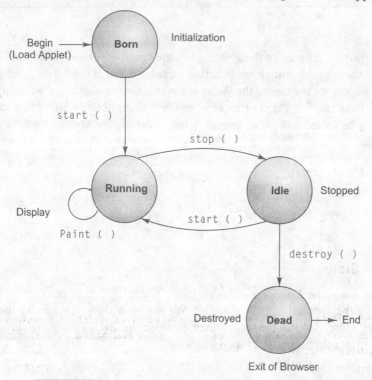

Fig. 14.5 *An applet's state transition diagram*

- Born on initialization state
- Running state
- Idle state
- Dead or destroyed state

Initialization State

Applet enters the *initialization* state when it is first loaded. This is achieved by calling the **init( )** method of **Applet** Class. The applet is born. At this stage, we may do the following, if required.

- Create objects needed by the applet
- Set up initial values
- Load images or fonts
- Set up colors

The initialization occurs only once in the applet's life cycle. To provide any of the behaviours mentioned above, we must override the **init( )** method:

```
public void init( )
{
    . . . . . . . . . .
    . . . . . . . . . .  (Action)
    . . . . . . . . . .
}
```

Running State

Applet enters the *running* state when the system calls the **start( )** method of **Applet** Class. This occurs automatically after the applet is initialized. Starting can also occur if the applet is already in 'stopped" (idle) state. For example, we may leave the Web page containing the applet temporarily to another page and return back to the page. This again starts the applet running. Note that, unlike **init( )** method, the **start( )** method may be called more than once. We may override the **start( )** method to create a thread to control the applet.

```
public voids start( )
{
    . . . . . . . . . .
    . . . . . . . . . .  (Action)
    . . . . . . . . . .
}
```

Idle or Stopped State

An applet becomes *idle* when it is stopped from running. Stopping occurs automatically when we leave the page containing the currently running applet. We can also do so by calling the **stop( )** method explicitly. If we use a thread to run the applet, then we must use **stop( )** method to terminate the thread. We can achieve this by overriding the **stop( )** method;

```
public void stop( )
{
    . . . . . . . . . .
    . . . . . . . . . .  (Action)
    . . . . . . . . . .
}
```

Dead State

An applet is said to be *dead* when it is removed from memory. This occurs automatically by invoking the **destroy( )** method when we quit the browser. Like initialization, destroying stage occurs only once in the applet's life cycle. If the applet has created any resources, like threads, we may override the **destroy( )** method to clean up these resources.

```
public void destroy( )
{
    . . . . . . . . . .
    . . . . . . . . . .  (Action)
    . . . . . . . . . .
}
```

Display State

Applet moves to the *display* state whenever it has to perform some output operations on the screen. This happens immediately after the applet enters into the running state. The **paint( )** method is called to accomplish this task. Almost every applet will have a **paint( )** method. Like other methods in the life cycle, the default version of **paint( )** method does absolutely nothing. We must therefore override this method if we want anything to be displayed on the screen.

```
public void paint (Graphics g)
{
    . . . . . . . . . .
    . . . . . . . . . .   (Display statements)
    . . . . . . . . . .
}
```

It is to be noted that the display state is not considered as a part of the applet's life cycle. In fact, the **paint( )** method is defined in the **Applet** class. It is inherited from the **Component** class, a super class of **Applet.**

14.6   Creating an Executable Applet

Executable applet is nothing but the **.class** file of the applet, which is obtained by compiling the source code of the applet. Compiling an applet is exactly the same as compiling an application. Therefore, we can use the Java compiler to compile the applet.

Let us consider the **HelloJava** applet created in Section 14.4. This applet has been stored in a file called **HelloJava.java**. Here are the steps required for compiling the **HelloJava** applet.

1. Move to the directory containing the source code and type the following command:
   ```
   javac HelloJava.java
   ```
2. The compiled output file called **HelloJava.class** is placed in the same directory as the source.
3. If any error message is received, then we must check for errors, correct them and compile the applet again.

14.7   Designing a Web Page

Recall the Java applets are programs that reside on Web pages. In order to run a Java applet, it is first necessary to have a Web page that references that applet.

A Web page is basically made up of text and HTML tags that can be interpreted by a Web browser or an applet viewer. Like Java source code, it can be prepared using any ASCII text editor. A Web page is also known as HTML page or HTML document. Web pages are stored using a file extension **. html** such as **MyApplet.html**. Such files are referred to as HTML files. HTML files should be stored in the same directory as the compiled code of the applets.

As pointed out earlier, Web pages include both text that we want to display and HTML tags (commands) to Web browsers. A Web page is marked by an opening HTML tag < HTML> and a closing HTML tag </HTML> and is divided into the following three major sections:

1. Comment section (Optional)
2. Head section (Optional)
3. Body section

A Web page outline containing these three sections and the opening and closing HTML tags is illustrated in Fig. 14.6.

Comment Section

This section contains comments about the Web page. It is important to include comments that tell us what is going on in the Web page. A comment line begins with a <! and ends with a >. Web browsers will ignore the text enclosed between them. Although comments are important, they should be kept to a minimum as they will be downloaded along with the applet. Note that comments are optional and can be included anywhere in the Web page.

Head Section

The head section is defined with a starting <HEAD> tag and a closing </HEAD> tag. This section usually contains a title for the Web page as shown below:

```
<HEAD>
        <TITLE> Welcome to Java Applets </TITLE>
</HEAD>
```

The text enclosed in the tags <TITLE> and </TITLE> will appear in the title bar of the Web browser when it displays the page. *The head section is also optional.*

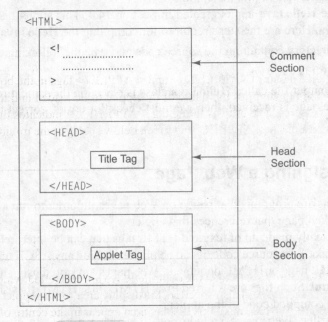

Fig. 14.6   *A Web page template*

Note that tags <....> containing HTML commands usually appear impairs such as <HEAD> and </HEAD>, and <TITLE> and </TITLE>. A slash (/) in a tag signifies the end of that tag section.

Body Section

After the head section comes the body section. We call this as body section because this section contains the entire information about the Web page and its behaviour. We can set up many options to indicate how our page must appear on the screen (like colour, location, sound, etc.,). Shown below is a simple body section:

```
<BODY>
  <CENTER>
        <H1> Welcome to the World of Applets </H1>
  </CENTER>
  <BR>
  <APPLET ...>
  </APPLET>
</BODY>
```

The body shown above contains instructions to display the message

```
Welcome to the World of Applets
```

followed by the applet output on the screen. Note that the <CENTER> tag makes sure that the text is centered and <H1> tag causes the text to be of the largest size. We may use other heading tags <H2> to <H6> to reduce the size of letters in the text.

14.8 Applet Tag

Note that we have included a pair of <APPLET...> and </APPLET> tags in the body section discussed above. The <APPLET ...> tag supplies the name of the applet to be loaded and tells the browser how much space the applet requires. The ellipsis in the tag < APPLET ...> indicates that it contains certain attributes that must specified. The <APPLET> tag given below specifies the minimum requirements to place the **HelloJava** applet on a Web page:

```
<APPLET
   CODE = helloJava.class
   WIDTH = 400
   HEIGHT = 200 >
</APPLET >
```

This HTML code tells the browser to load the compiled Java applet **HelloJava.class**, which is in the same directory as the HTML file. And also specifies the display area for the applet output as 400 pixels width and 200 pixels height. We can make this display area appear in the centre of the screen by using the CENTER tags shown as follows:

```
<CENTER>
    <APPLET
    . . . . . . . . . .
    . . . . . . . . . .
    . . . . . . . . . .
    </APPLET>
</CENTER>
```

Note that <APPLET> tag discussed above specifies three things:

1. Name of the applet
2. Width of the applet (in pixels)
3. Height of the applet (in pixels)

14.9 Adding Applet to HTML File

Now we can put together the various components of the Web page and create a file known as HTML file. Insert the <APPLET> tag in the page at the place where the output of the applet must appear. Following is the content of the HTML file that is embedded with the <APPLET> tag of our **HelloJava** applet.

```
<HTML>
    <! This page includes a welcome title in the title bar and also
    displays a welcome message. Then it specifies the applet to be
    loaded and executed.
    >
<HEAD>
        <TITLE>
                Welcome to Java Applets
        </TITLE>
</HEAD>
<BODY>
        <CENTER>
                <H1> Welcome to the World of Applets </H1>
        </CENTER>
        <BR>
        <CENTER>
            <APPLET
                CODE = HelloJava.class
                WIDTH = 400
                HEIGHT = 200>
            </APPLET>
        </CENTER>
        </BODY>
    </HTML>
```

We must name this file as **HelloJava.html** and save it in the same directory as the compiled applet.

14.10 Running the Applet

Now that we have created applet files as well as the HTML file containing the applet, we must have the following files in our current directory:

```
HelloJava.java
HelloJava.class
HelloJava.html
```

To run an applet, we require one of the following tools:

1. Java-enabled Web browser (such as HotJava or Netscape)
2. Java appletviewer

If we use a Java-enabled Web browser, we will be able to see the entire Web page containing the applet. If we use the **appletviewer** tool, we will only see the applet output. Remember that the **appletviewer** is not a full-fledged Web browser and therefore it ignores all of the HTML tags except the part pertaining to the running of the applet.

The **appletviewer** is available as a part of the Java Development Kit that we have been using so far. We can use it to run our applet as follows:

```
appletviewer HelloJava.html
```

Notice that the argument of the **appletviewer** is not the **.java** file or the **.class** file, but rather **.html** file. The output of our applet will be as shown in Fig. 14.7.

Applet Viewer: HelloJava.class	
Applet	
Hello Java	
appletloader.started	

Fig. 14.7 *Output of HelloJava applet by using appletviewer*

14.11 More About Applet Tag

We have used the <APPLET> tag in its simplest form. In its simplest form, it merely creates a space of the required size and then displays the applet output in that space. The syntax of the <APPLET> tag is a little more complex and includes several attributes that can help us better integrate our applet into the overall design of the Web page. The syntax of the <APPLET> tag in full form is shown as follows:

```
<APPLET
    [ CODEBASE = codebase_URL ]
    CODE = AppletFileName.class
    [ ALT = alternate_text ]
    [ NAME = applet_instance_name ]
    WIDTH = pixels
    HEIGHT = pixels
    [ ALIGN = alignment ]
    [ VSPACE = pixels ]
    [ HSPACE = pixels ]
>
[ < PARAM NAME = name1 VALUE = value1> ]
[ < PARAM NAME = name2 VALUE = value2> ]
. . . . . . . . .
. . . . . . . . .
[ Text to be displayed in the absence of Java ]
</APPLET>
```

The various attributes shown inside [ ] indicate the options that can be used when integrating an applet into a Web page. Note that the minimum required attributes are:

```
CODE = AppletFileName.class
WIDTH = pixels
HEIGHT = pixels
```

Table 14.1 lists all the attributes and their meaning.

Table 14.1 Attributes of APPLET Tag

Attribute	*Meaning*
CODE=AppletFileName.class	Specifies the name of the applet class to be loaded. That is, the name of the already-compiled .class file in which the executable Java bytecode for the applet is stored. This attribute must be specified.
CODEBASE=codebase_URL (Optional)	Specifies the URL of the directory in which the applet resides. If the applet resides in the same directory as the HTML file, then the CODEBASE attribute may be omitted entirely.
WIDTH=pixels HEIGHT=pixels	These attributes specify the width and height of the space on the HTML page that will be reserved for the applet.
NAME=applet_instance_name (Optional)	A name for the applet may optionally be specified so that other applets on the page may refer to this applet. This facilitates inter-applet communication.
ALIGN=alignment (Optional)	This optional attribute specifies where on the page the applet will appear. Possible values for alignment are: TOP, BOTTOM, LEFT, RIGHT, MIDDLE, ABSMIDDLE, ABSBOTTOM, TEXTTOP, and BASELINE.

(Continued)

Table 14.1 *(Continued)*

HSPACE=pixels (Optional)	Used only when ALIGN is set to LEFT or RIGHT, this attribute specifies the amount of horizontal blank space the browser should leave surrounding the applet.
VSPACE=pixels (Optional)	Used only when some vertical alignment is specified with the ALIGN attribute (TOP, BOTTOM, etc.,) VSPACE specifies the amount of vertical blank space the browser should leave surrounding the applet.
ALT=alternate_text (Optional)	Non-Java browsers will display this text where the applet would normally go. This attribute is optional.

We summarise below the list of things to be done for adding an applet to a HTML document:

1. Insert an <APPLET> tag at an appropriate place in the Web page.
2. Specify the name of the applet's **.class** file.
3. If the **.class** file is not in the current directory, use the codebase parameter to specify
   - the relative path if file is on the local system, or
   - the Uniform Resource Locator (URL) of the directory containing the file if it is on a remote computer.
4. Specify the space required for display of the applet in terms of width and height in pixels.
5. Add any user-defined parameters using <PARAM> tags.
6. Add alternate HTML text to be displayed when a non-Java browser is used.
7. Close the applet declaration with the </APPLET> tag.

14.12 Passing Parameters to Applets

We can supply user-defined parameters to an applet using <PARAM...> tags. Each <PARAM...> tag has a *name* attribute such as *color*, and a *value* attribute such as *red*. Inside the applet code, the applet can refer to that parameter by name to find its value. For example, we can change the colour of the text displayed to red by an applet by using a <PARAM...> tag as follows:

```
<APPLET .....>
<PARAM = color VALUE = "red">
</APPLET>
```

Similarly, we can change the text to be displayed by an applet by supplying new text to the applet through a <PARAM...> tag as shown below:

```
<PARAM NAME = text VALUE = "I love Java">
```

Passing parameters to an applet code using <PARAM> tag is something similar to passing parameters to the **main( )** method using command line arguments. To set up and handle parameters, we need to do two things:

1. Include appropriate <PARAM...> tags in the HTML document.
2. Provide Code in the applet to parse these parameters.

Parameters are passed on an applet when it is loaded. We can define the **init( )** method in the applet to get hold of the parameters defined in the <PARAM> tags. This is done using the **getParameter( )** method, which takes one string argument representing the **name** of the parameter and returns a string containing the value of that parameter.

Program 14.2 shows another version of **HelloJava** applet. Compile it so that we have a class file ready.

Program 14.2 *Applet HelloJavaParam*

```
import java.awt.*;
import java.applet.*;
public class HelloJavaParam extends Applet
{
  String str;
  public void init( )
  {
      str = getParameter("string");    // Receiving parameter value
      if (str == null)
          str = "Java";
      str = "Hello" + str;                // Using the value
  }
  public void paint (Graphics g)
  {
      g.drawString(str, 10, 100).
  }
}
```

Now, let us create HTML file that contains this applet. Program 14.3 shows a Web page that passes a parameter whose NAME is "string" and whose VALUE is "APPLET!" to the applet **HelloJavaParam**.

Program 14.3 *The HTML file for HelloJavaParam applet*

```
<HTML>
      <! Parameterized HTML file >
      <HEAD>
      <TITLE> Welcome to Java Applets </TITLE>
      <HEAD>
      <BODY>
            <APPLET CODE = HelloJavaParam.class
                  WIDTH = 400
                  HEIGHT = 200>
            <PARAM NAME = "string"
                  VALUE = "Applet! ">
            </APPLET>
      </BODY>
</HTML>
```

Save this file as **HelloJavaParam.html** and then run the applet using the applet viewer as follows:

```
appletviewer HelloJavaParam.html
```

This will produce the result as shown in Fig. 14.8.

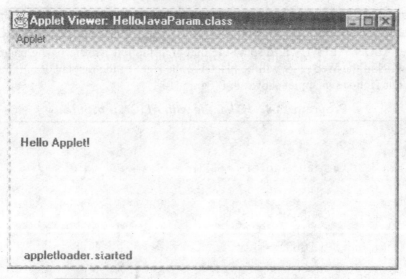

Fig. 14.8   *Displays of HelloJavaParam applet*

Now, remove the <PARAM> tag from the HTML file and then run the applet again. The result will be as shown in Fig. 14.9.

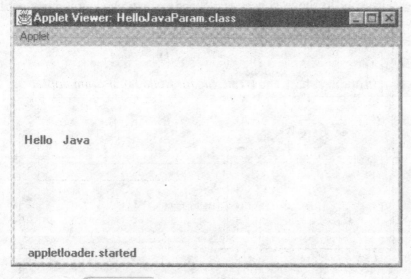

Fig. 14.9   *Output without PARAM tag*

14.13 Aligning the Display

We can align the output of the applet using the ALIGN attribute. This attribute can have one of the nine values:

LEFT, RIGHT, TOP, TEXT TOP, MIDDLE, ABSMIDDLE, BASELINE, BOTTOM, ABSBOTTOM.

For example, ALGN = LEFT will display the output at the left margin of the page. All text that follows the ALIGN in the Web page will be placed to the right of the display. Program 14.4 shows a HTML file for our **HelloJava** applet shown in Program 14.1.

Program 14.4   *HTML file with ALIGN attribute*

```
<HTML>
    <HEAD>
    <TILTE> Here is an applet </TITLE>
    </HEAD>
    <BODY>
            <APPLET CODE    = HelloJava.class
                    WIDTH   = 400
                    HEIGHT  = 200
                    ALIGN   = RIGHT >
            </APPLET>
    </BODY>
</HTML>
```

The alignment of applet will be seen and appreciated only when we run the applet using a Java-capable browser. Figure 14.10 shows how an applet and text surrounding it might appear in a Java-capable browser. All the text following the applet appears to the left of that applet.

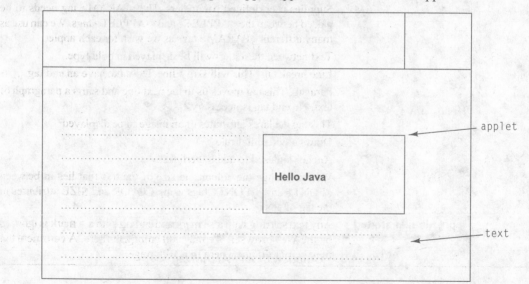

Hello Java

applet

text

Fig. 14.10   *An applet aligned right*

14.14　More About HTML Tags

We have seen and used a few HTML tags. HTML supports a large number of tags that can be used to control the style and format of the display of Web pages. Table 14.2 lists important HTML tags and their functions.

Table 14.2　HTML Tags and Their Functions	
Tag	*Function*
<HTML> ..... </HTML>	Signifies the beginning and end of a HTML file.
<HEAD> ..... </HEAD>	This tag may include details about the Web page. Usually contains <TITLE> tag within it.
<TITLE> ..... </TITLE>	The text contained in it will appear in the title bar of the browser.
<BODY> ..... </BODY>	This tag contains the main text of the Web page. It is the place where the <APPLET> tag is declared.
<H1> ..... </H1>	Header tags. Used to display headings. <H1> creates the largest font header, while <H6> creates the smallest one.
<H6> ..... <H/6>	
<CENTER> ... <CENTER>	Places the text contained in it at the centre of the page.
<APPLET ....>	<APPLET ...> tag declares the applet details as its attributes.
<APPLET> ... </APPLET)	May hold optionally user-defined parameters using <PARAM> Tags.
<PARAM ....>	Supplies user-defined parameters. The <PARAM> tag needs to be placed between the <APPLET> and </APPLET> tags. We can use as many different <PARAM> tags as we wish for each applet.
<B> .... <B>	Text between these tags will be displayed in bold type.
 	Line break tag. This will skip a line. Does not have an end tag.
<P>	Para tag. This tag moves us to the next line and starts a paragraph of text. No end tag is necessary.
<IMG ...>	This tag declares attributes of an image to be displayed.
<HR>	Draws a horizontal rule.
<A ....> </A>	Anchor tag used to add hyperlinks.
<FONT ...> .... </FONT>	We can change the colour and size of the text that lies in between <FONT> and </FONT> tags using COLOR and SIZE attributes in the tag <FONT ...>.
<! ....>	Any text starting with a <! mark and ending with a > mark is ignored by the Web browser. We may add comments here. A comment tag may be placed anywhere in a Web page.

14.15　Displaying Numerical Values

It applets, we can display numerical values by first converting them into strings and then using the **drawString( )** method of **Graphics** class. We can do this easily by calling the **ValueOf( )** method of **String** class. Program 14.5 illustrates how an applet handles numerical values.

Program 14.5   *Displaying numerical values*

```java
import java.awt.*;
import java.applet.*;
public class NumValues extends Applet
{
    public void paint (Graphics g)
    {
        int value1 = 10;
        int value2 = 20;
        int sum = value1 + value2;
        String s = "sum: " + String.valueOf(sum);
        g.drawString(s, 100, 100);
    }
}
```

The applet Program 14.5 when run using the following HTML file displays the output as shown in Fig. 14.11.

```html
<html>
<applet
    code = NumValues.class
    width = 300
    height = 300 >
</applet>
</html>
```

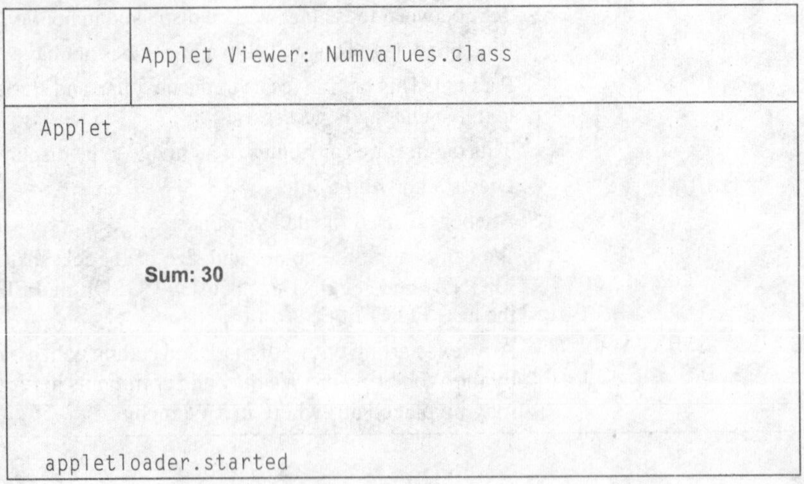

```
Applet Viewer: Numvalues.class



Applet




       Sum: 30




appletloader.started
```

Fig. 14.11   *Output of Program 14.5*

14.16   Getting Input from the User

Applets work in a graphical environment. Therefore, applets treat inputs as text strings. We must first create an area of the screen in which user can type and edit input items (which may be any data type). We can do this by using the **TextField** class of the applet package. Once text fields are created for receiving input, we can type the values in the fields and edit them, if necessary.

Next step is to retrieve the items from the fields for display of calculations, if any. Remember, the text fields contain items in string form. They need to be converted to the right form, before they are used in any computations. The results are then converted back to strings for display. Program 14.6 demonstrates how these steps are implemented.

Program 14.6   *Interactive input to an applet*

```
import java.awt.*;
import java.applet.*;
public class UserIn extends Applet
{
  TextField text1, text2;
  public void init( )
  {
      text1 = new TextField(8);
      text2 = new TextField(8);
      add (text1);
      add (text2);
      text1.setText ("0");
      text2.setText ("0");
  }
  public void paint (Graphics g)
  {
      int x=0, y=0, z=0;
      String s1, s2, s;
      g.drawString("Input a number in each box ", 10, 50);
      try
      {
          s1 = text1.getText( );
          x = Integer.parseInt(s1);
          s2 = text2.getText( );
          y = Integer.parseInt(s2);
      }
      catch (Exception ex) { }
      z = x + y;
      s = String.valueOf (z);
      g.drawString ("THE SUM IS: ", 10, 75);
      g.drawString (s, 100, 75);
  }
```

(Continued)

Program 14.6 (*Continued*)

```
public Boolean action (Event event, Object object)
{
    repaint ( );
    return true;
}
}
```

Run the applet **UserIn** using the following steps:

1. Type and save the program (.java file)
2. Compile the applet (.class file)
3. Write a HTML document (.html file)

```
<html>
<applet
        code = UserIn.class
        width = 300
        height = 200 >
</applet>
</html>
```

4. Use the **appletviewer** to display the results

When the applet is up and running, enter a number into each text field box displayed in the applet area, and then press the Return Key. Now, the applet computes the sum of these two numbers and displays the result as shown in Fig. 14.12.

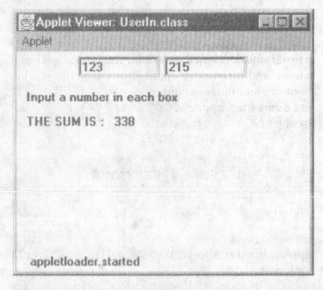

Fig. 14.12   *Interactive computing with applets*

Program Analysis

The applet declares two **TextField** objects at the beginning.

```
TextField text1, text2;
```

These two objects represent text boxes where we type the numbers to be added.

Next, we override the **init( )** method to do the following:

1. To create two text field objects to hold strings (of eight character length).
2. To add the objects to the applet's display area.
3. To initialize the contents of the objects to zero.

Then comes the **paint( )** method where all the actions take place. First, three integer variables are declared, followed by three string variables. Remember, the numbers entered in the text boxes are in string form and therefore they are retrieved as strings using the **getText( )** method and then they are converted to numerical values using the **parseInt( )** method of the **Integer** class.

After retrieving and converting both the strings to integer numbers, the **paint( )** method sums them up and stores the result in the variable **z**. We must convert the numerical value in **z** to a string before we attempt to display the answer. This is done using the **ValueOf( )** method of the **String** class.

14.17   Summary

Applets are Java programs developed for use on the Internet. They provide a means to distribute interesting, dynamic, and interactive applications over the World Wide Web. We have learned the following about applets in this chapter:

How do applets differ from applications,
How to design applets,
How to design a Web page using HTML tags,
How to execute applets, and
How to provide interactive input to applets.

 Key Terms

Applet, Local applet, Remote applet, Web page, HTML tag, APPLET tag, Applet life cycle.

REVIEW QUESTIONS

14.1   What is an applet?
14.2   What is a local applet?
14.3   What is a remote applet?
14.4   Explain the client/server relationship as applied to Java applets.
14.5   How do applets differ from application programs?
14.6   Discuss the steps involved in developing and running a local applet.
14.7   Discuss the steps involved in loading and running a remote applet.
14.8   Describe the various sections of Web page.
14.9   How many arguments can be passed to an applet using <PARAM> tags?

14.10 Why do applet classes need to be declared as public?

14.11 Describe the different stages in the life cycle of an applet. Distinguish between **init( )** and **start( )** methods.

14.12 Develop an applet that receives three numeric values as input from the user and then displays the largest of the three on the screen. Write a HTML page and test the applet.

DEBUGING EXERCISES

14.1 Find errors in the following code for drawing set of nested Rectangles.

```java
importjava.awt.*;
importjava.applet.Applet;
public class Rectangles extends Applet
{
    public void paint(Graphics g)
    {
        int inset;
        int rectWidth, rectHeight;

        g.SetColor(Color.blue);
        g.fillRect(0,0,300,160);

        inset = 0;
        rectWidth = 299;
        rectHeight= 159;
        g.setColor(Color.red);
        g.drawStr("Rectangles",150,200);

        while (rectWidth> = 0 && rectHeight> = 0)
        {
            g.drawRect(inset, inset, rectWidth, rectHeight)
            inset += 15;
            rectWidth -= 30;
            rectHeight -= 30;
        }
    }
}
```

14.2 The following code converts temperature values. Will the code display the new value on moving the scrollbar?

```java
import java.awt.*;
import java.applet.Applet;
import java.awt.event.*;
public class CelsiusValue extends Applet implements AdjustmentListener
{
    private Scrollbar bar;
    private int old, newtemp = 0;
    private inft fahr = 32;
    public void init( )
    {
```

```
      bar = new Scrollbar(Scrollbar.HORIZONTAL, 0, 1, 0, 100);
      bar.addAdjustmentListener(this);
      setLayout(new BorderLayout( ) );
      add("North", bar);
   }
   public void paint(Graphics g)
   {
      g.drawSTring("Celsius = " + newtemp, 30, 50);
      g.drawString ("Fahrenheit = " + fahr, 30, 70);
   }
   public void adjustmentValueChanged(AdjustmentEvent e)
   {
      newtemp = bar.getValue( );
      if (newtemp ! = old)
      {
         fahr = newtemp * 9 / 5 + 32;
         old = newtemp;
      }
   }
}
```

14.3 Given code creates an expanding ring on mouse click event. Does the code show the desired output?

```
import java.awt.*;
import java.awt.event.*;
import java.applet.Applet;
public class MouseRing extends Applet implements MouseListener
{
   private int x = 100, y = 100;
   private int pauseLength;
   public void init( )
   {
      pauseLength = Integer.parseInt(getParameter("PauseLength"));
      setBackground(Color.white);
   }
   public void paint(Graphics g)
   {
      int count = 0;
      while (count < 100)
      {
         int radius = 5*count;
         int diameter = 2*radius;
         g.setColor(Color.black);
         g.drawOval(x-radius, y-radius, diameter, diameter); // Draw
         pause(pauseLength);
         g.setColor(Color.white);
         g.drawOval(x-radius, y-radius, diameter, diameter); // Erase!
         count = count+1;
      }
   }
}
```

```
     private void pause(int howLong)
     {
        for (int count = 0; count < howLong; count++);
     }
     public void mouseClicked(MouseEvent e)
     {
        x = e.getX();
        y = e.getY();
        repaint();
     }
     public void mouseExited(MouseEvent e) { }
     public void mouseEntered(MouseEvent e) { }
     public void mousePressed(MouseEvent e) { }
     public void mouseReleased(MouseEvent e) { }
}
```

14.4   Using parameter, an applet provides answers to different questions. Correct the code.

Question.html

```
<html>
<head>
<title>Questions and Answers</title>
</hnead>
<body>
<APPLET CODE=Question.class
     WIDTH=400 HEIGHT = 100>
  <PARAM NAME=question VALUE="What is Inheritance?">
  <PARAM NAME=answer VALUE="Getting the properties of one class into another">
</APPLET>
</body>
</html>
```

Question.java

```
import java.awt.*;
import java.awt.event.*;
import java.applet.Applet;
public class Question extends Applet implements ActionListener
{
   String theQuestion;
   String theAnswer = "   ";
   Button reveal = new Button("Click to know the answer");
   public void init()
   {
      theQuestion = getParameter("ques");
      add(reveal);
      reveal.addActionListener(this);
   }
   public void paint(Graphics g)
```

```
    {
        g.setColor(Color.black);
        g.drawString(theQuestion, 10, 50);
        g.setColor(Color.red);
        g.drawString(theAnswer, 10, 70);
    }
    public void actionPerformed(ActionEvent e)
    {
        theAnswer = getParameter("answer");
        repaint();
    }
}
```

14.5 Given applet shows the sequence of events called in an applet. Will the message defined in destroy() event be shown?

```
import java.awt.*;
importjava.applet.Applet;
public classAllMethodsApplet extends Applet
{
    TextrArea messages = new TextArea(8, 30);
    public AllMethodsApplet()
    {
        messages.append("Constructor called/n");
    }
    public void init()
    {
        add( messages );
        messages.append ( "Init called/n" );
    }
    public void start()
    {
        messages.append( "Start calld/n" );
    }
    public void stop()
    {
        messages.append ( "Stop called/n" );
    }
    public void destory()
    {
        messages.append ( "Destroy called/n" );
    }
    public void paint( Graphics display )
    {
        messages.append( "Paint called/n" );
        Dimension size = getSize();
        display.drawRect( 0, 0, size.widtrh-1, size.height-1);
    }
}
```

15

Graphics Programming

15.1 Introduction

One of the most important features of Java is its ability to draw graphics. We can write Java applets that draw lines, figures of different shapes, images, and text in different fonts and styles. We can also incorporate different colours in display.

Every applet has its own area of the screen known as *canvas*, where it creates its display. The size of an applet's space is decided by the attributes of the <APPLET...> tag. A Java applet draws graphical image inside its space using the coordinate system as shown in Fig. 15.1.

Java's coordinate system has the origin (0, 0) in the upper-left corner. Positive x values are to the right, and positive y values are to the bottom. The values of coordinates x and y are in pixels.

15.2 The Graphics Class

Java's **Graphics** class includes methods for drawing many different types of shapes, from simple lines to polygons to text in a variety of fonts. We have already seen how to display text using the **point( )** method and a **Graphics** object.

To draw a shape on the screen, we may call one of the methods available in the **Graphics** class. Table 15.1 shows the most commonly used drawing methods in the **Graphics** class. All the drawing methods have arguments representing end points, corners, or starting locations of a shape as values in the applet's coordinate system. To draw a shape, we only need to use the appropriate method with the required arguments.

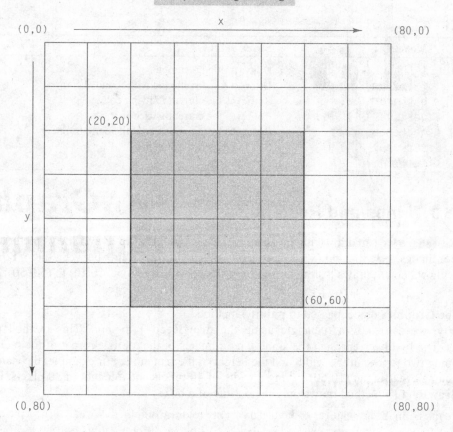

Fig. 15.1 Coordinate system of Java

Table 15.1 Drawing Methods of the Graphics Class

Method	Description
clearRect ( )	Erases a rectangular area of the canvas.
copyArea ( )	Copies a rectangular area of the canvas to another area.
drawArc ( )	Draws a hollow arc.
drawLine ( )	Draws a straight line.
drawOval ( )	Draws a hollow oval.
drawPolygon ( )	Draws a hollow polygon.
drawRect ( )	Draws a hollow rectangle.
drawRoundRect ( )	Draws a hollow rectangle with rounded corners.
drawString ( )	Displays a text string.
fillArc ( )	Draws a filled arc.
fillOval ( )	Draws a filled oval.
fillPolygon ( )	Draws a filled polygon.

(Continued)

Table 15.1 *(Continued)*

Method	Description
fillRect ( )	Draws a filled rectangle.
fillRoundRect ( )	Draws a filled rectangle with rounded corners.
getColor ( )	Retrieves the current drawing colour.
getFont ( )	Retrieves the currently used font.
getFontMetrics ( )	Retrieves information about the current font.
setColor ( )	Sets the drawing colour.
setFont ( )	Sets the font.

 ## 15.3   Lines and Rectangles

The simplest shape we can draw with the **Graphics** class is a line. The **drawLine ( )** method takes two pair of coordinates, (x1, y1) and (x2, y2) as arguments and draws a line between them. For example, the following statement draws a straight line from the coordinate point (10,10) to (50, 50):

```
g.drawLine (10,10, 50,50) ;
```

The **g** is the **Graphics** object passed to **paint( )** method.

Similarly, we can draw a rectangle using the **drawRect( )** method. This method takes four arguments. The first two represent the x and y coordinates of the top left corner of the rectangle, and the remaining two represent the width and the height of the rectangle. For example, the statement will draw a rectangle starting at (10,60) having a width of 40 pixels and a height of 30 pixels. Remember that the **drawRect ( )** method draws only the outline of a box.

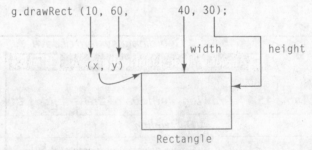

We can draw a solid box by using the method **fillRect ( )**. This also takes four parameters (as drawRect) corresponding to the starting point, the width and the height of the rectangle. For example, the statement

```
g.fillRect (60, 10, 30, 80) ;
```

will draw a solid rectangle starting at (60,10) with a width of 30 pixels and a height of 80 pixels.

We can also draw rounded rectangles (which are rectangles with rounded edges), using the methods **drawRoundRect( )** and **fillRoundRect( )**. These two methods are similar to **drawRect( )** and **fillRect ( )** except that they take two extra arguments representing the width and height of the angle of corners. These extra parameters indicate how much of corners will be rounded. Example:

```
g.drawRoundRect (10, 100, 80, 50, 10, 10) ;
g.fillRoundRect (20, 110, 60, 30, 5, 5) ;
```

Program 15.1 is an applet code that draws three lines, a rectangle, a filled rectangle, a rounded rectangle and a filled rounded rectangle. Note that the filled rounded one is drawn inside the rounded rectangle. Program 15.2 shows a HTML file that displays the applet. The output of the applet. **LineRect** under **appletviewer** is shown in Fig. 15.2.

Program 15.1   *Drawing lines and rectangles*

```
import java.awt.*;
import java.applet.*;
public class LineRect extends Applet
{
    public void paint (Graphics g)
    {
        g.drawLine (10, 10, 50, 50) ;
        g.drawRect (10, 60, 40, 30) ;
        g.fillRect (60, 10, 30, 80) ;
        g.drawRoundRect (10, 100, 80, 50, 10, 10) ;
        g.fillRoundRect (20, 110, 60, 30, 5, 5) ;
        g.drawLine (100, 10, 230, 140) ;
        g.drawLine (100, 140, 230, 10) ;
    }
}
<APPLET
    CODE = LineRect.class
    WIDTH = 250
    HEIGHT = 200>
</APPLET>
```

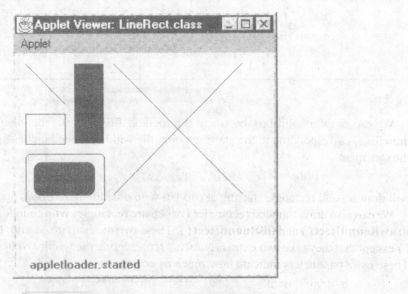

Fig. 15.2   *Output of LineRect applet*

15.4 Circles and Ellipses

The **Graphics** class does not have any method for circles or ellipses. However, the **drawOval( )** method can be used to draw a circle or an ellipse. Ovals are just like rectangles with overly rounded corners as shown in Fig. 15.3. Note that the figure is surrounded by a rectangle that just touches the edges. The **drawOval( )** method takes four arguments: the first two represent the top left corner of the imaginary rectangle and the other two represent the width and height of the oval itself. Note that if the width and height are the same, the oval becomes a circle. The oval's coordinates are actually the coordinates of an enclosing rectangle.

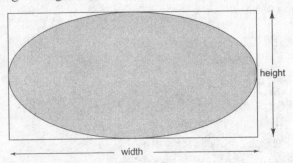

Fig. 15.3   *Oval within an imaginary rectangle*

Like rectangle methods, the **drawOval( )** method draws outline of an oval, and the **fillOval( )** method draws a solid oval. The code segment shown below draws a filled circle within an oval (see Fig. 15.4).

```
public void paint (Graphics g)
{
        g.drawOval (20, 20, 200, 120) ;
        g.setColor (Color.green);
        g.fillOval (70, 30, 100, 100) ; // This is a circle.
}
```

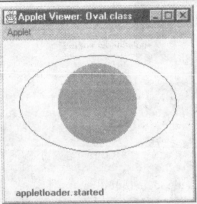

Fig. 15.4   *A filled circle within an ellipse*

We can draw an object using a color object as follows:

```
g.setColor (Color.green) ;
```

After setting the color, all drawing operations will occur in that color.

15.5 Drawing Arcs

An arc is a part of an oval. In fact, we can think of an oval as a series of arcs that are connected together in an orderly manner. The **drawArc( )** designed to draw arcs takes six arguments. The first four are the same as the arguments for **drawOval( )** method and the last two represent the starting angle of the arc and the number of degrees (sweep angle) around the arc.

In drawing arcs, Java actually formulates the arc as an oval and then draws only a part of it as dictated by the last two arguments. Java considers the three O'clock position as zero degree position and degrees increase in anti-clockwise direction as shown in Fig. 15.5. So, to draw an arc from 12:00 O'clock position to 6:00 O'clock position, the starting angle would be 90, and the sweep angle would be 180.

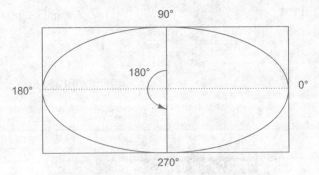

Fig. 15.5   *Arc as a part of an oval*

We can also draw an arc in backward direction by specifying the sweep angle as negative. For example, if the last argument is −135° and the starting angle is 45°, then the arc is drawn as shown in Fig. 15.6.

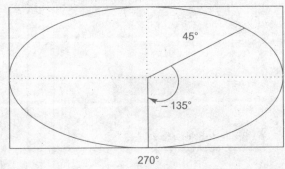

Fig. 15.6   *Drawing an arc in clockwise direction*

We can use the **fillArc( )** method to fill the arc. Filled arcs are drawn as if they were sections of a pie. Instead of joining the two end points, they are joined to the centre of the oval. Program 15.3 shows an applet that draws a human face as shown in Fig. 15.7.

Program 15.3 *Applet for drawing a human face*

```
import java.awt.*;
import java.applet.*;
public class Face extends Applet
{
    public void paint (Graphics g)
    {
        g.drawOval (40, 40, 120, 150) ;        // / Head
        g.drawOval (57, 75, 30, 20) ;          // / Left eye
        g.drawOval (110, 75, 30, 20) ;         // / Right eye
        g.fillOval (68, 81, 10, 10) ;          // / Pupil (left)
        g.fillOval (121, 81, 10, 10) ;         // / Pupil (right)
        g.drawOval (85, 100, 30, 30) ;         // / Nose
        g.fillArc (60, 125, 80, 40, 180, 180) ; // / Mouth
        g.drawOval (25, 92, 15, 30) ;          // / Left ear
        g.drawOval (160, 92, 15, 30) ;         // / Right ear
    }
}
```

Fig. 15.7 *Output of the Face applet*

15.6 Drawing Polygons

Polygons are shapes with many sides. A polygon may be considered a set of lines connected together. The end of the first line is the beginning of the second line, the end of the second is the beginning of the third, and so on. This suggests that we can draw a polygon with n sides using the **drawLine( )** method n times in succession. For example, the code given below will draw a polygon of three sides. The output of this code is shown in Fig. 15.8.

```
public void paint (Graphics g)
{
      g.drawLine (10, 20, 170, 40) ;
      g.drawLine (170, 40, 80, 140) ;
      g.drawLine (80, 140, 10, 20) ;
}
```

Note that the end point of the third line is the same as the starting point of the polygon.

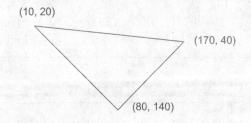

Fig. 15.8   *A polygon with three sides*

We can draw polygons more conveniently using the **drawPolygon( )** method of **Graphics** class. This method takes three arguments:

- An array of integers containing x coordinates
- An array of integers containing y coordinates
- An integer for the total number of points

It is obvious that x and y arrays should be of the same size and we must repeat the first point at the end of the array for closing the polygon. The polygon shown in Fig. 15.8 can be drawn using the **drawPolygon( )** method as follows:

```
public void paint (Graphics g)
{
      int xPoints [ ] = {10, 170, 80, 10};
      int yPoints [ ] = {20, 40, 140, 20};
      int nPoints [ ] = xPoints.length;
      g.drawPolygon (xPoints, yPoints, nPoints) ;
}
```

We can also draw a filled polygon by using the **fillPolygon( )** method. Program 15.4 illustrates the use of polygon methods to draw both the empty polygons and the filled polygons. Its output is shown in Fig. 15.9.

Program 15.4 *Drawing polygons*

```
import java.awt.*;
import java.applet.*;
public class Poly extends Applet
{
    int x1 [ ] = {20, 120, 220, 20};
    int y1 [ ] = {20, 120, 20, 20};
    int n1 = 4;
    int x2 [ ] = {120, 220, 220, 120};
    int y2 [ ] = {120, 20, 220, 120};
    int n2 = 4;
    public void paint (Graphics g)
    {
        g.drawPolygon (x1, y1, n1) ;
        g.fillPolygon (x2, y2,n2) ;
    }
}
```

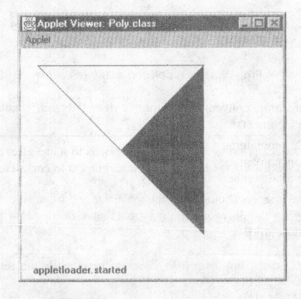

Fig. 15.9   *Output of Program 15.4*

Another way of calling the methods **drawPolygon( )** and **fillPolygon( )** is to use a **Polygon** object. The **Polygon** class enables us to treat the polygon as an object rather than having to deal with individual arrays. This approach involves the following steps:

1. Defining x coordinate values as an array
2. Defining y coordinate values as an array
3. Defining the number of points n
4. Creating a Polygon object and initializing it with the above x, y and n values.
5. Calling the method **drawPolygon( )** or **fillPolygon( )** with the polygon object as arguments

The following code illustrates these steps:

```
public void paint (Graphics g)
{
    int x [ ] = {20, 120, 220, 20};
    int y [ ] = {20, 120, 20, 20};
    int n = x.length;
    Polygon poly = new Polygon (x, y, n) ;
    g.drawPolygon (poly) ;
}
```

The **Polygon** class is useful if we want to add points to the polygon. For example, if we have a polygon object existing, then we can add a point to it as follows:

```
poly.addPoint (x, y) ;
```

The above code may be rewritten using the **addPoint( )** method as follows:

```
public void paint (Graphics g)
{
    Polygon poly = new Polygon ( ) ;
    poly.addPoint (20, 20) ;
    poly.addPoint (120, 120) ;
    poly.addPoint (220, 20) ;
    poly.addPoint (20, 20) ;
    d.drawPolygon (poly) ;
}
```

Here, we first create an empty polygon and then add points to it one after another. Finally, we call the **drawPolygon( )** method using the **poly** object as an argument to complete the process of drawing the polygon.

15.7 Line Graphs

We can design applets to draw line graphs to illustrate graphically the relationship between two variables. Consider the table of values shown as follows:

X	0	60	120	180	240	300	360	400
Y	0	120	180	260	340	340	300	180

The variation of Y, when X is increased can be shown graphically using the Program 15.5. The graph is drawn in an area 400 x 400 pixels. As we know, X increases to the right and Y increases downwards. This is different from the normal graphical systems that have their origin in the bottom left corner. In order to convert the Java coordinate system to the normal systems, we transform the Y values to N-Y where N is the height of the display area. For example, if the vertical height of the display area is 400 pixels, then the point (5, 5) would be (5, 395) in the new system. The table below shows the new values of X and Y and Program 15.5 gives the applet code that draws a line graph showing the relationship between X and Y. Figure 15.10 shows the graph.

X	0	60	120	180	240	300	360	420
Y	400	280	220	140	60	60	100	220

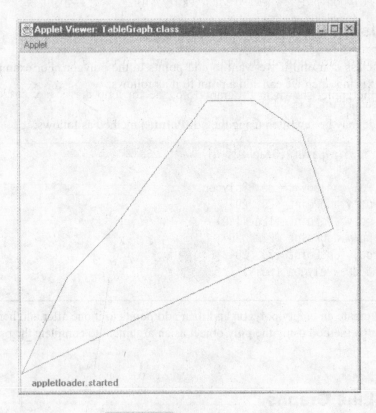

Fig. 15.10 *A line graph*

Program 15.5 *Applet to draw a line graph*

```
import java.awt.*;
import java.applet.*;
```

(*Continued*)

Program 15.5 *(Continued)*

```
public class TableGraph extends Applet
{
    int x [ ] = {0, 60, 120, 180, 240, 300, 360, 400} ;
    int y [ ] = {400, 280, 220, 140, 60, 60, 100, 220};
    int n = x.length;
    public void paint (Graphics g)
    {
        g.drawPolygon (x, y, n) ;
    }
}
```

15.8 Using Control Loops in Applets

We can use all control structures in an applet. Program 15.6 uses a **for** loop for drawing circles repeatedly.

When we run the applet shown in Program 15.6, the for loop draws five circles as shown in Fig. 15.11.

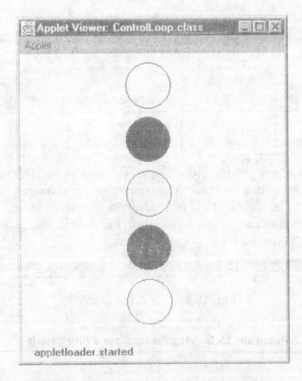

Fig. 15.11   *Output of Program 15.6*

Program 15.6   *Using control loops in applets*

```java
import java.awt.*;
import java.applet.*;
public class ControlLoop extends Applet
{
    public void paint (Graphics g)
    {
        for (int i=0; i<=4; i++)
        {
            if(i%2) == 0)
                g.drawOval (120, i*60+10, 50, 50) ;
            else
                g.fillOval (120, i*60+10, 50, 50) ;
        }
    }
}
```

15.9   Drawing Bar Charts

Applets can be designed to display bar charts, which are commonly used in comparative analysis of data. The table below shows the annual turnover of a company during the period 1991 to 1994. These values may be placed in a HTML file as PARAM attributes and then used in an applet for displaying a bar chart.

Year	1991	1992	1993	1994
Turnover (Rs. Crores)	110	150	100	170

Program 15.7 shows an applet that receives the data values from the HTML page shown in Program 15.8 and displays an appropriate bar chart. The method **getParameter( )** is used to fetch the data values from the HTML file. Note that the method **getParameter( )** returns only string values and therefore we use the wrapper class method **parseInt( )** to convert strings to integer values. Figure 15.12 shows the result of Program 15.7.

Program 15.7   *An applet for drawing bar charts*

```java
import java.awt.*;
import java.applet.*;
public class BarChart extends Applet
{
    int n = 0;
    String label [ ] ;
    int value [ ] ;
```

(Continued)

Program 15.7 (*Continued*)

```
    public void init ( )
    {
        try
        {
            n = Integer.parseInt (getParameter ("columns") ) ;
            label = new String [n] ;
            value = new int [n] ;

            label [0] = getParameter ("label1") ;
            label [1] = getParameter ("label2") ;
            label [2] = getParameter ("label3") ;
            label [3] = getParameter ("label4") ;
            value [0] = Integer.parseInt (getParameter ("c1") ) ;
            value [1] = Integer.parseInt (getParameter ("c2") ) ;
            value [2] = Integer.parseInt (getParameter ("c3") ) ;
            value [3] = Integer.parseInt (getParameter ("c4") ) ;
        }
        catch (NumberFormatException e) { }
    }
    public void paint (Graphics g)
    {
        for (int i = 0; i < n; i++)
        {
            g.setColor (Color.red) ;
            g.drawString (label [i], 20,i*50+30) ;
            g.fillRect (50, i*50+10, value [i], 40) ;
        }
    }
}
```

Program 15.8 *HTML file for running the BarChart applet*

```
<HTML>
    <APPLET
        CODE = BarChart.class
        WIDTH = 300
        HEIGHT = 250>

    <PARAM NAME = "columns" VALUE = "4">

    <PARAM NAME = "c1" VALUE = "110">
    <PARAM NAME = "c2" VALUE = "150">
    <PARAM NAME = "c3" VALUE = "100">
    <PARAM NAME = "c4" VALUE = "170">
    <PARAM NAME = "label1" VALUE = "91">
```

(*Continued*)

Program 15.8   (*Continued*)

```
    <PARAM NAME = "label2" VALUE = "92">
    <PARAM NAME = "label3" VALUE = "93">
    <PARAM NAME = "label4" VALUE = "94">

    </APPLET>
</HTML>
```

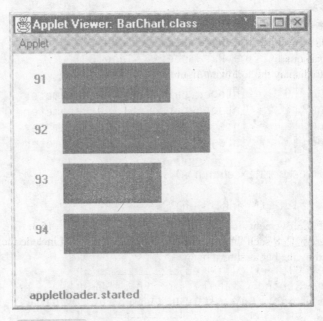

Fig. 15.12   *Barchart produced by Program 15.7*

 ## 15.10   Summary

Java's **Graphics** class supports many methods that enable us to draw many types of shapes, including lines, rectangles, ovals, and arcs. We can use these methods to enhance the appearance of outputs of applets, to draw frames around objects, and to put together simple illustrations. We have also seen how the graphics capability of Java can be used to draw line graphs and bar charts.

 ### *Key Terms*

Canvas, Coordinate system, Line graph, Bar graph, Polygon, Arc.

REVIEW QUESTIONS

15.1 How is Java's coordinate system organized?

15.2 Describe the arguments used in the method **drawRoundRect( )**.

15.3 Explain the purpose of each argument used in the method **drawArc( )**.

15.4 Describe the three ways of drawing polygons.

15.5 Write applets to draw the following shapes:
(a) Cone
(b) Cylinder
(c) Cube
(d) Square inside a circle
(e) Circle inside a square

15.6 Write an applet to display the following figure:

15.7 Suggest possible improvements in the human face drawn by Program 15.3.

15.8 Modify the Program 15.8 such that the display for each year would include the year, bar graph and the value represented by the bar as shown below

Year 91 110

DEBUGGING EXERCISES

15.1 Find errors in the following code which draws an arc.

```
import java.awt.*;
import java.applet.*;
public class arc extends Applet
{
    public void paint(Graphics g)
    {
        g.drawArc(60,125,80,40,180,180);
        g.fillArc(60,125,80,40,180,180);
        g.setFont("Arial");
        g.drawString("Arc Example",50,50);
    }
}
```

15.2 The following code draws a line. Will the code work? If not, why?

```
import java.awt.*;
import java.applet.*;
class line extends Applet
{
public void paint(Graphics g)
    {
        g.drawLine(10,10,100,100,45);
    }
}
```

15.3 The program given below should create a square using drawLine() method. Does the code show the desired output?

```
import java.awt.*;
import java.applet.*;
public class lineSquare extends Applet
{
    public void paint(Graphics g)
    {
        g.drawLine(10,10,10,200);
        g.drawLine(10,10,200,10);
        g.drawLine(10,200,200,200);
        g.drawLine(200,10,200,200);
```

15.4 An oval, line and rectangle are being created using this code. Correct the code.

```
import java.awt.*;
import java.applet.*;
class roundrect extends Applet
{
    public void paint(Graphics g)
    {
        g.drawOval(20,20,120,120);
        g.drawLine(10,10,100,100);
        g.drawRect(10,10,100,100,10,50);
    }
}
```

15.5 The following code is designed to draw a rectangle with pink color. What is wrong with the code?

```
import java.awt.*;
import java.applet.*;
public class colorrect extends Applet
{
    public void paint(Graphics g)
    {
        Color c=g.getColor();
        g.setColor(pink);
        g.drawOval(20,20,100,100);
        g.setColor(c);
        g.fillRect(120,120,50,50);
    }
}
```

16

Managing Input/ Output Files in Java

16.1 Introduction

So far we have used variables and arrays for storing data inside the programs. This approach poses the following problems.

1. The data is lost either when a variable goes out of scope or when the program is terminated. That is, the storage is temporary.
2. It is difficult to handle large volumes of data using variables and arrays.

We can overcome these problems by storing data on *secondary storage devices* such as floppy disks or hard disks. The data is stored in these devices using the concept of *files*. Data stored in files is often called *persistent* data.

A file is a collection of related *records* placed in a particular area on the disk. A record is composed of several fields and a field is a group of characters as illustrated in Fig. 16.1. Characters in Java are *Unicode* characters composed of two *bytes*, each byte containing eight binary digits, 1 or 0.

Storing and managing data using files is known as *file processing* which includes tasks such as creating files, updating files and manipulation of data. Java supports many powerful features for managing input and output of data using files. Reading and writing of data in a file can be done at the level of bytes or characters or fields depending on the requirements of a particular application. Java also provides capabilities to read and write class objects directly. Note that a record may be represented as a class object in Java. The process of reading and writing objects is called *object serialization*. In this chapter, we discuss various features supported by Java for file processing.

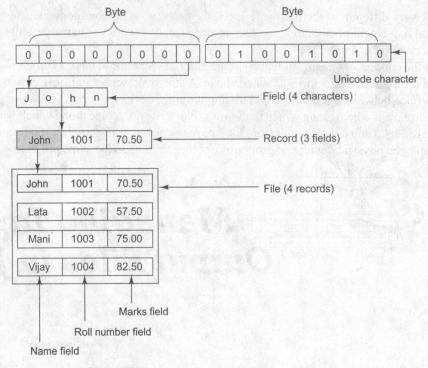

Fig. 16.1   *Data representation in Java files*

16.2   Concept of Streams

In file processing, input refers to the flow of data into a program and output means the flow of data out of a program. Input to a program may come from the keyboard, the mouse, the memory, the disk, a network, or another program. Similarly, output from a program may go to the screen, the printer, the memory, the disk, a network, or another program. This is illustrated in Fig. 16.2. Although these

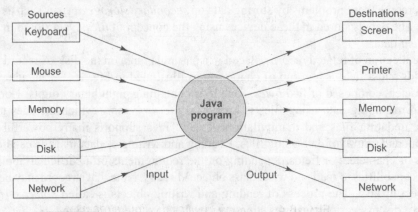

Fig. 16.2   *Relationship of Java program with I/O devices*

devices look very different at the hardware level, they share certain common characteristics such as unidirectional movement of data, treating data as a sequence of bytes or characters and support to the sequential access to the data.

Java uses the concept of streams to represent the ordered sequence of data, a common characteristic shared by all the input/output devices as stated above. A stream presents a uniform, easy-to-use, object-oriented interface between the program and the input/output devices.

A stream in Java is a path along which data flows (like a river or a pipe along which water flows). It has a *source* (of data) and a *destination* (for that data) as depicted in Fig. 16.3. Both the source and the destination may be physical devices or programs or other streams in the same program.

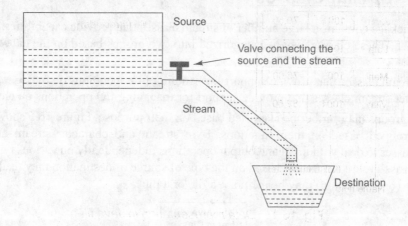

Fig. 16.3   *Conceptual view of a stream*

The concept of sending data from one stream to another (like one pipe feeding into another pipe) has made streams in Java a powerful tool for file processing. We can build a complex file processing sequence using a series of simple stream operations. This feature can be used to filter data along the pipeline of streams so that we obtain data in a desired format. For example, we can use one stream to get raw data in binary format and then use another stream in series to convert it to integers.

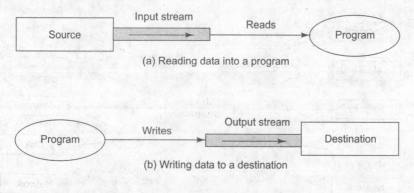

Fig. 16.4   *Using input and output streams*

Java streams are classified into two basic types, namely, *input stream* and *output stream*. An input stream extracts (i.e. *reads*) data from the source (file) and sends it to the program. Similarly, an output stream takes data from the program and sends (i.e. *writes*) it to the destination (file). Figure 16.4 illustrates the use of input and output streams. The program connects and opens an input stream on the data source and then reads the data serially. Similarly, the program connects and opens an output stream to the destination place of data and writes data out serially. In both the cases, the program does not know the details of end points (i.e. source and destination).

16.3 Stream Classes

The **java.io** package contains a large number of stream classes that provide capabilities for processing all types of data. These classes may be categorized into two groups based on the data type on which they operate.

1. Byte stream classes that provide support for handling I/O operations on bytes.
2. Character stream classes that provide support for managing I/O operations on characters.

These two groups may further be classified based on their purpose. Figure 16.5 shows how stream classes are grouped based on their functions. Byte stream and character stream classes contain specialized classes to deal with input and output operations independently on various types of devices. We can also cross-group the streams based on the type of source or destination they read from or write to. The source (or destination) may be memory, a file or a pipe.

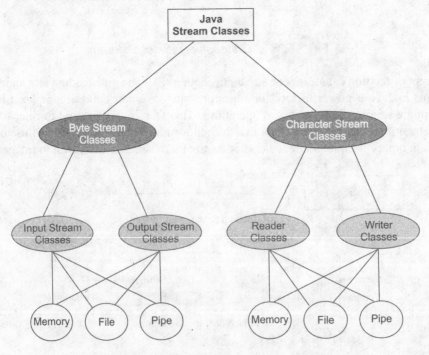

Fig. 16.5   *Classification of Java stream classes*

16.4 Byte Stream Classes

Byte stream classes have been designed to provide functional features for creating and manipulating streams and files for reading and writing bytes. Since the streams are unidirectional, they can transmit bytes in only one direction and, therefore, Java provides two kinds of byte stream classes: *input stream classes* and *output stream* classes.

Input Stream Classes

Input stream classes that are used to read 8-bit bytes include a super class known as **InputStream** and a number of subclasses for supporting various input-related functions. Figure 16.6 shows the class hierarchy of input stream classes.

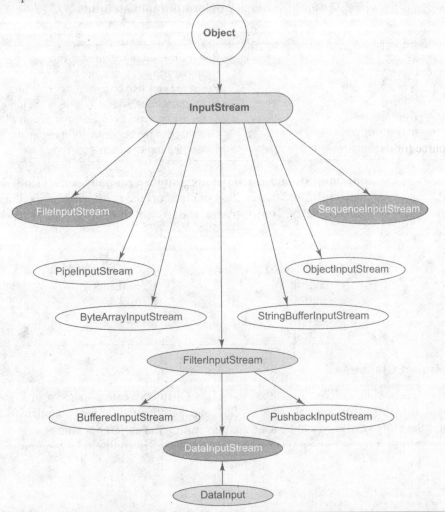

Fig. 16.6 *Hierarchy of input stream classes*

The super class **InputStream** is an abstract class, and, therefore, we cannot create instances of this class. Rather, we must use the subclasses that inherit from this class. The **InputStream** class defines methods for performing input functions such as

- Reading bytes
- Closing streams
- Marking positions in streams
- Skipping ahead in a stream
- Finding the number of bytes in a stream

Table 16.1 gives a brief description of all the methods provided by the **InputStream** class.

Table 16.1 Summary of InputStream Methods

Method	Description
1. read( )	Reads a byte from the input stream
2. read (byte b[ ])	Reads an array of bytes into b
3. read (byte b[ ], int n, int m)	Reads m bytes into b starting from nth byte.
4. available( )	Gives number of bytes available in the input
5. skip(n)	Skips over n bytes from the input stream
6. reset( )	Goes back to the beginning of the stream
7. close( )	Closes the input stream

Note that the class **DataInputStream** extends **FilterInputStream** and implements the interface **DataInput**. Therefore, the **DataInputStream** class implements the methods described in **DataInput** in addition to using the methods of **InputStream** class. The **DataInput** interface contains the following methods:

- readShort( )
- readInt( )
- readLong( )
- readFloat( )
- readUTF( )

- readDouble( )
- readLine( )
- readChar( )
- readBollean( )

Output Stream Classes

Output stream classes are derived from the base class **OutputStream** as shown in Fig. 16.7. Like **InputStream,** the **OutputStream** is an abstract class and therefore we cannot instantiate it. The several subclasses of the **OutputStream** can be used for performing the output operations.

The **OutputStream** includes methods that are designed to perform the following tasks:

- Writing bytes
- Closing streams
- Flushing streams

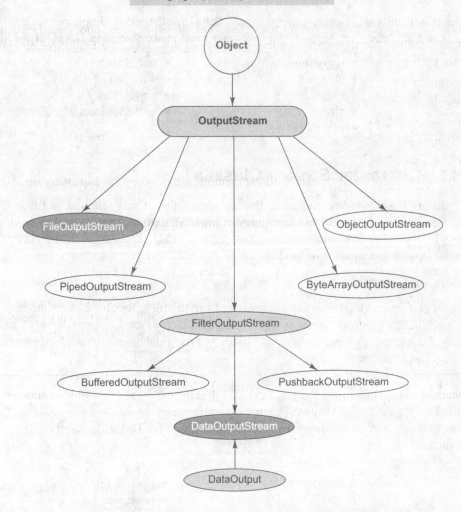

Fig. 16.7 *Hierarchy of output stream classes*

Table 16.2 gives a brief description of all the methods defined by the **OutputStream** class.

Table 16.2	Summary of OutputStream Methods
Method	*Description*
1. write( )	Writes a byte to the output stream
2. write(byte[ ] b)	Writes all bytes in the array b to the output stream
3. write(byte b[ ], int n, int m)	Writes m bytes from array b starting from nth byte
4. close( )	Closes the output stream
5. flush( )	Flushes the output stream

The **DataOutputStream**, a counterpart of **DataInputStream**, implements the interface **DataOutput** and, therefore, implements the following methods contained in **DataOutput** interface.

• writeShort( )	• writeDouble( )
• writeInt( )	• writeBytes( )
• writeLong( )	• writeChar( )
• writeFloat( )	• writeBoolean( )
• writeUTF( )	

16.5   Character Stream Classes

Character stream classes were not a part of the language when it was released in 1995. They were added later when the version 1.1 was announced. Character streams can be used to read and write 16-bit Unicode characters. Like byte streams, there are two kinds of character stream classes, namely, *reader stream* classes and *writer stream* classes.

Reader Stream Classes

Reader stream classes are designed to read character from the files. **Reader** class is the base class for all other classes in this group as shown in Fig. 16.8. These classes are functionally very similar to the input stream classes, except input streams use bytes as their fundamental unit of information, while reader streams use characters.

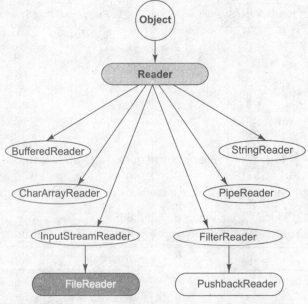

Fig. 16.8   *Hierarchy of reader stream classes*

The **Reader** class contains methods that are identical to those available in the **InputStream** class, except **Reader** is designed to handle characters (see Table 16.1). Therefore, reader classes can perform all the functions implemented by the input stream classes.

Writer Stream Classes

Like output stream classes, the writer stream classes are designed to perform all output operations on files. Only difference is that while output stream classes are designed to write bytes, the writer stream classes are designed to write characters.

The **Writer** class is an abstract class which acts as a base class for all the other writer stream classes as shown in Fig. 16.9. This base class provides support for all output operations by defining methods that are identical to those in **OutputStream** class (see Table 16.2).

16.6 Using Streams

We have seen briefly various types of input and output stream classes used for handling both the 16-bit characters and 8-bit bytes. Although all the classes are known as i/o classes, not all of them are used for reading and writing operations only. Some perform operations such as buffering, filtering, data conversion, counting and concatenation while carrying out i/o tasks.

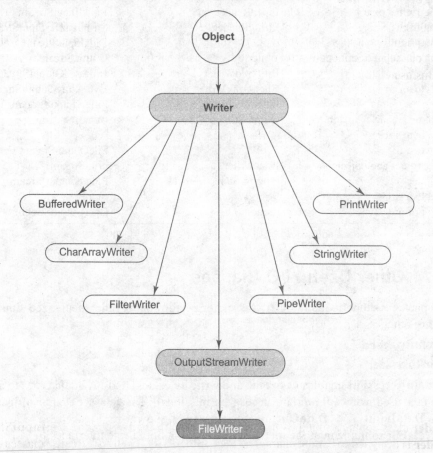

Fig. 16.9 *Hierarchy of writer stream classes*

As pointed out earlier, both the character stream group and the byte stream group contain parallel pairs of classes that perform the same kind of operation but for the different data type. Table 16.3 gives a list of tasks and the character streams and byte streams that are available to implement them.

Table 16.1 *List of Tasks and Classes Implementing Them*		
Task	*Character Stream Class*	*Byte Stream Class*
Performing input operations	Reader	InputStream
Buffering input	BufferedReader	BufferdInputStream
Keeping track of line numbers	LineNumberReader	LineNumberInputStream
Reading from an array	CharArrayReader	ByteArrayInputStream
Translating byte stream into a character stream	InputStreamReader	(none)
Reading from files	FileReader	FileInputStream
Filtering the input	FilterReader	FilterInputStream
Pushing back characters/bytes	PushbackReader	PushbackInputStream
Reading from a pipe	PipedReader	PipedInputStream
Reading from a string	StringReader	StringBufferInputStream
Reading primitive types	(none)	DataInputStream
Performing output operations	Writer	OutputStream
Buffering output	BufferedWriter	BufferedOutputStream
Writing to an arry	CharArrayWriter	ByteArrayOutputStream
Filtering the output	FilterWriter	FilterOutputStream
Translating character stream into a byte stream	OutputStreamWriter	(none)
Writing to a file	FileWriter	FileOutputStream
Printing values and objects	PrintWriter	printStream
Writing to a pipe	PipedWriter	PipedOutputStream
Writing to a string	StringWriter	(none)
Writing primitive types	(none)	DataOutputStream

16.7   Other Useful I/O Classes

The **java.io** package supports many other classes for performing certain specialized functions. They include among others:

- RandomAccessFile
- StreamTokenizer

The **RandomAccessFile** enables us to read and write bytes, text and Java data types to any location in a file (when used with appropriate access permissions). This class extends **object** class and implements **DataInput** and **DataOutput** interfaces as shown in Fig. 16.10. This forces the **RandomAccessFile** to implement the methods described in both these interfaces.

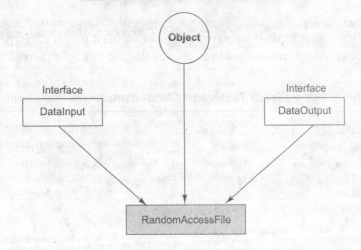

Fig. 16.10 *Implementation of the RandomAccessFile*

The class **Stream Tokenizer,** a subclass of **object** can be used for breaking up a stream of text from an input text file into meaningful pieces called *tokens*. The behaviour of the **StreamTokenizer** class is similar to that of the **StringTokenizer** class (of **java.util** package) that breaks a string into its component tokens.

16.8 Using the File Class

The **java.io** package includes a class known as the **File** class that provides support for creating files and directories. The class includes several constructors for instantiating the **File** objects. This class also contains several methods for supporting the operations such as

- Creating a file
- Opening a file
- Closing a file
- Deleting a file
- Getting the name of a file
- Getting the size of a file
- Checking the existence of a file
- Renaming a file
- Checking whether the file is writable
- Checking whether the file is readable

16.9 Input/Output Exceptions

When creating files and performing i/o operations on them, the system may generate i/o related exceptions. The basic i/o related exception classes and their functions are given in Table 16.4.

Table 16.4 Important I/O Exception Classes and their Functions

I/O Exception class	Function
EOFException	Signals that an end of the file or end of stream has been reached unexpectedly during input
FileNotFoundException	Informs that a file could not be found
InterruptedIOException	Warns that an I/O operations has been interrupted
IOException	Signals that an I/O exception of some sort has occurred

Each i/o statement or group of i/o statements must have an exception handler around it as shown below or the method must declare that it throws an IOException.

```
try
{
.........
.........     //   I/O statements
.........
}
catch (IOException e)
{
.........     //   Message output statement
}
```

Proper use of exception handlers would help us identify and locate i/o errors more effectively.

16.10 Creation of Files

If we want to create and use a disk file, we need to decide the following about the file and its intended purpose:

- Suitable name for the file
- Data type to be stored
- Purpose (reading, writing, or updating)
- Method of creating the file

A filename is a unique string of characters that helps identify a file on the disk. The length of a filename and the characters allowed are dependent on the OS on which the Java program is executed. A filename may contain two parts, a primary name and an optional period with extension. Examples:

input.data	salary
test.doc	student.txt
inventory	rand.dat

Data type is important to decide the type of file stream classes to be used for handling the data. We should decide whether the data to be handled is in the form of characters, bytes or primitive type.

The purpose of using a file must also be decided before using it. For example, we should know whether the file is created for reading only, or writing only, or both the operations.

As we know, for using a file, it must be opened first. This is done by creating a file stream and then linking it to the filename. A file stream can be defined using the classes of **Reader/InputStream** for reading data and **Writer/OutputStream** for writing data. The common stream classes used for various i/o operations are given in Table 16.5. The constructors of stream classes may be used to assign the desired filenames to the file stream objects.

Table 16.5 Common Stream Classes used for I/O Operations

Source or Destination	Characters		Bytes	
	Read	Write	Read	Write
Memory	CharArrayReader	CharArrayWriter	ByteArrayInputStream	ByteArrayOutputStream
File	FileReader	FileWriter	FileInputStream	FileOutputStream
Pipe	PipedReader	PipedWriter	PipedInputStream	PipedOutputStream

There are two ways of initializing the file stream objects. All of the constructors require that we provide the name of the file either *directly*, (as a literal string or variable), or *indirectly* by giving a file object that has already been assigned a filename. The following code segment illustrates the use of direct approach.

```
FileInputStream fis;      //  Declare a file stream object
try
{
    //  Assign the filename to the file stream object
    fis = new FileInputStream ("test.dat") ;
    ....
}
catch (IOException e)
....
....
```

The indirect approach uses a file object that has been initialized with the desired filename. This is illustrated by the following code.

```
..........
File inFile;                         // Declare a file object
InFile = new File ("test.dat") ;     // Assign the filename to
                                     // the file object

FileInputStream fis;
try
{
    //  Give the value of the file object
    //  to the file stream object
    fis = new FileInputStream (inFile) ;
        ..........
}
```

```
catch (.........)
..........
..........
```

The code above includes five tasks:

- Select a filename
- Declare a file object
- Give the selected name to the file object declared
- Declare a file stream object
- Connect the file to the file stream object

Both the approaches are illustrated in Fig. 16.11.

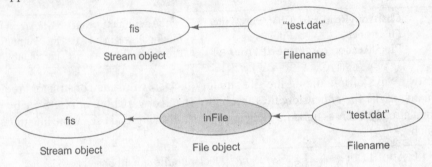

Fig. 16.11   *Instantiating file stream objects*

16.11   Reading/Writing Characters

As pointed out earlier, subclasses of **Reader** and **Writer** implement streams that can handle characters. The two subclasses used for handling characters in files are **FileReader** (for reading characters) and **FileWriter** (for writing characters). Program 16.1 uses these two file stream classes to copy the contents of a file named "input.dat" into a file called "output.dat".

Program 16.1   *Copying characters*

```
//  Copying characters from one file into another
import java.io.*:
class CopyCharacters
{   public static void main (String args [ ] )
    {
        //  Declare and create input and output files
        File inFile = new File ("input.dat") ;
        File outFile  = new File ("output.dat") ;
        FileReader ins = null;              //  Creates file stream ins
        FileWriter outs = null;             //  Creates file stream outs
        try
```

(Continued)

Program 16.1 (*Continued*)

```
        {
                ins = new FileReader (inFile) ;      //  Opens inFile
                outs = new FileWriter (outFile) ;    //  Opens outFile
                //  Read and write till the end
                int ch;
                while ( (ch = ins.read( ) ) != - 1)
                {
                        outs.write (ch) ;
                }
        }
        catch (IOException e)
        {
                System.out.println (e) ;
                System.exit (- 1) ;
        }
        finally   //  Close files
        {
                try
                {
                        ins.close ( ) ;
                        outs.close ( ) ;
                }
                catch (IOException e) { }
        }
    }
}
```

This program is very simple. It creates two file objects **inFile** and **outFile** and initializes them with "input.dat" and "output.dat" respectively using the following code:

```
File inFile  = new File ("input.dat");
File outFile = new File ("output.dat");
```

The program then creates two file stream objects ins and outs and initializes them with "null" as follows:

```
FileReader ins  = null;
FileWriter outs = null;
```

These streams are then connected to the named files using the following code:

```
ins  = new FileReader (inFile) ;
outs = new FileWriter (outFile) ;
```

This connects **inFile** to the **FileReader** stream **ins** and **outFile** to the **FileWriter** stream **outs**. This essentially means that the files "input.dat" and "output.dat" are opened. The statements

```
ch = ins.read ( )
```

reads a character from the **inFile** through the input stream **ins** and assigns it to the variable **ch.** Similarly, the statement

```
outs.write (ch) ;
```

writes the character stored in the variable **ch** to the **outFile** through the output stream **outs.** The character –1 indicates the end of the file and therefore the code

```
while ( (ch=ins.read( ) ) != –1)
```

causes the termination of the while loop when the end of the file is reached. The statements

```
ins.close ( ) ;
```

```
outs.close ( ) ;
```

enclosed in the **finally** clause close the files created for reading and writing. When the program catches an I/O exception, it prints a message and then exits from execution.

The concept of using file streams and file objects for reading and writing characters in Program 16.1 is illustrated in Fig. 16.12.

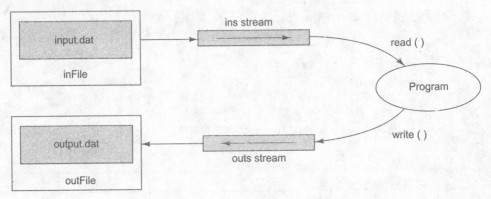

Fig. 16.12 *Reading from and writing to files*

16.12   Reading/Writing Bytes

In Program 16.1 we have used **FileReader** and **FileWriter** classes to read and write 16-bit characters. However, most file systems use only 8-bit bytes. As pointed out earlier, Java i/o system provides a number of classes that can handle 8-bit bytes. Two commonly used classes for handling bytes are **FileInputStream** and **FileOutputStream** classes. We can use them in place of **FileReader** and **FileWriter**.

Program 16.2 demonstrates how **FileOutputStream** class is used for writing bytes to a file. The program writes the names of some cities stored in a byte array to a new file named "city.txt". We can verify the contents of the life by using the command

```
type city.txt
```

Program 16.2   *Writing bytes to a file*

```
//   Writing bytes to a file
import java.io.*;
class WriteBytes
{
    public static void main (String args [ ] )
    {
        //   Declare and initialize a byte array
        byte cities [ ] = {'D', 'E', 'L', 'H', 'I', '\n', 'M', 'A', 'D',
             'R', 'A', 'S', '\n', 'L', 'O', 'N', 'D', 'O', 'N', '\n' } ;
        //   Create an output file stream
        FileOutputStream outfile = null;
        try
        {
            //   Connect the outfile stream to "city.txt"
            outfile = new FileOutputStream ('city.txt") ;
            //   Write data to the stream
            outfile.write (cities) ;
            outfile.close ( ) ;
        }
        catch (IOException ioe)
        {
            System.out.println (ioe) ;
            System.exit (-1) ;
        }
    }
}
```

```
type city.txt
DELHI
    MADRAS
        LONDON
```

Note that a instantiating a **FileOutputStream** object with the name of the file creates and opens the file. We may also supply the filename as a command line argument at the time of execution.

Remember, there are several forms of **write( )** method. The one we have used here writes the entire byte array to the file. Finally, we close the file opened for writing.

Program 16.3 shows how **FileInputStream** class is used for reading bytes from a file. The program reads an existing file and displays its bytes on the screen. Remember, before we run this program, we must first create a file for it to read. We may use this program to read the file "city.txt" created in Program 16.2.

Program 16.3   *Reading bytes from a file*

```
//   Reading bytes from a file
import java.io.*;
class ReadBytes
```

(*Continued*)

Program 16.3 *(Continued)*

```
    {
        public static void main (String args [ ] )
        {
            //  Create an input file stream
            FileInputStream infile = null;
            int b;
            try
            {
                //  Connect infile stream to the required file
                infile = new FileInputStream (args [ 0 ] ) ;
                //  Read and display data
                while ( (b = infile.read ( ) ) != -1)
                {
                    System.out.print ( ( char) b) ;
                }
                infile.close ( ) ;
            }
            catch (IOException ioe)
            {
                System.out.println (ioe) ;
            }
        }
    }
```

Note that the program requires the filename to be given as a command line argument. Program 16.3 displays the following when we supply the filename "city.txt".

```
Prompt>java ReadBytes city.txt
    DELHI
        MADRAS
            LONDON
```

Another example code given in Program 16.4 uses both **FileInputStream** and **FileOutputStream** classes to copy files. We need to provide a source filename for reading and a target filename for writing. In the example code, we have supplied file names directly to the constructors while creating file streams. We may also supply them as command line arguments. Note that the file "in.dat" already exists and contains the following text.

```
Java programming for Internet.
Javascript for Web page development.
Perl for Server-side scripting.
```

Program 16.4 *Copying bytes from one file to another*

```
//  Copying bytes from one file to another
import java.io.*;
class CopyBytes
{
```

Program 16.4 *(Continued)*

```java
        public static void main (String args [ ] )
        {
            //   Declare input and output file streams
            FileInputStream infile = null;   //  Input stream
            FileOutputStream outfile = null; //  Output stream
            //   Declare a variable to hold a byte.
            byte byteRead;
            try
            {
                //   Connect infile to in.dat
                infile = new FileInputStream ("in.dat") ;
                //   Connect outfile to out.dat
                outfile = new FileOutputStream ("out.dat") ;
                //   Reading bytes from in.dat and
                //   writing to out.dat
                do
                {
                    byteRead = (byte) infile.read ( ) ;
                    outfile.write (byteRead) ;
                }
                while (byteRead != -1) ;
            }
            catch (FileNotFoundException e)
            {
                System.out.println ("File not found") ;
            }
            catch (IOException e)
            {
                System.out.println (e.getMessage ( ) ) ;
            }
            finally   //   Close files
            {
                try
                {
                    infile.close ( ) ;
                    outfile.close ( ) ;
                }
                catch (IOExcedption e) { }
            }
        }
    }
```

The command `type out.dat` will produce the following output:

```
        Java programming for Internet.
        Javascript for Web page development.
        Perl for Server-side scripting.
```

Program 16.4 creates **infile** and **outfile** streams for handling the input/output operations. The program then continuously reads a byte from "in.dat" file (using **infile** stream) and writes it to "out.dat" file (using **outfile** stream) until the end of file condition is reached. We should avoid writing to an existing file. We may use the **exists( )** method in the **File** class to check whether the named file already exists. Example:

```
File fout        =    new File ("out.dat") ;
if (fout.exists ( ) )
      return ( ) ;
```

This program could also be written using **FileReader** and **FileWriter** classes.

16.13   Handling Primitive Data Types

The basic input and output streams provide read/write methods that can only be used for reading/writing bytes or characters. If we want to read/write the primitive data types such as integers and doubles, we can use filter classes as wrappers on existing input and output streams to filter data in the original stream. The two filter classes used for creating "data streams" for handling primitive types are **DataInputStream** and **DataOutputStream**. These classes use the concept of multiple inheritance as illustrated in Fig. 16.13 and therefore implements all the methods contained in both the parent class and the interface.

A data stream for input can be created as follows:

```
FileInputStream fis = new FileInputStream (infile) ;
DataInputStream dis = new DataInputStream (fis) ;
```

These statements first create the input file stream fis and then create the input data stream **dis**. These statements basically wrap **dis** on **fis** and use it as a "filter". Similarly, the following statements create the output data stream **dos** and wrap it over the output file stream **fos**.

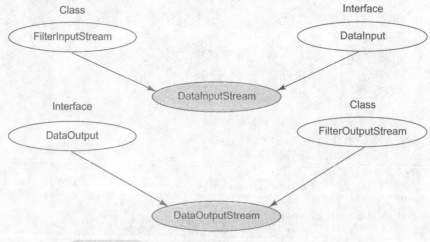

Fig. 16.13   *Hierarchy of data stream classes*

```
FileOutputStream fos = new FileOutputStream (outfile) ;
DataOutputStream dos = new DataOutputStream (fos) ;
```

Note that the file objects **infile** and **outfile** must be initialized with appropriate file names before they are used. We may also use file names directly in place of file objects.

Program 16.5 demonstrates the use of data streams for reading and writing primitive data types. The program first creates "prim.dat" file and then writes a few primitive data types into it using data output stream. At the end of writing, the streams are closed.

The program also creates a data input stream, and connects it to "prim.dat" file. It then reads data from the file and displays them on the screen. Finally, it closes the streams. Note that the **main** method declares that it throws IOException and therefore we need not use **try .... catch** statements.

Program 16.5 *Reading and writing primitive data*

```
//   Reading and writing primitive data
import java.io.*;
Class ReadWritePrimitive
{
    public static void main (String args [ ] ) throws IOException
    {
        File primitive = new File ("prim.dat") ;
        FileOutputStream fos = new FileOutputStream (primitive) ;
        DataOutputStream dos = new DataOutputStream (fos) ;

        //   Write primitive data to the "prim.dat" file
        dos.writeInt (1999) ;
        dos.writeDouble (375.85) ;
        dos.writeBoolean (false) ;
        dos.writeChar ('X') ;
        dos.close ( ) ;
        fos.close ( ) ;

        //   Read data from the "prim.dat" file
        FileInputStream fis = new FileInputStream (primitive) ;
        DataInputStream dis = new DataInputStream (fis) ;
        System.out.println (dis.readInt( ) ) ;
        System.out.println (dis.readDouble ( ) ) ;
        System.out.println (dis.readBoolean ( ) ) ;
        System.out.println (dis.readChar ( ) ) ;
        dis.close ( ) ;
        fis.close ( ) ;
    }
}
```

Program 16.5 displays the following:
```
1999
375.85
false
X
```

The data streams used in Program 16.5 and their functions are illustrated in Fig. 16.14.

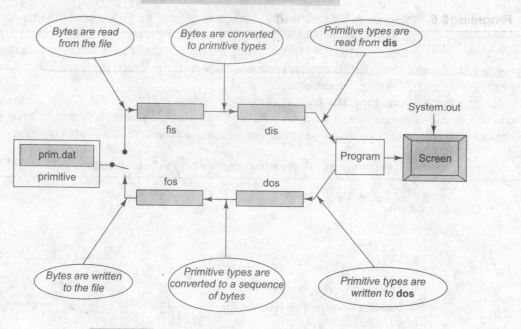

Fig. 16.14　　*Data streams used in Program 16.5*

Another example code shown in Program 16.6 generates random integers and stores them in a file named "rand.dat". The program then reads the integers from the file and displays on the screen.

Program 16.6　*Using a single file for storing and retrieving*

```
// Storing and retrieving integers using data streams
// on a single file

import java.io.*;
class ReadWriteIntegers
{
    public static void main (String args [ ] )
    {
        // Declare data streams
        DataInputStream dis = null;    // Input stream
        DataOutputStream dos = null; // Output stream

        // Construct a file
        File intFile = new File ("rand.dat") ;

        // Writing integers to rand.dat file
        try
        {
            // Create output stream for intFile file
            dos = new DataOutputStream (new
```

(Continued)

Program 16.6 (*Continued*)

```
FileOutputStream (intFile) ) ;
            for (int i = 0; i<20;i++)
                    dos.writeInt ( (int) (math.random ( ) *100) ) ;
        }
        catch (IOException ioe)
        {
            System.out.println (ioe.getMessage ( ) ) ;
        }
        finally
        {
            try
            {
                dos.close ( ) ;
            }
            catch (IOException ioe) { }
        }

        // Reading integers from rand.dat file
        try
        {
            // Create input stream for intFile file
            dis = new DataInputStream (new
                    FileInputStream (intFile) ) ;
            for (int i=0; i < 20; i++)
            {
                int n = dis.readInt ( ) ;
                System.out.print (n + "   ") ; }
        }
        catch (IOException ioe)
        {
            System.out.println (ioe.getMessage ( ) ) ; }
        finally
        {
            try
            {
                dis.close ( ) ;
            }
            catch (IOException ioe) { }
        }
    }
}
```

Output of Program 16.6

```
78  62  54  56  55  48  48  35  13  64  13  90  10  78  91  42  9  44  84  66
```

16.14   Concatenating and Buffering Files

It is possible to combine two or more input streams (files) into a single input stream (file). This process is known as *concatenation* of files and is achieved using the **SequenceInputStream class**. One of the constructors of this class takes two **InputStream** objects as arguments and combines them to construct a single input stream.

Java also supports creation of buffers to store temporarily data that is read from or written to a stream. The process is known as *buffered i/o* operation. A buffer sits between the program and the source (or destination) and functions like a filter. Buffers can be created using the **BufferedInputStream** and **BufferedOutputStream** classes.

Program 16.7   *Example of concatenation and buffering*

```
// Concatenating and buffering files
import java.io.*;
class SequenceBuffer
{
    public static void main (String args [ ] )
    throws IOException
    {
        // Declare file streams
        FileInputStream file1 = null;
        FileInputStream file2 = null;

        // Declare file3 to store combined files
        SequenceInputStream file3 = null;

        // Open the files to be concatenated
        file1 = new FileInputStream ("text1.dat") ;
        file2 = new FileInputStream ("text2.dat") ;

        // Concatenate file1 and file2 into file3
        file3 = new SequenceInputStream (file1, file2) ;

        // Create buffered input and output streams
        BufferedInputStream inBuffer =
                new BufferedInputStream (file3) ;
        BufferedOutputStream outBuffer =
                new BufferedOutputStream (System.out) ;

        // Read and write till the end of buffers
        int ch;
        while ( (ch = inBuffer.read ( ) ) != - 1)
        {
            outBuffer.write ( (char) ch) ;
        }
```

(Continued)

Program 16.7 (*Continued*)

```
            inBuffer.close ( ) ;
            outBuffer.close ( ) ;
            file1.close ( ) ;
            file2. close ( ) ;
        }
    }
```

Program 16.7 illustrates the process of concatenation as well as buffering. The program creates two objects of class **FileInputStream** for the files "text1.dat" and "text2.dat". The two **FileInputStream** objects **file1** and **file2** are used as arguments to the **SequenceInputStream** constructor to obtain a single input stream object **file3**. The file **file3** now contains the contents of **file1** and **file2**.

The program now creates an input buffer named **inBuffer** and connects it to **file3** and creates and output buffer named **outBuffer** and connects it to **system.out** that represents screen. It then uses a while loop to read all bytes in the input buffer and display them through the output buffer.

The entire process of concatenation, buffering and displaying the contents of two independent files is illustrated in Fig. 16.15.

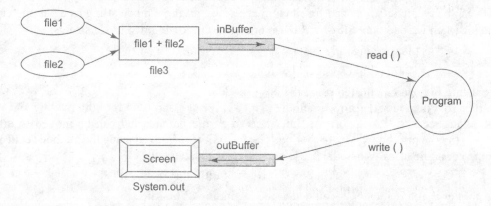

Fig. 16.15   *Illustration of concatenation and buffering*

Given the contents of "text1.dat" and "text2.dat" as follows:

Contents of "text1.dat":

```
        Java (tm) Development Kit
            Version 1.2
        Binary Code License
```

Contents of "text2.dat":

```
This binary code license ("License") contains rights and restrictions associated with
use of the accompanying software and documentation ("Software"). Read the License
carefully before installing the Software. By installing the Software you agree to the
terms and conditions of this License.
```

Then, the output of Program 16.7 would be:

```
Java (tm) Development Kit
      Version 1.2
         Binary Code License
```

The binary code license ("License") contains rights and restrictions associated with use of the accompanying software and documentation ("Software"). Read the License carefully before installing the Software. By installing the Software you agree to the terms and conditions of this License.

16.15　Random Access Files

So far we have discussed files that can be used either for "read only" or for "write only" operations and not for both purposes simultaneously. These files are read or written only sequentially and, therefore, are known as *sequential* files.

As stated earlier, the **RandomAccessFile** class supported by the **Java.io** package allows us to create files that can be used for reading and writing data with random access. That is, we can "jump around" in the file while using the file. Such files are known as *random access* files.

A file can be created and opened for random access by giving a mode string as a parameter to the constructor when we open the file. We can use one of the following two mode strings:

- " r " for reading only
- " rw " for both reading and writing

An existing file can be updated using the "rw" mode.

Program 16.8 demonstrates how a random access is created and used for both reading and writing data. Random access files support a pointer known as *file pointer* that can be moved to arbitrary positions in the file prior to reading or writing. The file pointer is moved using the method **seek( )** in the **RandomAccessFile** class. When the file is opened by the statement

```
file = new RandomAccessFile ("rand.dat", "rw");
```

the file pointer is automatically positioned at the beginning of the file.

Program 16.8　*Reading/Writing using a random access file*

```
// Writing and reading with random access
import java.io.*;
class RandomIO
{
    public static void main (string args [ ] )
    {
        RandomAccessFile file = null;
        try
        {
            file = new RandomAccessFile ("rand.dat", "rw") ;
            // Writing to the file
            file.WriteChar ('X') ;
```

(Continued)

Program 16.8   (*Continued*)

```
                file.writeInt (555) ;
                file.writeDouble (3.1412) ;

                file.seek (0) ; // Go to the beginning
                // Reading from the file
                System.out.println (file.readChar ( ) ) ;
                System.out.println (file.readInt ( ) ) ;
                System.out.println (file.readDouble ( ) ) ;

                file.seek (2) ; // Go to the second item
                System.out.println   (file.readInt ( ) ) ;

                // Go to the end and append false to the file
                file.seek (file.length ( ) ) ;
                file.writeBoolean (false) ;

                file.seek (4) ;
                System.out.println (file.readBoolean ( ) ) ;
                file.close ( ) ;
        }
        catch (IOException e) { System.out.println (e) ; }
    }
}
```

The program opens a random access file and then performs the following operations.

1. Writes three items of data

    ```
    X
    555
    3.1412
    ```

2. Brings the file pointer to the beginning
3. Reads and displays all the three items

    ```
    X
    555
    3.1412
    ```

4. Takes the pointer to the second item and then reads and displays the second item in the file.

    ```
    555
    ```

5. Places the pointer at the end using the method **length( )** and then adds a Boolean item to the file. (Now there are four items in the file and the pointer is at the end, that is, beyond the fourth item).
6. Finally, takes the pointer to the fourth item and displays it.
7. At the end, closes the file.

    The output on the screen would appear as follows:

    ```
    X
    555
    3.1412
    555
    false
    ```

Program 16.9 shows how we could append items to an existing file using the **RandomAccessFile** class. This program opens the file "city.text" created earlier by Program 16.2 and then appends MUMBAI to the end.

Program 16.9   *Appending to an existing file*

```
// Appending to a text file using random access
import java.io.*;

class RandomAccess
{
  static public void main (String args [ ] )
  {
    RandomAccessFile rFile;
    try
    {
      rFile = new RandomAccessFile ("city.txt", "rw") ;
      rFile.seek (rFile.length ( ) ) ;  // Go to the end
      rFile.writeBytes ("MUMBAI/n") :    // Append MUMBAI
      rFile.close ( ) :
    }
    catch (IOExceptionioe)
    {
      System.out.println (ioe) ;
    }
  }
}
```

16.16   Interactive Input and Output

In all the examples discussed so far, we generated data for writing to files within the programs or used data from other files stored in the memory. What if the data is to be provided through the keyboard? We can do this in Java by using an object of the **DataInputStream** class. The process of reading data from the keyboard and displaying output on the screen is known as *interactive i/o*. There are two types of interactive i/o. First one is referred to as simple interactive i/o which involves simple input from the keyboard and simple output in a pure text form. The second type is referred to as graphical interactive i/o which involves input from various input devices and output to a graphical environment on frames and applets.

We have used data stream object to read data from the keyboard in Chapter 4 and graphical interactive input and output for applets in Chapter 14. In this section we shall consider how to use interactive i/o while handling files.

Simple Input and Output

The **System** class contains three i/o objects, namely **System.in, System.out**, and **System. err** where **in, out**, and **err** are static variables. The variable **in** is of **InputStream** type and the other two are of

PrintStream type. We can use these objects to input from the keyboard, output to the screen, and display error messages. **System** class is stored in **java.lang** package which is imported into a Java program automatically.

To perform keyboard input for primitive data types, we need to use the objects of **DataInputStream** and **StringTokenizer** classes. The following code illustrates the reading of an integer value from the keyboard.

```
static DataInputStream din =
                new DataInputStream (System.in) ;
static StringTokenizer st;
..........
..........
st = new StringTokenizer (din.readLine) ;
int code = Integer.parseInt (st.nextToken) ;
```

The first line of code wraps **din** over the input stream object **System.in** thus enabling the object **din** to read data from the keyboard. For example, the method call

```
din.readLine ( )
```

will fetch an entire string (up to a newline which will be discarded) from the console. The statement

```
st = new StringTokenizer (din.readLine ( ) ) ;
```

initializes the **StringTokenizer** object **st** with the string read by the **readLine( )** method. Finally, the line

```
int code = Integer.parseInt (st.nextToken) ;
```

takes the string, converts it into the corresponding integer value, and then assigns the result to the integer type variable **code.** A similar algorithm may be used for reading all the other primitive type data from the console.

Program 16.10 demonstrates how data is read from the keyboard for writing to a file and how the data is read back from the file for display on the screen.

Program 16.10 *Interactive input and output*

```
// Creating files interactively from keyboard input
import java.util.*;    // For using StringTokenizer class
import java.io*;

class Inventory
{
    static DataInputStream din = new DataInputStream (System.in) ;
    static StringTokenizer st;

    public static void main (String args [ ] ) throws IOException
    {
        DataOutputStream dos = new DataOutputStream (new
                    FileOutputStream ("invent.dat") ) ;
        // Reading from console
```

(Continued)

Program 16.10   *(Continued)*

```
System.out.println ("Enter code number") ;
st = new StringTokenizer (din.readLine ( ) ) ;
int code = Integer.parseInt (st.nextToken ( ) ) ;

System.out.println ("Enter number of items") ;
st = new StringTokenizer (din.readLine ( ) ) ;
int items = Integer.parseInt (st.nextToken ( ) ) ;

System.out.println ("Enter cost") ;
st = new StringTokenizer (din.readLine ( ) ) ;
double cost = new Double (st.nextToken ( ) ). doubleValue ( );

// Writing to the file "invent.dat"
dos.writeInt (code) ;
dos.writeInt (items) ;
dos.writeDouble (cost) ;
dos.close ( ) ;

// Processing data from the file
DataInputStream dis = new DataInputStream (new
                        FileInputStream ("invent.dat") ) ;
int codeNumber = dis.readInt ( ) ;
int totalItems = dis.readInt ( ) ;
double itemCost = dis.readDouble ( ) ;
double totalCost = totalItems * itemCost;
dis.close ( ) ;

// Writing to console
System.out.println ( ) ;
System.out.println ("Code Number: " + codeNumber) ;
System.out.println ("Item Cost:    " + itemCost) ;
System.out.println ("Total Items: " + totalItems) ;
System.out.println ("Total Cost: " + totalCost) ;
    }
}
```

The screen would look as follows when the program is executed.

```
Enter code number
1001
Enter number of items
193
Enter cost
452

Code Number : 1001
Item cost    : 452.0
Total Items : 193
Total Cost  : 87236.0
```

Graphical Input and Output

Program 16.11 creates a simple sequential student file interactively using window frames. The program uses the **TextFiled** class to create text fields that receive information from the user at the keyboard and then writes the information to a file. A record of information contains roll number, name, and marks obtained by a student in a test.

Program 16.11 *Creating a file using text fields in windows*

```java
import java.io.*;
import java.awt.*;
class StudentFile extends Frame
{
    // Defining window components
    TextField number, name, marks;
    Button enter, done;
    Label numLabel, namelabel, markLabel;

    DataOutputStream dos;

    // Initialize the Frame
    public StudentFile ( )
    {
        super ("Create Student File") ;
    }
    // Setup the window
    public void setup ( )
    {
        resize (400, 200) ;
        setLayout (new GridLayout (4, 2) ) ;
        // Create the components of the Frame
        number = new TextField (25) ;
        numLabel = new Label ("Roll Number") ;
        name = new TextField (25) ;
        nameLabel = new Label ("Student name") ;
        marks = new TextField (25) ;
        markLabel = new Label ("Marks") ;
        enter = new Button ("ENTER") ;
        done = new Button ("DONE") ;

        // Add the components to the Frame
        add (numLabel) ;
        add (number) ;
        add (nameLabel) ;
        add (name) ;
        add (markLabel) ;
        add (marks) ;
        add (enter) ;
```

(Continued)

Program 16.11   (*Continued*)

```
        add (done) ;
        // Show the Frame
        show ( ) ;
        // Open the file
        try
        {
            dos = new DataOutputStream (
                    new FileOutputStream ("student.dat") ) ;
        }
        catch (IOException e)
        {
            System.err.println (e.toString ( ) ) ;
            System.exit (1) ;
        }
    }

    // Write to the file
    public void addRecord ( )
    {
        int num;
        Double d;
        num = (new Integer (number.getText ( ) ) ) . intValue ( ) ;
        try
        {
            dos.writeInt (num) ;
            dos.writeUTF (name.getText ( ) ) ;
            d = new Double (marks.getText ( ) ) ;
            dos.writeDouble (d.doubleValue ( ) ) ;
        }
        catch (IOException e) {    }

        // Clear the text fields
        number.setText (" ") ;
        name.setText (" ") ;
        marks.setText (" ") ;
    }

    // Adding the record and clearing the TextFields
    public void cleanup ( )
    {
        if (! number.getText ( ) . equals (" ") )
        {
            addRecord ( ) ;
        }
        try
        {
```

Program 16.11 *(Continued)*

```
            dos.flush ( ) ;
            dos.close ( ) ;
        }
        catch (IOException e) { }
    }

    // Processing the event
    public boolean action (Event event, object o)
    {
        if (event.teg instanceof Button)
        {
            if (event.arg.equals ("ENTER") )
            {
                addRecord ( ) ;
                return true;
            }
        }
        return super.action (event, o) ;
    }
    public boolean handleEvent (Event event)
    {
        if (event.get instanceof Button)
        {
            if (event.arg.equals ("DONE") )
            {
                cleanup ( ) ;
                System.exit (0) ;
                return true;
            }
        }
        return super.handleEvent (event) ;
    }

    // Execute the program
    public static void main (String args [ ] )
    {
        StudentFile student = new StudentFile ( ) ;
        student.setup ( ) ;
    }
}
```

The program uses classes **Frame**, **TextField**, **Button**, and **Label** of **java.awt** package to create the window and the text fields required to receive a student record. The method **setup( )** does the job of setting up the window. The method **addRecord( )** writes the information to the "student.dat" file created earlier.

When we execute the program, a window appears on the screen to enable us to enter data (Fig. 16.16).

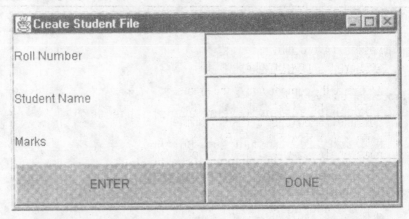

Fig. 16.16   *Screen output produced by Program 16.11*

After entering data in the appropriate text fields, we must click the **ENTER** button to write data to the file. This invokes the **addRecord( )** which performs the task of writing to the file. When we clock the "DONE" button, the program will call the method **cleanup( )** which will close the file stream and terminate the program execution.

Program 16.12 reads the data stored in "student.dat" file by the previous program. The program opens the file for reading and sets up a window that is similar to the one created for writing. When we click the **NEXT** button, the program reads a record from the file and displays its content in the text fields of the window. A clock on the **DONE** button closes the file stream and then terminates the execution.

Program 16.12   *Reading a file using text fields*

```
import java.io.*;
import java.awt.*;
class ReadStudentFile extends Frame
{
    // Defining window components
    TextField number, name, marks;
    Button next,done;
    Label numLabel, nameLabel, markLabel;
    DataInputStream dis;
    boolean moreRecords = true;

    // Initialize the Frame
    public ReadStudentFile ( )
    {
        super ("Create Student File") ;
    }
    // Setup the window
```

(Continued)

Program 16.12   (*Continued*)

```java
public void setup ( )
{
    resize (400, 200) ;
    setLayout (new GridLayout (4, 2) ) ;

    // Create the components of the Frame
    number = new TextField (25) ;
    numLabel =new Label ("Roll Number") ;
    name = new TextField (25) ;
    nameLabel = new Label ("Student Name") ;
    marks = new TextField (25) ;
    markLabel = new Label ("Marks") ;
    next = new Button ("NEXT") ;
    done = new Button ("DONE") ;

    // Add the components to the Frame
    add (numLabel) ;
    add (number) ;
    add (nameLabel) ;
    add (name) ;
    add (markLabel) ;
    add (marks) ;
    add (next) ;
    add (done) ;

    // Show the Frame
    show ( )

    // Open the file
    try
    {
        dis = new DataInputStream (
        new FileInputStream ("student.dat") ) ;
    }
    catch (IOException e)
    {
        System.err.println (e.toString ( ) ) ;
        System.exit (1) ;
    }
}

// Read from the file
public void readRecord ( )
{
    int n;
    String s;
```

Program 16.12 (*Continued*)

```
        double d;
        try
        {
            n = dis.readInt ( ) ;
            s = dis.readUTF ( ) ;
            d = dis.readDouble ( ) ;
            number.setText (String.valueOf (n) ) ;
            name.setText (String.valueOf (s) ) ;
            marks.setText (String.valueOf (d) ) ;
        }
        catch (EOFException e)
        {
            moreRecords = false;
        }
        catch (IOException ioe)
        {
            System.out.println ("IO Error") ;
            System.exit (1) ;
        }
    }

    // Closing the input file
    public void cleanup ( )
    {
        try
        {
            dis.close ( ) ;
        }
        catch (IOException e) { }
    }

    // Processing the event
    public boolean action (Event event, Object o)
    {
        if (event.target instanceof Button)
        {
            if (event.arg.equals ("NEXT") )
                    readRecord ( ) ;
        }
        return true;
    }
    public boolean handleEvent (Event event)
    {
        if (event.target instanceof Button)
```

(*Continued*)

Program 16.12 *(Continued)*

```
        {
            if (event.arg.equals ("DONE") ||
                 moreRecords == false)
            {
                cleanup ( ) ;
                System.exit (0) ;
                return true;
            }
        }
        return super.handleEvent (event) ;
    }
    // Execute the program
    public static void main (String args [ ] )
    {
        ReadStudentFile student = new ReadStudentFile ( ) ;
        student.set up ( ) ;
    }
}
```

16.17   Other Stream Classes

Java supports many other input/output streams that we might find useful in some situations. A brief discussion of some of these streams is given as follows.

Object Streams

We have seen in this chapter how we can read and write characters, bytes, and primitive data types. It is also possible to perform input and output operations on objects using the object streams. The object streams are created using the **ObjectInputStream** and **ObjectOuputStream** classes. In this case, we may declare records as objects and use the object classes to write and read these objects from files. As mentioned in the beginning, this process is known as *object serialization*.

Piped Streams

Piped streams provide functionality for threads to communicate and exchange data between them. Figure 16.17 shows how two threads use *pipes* for communication. The write thread sends data to the read thread through a pipeline that connects an object of **PipedInputStream** to an object of **PipedOutputStream**. The objects **inputPipe** and **outputPipe** are connected using the **connect( )** method.

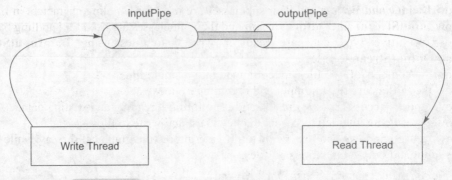

Fig. 16.17   *Threads using pipes to communicate*

Pushback Streams

The pushback streams created by the classes **PushbackInputStream** and **PushbackReader** can be used to push a single byte or a character (that was previously read) back into the input stream so that it can be reread. This is commonly used with parsers. When a character indicating a new input token is read, it is pushed back into the input stream until the current input token is processed. It is then reread when processing of the next input token is initiated.

Filtered Streams

Java supports two abstract classes, namely, **FilterInputStream** and **FilterOutputStream** that provide the basic capability to create input and output streams for filtering input/output in a number of ways. These streams, known as *filters*, sit between an input stream and an output stream and perform some optional processing on the data they transfer. We can combine filters to perform a series of filtering operations as shown in Fig. 16.18. Note that we used **DataInputStream** and **DataOutputStream** as filters in the Program 16.5 for handling primitive type data.

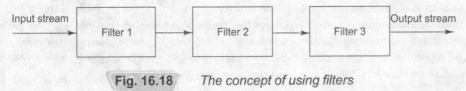

Fig. 16.18   *The concept of using filters*

16.18 Summary

In this chapter we have learned how to work with files for storing and retrieving data. We have discussed in detail the following:

- How the concept of streams are used for handling all input and output operations.
- How stream classes provide capabilities for processing files.
- How stream classes are classified into different groups to handle different data types.
- How the classes in each group are hierarchically related.
- What are the basic methods used for input and output operation.
- How files are created and opened for input and output operations.

- How **Reader** and **Writer** and their subclasses are used for handling characters in files.
- How **InputStream** and **OutputStream** and their subclasses are used for handling bytes in files.
- How primitive type data are read or written to files using **DataInputStream** and **DataOutputStream** classes.
- How the contents of two files are combined into a single file.
- How the buffers are used in input and output operations.
- How random access files are created and used for both reading and writing data.
- How to read data interactively from the keyboard and write to files.
- How to use windows and text fields to provide interactive graphical display while performing the input and output operations on files.

 ## Key Terms

Files, Persistent Data, Unicode, Secondary Storage, File Processing, Object Serialization, Records, Bytes, Fields, Stream, Source, Destination, Input Stream, Output Stream, Reader Stream, Writer Stream, Tokens, Concatenation, Buffering, Sequential File, Random Access File, File Pointer, Interactive Input, Graphical Interactive I/O, Windows, Text Fields, Pipes, Filters.

REVIEW QUESTIONS

16.1 What is a file? Why do we require files to store data?

16.2 What is a stream? How is the concept of streams used in Java?

16.3 What are input and output streams? Explain them with illustrations.

16.4 What is a stream class? How are the stream classes classified?

16.5 Describe the major tasks of input and output stream classes.

16.6 Distinguish between
  (a) InputStream and Reader classes
  (b) OutputStream and Writer classes

16.7 Describe the functions of the **File** class?

16.8 Describe the most commonly used classes for handling i/o related exceptions.

16.9 State the steps involved in creating a disk file.

16.10 What is meant by initializing a file stream object? What are the ways of doing it? Give example code for each of them.

16.11 Which streams must always be used to process external files? Why?

16.12 What is a random access file? How is it different from a sequential file? Why do we need a random access file?

16.13 Create a **DataInputStream** for the file named "student.dat".

16.14 Create a **RandomAccessFile** stream for the file "student.dat" for updating the student information in the file.

16.15 Write statements to create a file stream that concatenates two existing files.

16.16 Can we open an existing file for writing? If not, why?

16.17 How would you check whether a file to be opened for writing already exists?

16.18 While reading a file, how would you check whether you have reached the end of the file?

16.19 Write statements to create data streams for the following operations:
  (a) Reading primitive data from a file
  (b) Writing primitive data to a file

16.20 Describe, through appropriate statements, how a double type value is read from the keyboard interactively.

16.21 Write a program that will count the number of characters in a file.

16.22 Modify the above program so that it will also count the number of words, and lines in the file.

16.23 Rewrite Program 16.1 using the **FileInputStream** and **FileOutputStream** classes.

16.24 Rewrite Program 16.4 using the **FileReader** and **FileWriter** classes.

16.25 Write a program to create a sequential file that could store details about five products. Details include product code, cost, and number of items available and are provided through the keyboard.

16.26 Write a program to read the file created in Review Question 16.25 and compute and print the total value of all the five products.

16.27 Rewrite the program of Review Question 16.25 using a random access file so that we can add more products to the file, if necessary.

16.28 Write a program that will print the details of the alternate products stored in the random access file of Review Question 16.27.

DEBUGGING EXERCISES

16.1 Find errors in the following code which writes data of one file to another file.

```java
import java.io.*;
public class file1
{
    public static void main(String args[])
    {
        try
        {
            FileReader fr=new FileReader("in.dat");
            FileWriter fw=new FileWriter("out.dat");
            int ch;
            while((ch=fr.read())!=-1)
            {
                fr.write(ch);
            }
        }
        catch(Exception ex)
        {
            System.out.println(ex);
        }
    }
}
```

16.2 Debug the following code for reading a file using FileInputStream class.

```java
import java.io.*;
class file2
{
    public static void main(String args[])
    {
```

```
            if (args.length ==1)
            {
                try
                {
                    FileInputStream fstream = new FileInputStream(args[0]);
                    DataInputStream in = new DataInputStream();

                    while (in.available() !=0)
                    {
                        System.out.println(in.readLine());
                    }
                  in.close();
                }
                catch (Exception e)
                {
                    System.err.println("File input Error");
                }
            }
        else
            System.out.println()"Invalid parameters");
        }
    }
```

16.3 Find the compile-time error in the program given below.

```
import java.io.*;
class FileOutput
{
    public static void main(String args[])
    {
        FileOutputStream out;
        PrintStream p;
        try
        {
            out = new FileOutputStream();
            p = new PrintStream( out );
            p.println ("This is written to a file");

            p.close();
        }
        catch (Exception e)
        {
            System.err.println ("Error writing to file");
        }
    }
}
```

16.4 The program throws an exception. Correct the code to make it run successfully.

```java
import java.io.*;
public class randomAccess
{
    public static void main(Strinjg[] args) throws IOException
    {
        RandomAccessFile raf = new RandomAccessFile("random.text",
"rwasd");
        try
        {
            Writer out = new OutputStreamWriter(new
            FileOutputStream(raf.getFD()), "UTF-8");

            out.write("Programming in C");
            out.flush();

            raf.seek(12);
            out.write("Java");
            out.flush();
        }
        finally
        {
            raf.close();
        }
    }
}
```

16.5 Correct the code for reading a file byte by byte.

```java
import java.io.*;
class ByteRead
{
    public static void main(String args[]) throws IO Exception
    {
        int i;
        FileInputStream fin=new FileInputStream("c:\\input.text");
        do
        {
            i=fin.readByte();
            System.out.println((char)i);
        }
        while(i != -1);

        fin.close()
        fin = null;
    }
}
```

Chapter **17**

Assertion and Design by Contract

17.1   Introduction

The concept of Design By Contract (DBC) was first introduced in the Eiffel programming language. This technique specifies the interaction between various components of an application. To achieve this, it defines a contract, based on which the components of the application communicate with each other. The DBC technique uses assertions to check whether the application meets the requirements specified in the defined contract. These assertions can be used to test the assumptions made by a programmer in the Java programming language. In this chapter, we will discuss the concept of design by contract and assertion.

17.2   Design by Contract

The design by contract technique allows a programmer to provide a detailed specification to create a software according to the user requirements. Based on this specification, the programmer develops the software. DBC technique uses three types of assertions to check whether the software complies with the specification. The three types of assertions are:

- **Precondition:** An application must satisfy this specified condition before calling an external component.
- **Postcondition:** An application must satisfy this specified condition after the execution of the external component.
- **Invariant:** The application must always satisfy this specified condition.

For example, consider the operation of a stack that uses precondition, postcondition, and invariant assertions. When we need to extract an element from a stack, the stack should not be empty. This condition is checked before extracting an element from a stack. This type of condition is referred to as *precondition*. When we push an element into the stack, we need to check whether the element is correctly added to the specified index. This type of condition is referred to as *postcondition*. The number of elements in the stack is greater than or equal to zero and should not exceed the capacity of the stack. This type of condition is referred to as *invariant*.

17.3　Implementing Assertion

An assertion is a statement, which contains a Boolean expression that the programmer assumes to be true. If the result of the Boolean expression is true, the program execution continues. Here, the assertion ensures that the assumptions made by the programmer are correct and free from errors. If the result of the Boolean expression is false, the **AssertionError** exception will be thrown. This exception contains error information, such as file name and the line number in which the error has occurred in the program.

We use the assert statement to implement assertions in Java programs. The assert statement can be represented in two forms. One of the forms is:

```
assert Expression1;
```

Expression1 is a Boolean expression. If the result of the Boolean expression is false, the AssertionError exception is thrown without any information about the bugs that occurred in the program. Another form of the assert statement is:

```
assert Expression1 : Expression2;
```

Expression1 is a Boolean expression and Expression2 is a value, which is passed to the constructor of the **AssertionError** exception. The following code illustrates the use of the assert statement:

```
public void division()
{
double c=a/b;  //  b cannot be zero
}
```

In the above code, the comment line, "b cannot be equal to zero" can be replaced by using the assert statement, as shown below:

```
public void division()
{
assert b!=0;
double c=a/b;
}
```

If the expression in the assert statement is false, it specifies that the program contains errors and this process is referred to as assertion failure.

The value of the Expression2 in the second form must be a non-void expression. Consider the following example:

```
assert age>0 : "The age of a person should not be less than zero";
```

where, age>0 is a Boolean expression. The second expression in the assert statement is a String value and it is passed to the constructor of the **AssertionError** exception. If the assertion failure occurs, the string value acts as additional information about the errors that arise in the program.

Often readers may get confused with the usage of assertion and exception. The difference between the exception and assertion is:

- Exception is used to test the abnormal conditions, such as division by zero, ArrayIndexOutOf BoundsException occurred while executing the program and it does not ensure that the program is running correctly.
- Assertion is used to test the condition assumed by the programmer, and it ensures that the program is running correctly.

Compiling the Assert Statement

As we know, we use the following command to compile a Java program:

```
javac filename.java
```

The above command does not compile the programs that contain the assert statement. Therefore, we need to use the following command to compile the programs that use the assert statement:

```
java -source 1.4 filename.java
```

Enabling and Disabling Assertions

Java provides the command line parameters to enable and disable assertions. The syntax of using the command line parameter to enable assertion is:

```
-ea or -enableassertions
```

For example, the command used to run the Java file, Myfile.java, which enables assertion is:

```
java -enableassertions Myfile.java
```

Or

```
java -ea Myfile.java
```

The syntax of using the command line parameter to disable assertion is:

```
-da or disableassertions
```

For example, the command used to run the Java file, Myfile.java, which disables assertion is:

```
java -disableassertions Myfile.java
```

Or

```
java -da Myfile.java
```

17.4   Assertion Rules

Assertion is used to check the validity of an assumption, which is made by a programmer at the time of execution. There are certain rules that govern the usage of assertions in a program. The assertion rules are:

- Check the method arguments
- Use assertion in the default case of the Switch statement
- Make use of an assertion descriptive
- Avoid processing in an assertion condition
- Avoid catching assertion related exception
- Avoid the use of evaluating more than one condition in an assertion

Checking the Method Arguments

We need to check the values passed to the arguments of a method before performing any operation on these values. We check the argument values in the methods, public or protected, or the local package. For example, consider the following program to add two positive numbers.

```
public void addition(int a, int b)
{
   int c=a+b;
}
```

In the above code, the user may provide a negative value of the arguments that results in an inaccurate solution. Therefore, we need to check whether the values of the arguments are positive before performing the addition operation. The following code satisfies the first rule of assertion:

```
public void addition(int a, int b)
{
   if(a>0)
   {
     if(b>0)
     int c=a+b;
   }
}
```

Using Assertion in the Default Case of the Switch Statement

We can use assertions in the switch statement with no default case. In such cases, we add the default case to specify the assert statement. If none of the conditions are satisfied in the switch case and the assertion is enabled, the application causes the assertion failure and throws **AssertionError** exception.

For example, consider the following example:

```
public String Number()
{
String code;
String description;
```

```
        if (number >0)
        code="POSITIVE";
        IF(number<0)
        code="NEGATIVE";
        switch(code)
        {
        case POSITIVE:
        description="The Number is Positive"
        break;
        case NEGATIVE:
        description="The Number is Negative";
        break;
        default:
        assert false : "Unknown code" + code;
        }
        assert(description!= null) : "Provide description";
        return description;
        }
```

In the above code, we use the **assert** statement in the default case. This statement will be executed if the variable **code** does not match with any of the specified cases.

Make Use of an Assertion Descriptive

We need to provide a descriptive string message in an assert statement. It enables a programmer to understand the type of error in case the assertion failure occurs.

A program can contain a number of assert statements. If an assert statement does not contain description, the programmer cannot identify the error easily when the assertion failure occurs. For example, consider the following code segment, which contains an assert statement without description:

```
public void setName()
{
    if(name == null)
    throw new IllegalArgumentException();
}
private void setName()
{
    assert (name != null)
    ..........
}
```

In the above code, the assert statement does not contain the description. When the assertion fails, the programmer is not able to equate the error against the assertion. Therefore, the above code is rewritten as:

```
public void setName()
{
    if(name == null)
```

```
    throw new IllegalArgumentException("name cannot be null");
}
private void setName()
{
    assert (name != null) : "name cannot be null"
    . . . . . . . . . .
}
```

In the above code, if the assert statement fails, the message "name cannot be null" is reported to the programmer.

Avoid Processing in an Assertion Condition

When an assertion is disabled, JVM does not execute the assert statement. Therefore, the operation to be processed or performed in the assertion statement is not executed. For example, consider the following code:

```
        assert list.remove("Element") : " The assertion was not in the list";
```

This is an assert statement and the assertion is disabled. Therefore, "Element" is not removed from the list. We can rewrite the above code as:

```
        boolean stprocessed=list.remove("Element");
        assert stprocessed : " The Element was not in the list";
```

Avoid Catching Assertion Related Exception

The act of catching exceptions related to the assertion may discard the assertion and design by contract mechanism. Some of the assertion related exceptions are **AssetError** and **IllegalArgumentException.** Consider the following example of catching the IllegalArgumentException:

```
public void NamingInformation()
{
try
{
setName(null)
{
catch(IllegalArgumentException e)
{
}
}
public void setName(String name)
{
if(name==null)
{
throw new IllegalArgumentException("name cannot be null");
}
this.name = name;
}
```

The above code throws the IllegalArgumentException exception which arises when the name is specified as null.

Avoid Evaluating more than one Condition in an Assert Statement

We need to avoid using more than one condition in an assert statement. When we use more than one condition in an assert statement it may be difficult to find which of the conditions is not satisfied. For example, consider the following code which uses more than one condition in an assert statement:

```
public void setname(String firstName, String lastname)
{
  if((firstName==null)||(lastName==null))
  {
    throw new IllegalArgumentException("firstName or lastName cannot be null");
  }
}
private void setname(String firstName, String lastName)
{
  assert (firstName != null ) && ( lastName != null) : "FirstName or LastName cannot
  be null";
  ..........
  ..........
}
```

In the above code, if one of the conditions fails, it is difficult for the programmer to identify which of the assumptions causes failure. Therefore, the above code can be rewritten as:

```
public void setname(string firstName, String lastName)
{
if((firstName==null)
{
throw new IllegalArgumentException("firstName cannot be null");
}
if ((lastName=null)
{
throw new IllegalArgumentException("Last Name cannot be null");
}
}
private void setname(String firstName, String lastName)
{
assert (firstName != null ): "FirstName cannot be null";
assert(lastName != null): "Last name cannot be null";
..........

..........
}
```

17.5 Creating a Java Program Using Assertion

In this section, we will create a simple Java program to show the usage of assertion. This program helps the reader to implement assertion. For example, consider the division of two numbers as shown in Program 17.1. Here, the assert statement uses the assumption that the divisor should not be zero.

Program 17.1 *Using Assertion*

```
public class division
{
  void assertcheck(int a, int b)
  {
    assert b!=0: "The value b cannot be zero";
    double c=a/b;
    System.out.println("The result is "+c);
  }
  public static void main(String args[])
  {
    division div=new division();
    div.assertcheck(5, 0);
  }
}
```

When we compile and run the above program, the **assertcheck( )** method is called and value of the argument is passed to the parameters **a** and **b**. The value of **b** should be checked using the **assert** statement. If the assertion fails, the control will be transferred to the expression2 in the assert statement. Here, the control will not be transferred to the next statement after the assert statement. The output of the above program is:

The value **b** cannot be zero.

DEBUGGING EXERCISES

17.1 Find the compile-time error in the following program for dividing two numbers:

```
public class divide
{
    void division(int first, int second)
    {
        assert second: "The second value cannot be zero";
        double result=first/second;
        System.out.println("The result is " + result);
    }
    public static void main(String args[])
    {
```

```
                divide d=new divide();
                d.division(10, 2);
        }
}
```

Ans: The first expression passed to assert statement should return a Boolean value. In the above code, it is returning an int value, which will result in a compile-time error.

```
public class divide
{
        void division(int first, int second)
        {
                assert second!=0: "The second value cannot be zero";
                double result=first/second;
                System.out.println("The result is " + result);
        }
        public static void main(String args[])
        {
                divide d=new divide();
                d.division(10, 2);
        }
}
```

17.2 Debug the following code for checking negative values using the assert statement.

```
public class CheckNegative
{
        public void CheckAssert(int value)
        {
                assert 0 <= value ; "Value must be non-negative: value= " + value;
                System.out.println("OK");
        }
        public static void main( String[] args )
        {
                CheckNegative cn = new CheckNegative();
                System.out.print("cn.CheckAssert(2): ");
                cn.CheckAssert(2);
                System.out.print("cn.CheckAssert(-2): ");
                cn.CheckAssert(-2);
        }
}
```

Ans: The correct syntax for assert statement is *assert Expression1 : Expression2;* Replace ; with : in the above code to compile and run the program successfully.

```
public class CheckNegative
{
        public void CheckAssert(int value)
        {
                assert 0 <= value : "Value must be non-negative: value= " + value;
                System.out.println("OK");
```

```
        }
        public static void main(String[] args)
        {
                CheckNegative cn = new CheckNegative();
                System.out.print("cn.CheckAssert(2): ");
                cn.CheckAssert(2);
                System.out.print("cn.CheckAssert(-2): ");
                cn.CheckAssert(-2);
        }
}
```

17.3 On running the command *java –ea –da:superEx sub* for executing the program, what will be output of the program?.

```
class superEx
{
        public void check(boolean test)
        {
                assert test : "Assertion failed: test is " + test;
                System.out.println("OK");
        }
}
public class sub extends superEx
{
        public void checkTest(boolean test)
        {
                assert test : "Assertion failed: test is " + test;
                System.out.println("OK");
        }
        public static void printAssertionError(AssertionError ae)
        {
                StackTraceElement[] stackTraceElements = ae.getStackTrace();
                StackTraceElement stackTraceElement = stackTraceElements[ 0 ];
                System.err.println("AssertionError");
                System.err.println(" Class = " + stackTraceElement.getClassName());
                System.err.println(" Method = " + stackTraceElement.getMethodName());
                System.err.println(" Message= " + ae.getMessage());
        }
        public static void main(String[] args)
        {
                try
                {
                        sub subObj = new sub();
                        System.out.print("subObj.check( false ): ");
                        subObj.check(false);
                        System.out.print("subObj.checkTest( false ): ");
                        subObj.checkTest(false);
```

```
                }
                catch(AssertionError ae)
                {
                        printAssertionError(ae);
                }
        }
}
```

Ans: Assertions will be disabled for superEx class, but call to assertions in class sub will still be enabled. The output of the program will be:

```
subObj.check(false): OK
subObj.checkTest(false): AssertionError
    Class = sub
    Method = checkTest
    Message = Assertion failed: test is false
```

17.4 Correct the code for checking the value given in the code to make it run successfully.

```
public class ErrorCheck
{
        public static void main (String [ ] args)
        {
                try
                {
                        AssertValue ( ) ;
                }
                catch (AssertError error)
                {
                        error.printStackTrace ( );
                }
        }
        public static int AssertValue ( )
        {
                int value = 2;
                assert value!= 2 : "Value given is 2.";
                return value;
        }
}
```

Ans: assert statement throws an AssertionError error, instead of AssertError.

```
public class ErrorCheck
{
        public static void main (String [ ] args)
        {
                try
                {
                        AssertValue ( );
                }
                catch (AssertionError error)
```

```
                {
                        error.printStackTrace ( );
                }
        }
        public static int AssertValue ( )
        {
                int value = 2;
                assert value!= 2 : "Value given is 2.";
                return value;
        }
}
```

17.5 In the following program what condition will throw the java.lang.AssertionError error?

```
class Withdraw
{
        public static void main(String args[])
        {
                System.out.println(withdrawAmount(5000,1000));
                System.out.println(withdrawAmount(2000,3000));
        }
        public static double withdrawAmount(double balance , double amount)
        {
                assert balance >= amount;
                return balance - amount;
        }
}
```

Ans: withdrawAmount(2000,3000) will throw the java.lang.AssertionError error because balance is lesser than the amount to be withdrawn, so the assertion will fail.

Chapter **18**

Java Collections

18.1   Introduction

The *collections framework* which is contained in the **java.util** package is one of Java's most powerful sub-systems. The collections framework defines a set of interfaces and their implementations to manipulate collections, which serve as a container for a group of objects such as a set of words in a dictionary or a collection of mails. The collections framework also allows us to store, retrieve, and update a set of objects. It provides an API to work with the data structures, such as lists, trees, maps, and sets. In this chapter, we shall discuss the interfaces, classes, and algorithms available in the collections framework.

18.2   Overview of Interfaces

The collections framework contains many interfaces, such as Collection, Map, and Iterator. Other interfaces of the framework extend these interfaces. The interfaces available in the collections framework can be structured as shown in Fig. 18.1. The interfaces List and Set are the subinterfaces of the Collection interface. The SortedMap interface is the subinterface of the Map interface. The ListIterator interface is the subinterface of the Iterator interface. Brief description of these interfaces is provided in Table 18.1.

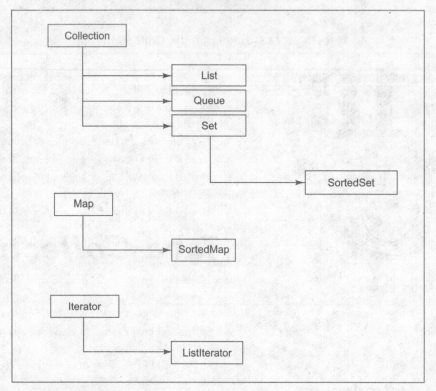

Fig. 18.1 *Interfaces defined in the Collections Framework*

Table 18.1 Description of Interfaces

Interface	Description
Collection	collection of elements.
List(extends Collection)	sequence of elements.
Queue (extends Collection)	special type of list
Set(extends Collection)	collection of unique elements.
SortedSet(extends Set)	sorted collection of unique elements.
Map	collection of key and value pairs, which must be unique.
SortedMap(extends Map)	sorted collection of unique key value pairs.
Iterator	object used to traverse through a collection.
ListIterator (extends Iterator)	object used to traverse through the sequence.

The Collection Interface

All collection classes must implement the Collection interface. The Collection interface defines some methods, which enable us to access the objects of a collection. Table 18.2 describes these methods.

Table 18.2   Methods Defined in the Collection Interface

Methods	Description
add(object o)	Returns true if the object is added to the specified collection.
addAll(collection c)	Returns true if the entire object in the collection is added to the specified collection.
clear()	Removes all elements from the specified collection.
contains(object o)	Returns true if the collection contains the specified element.
containsAll(collection c)	Returns true if the collection contains all the elements in the specified collection.
equals(object o)	Returns true if the specified object matches with the object in the collection.
hashCode()	Returns the hashcode for the collection.
isEmpty()	Return true if the collection is empty.
iterator()	Returns an iterator over the elements in the collection.
remove(object o)	Returns true, if the specified element is present in the collection and removes the object from the collection.
removeAll(collection c)	Returns true, if all the elements in collection c is removed from the specified collection.
retainAll(collection c)	Returns true, if all the elements in Collection c is retained in the specified collection.
size()	Returns the number of elements in the collection.
toArray()	Returns an array containing all of the elements in the collection.
toArray(object[] a)	Returns an array of object if the array contains all the elements in the specified collection.

The methods, **add( )**, **addAll( )**, and **remove( )** that modify the collection objects, will throw an exception, **UnsupportedOperationException**, when the collection does not support the respective operation. The methods of the Collection interface will throw the **ClassCastException** exception, when we add an incompatible element to a collection. For example, some collections may not support null elements.

The Set Interface

The Set interface extends the Collection interface and it contains the methods that are inherited from the Collection interface. The Set interface does not allow the use of duplicate elements in a collection. Hence, the **add( )** method returns false, if we add the duplicate element to the collection.

The List Interface

The List interface contains an ordered sequence of elements available in a collection. It allows duplicate elements in the List. The List interface inherits the methods of the Collection interface. In addition to these methods the List interface also contains the methods described in Table 18.3.

Table 18.3 Methods Defined in the List Interface	
Method	*Description*
add (int index, object o)	Adds the element, o in the specified index of the list.
addAll (int index, collection c)	Adds all the elements of collection, c in the specified index of the list.
get (int index)	Returns the element available in the specified index of the list.
indexOf (object o)	Returns the index of object o in the list. If there are more than one occurrence of object o, the method returns the index of the first occurrence. If the object o is not available in the list, the method returns –1.
lastIndexOf (object o)	Returns the last index of the object o in the list. If the object o is not available in the list, the method returns –1.
listIterator ()	Returns a list iterator of the elements.
listIterator (int index)	Returns a list iterator of the elements starting from the specified index of a list.
remove (int index)	Removes the element at the specified index of the list.
set (int index, object o)	Replaces the element in the specified index with the specified element.
subList (int startindex, int endindex)	Returns the elements available from the specified startindex to the endindex.

The SortedSet Interface

The SortedSet interface is used to sort the elements of a collection in ascending order. The SortedSet interface extends the Set interface, which in turn extends the Collection interface. The SortedSet interface does not allow duplicate elements in a set. In addition to the methods defined by the Set interface, the SortedSet interface contains the methods listed in Table 18.4.

Table 18.4 Methods Defined in the SortedSet Interface	
Methods	*Description*
comparator()	Returns the comparator object. If the elements in the SortedSet are in ascending order then it returns null.
first()	Returns the first element from the SortedSet.
headset(Object toElement)	Returns the number of elements less than that of the elements specified using the toElement object. The elements are returned from the sorted set.
last()	Returns the last element from the SortedSet.
subSet(Object FromElement, Object ToElement)	Returns the elements between the range specified by the objects, FromElement and ToElement. Here the returned set includes the FromElement and excludes the ToElement.
tailSet(Object FromElement)	Returns the elements from a sorted set that are greater than or equal to the FromElement.

The Queue Interface

The Queue interface extends Collection interface and declares the behaviour of a queue, which is often a first-in, first-out list. In a queue, elements can only be removed from the head of the queue. The Queue interface defines a few methods as listed in Table 18.5.

Table 18.5   Methods Defined in Queue

Methods	Description
element( )	Returns the element at the head of the queue. The element is not removed.
offer(Object o)	Attempts to add an element to the queue. Returns true if added, false otherwise.
peek( )	Returns the element at the head of the queue. The element is not removed.
poll( )	Returns the element at the head of the queue after removing the element.
remove( )	Returns the element at the head of the queue after removing the element.

Note: 1. The mothods **element()** and **peek( )** are similar but, if the queue is empty, **element( )** throws the exception **NoSuchElementException** while **peek( )** returns **null**.
2. The methods **poll( )** and **remove( )** perform the same job but, when the queue is empty, **poll( )** returns **null** while **remove( )** throws the exception **NoSuchElementException**.

The Map Interface

The Map interface maps unique key elements to their values. For example, in a mail server, each mail id is mapped to a unique password. The Map interface allows us to view the elements of a collection as set of keys, collection of values, and the mappings of key-value pairs. Table 18.6 describes the methods of the Map interface.

Table 18.6   Methods Defined in the Map Interface

Methods	Description
clear()	Removes all the mappings from a map.
containsKey(Object key)	Returns true if a map contains mapping for the specified key.
containsValue(Object value)	Returns true if the specified value maps with one or more key in a map interface.
entrySet()	Returns the key-value pair contained in this map.
equals(Object o)	Returns true if the specified object maps with an object of a map interface.
get(Object key)	Returns the value, which is mapped to the specified key.
isEmpty()	returns true if a map contains no key-value mapping.
keySet()	Returns the keys in a map. If we remove a key from the map, the corresponding value will also be removed.

(Continued)

Table 18.6   (*Continued*)

put(Object key, Object value)	Maps the specified key with the specified value.
putAll(Map t)	Copied all the specified key value pair from a specified map to the map with which we are currently working.
remove(Object key)	Removes the specified key from the map.
size()	Returns the number of key-value mappings available in a map.

The SortedMap Interface

The SortedMap interface extends the Map Interface. The SortedMap interface contains elements in ascending order. In this, the sorting is based on the keys. The functionality of the SortedMap is analogous to the functionality of the SortedSet interface. This Map interface is implemented in the TreeMap class. Table 18.7 describes the methods of the SortedMap Interface.

Table 18.7   Methods Defined in the SortedMap Interface

Methods	*Description*
comparator()	Returns the comparator of the sorted map. It returns null, if the sorted map uses natural ordering for their keys.
firstKey()	Returns the first key of the sorted map.
headMap(Object end)	Returns the keys of the sorted map that are less than the specified end object.
lastKey()	Returns the last key of the sorted map.
subMap(Object start, Object end)	Returns the keys of the sorted map that are greater than or equal to the specified start object and less than are equal to the specified end object.
tailMap (Object start)	Returns the keys of the sorted map that are greater than or equal to the start object.

The Iterator Interface

The Iterator interface enables us to sequentially traverse and access the elements contained in a collection. The elements of a collection can be accessed using the methods defined by the Iterator interface. Table 18.8 describes the methods of the Iterator interface.

Table 18.8   Methods Defined in the Iterator Interface

Method	*Description*
hasNext()	Returns true if the collection contains more than one element.
next()	Returns the next element from the collection.
remove()	Remove the current element from the collection.

The **next( )** method of the Iterator interface returns the next element if it is available in the collection. If there is no such element in the collection, it will throw the exception **NoSuchElementException**. The **remove( )** method throws the exception **IllegalStateException** when there is no element in the collection. Using the Iterator interface, we can insert elements only at the end of a list. If we need to insert elements at the required location of the list, we should use the ListIterator interface, which extends the Iterator interface. The ListIterator interface contains a method named **add(int index, Object obj)**. This method allows us to add an element at the required location based on the index value.

18.3 Overview of Classes

The classes available in the collections framework implement the collection interface and the subinterfaces. These classes also implement the Map and Iterator interfaces. Table 18.9 lists out the classes and their corresponding implementations.

Table 18.9

Class	Name of the interface
AbstractCollection	Collection
AbstractList	List
AbstractQueue	Queue
AbstractSequentialList	List
LinkedList	List
ArrayList	List, Cloneable, and Serializable
AbstractSet	Set
EnumSet	Set
HashSet	Set
PriorityQueue	Queue
TreeSet	Set
Vector	List, Cloneable, and Serializable
Stack	List, Cloneable, and Serializable
Hashtable	Map, Cloneable, and Serializable

The AbstractCollection Class

The AbstractCollection class implements the Collection interface. Therefore it contains all the methods available in the Collection Interface. We use the AbstractCollection class to implement a collection, which cannot be modified. For example, a collection containing the months of a year cannot be modified.

We can also implement collection using the AbstractCollection class by overriding the **add(object o)** method and implementing the **remove (object o)** method. The constructor for this class is represented as:

```
Protected   AbstractCollection()
```

The AbstractList Class

The AbstractList class extends the AbstractCollection class and implements the List interface. We use the AbstractList class to access the data randomly. For example, we can use the index values to access the elements of an array at random. The Constructor for this class is represented as:

```
Protected AbstractList( )
```

The AbstractList class extends the methods, such as **add(Object o)**, **clear()**, **iterator()** of the AbstractCollection class. It also inherits the methods from the List interface.

Note The AbstractSequentialList class is used to access the elements of an array sequentially.

The ArrayList Class

The ArrayList class extends the AbstractList class and implements the interfaces, such as List, Cloneable and Serializable. Using the ArrayList class, we can use dynamic array in Java applications. The dynamic array is an array in which the array size is not fixed in advance. Therefore, we can change the size of an array at run time using the ArrayList class. Every instance of the ArrayList class is allowed to store a set of elements in the list. The capacity increases automatically as we add elements to the list.

The constructor of the ArrayList takes three forms:

- **ArrayList():** Creates an empty list. The capacity of the list is initialized to ten.
- **ArrayList(Collection c):** Creates a list to which the elements of the specified collection are added.
- **ArrayList(int capacity):** Creates an empty list. The capacity of the list is initialized to the specified value.

The ArrayList class inherits the methods from the List interface. The elements of an array can be accessed directly using the **get()** and **set()** methods. The **add()** method is used to add an element to the array list and the **remove()** method is used to remove an element from the array list. Program 18.1 that illustrates the usage of the **add()** and **remove()** methods of the ArrayList class:

Program 18.1 *Using the methods of the ArrayList Class*

```java
import java.util.*;
public class ArrayListExample
{
  public static void main(String args[])
  {
    ArrayList arraylist=new ArrayList();
    System.out.println("Initial size of arraylist" +arraylist.size());
    arraylist.add("A");
    arraylist.add("B");
    arraylist.add("C");
    arraylist.add("D");
    System.out.println("Size of arraylist after adding the element"+ arraylist.size());
    System.out.println("Contents of arraylist"+arraylist);
    arraylist.add(2, "E");
    System.out.println("changed contents of arraylist by adding element at
                 the given index: "+arraylist);
```

(*Continued*)

Program 18.1 (*Continued*)

```
arraylist.remove(3);
arraylist.remove("A");
System.out.println("Changed contents of arraylist by removing element from
                   the list: "+arraylist);
    }
}
```

The output of Program 18.1 is:

```
Initial size of arraylist 0
Size of arraylist after adding the element 4
Contents of arraylist[A, B, C, D]
Changed contents of arraylist by adding element at the given index: [A, B,
E, C, D]
Changed contents of arraylist by removing element from the list: [B, E, D]
```

The LinkedList Class

The LinkedList class extends the AbstractSequentialList class and implements the List interface. This class supports the methods shown in Table 18.10.

These methods allow us to insert and remove elements in a list. We can use the list as a stack, queue, and doubly linked list. The constructor of the LinkedList class are:

- **LinkedList()**
- **LinkedList(Collection c)**

Table 18.10   Some of the Methods Supported by the LinkedList Class

Methods	Description
addFirst(Object obj)	Adds the specified element to the first position of the list.
addLast(Object obj)	Used to add element at last of the list.
getFirst()	Used to get the element at first from the list.
getLast()	Used to get the element at last from the list.
removeFirst()	Used to remove the element at first from the list.
removeLast()	Used to remove the element at last from the list.

Program 18.2 illustrates the usage of methods supported by the LinkedList class:

Program 18.2   *Using the methods of the LinkedList Class*

```
import java.util.*;
public class MyStack
{
  private LinkedList list = new LinkedList();
  public void push1(Object o)
  {
```

Program 18.2 _(Continued)_

```
        list.addFirst(o);
    }
    public void push2 (Object obj)
    {
        list.addLast(obj);
    }
    public Object bottom()
    {
        return list.getLast();
    }
    public Object pop()
    {
        return list.removeFirst();
    }
    public static void main(Strings args[])
    {
        Car myCar;
        Bird myBird;
        MyStack s = new MyStack();
        s.push1 (new Car());
        s.push2(new Bird());
        myCar = (Car)s.pop();
        System.out.println("The first element in the list: "+myCar);
        myBird=(Bird)s.bottom();
        System.out.println("The last element in the list: "+myBird);
    }
}
class Car
{
    String car1, car2, car3, car4;
    Car()
    {
        car1="Benz";
        car2="Toyoto";
        car3="Qualis";
        car4="Santro";
    }
}
class Bird
{
    String bird1, bird2, bird3;
    Bird()
    {
```

Program 18.2 (*Continued*)

```
        bird1="parrot";
        bird2="duck";
        bird3="raven";
    }
}
```

The output of Program 18.2 is:

```
The first element in the list: Benz
The last element in the list: raven
```

The HashSet Class

The HashSet class extends the AbstractSet class and implements the Set interface. The AbstractSet class itself extends the AbstractCollection class. The HashSet class is used to create a collection and store it in a hash table. Each collection refers to a unique value called hash code. The hash code is used as an index to associate with the object, which is stored in the hash table. This type of storing information in a hash table is called *hashing*. Constructors for the HashSet class are:

- **HashSet():** Constructs an empty HashSet.
- **HashSet(Collection c):** Initializes the HashSet using the element c
- **HashSet(int capacity):** Initializes the capacity of the HashSet
- **HashSet(int capacity, float fillratio):** Initializes the capacity and the fill ratio of the HashSet.

The value of the fill ratio ranges from 0.0 to 1.0. This value is used to set the initial size of the hash set. If the number of elements is greater than the capacity of the hash set, the size of the hash set is expanded automatically by multiplying the capacity with the fill ratio. The default value of the fill ratio is 0.75.

The HashSet class inherits the methods of its parent classes and the methods of the implemented interface. Program 18.3 illustrates the use of methods of the HashSet class. It is important to note that **HashSet** does not guarantee the order of its elements. Elements may be stored in any order.

Program 18.3 *Using the methods of the HashSet Class*

```
import java.util.*;
class HashSetExample
{
    public static void main(String args[])
    {
        HashSet hs=new HashSet();
        hs.add("D")
        hs.add("A");
        hs.add("C");
        hs.add("B");
        hs.add("E");
        System.out.println("The elements available in the hash set are: "+hs);
    }
}
```

The output of Program 18.3 is:

```
        The elements available in the hash set are: [D, A, C, B, E]
```

The TreeSet Class

The TreeSet Class implements the Set interface. The sorted elements are stored in a tree structure. This class allows us to access and retrieve the elements from a tree in less time. The constructor for the TreeSet class can take the following forms:

- **TreeSet( ):** Builds an empty tree set. This empty constructor will sort the elements in ascending order.
- **TreeSet(Collection c):** Builds a tree set, which contains a collection of elements.
- **TreeSet(Comparator comp):** Builds a tree set based on the specified comparator.
- **TreeSet(SortedSet s):** Builds a tree set, which contains elements in the specified order.

Program 18.4 illustrates the usage of the TreeSet class.

Program 18.4 *Using the TreeSet Class*

```
import java.util.*;
public class TreeSetExample
{
  public static void main(String args[])
  {
    TreeSet ts=new TreeSet();
    Ts.add("B");
    Ts.add("C");
    Ts.add("A");
    Ts.add("E");
    Ts.add("D");
    System.out.println("The elements in the TreeSet are: "+ ts);
  }
}
```

The output of Program 18.4 is:

        The elements in the TreeSet are: [A, B, C, D, E]

Note that the elements are automatically arranged in sorted order.

The Vector Class

The Vector class extends the AbstractList class and implements the interfaces, such as List, Cloneable, and Serializable. The Vector class is similar to the ArrayList class except that the Vector class is synchronized. As the Vector class is synchronized, multiple threads cannot access the vector objects simultaneously. Only one thread can access the Vector object at the specific time. The Vector class implements the dynamic array. The constructors of the Vector class are:

- **Vector():** Serves as a default constructor with an array size of 10.
- **Vector(int size):** Builds a vector with the specified size.
- **Vector(int size, int increment):** Builds a vector of the specified size. The specified increment value is used to increase the size of the vector. If the increment value is not specified, then the size of the vector is doubled for each allocation.
- **Vector(Collection c):** Builds a vector that consists of elements available in the specified collection c.

Table 18.11 illustrates the methods and the task performed by these methods of the Vector class:

Table 18.11   Methods Defined in the Vector Class

Methods	Description
addElement(Object element)	Adds the specified element to the end of the vector and increments the size of the vector by one.
capacity()	Returns the current capacity of the vector.
contains(Object element)	Returns true if the specified object is present in the vector.
containsAll(Collection c)	Returns true if the vector contains all the elements specified in the collection.
elementAt(int index)	Returns an element at the specified index.
ensureCapacity(int minimumcapacity)	Sets the specified minimum capacity to the size of the vector.
get(int index)	Returns the object, which is available in the specified position of the vector.
setElementAt(Object e,int index)	Replaces the element at the specified index with specified element.
setSize(int newsize)	Sets the size of the vector to the specified size, newsize.
size()	Returns the size of the vector.
toString()	Return a String representation of this vector.

Program 18.5   *Example of using the Vector Class*

```java
import java.util.Iterator;
import java.util.Vector;
public class VectorExample
{
  public static void main(String[] args)
  {
    Vector fruits = new Vector();
    fruits.add("Apple");
    fruits.add("Orange");
    fruits.add("Grapes");
    fruits.add("Pine");

    Iterator it = fruits.iterator();
    while(it.hasNext())
        System.out.println(it.next());
  }
}
```

The output of Program 18.5 is:

```
Apple
Orange
Grapes
Pine
```

The Stack Class

The Stack class extends the Vector class. In addition to the inherited methods from the Vector class, the Stack class contains some methods to perform operations, such as push, pop, peek, and search. The constructor of Stack class can be represented as:

```
Stack()
```

The above constructor is used to create an empty stack. The Stack class uses the First In Last Out (FILO) mechanism. Table 18.12 describes some of the methods of the Stack class:

Table 18.12　Methods Defined in the Stack Class

Methods	Description
empty()	Returns true if the stack is empty.
peek()	Returns the element at the top of the Stack.
pop()	Removes the element at the top of the Stack and returns the element that is removed from the Stack.
push()	Adds an item to the top of the Stack.

For example, consider the Program 18.6 that adds string values to a stack.

Program 18.6　*Example of using the Stack Class*

```java
import java.util.*;
public class stackex
{
  public static void main(String args[])
  {
    Stack st=new Stack();
    st.push("Java");
    st.push("latest");
    st.push("Edition");
    st.push("-fifth");
    System.out.println("The elements in the Stack: "+st);
    System.out.println("The element at the top: "+st.peek());
    System.out.println("The element poped out of the stack: "+st.pop());
    System.out.println("The element in a stack after pop out an element: "+st);
    System.out.println("The result of searching: "+st.search("r u"));
  }
}
```

The output of Program 18.6 is:

```
The element in the Stack: [Java, latest, Edition, -fifth]
The element at the top: -fifth
The element popped out of the Stack: -fifth
The element in a stack after pop out an element: [Java, latest, Edition]
The result of searching: -1
```

The Hashtable Class

The Hashtable class implements the interfaces, such as Map, Cloneable, and Serializable. The hashtable is used to store values in the form of map key with value. The key should implement the hashcode and equals methods to store and retrieve values in a hashtable. The constructors of the Hashtable class are:

- **Hashtable():** Creates an empty hashtable with the default initial capacity as 11 and the loadFactor as 0.75.
- **Hashtable(int initialCapacity):** Creates an empty hashtable with the specified initial capacity and the default loadFactor.
- **Hashtable(int initialCapacity, float loadFactor):** Creates an empty hashtable, which has the specified initial capacity and loadFactor.
- **Hashtable(Map m):** Creates a new hashtable with the specified map.

Program 18.7   *Using the Hashtable Class*

```
import java.util.Enumeration;
import java.util.Hashtable;
public class HashTableExample
{
  public static void main(String[] args)
  {
    Hashtable ht = new Hashtable();
    ht.put("Item1", "Apple");
    ht.put("Item2", "Orange");
    ht.put("Item3", "Grapes");
    ht.put("Item4", "Pine");
    Enumeration e = ht.keys();
    while(e.hasMoreElements())
    {
      String str = (String) e.nextElement();
      System.out.println(ht.get(str));
    }
  }
}
```

The output of the above program is:

```
Apple
Orange
Grapes
Pine
```

18.4   Overview of Algorithms

The collections framework supports several algorithms that allow us to operate on collections. We can use these algorithms to sort, shuffle, manipulate, and search a set of elements in a collection. Some of the algorithms available in the collections framework are:

- Sorting
- Shuffling
- Manipulating
- Searching

These algorithms are contained in the Collections class. Table 18.13 shows some algorithms defined in the Collection class.

Table 18.13   Algorithms Defined in the Collections Class

Methods	*Description*
binarySearch(Listl,Object v)	Searches the specified object in the specified list. It returns the position of the specified object in the list. If the specified object is not in the list, then it returns -1.
copy(List src, List dest)	Copies elements from one list to another.
disjoint(Collection c1, Collection c2)	Returns true if no common element is available in the two specified collections.
frequency(Collection c, Object o)	Returns the number of elements that equal to the specified object in the specified collection.
indexOfSubList(List src, List dest)	Returns the index of the first occurrence of the specified destination list in the specified source list and -1 if the source list does not contain the occurrence.
lastIndexOfSubList(List src, List dest)	Returns the index of the last occurrence of the specified destination list in the specified source list and -1 if the source list does not contain the occurrence.
replaceAll(List 1, old_val, new_val)	Replaces all occurrences of the old value in the list with the new value.
reverse(List 1)	Reverses the order of elements in the list.
shuffle(List 1, Random r)	Shuffles the elements in the list by using r as a source to generate random values.
swap(List1, index i1, index i2)	Interchanges the elements in the specified indexes of the list.

The Sort Algorithm

The sort algorithm enables us to arrange the elements of a list in a certain order. The ordering depends on the type of elements. If the list contains a set of string elements, the sorting is done alphabetically. If the list contains a set of numeric elements, the elements are arranged in ascending order.

The Shuffle Algorithm

The shuffle algorithm shuffles the elements of a list such that the current order of the list is destroyed. This algorithm arranges the elements using all possible permutations. For example, we can use this algorithm to shuffle objects in a memory game.

Manipulating Algorithms

The Collections class provides algorithms to perform operations, such as fill, reverse, copy, swap, and add on a list of elements on a collection. The reverse operation reverses the order of elements in the list. The fill operation replaces the elements of a list with a specified elements. The copy operation copies the elements of one list to another. The swap operation swaps the specified elements in a list. The addAll operation adds the specified elements to a list.

The Search Algorithm

The search algorithm allows us to search an element in a collection. Here we use the binary search algorithm. To find an element from a list, we need to traverse the entire list. We can use the binary search algorithm in a sorted list. The steps to find an element from a list using binary search algorithm are:

Step 1: Sort the elements in the collection.
Step 2: Find the middle element of the collection.
Step 3: Compare the specified element with the middle element of the collection.
Step 4: If the middle element is greater than the specified element, traverse the first half of the list.
Else traverse the second half of the list.

The **binarySearch()** method of the Collections class implement the binary search algorithm. We need to pass the collection and the element to be searched from the specified collection as arguments to the **binarySearch()** method.

If the element in the collection is not available in the sorted order, we need to pass the comparator as an additional argument to the **binarySearch()** method. This comparator is used to sort the elements of the collection according to the condition specified in the comparator.

Program 18.8 *Use of binarySearch method*

```
Import java.util.*;
Class algorithmdemo
{
  public static void main(String args[])
  {
    LinkedList l=new LinkedList();
    l.add(new String("Java"));
    l.add(new String("is"));
    l.add(new String("platform"));
    l.add(new String("Independent"));
    Comparator r=Collections.reverseOrder();
    Collections.sort(l, r);
    Iterator iter=l.iterator();
    System.out.println("List sorted in reverse order");
    While(iter.hasNext())
    System.out.println(iter.next() + "");
    Collections.shuffle(l);
    Iter= l.iterator();
    System.out.println("List shuffled : ");
    While(iter.hasNext())
    System.out.println(iter.next() + "");
    System.out.println();
    System.out.println("Minimum :" + Collections.min(l));
    System.out.println("Maximum: "+ Collection.max(l));
  }
}
```

The output for the above program is:

```
List sorted in reverse order: Java is platform independent
List shuffled:
Minimum: independent
Maximum: platform
```

DEBUGGING EXERCISES

18.1 The following code creates an object of List interface and adds and removes items from it. Will this code compile successfully?

```java
import java.util.*;
public class ListInterfaceExample
{
    public static void main(String[] args)
    {
        List<String> list;
        list = new ArrayList<String>();
        list.add("a");
        list.add(0,"b");
        list.add(1,"c");
        list.add(1,"d");
        list.add(3,"d");
        System.out.println("List is "+list);
        int size = list.size();
        Object element = list.get(list.size()-1);
        System.out.println("Element at "+list.size()+" location is "+element);
        element = list.getItem(0);
        System.out.println("Element at 0 location is "+element);
        Collections.sort(list);
        Collections.sort(list, String.CASE_INSENSITIVE_ORDER);
        System.out.println("List after sort is "+list);
        boolean b = list.remove("c");
        element = list.delete(0);
        System.out.println("List after removal of c and 1st element "+list);
    }
}
```

Ans: No, list object does not contain any function with the name of getItem and delete.

```java
import java.util.*;
public class ListInterfaceExample
{
    public static void main(String[] args)
    {
        List<String> list;
        list = new ArrayList<String>();
        list.add("a");
        list.add(0,"b");
        list.add(1,"c");
        list.add(1,"d");
        list.add(3,"d");
        System.out.println("List is "+list);
```

```
        int size = list.size();
        Object element = list.get(list.size()-1);
        System.out.println("Element at "+list.size()+" location is "+element);
        element = list.get(0);
        System.out.println("Element at 0 location is "+element);
        Collections.sort(list);
        Collections.sort(list, String.CASE_INSENSITIVE_ORDER);
        System.out.println("List after sort is "+list);
        boolean b = list.remove("c");
        element = list.remove(0);
        System.out.println("List after removal of c and 1st element "+list);
    }
}
```

18.2 The following code will play with the objects of Set interface. Will this code compile successfully?

```
import java.util.*;
public class SetsExample
{
    public static void main(String[] args)
    {
        Set<String> set1 = new HashSet<String>();
        set1.add("a");
        set1.add("b");
        set1.add("c");
        System.out.println("Set1 is "+set1);
        set1.remove("c");
        System.out.println("Set1 after removing c is "+set1);
        int size = set1.size();
        System.out.println("Size of set1 is "+size);
        set1.add("a");
        size = set1.size();
        System.out.println("Size of set1 after adding duplicate item is "+size);
        boolean b = set1.isContains("a");
        System.out.println("Is Set1 contains a "+b);
        System.out.println("Is Set1 contains c "+set1.contains("c"));
        Set<String> set2 = new HashSet<String>();
        set2.add("e");
        set2.add("d");
        set2.add("f");
        System.out.println("Set2 is "+set2);
        set2.add(set1);
        System.out.println("Set2 is after merging set1 elements"+set2);
        set2.removeAll(set1);
        System.out.println("Set2 is after deleting set1 elements"+set2);
        set2.addAll(set1);
```

```
            set2.retainAll(set1);
            System.out.println("Set2 is after deleting all elements except set1
            elements"+set2);
        }
}
```

Ans: No, there is no function with the name of isContains in set interface and add function does not add a complete set into another set. Add function only add a single element in a set.

```java
import java.util.*;
public class SetsExample
{
        public static void main(String[] args)
        {
            Set<String> set1 = new HashSet<String>();
            set1.add("a");
            set1.add("b");
            set1.add("c");
            System.out.println("Set1 is "+set1);
            set1.remove("c");
            System.out.println("Set1 after removing c is "+set1);
            int size = set1.size();
            System.out.println("Size of set1 is "+size);
            set1.add("a");
            size = set1.size();
            System.out.println("Size of set1 after adding duplicate item is "+size);
            boolean b = set1.contains("a");
            System.out.println("Is Set1 contains a "+b);
            System.out.println("Is Set1 contains c "+set1.contains("c"));
            Set<String> set2 = new HashSet<String>();
            set2.add("e");
            set2.add("d");
            set2.add("f");
            System.out.println("Set2 is "+set2);
            set2.addAll(set1);
            System.out.println("Set2 is after merging set1 elements"+set2);
            set2.removeAll(set1);
            System.out.println("Set2 is after deleting set1 elements"+set2);
            set2.addAll(set1);
            set2.retainAll(set1);
            System.out.println("Set2 is after deleting all elements except set1
            elements"+set2);
        }
}
```

18.3 The following code will create a vector object and convert it to array. What will be the size and capacity of v after execution of this program?

```java
import java.util.*;
class VectorExample
{
    public static void main (String [ ] args)
    {
        Vector<String> v = new Vector<String>(15);
        int i;
        System.out.println("starting...");
        for( i=0;i<2;i++)
        {
            v.add(args[i]);
            System.out.println(args[i]+" added to vector");
        }
        System.out.println ("Converting to array");
        String[] list = new String[v.size()];
        v.copyInto(list);
        System.out.println ("Printing array");
        for (i=0;i < v.size ( );i++)
        {
            System.out.println ("Element at "+i+" location is "+ list [ i ]);
        }
    }
}
```

Ans: Size of the v will be 2 and the capacity of the v will be 15.

18.4 The following code will create a Hashtable object and add some values in it and add it into vector to perform sort using Collections.sort method. Will this code execute successfully? If yes, what will be the output of this?

```java
import java.util.*;
public class HashTableExamples
{
    public static void main(String[] s)
    {
        Hashtable<String,Integer> hash= new Hashtable<String,Integer> ( 4 );
        String ob = "ABC";
        Integer in = new Integer(563);
        hash.put (ob,in);
        ob= "XYZ";
        in = new Integer(129);
        hash.put ( ob ,in);
        ob = "MNO";
        in = new Integer (6564);
        hash.put (ob ,in);
        System.out.println(hash);
        Vector<String> v = new Vector<String>(hash.keySet());
```

```
        Collections.sort(v);
        for (Enumeration e = v.elements(); e.hasMoreElements();)
        {
            String key = (String)e.nextElement();
            Integer val = (Integer)hash.get(key);
            System.out.println("Key: " + key + " Val: " + val);
        }
    }
}
```

Ans: Yes, this will execute successfully and display sorted data on string values of hashtable.

18.5 The following code will create a String type array to perform binary search for word "Hello". Will this code compile successfully?

```
public class BinarySearchExample
{
    public int binarySearch(String[] sorted, String key)
    {
        int first = 0;
        int last = sorted.length;
        while (first < last)
        {
            int mid = (first + last) / 2;
            if (key.compareTo(sorted[mid]) < 0)
            {
                last = mid;
            }
            else if (key.compareTo(sorted[mid]) > 0)
            {
                first = mid + 1;
            }
            else
            {
                return mid;
            }
        }
        return -(first + 1);
    }
    public static void main(String[] args)
    {
        int i=binarySearch(args,"Hello");
        if(i<0)
            System.out.println("Not found");
        else
            System.out.println("Found at "+(i+1)+" location.");
    }
}
```

Ans: No, this will give a compile time error in function main which is referencing a non-static method binarySearch. binarySearch method should be static to call it from static function main without creating any object of this class.

```java
public class BinarySearchExample
{
    public static int binarySearch(String[] sorted, String key)
    {
        int first = 0;
        int last = sorted.length;
        while (first < last)
        {
            int mid = (first + last) / 2;
            if (key.compareTo(sorted[mid]) < 0)
            {
                last = mid;
            }
            else if (key.compareTo(sorted[mid]) > 0)
            {
                first = mid + 1;
            }
            else
            {
                return mid;
            }
        }
        return -(first + 1);
    }
    public static void main(String[] args)
    {
        int i=binarySearch(args,"Hello");
        if(i<0)
            System.out.println("Not found");
        else
            System.out.println("Found at "+(i+1)+" location.");
    }
}
```

Java Language Reference

Important Keywords

Data-declaration keywords:

byte	int	float	char	double

Loop keywords:

do	while	for	break	continue

Conditional keywords:

if	else	switch

Exception keywords:

throw	try	catch

Structure keywords:

class	extends	interface	implements

Access keywords:

public	private	protected

Specifying Character Literals		
Description or Escape Sequence	*Sequence*	*Output*
any character	'y'	y
backspace BS	'\b'	back space
Horizontal tab HT	'\t'	tab

(Continued)

Description or Escape Sequence	Sequence	Output
line feed LF	'\n'	linefeed
form feed FF	'\f'	form feed
carriage return CR	'\r'	carriage return
double quote	'\"'	` `` `
single quote	'\''	` `
backslash	'\\'	\
octal bit pattern	'0ddd'	(octal value of ddd)
hex bit pattern	'0xdd'	(hex value of dd)
Unicode character	'\dddd'	(actual Unicode character of dddd)

Arithmetic Operators

Operator	Operation	Example
+	Addition	x + y
–	Subtraction	x – y
*	Multiplication	x * y
/	Division	x / y
%	Modulus	x % y

Assignment Operators

Operator	Operation	Example	Meaning
+ =	add to current variable	x + = y	x = x + y
– =	subtract from current variable	x – = y	x = x – y
* =	multiply by current variable	x * = y	x = x * y
/ =	divide by current variable	x / = y	x = x / y

Increment and Decrement Operators

Operator	Operation	Example	Meaning
+ +	increment by 1	x + +	x = x + 1
– –	decrement by 1	x – –	x = x – 1

Comparison Operators (return true or false)

Operator	Operation	Example	Meaning
= =	Equal	x = = y	Is x equal to y?
! =	Not equal	x ! = y	Is x not equal to y?
<	Less than	x < y	Is x less than y?
>	Greater than	x > y	Is x greater than y?
< =	Less than or equal to	x < = y	Is x less than or equal to y?
> =	Greater than or equal to	x > = y	Is x greater than or equal to y?

Bitwise Operators

Operator	Operation
&	Bitwise AND
|	Bitwise OR
^	Bitwise XOR
< <	Left shift
> >	Right shift
> > >	Zero fill right shift
_	Bitwise complement
< < =	Left shift assignment
> > =	Right shift assignment
> > > =	Zero fill right shift assignment
x & = y	AND assignment
x | = y	OR assignment
x ^ = y	NOT assignment

Comment Indicators

Start	Text	End Comment
/ *	text	* /
/ **	text	* /
/ /	text	(everything to the end of the line is ignored by the compiler)

Primitive Data Type Keywords

```
boolean   char   byte   short   int   long   float   double
```

Integer Data Type Ranges

Type	Length	Minimum Value	Maximum Value
byte	8 bits	− 128	127
Short	16 bits	− 32768	32767
Int	32 bits	− 2147483648	2147483647
long	64 bits	− 9223372036854775808	9223372036854775807

Unary operators

Operator	Operation
−	Unary negation
~	Bitwise complement
+ +	Increment
− −	Decrement
!	Not

Operator Precedence

+ +	– –	!	~	instanceof	*
/	%	+	–	<<	>>
>>>	<	>	<=	>=	==
!=	&	^	&&	||	?:
=	op=				

Control Statements

Statement	*Example*
A simple if statement	`if   (booleanTest)` `    callfunction  ( );`

A multiline `if` statement	`if   (booleanTest)`
	`{`
	`    // set of statements`
	`}`

The `if...else` statement	`if  .(booleanTest)`
	`{`
	`    // True block statements`
	`}`
	`else`
	`{`
	`    // False block statements`
	`}`

The `while` statement	`while   (booleanTest)`
	`{`
	`    // Loop statements`
	`}`

The `do...while` loop	`do`
	`{`
	`    // Loop statements`
	`}`
	`while (booleanTest)  ;`

The `switch` statement	`switch   (expression)`
	`{`
	`  case  FirstCase :`
	`    // First set of statements`
	`    break;`
	`  case  SecondCase :`
	`    // Second set of statements`
	`    break;`
	`  case  ThirdCase :`
	`    // Third set of statements`
	`    break;`
	`  default :`

(Continued)

Statement	Example

	`// Default statement`
	`break;`
	`}`

The `for` loop	`for (initialization; condition;` `increment) statement;`

Defining Classes

The basic structure of defining a class is as follows:

```
Scope class ClassName [extends class]
{
    // Class implementation statements
}
```

When declaring the scope of the class, we have several options to control how other classes can access this class:

`public`	The class can be used by code outside of the file. Only one class in a file may have this scope. The file must be named with the class name followed by further four-letter .java extension.
`private`	The class can only be used within a file.
`abstract`	The class cannot be used by itself and must be subclassed.
`final`	The class cannot be used by a subclass.
`synchronizable`	Instances of this class can be made arguments.

If a scope modifier is not used, the class is only accessible within the current file.

Defining Methods

A *method* is the code that acts on data inside a class and is always declared inside the class declaration. A method has the following syntax:

```
Scope ReturnType methodName (arguments)
{
    // Method implementation statements
}
```

The scope allows the programmer to control access to methods and can be one of the following:

`public`	The method is accessible by any system object.
`protected`	The method is only accessible by subclasses and the class in which it is declared.
`private`	The method is accessible only within current class.
`final`	The method cannot be overridden by any subclass.
`static`	The method is shared by all instances of the class.

If a method is not given a scope, it is only accessible within the scope of the current file. We can also use these scope operators when declaring variables.

Exception Handling

An exception has two parts: signalling an exception and setting up an exception handler. To signal an exception, use the **try** keyword. To set up an exception handler, we use the **catch** keyword. We use the **finally** keyword to specify a block of statements that will execute no matter what. To tell the system that an error has occurred, use the **throw** keyword.

```
try
{
        // Try this block of code and throw exception
}
catch (Exception e)
{
        // Handle error
}
finally
{
        // Executed no matter what happens
}
```

General Applet Construction

A minimal Java Applet has the following construction:

```
/*
*    JavaApplet.java   -   Sample   Applet
*
*/
import java.applet.*;
import java.awt.Graphics;
public class JavaApplet extends java.applet.Applet
{
    public void init ( )
    {
        // Called first time applet is executed
    }
    public void start ( )
    {
        // Called after init( ) and whenever Web page is revisited
    }
    public void stop ( )
    {
        // Called when Web page disappears
    }
    public void destroy ( )
    {
```

(Continued)

(*Continued*)

```
        // Called when applet is being removed from memory
    }
    public  void  paint  (Graphics  g)
    {
        g.drawString  ("Goodbye  !",  100,  100)  ;
    }
}
```

Java Keywords

This appendix lists the keywords in Java. They are grouped according to their meaning/function.

Group	Keyword	Meaning/Function
Class Organization	package	specifies the class in a particular source file should belong to the named package.
	import	requests the named class or classes be imported into the current application.
Class Definition	interface	defines global data and method signatures that can be shared among classes.
	class	defines a collection of related data behaviour.
	extends	indicates which class to subclass.
	implements	indicates the interface for which a new class will supply methods.
Keywords for Classes and Variables	abstract	specifies the class cannot be instantiated directly.
	públic	means the class, method, or variable can be accessed from anywhere.
	private	means only the class defining the method or variable can access it.
	protected	means only the defining class and its subclasses can access the method or variable.
	static	specifies a class method or variable.
	synchronized	indicates only one object or class can access this variable or method at a time.

(*Continued*)

(*Continued*)

Group	Keyword	Meaning/Function
	volatile	tells the compiler this variable may change asynchronously due to threads.
	final	means this variable or method cannot be changed by subclasses.
	const	means this variable cannot be changed.
	native	links a method to native code.
Simple Data Types	long	is a 64-bit integer value.
	int	is a 32-bit integer value.
	short	is a 16-bit integer value.
	byte	is a 8-bit integer value.
	double	is a 64-bit floating-point value.
	float	is a 32-bit floating-point value.
	char	is a 16-bit Unicode character.
	boolean	is a true or false value.
	void	indicates a method does not return a value.
Values and Variables	false	is a Boolean value.
	true	is a Boolean value.
	this	refers to the current instance in an instance method.
	super	refers to the immediate superclass in an instance method.
	null	represents a nonexistent instance.
Exception Handling	throw	throws an exception
	throws	throws an exception.
	try	marks a stack so that if an exception is thrown, it will unwind to this point.
	catch	catches an exception.
	finally	says execute this block of code regardless of exception error handling flow.
Instance Creating and Testing	new	creates new instances.
	instanceof	tests whether an instance derives from a particular class or interface.
Control Flow	switch	tests a variable.
	case	executes a particular block of code according to the value tested in the switch.
	default	means the default block of code executes if no matching case statement was found.
	break	breaks out of a particular block of code.

(*Continued*)

(*Continued*)

Group	Keyword	Meaning/Function
	continue	continues with the next iteration of a loop.
	goto	directs control to a specified place.
	return	returns from a method, optionally passing back a value.
	do	performs some statement or set of statements.
	if	tests for a condition and performs some action if true.
	else	performs some action if the above test was false.
	for	signifies iteration.
	while	performs some action while a condition is true.

- **Keywords not available from C**
  auto, enum, extern, register, signed, sizeof, struct, typedef, union, unsigned.
- **Keywords not available from C++**
  delete, friend, inline, mutable, template, using, virtual.

Appendix **C**

Differences Between Java and C/C++

C.1 Data Types

- All Java primitive data types (char, int, short, long, byte, float, double and boolean) have specified sizes and behaviour that are machine-independent.
- Conditional expressions can only be Boolean, not integral.
- Casting between data types is much more controlled in Java. Automatic conversion occurs only when there is no loss of information. All other casts must be explicit.
- Java supports special methods to convert values between class objects and primitive types.
- Composite data types are accomplished in Java using only classes. Structures and unions are not supported.
- Java does not support **typedef** keyword.
- All non-primitive types can only be created using **new** operator.
- Java does not define the type modifiers **auto, extern, registor, signed,** and **unsigned**.

C.2 Pointers

- Java does not support pointers. Similar functionality is accomplished by using implicit references to objects. Pointer arithmetic is not possible in Java.

C.3　Operators

- Java adds a new right shift operator > > > which inserts zeros at the top end.
- The + operator can be used to concatenate strings.
- Operators overloading is not possible in Java.
- The , operator of C has been deleted.
- Java adds another operator **instanceof** to identify objects.
- The modulo division may be applied to float values in Java which is not permitted in C/C++.

C.4　Functions and Methods

- All functions are defined in the body of the class. There are no independent functions.
- The functions defined inside a class are known as methods.
- Although function overloading in Java works virtually identical to C++ function overloading, there are no default arguments to functions.
- No inline functions in Java.
- Java requires that methods with no arguments must be declared with empty parenthesis, (not with **void** keyword).

C.5　Preprocessor

- Java does not have a preprocessor, and as such, does not support **#define** or macros.
- Constants can be created using the **final** modifier when declaring class and instance variables.
- Java programs do not use header files.

C.6　Classes

- Class definitions take the similar form in Java as in C++, but there is no closing semicolon.
- There is no scope resolution operator :: in Java.
- No forward references of classes are necessary in Java.
- No destructors in Java.
- Java has no templates.
- No nested classes in Java.
- Inheritance in Java has the same effect as in C++, but the syntax is different.
- Java does not provide direct support for multiple inheritance. We can accomplish multiple inheritance by using interfaces.
- Access specifiers (public, private, protected and private protected) are placed on each definition for each member of a class.

- A class in Java can have an access specifier to determine whether it is visible outside the file.
- There is no **virtual** keyword in Java. All non-static methods always use dynamic binding.
- Initialization of primitive class data member is guaranteed in Java. We can initialize them directly when we define them in the class, or we can do it in the constructor.
- We need not externally define storage for **static** members like we do in C++.

C.7　Strings

- Strings in C and C++ are arrays of characters, terminated by a null character. But strings in Java are objects. They are not terminated by a null. Therefore, strings are treated differently in C++ and Java.
- Strings can be concatenated using + operator.

C.8　Arrays

- Arrays are quite different in Java. Array boundaries are strictly enforced. Attempting to read past the end of an array produces an error.
- One array can be assigned to another in Java.
- Java does not support multidimensional arrays as in C and C++. However, it is possible to create arrays of arrays to represent multidimensional arrays.

C.9　Control Flow

- The test expressions for control flow constructs return a Boolean value (true or false) in Java. In C and C++, they return an integer value.
- The control variable declared in **for** loop is not available after the loop is exited in Java.

C.10　Command-Line Arguments

- The command line arguments passed from the system into a Java program differ in a couple of ways compared to that of C++ program.
- In C and C++, two arguments are passed. One specifies the number of arguments and the other is a pointer to an array of characters containing the actual arguments. In Java, a single argument containing an array of strings is passed.
- The first element in the arguments vector in C and C++ is the name of the program itself. In Java, we do not pass the name of the program as an argument. We already know the name of the program because it is the same name as the class.

C.11 Other Differences

- Java supports multithreading.
- Java supports automatic garbage collection and makes a lot of programming problems simply vanish.
- The destructor function is replaced with a finalize function.
- Exception handling in Java is different because there are no destructors. A **finally** clause is always executed to perform necessary cleanup.
- Java has built-in support for comment documentation, so the source code file can also contain its own documentation.

Appendix **D**

Bit-level Programming

D.1 Introduction

One of the unique features of Java language as compared to other high-level languages is that it allows direct manipulation of individual bits within a word. Bit-level manipulations are used in setting a particular bit or group of bits to 1 or 0. They are also used to perform certain numerical computations faster. As pointed out in Chapter 5, Java supports the following operators:

1. Bitwise logical operators
2. Bitwise shift operators
3. One's complement operator

All these operators work only on integer type operands.

D.2 Bitwise Logical Operators

There are three logical Bitwise operators. They are:

- Bitwise AND (&)
- Bitwise OR (|)
- Bitwise *exclusive* OR (^)

These are binary operators and require two integer-type operands. These operators work on their operands bit by bit starting from the least significant (i.e. the rightmost) bit, setting each bit in the result as shown in Table D.1.

Table D.1   Java Milestones

op1	op2	op1 & op2	op1 | op2	op1 ^ op2
1	1	1	1	0
1	0	0	1	1
0	1	0	1	1
0	0	0	0	0

Bitwise AND

The bitwise AND operator is represented by a single ampersand (&) and is surrounded on both sides by integer expressions. The result of ANDing operation is 1 if both the bits have a value of 1; otherwise it is 0. Let us consider two variables x and y whose values are 13 and 25. The binary representation of these two variables are

$$x \longrightarrow 0000 \quad 0000 \quad 0000 \quad 1101$$
$$y \longrightarrow 0000 \quad 0000 \quad 0001 \quad 1001$$

If we execute statement

z = x & y;

then the result would be:

$$z \longrightarrow 0000 \quad 0000 \quad 0000 \quad 1001$$

Although the resulting bit pattern represents the decimal number 9, there is no apparent connection between the decimal values of these three variables. Program D.1 shows how to use the bitwise operators.

Program D.1   *Demonstration of bitwise operators*

```
Class Bitwise
{
    public static void main (String args[])
    {
        int a=13, b=25;
        System.out.println ("a = " + a);
        System.out.println ("b = " + b);
        System.out.println ("a & b = " + (a & b) );
        System.out.println ("a | b = " + (a | b) );
        System.out.println ("a ^ b = " + (a ^ b) );
    }
}
```

The output would be:

```
a = 13
b = 25
a & b = 9
a | b = 29
a ^ b = 20
```

Bitwise ANDing is often used to test whether a particular bit is 1 or 0. For example, the following program tests whether the fourth bit of the variable **flag** is 1 or 0.

```
Class Bit1
{
    Static final TEST = 8;              /* represents 00....01000 */
    public static void main (String args[])
    {
        int flag:
        ..........
        ..........
        if ( (flag & TEST) ! = 0)       /* test 4th bit */
        {
                System.out.println ("Fourth bit is set \n") ;
        }
        ..........
        ..........
    }
}
```

Note that the bitwise logical operators have lower precedence than the relational operators and therefore additional parentheses are necessary as shown above.

The following program tests whether a given number is odd or even.

```
Class Bit2
{
    public static void main (String args [])
    {
        int test = 1;
        int number:
    // Input a number here
        ..........
        ..........
        while (number ! = -1)
        {
            if (number & test)
                System.out.println ("Number is odd\n\n");
            else
                System.out.println ("Number is even\n\n");
            // Input a number here
            ..........
            ..........
        }
    }
}
```

Output:
```
Input a number
20
Number is even
Input a number
9
Number is odd
Input a number
-1
```

Bitwise OR

The bitwise OR is represented by the symbol | (vertical bar) and is surrounded by two integer operands. The result of OR operation is 1 if *at least* one of the bits has a value of 1; otherwise it is zero. Consider the variables **x** and **y** discussed above.

x	►	0000	0000	0000	1101
y	⟶	0000	0000	0001	1001
x|y	⟶	0000	0000	0001	1101

The bitwise inclusion OR operation is often used to set a particular bit to 1 in a flag. Example:

```
Class Bit3
{
    final static SET = 8;
    public static void main (String args[])
    {
        int flag;
        ..........
        ..........
        flag = flag | SET;
        if ((flag & SET) ! = 0)
        {
            System.out.println ("flag is set \n");
        }
        ..........
        ..........
    }
}
```

The statement

```
        flag = flag | SET;
```

causes the fourth bit of flag to set 1 if it is 0 and does not change it if it is already 1.

Bitwise Exclusive OR

The bitwise *exclusive* OR is represented by the symbol ^. The result of exclusive OR is 1 if *only one* of the bits is 1; otherwise it is 0. Consider again the same variables **x** and **y** discussed above.

```
x    ⟶    0000    0000    0000    1101
y    ⟶    0000    0000    0001    1001
         _____
x^y  ⟶    0000    0000    0001    1101
```

D.3 Bitwise Shift Operators

The shift operators are used to move bit patterns either to the left or to the right. The shift operators are represented by the symbols < and > and are used in the following form:

```
Left shift:op << n
Right shift:    op >> n
```

op is the integer expression that is to be shifted and *n* is the number of bit positions to be shifted.

The left-shift operation causes all the bits in the operand *op* to be shifted to the left by *n* positions. The leftmost *n* bits in the original bit pattern will be lost and rightmost *n* bits positions that are vacated will be filled with 0s.

Similarly, the right-shift operation causes all the bits in the operand *op* to be shifted to the right by *n* positions. The rightmost *n* bits will be lost. The leftmost *n* bit positions that are vacated will be filled with zero, if the *op* is a *positive integer*. If the variable to be shifted is *negative*, then the operation preserves the high-order bit of 1 and shifts only the lower 31 bits to the right.

Both the operands *op* and *n* can be constants or variables. There are two restrictions on the value of *n*. It may not be negative and it may not exceed the number of bits used to represent the left operand *op*.

Let us suppose **x** is a positive integer whose bit pattern is

```
    0100    1001    1100    1011
```

then,

```
                                              Vacated
                                            positions
                                          ↙
x << 3 = 0100    1110    0101    1000
x >> 3 = 0000    1001    0011    1001
            ↑
        Vacated
        positions
```

Shift operators are often used for multiplication and division by powers of two.

Consider the following statement:

```
x = y << 1;
```

This statement shifts one bit to the left in **y** and then the result is assigned to **x**. The decimal value of **x** will be the value of y multiplied by 2. Similarly, the statement

```
x = y >> 1;
```

shifts **y** one bit to the right and assigns the result to **x**. In this case, the value of **x** will be the value of **y** divided by 2.

Java supports another shift operator >>> known as zero-fill-right-shift operator. When dealing with positive numbers, there is no difference between this operator and the right-shift operator. They both shift zeros into the upper bits of a number. The difference arises when dealing with negative numbers. Note that negative numbers have the high-order bit set to 1. The right-shift operator preserves the high-order bit as 1. The zero-fill-right-shift operator shifts zeros into all the upper bits, including the high-order bit, thus making a negative number into positive. Program D.2 demonstrates the use of shift operators.

Program D.2 *Demonstration of Shift operators*

```
Class Shift
{
    public static void main (String args[])
    {
        int a=8, b=-8;
        System.out.println ("a = " + a + " b = " + b);
        System.out.println ("a >> 2 = " + (a >> 2));
        System.out.println ("a << 1 = " + (a << 1));
        System.out.println ("a >>> 1 = " + (a >>> 1));
        System.out.println ("b >> 1 = " + (b >> 1));
        System.out.println ("b >>> 1 = " + (b >>> 1));
    }
}
```

The output would be:
```
a = 8        b =    - 8
a >> 2    =        2
a << 1    =        16
a >>> 1   =        4
b >> 1    =        - 4
b >>> 1   =        2147483644
```

D.4 Bitwise Complement Operators

The complement operator ~ (also called the one's complement operator) is an unary operator and inverts all the bits represented by its operand. That is, 0s become 1s and 1s become zero. Example:

```
x    = 1001 0110 1100 1011
~x   = 0110 1001 0011 0100
```

This operator is often combined with the bitwise AND operator to turn off a particular bit. For example, the statements

```
x    = 8;           /* 0000 0000 00000 1000 */
flag = flag & ~x;
```

would turn off the fourth bit in the variable **flag**.

Java API Packages

Java API is implemented as packages, which contain groups of related classes. Along with classes, they also include interfaces, exception definitions and error definitions. Java API is composed of a large number of packages. The most commonly used packages are:

Stand-alone Application Programming

1. java.lang
2. java.util
3. java.io

Applet and Network Programming

4. java.awt
5. java.applet
6. java.net

This appendix lists the frequently used interfaces and classes contained in the above packages.

Table E.1 Java.lang Package	
Interfaces	
Cloneable	Interface indicating that an object may be copied or cloned
Runnable	Methods for classes that want to run as threads
Classes	
Boolean	Object wrapper for boolean values
Byte	Object wrapper for byte values

(Continued)

Table E.1 (*Continued*)

Character	Object wrapper for char values
Class	Run-time representations of classes
ClassLoader	Abstract behaviour for handling loading of classes
Compiler	System class that gives access to the Java compiler
Double	Object wrapper for double values
Float	Object wrapper for float values
Integer	Object wrapper for int values
Long	Object wrapper for long values
Math	Utility class for math operations
Number	Abstract superclass of all number classes (Integer, Float, and so on)
Object	Generic object class, at top of inheritance hierarchy
Process	Abstract behaviour for processes such as those spawned using methods in the System class
Runtime	Access to the Java runtime
SecurityManager	Abstract behaviour for implementing security policies
String	Character strings
StringBuffer	Mutable strings
System	Access to Java's system-level behaviour, provided in a platform independent way
Thread	Methods for managing threads and classes that run in threads
ThreadDeath	Class of object thrown when a thread is asynchronously terminated
ThreadGroup	A group of threads
Throwable	Generic exception class; all objects thrown must be a Throwable.

Table E.2   Java.util Package

Interfaces

Enumeration	Methods for enumerating sets of values
Observer	Methods for enabling classes to be Observable objects

Classes

BitSet	A set of bits
Date	The current system date, as well as methods for generating and parsing dates
Dictionary	An abstract class that maps between keys and values (superclass of HashTable)
Hashtable	A hash table
Observable	An abstract class for observable objects
Properties	A hash table that contains behaviour for setting and retrieving persistent properties of the system or a class
Random	Utilities for generating random numbers
Stack	A stack (a last-in-first-out queue)
StringTokenizer	Utilities for splitting strings into individual "token"
Vector	A growable array of Objects

Table E.3   Java.io Package

Interfaces

DataInput	Methods for reading machine-independent typed input streams
DataOutput	Methods for writing machine-independent typed output streams
FilenameFilter	Methods for filtering file names

Classes

BufferedInputStream	A buffered input stream
BufferedOutputStream	A buffered output stream
ByteArrayInputStream	An input stream from a byte array
ByteArrayOutputStream	An output stream to a byte array
DataInputStream	Enables you to read primitive Java types (ints, chars, booleans, and so on) from a stream in a machine-independent way
DataOutputStream	Enables you to write primitive Java data types (ints, chars, booleans, and so on) to a stream in a machine-component way
File	Represents a file on the host's file system
FileDescriptor	Holds onto the UNIX-like file descriptor of a file or socket
FileInputStream	An input stream from a file, constructed using a filename of descriptor
FileOutputStream	An output stream to a file, constructed using a filename or descriptor
FilterInputStream	Abstract class which provides a filter for input streams (and for adding stream functionality such as buffering)
FilterOutputStream	Abstract class which provides a filter for output streams (and for adding stream functionality such as buffering)
Input Stream	An abstract class representing an input stream of bytes; the parent of all input streams in this package
LineNumberInputStream	An input stream that keeps track of line numbers
OutputStream	An abstract class representing an output stream of bytes; the parent of all output stream in this package
PipedInputStream	A piped input stream, which should be connected to a PipedOutputStream to be useful
PipedOutputStream	A piped output stream, which should be connected to a PipedInputStream to be useful (together they provide safe communication between threads)
PrintStream	An output stream for printing (used by System.out.println(...))
PushbackInputStream	An input stream with a 1-byte push back buffer
RandomAccessFile	Provides random access to a file, constructed from filenames, descriptors or objects
SequenceInputStream	Converts a sequence of input streams into a single input stream
StreamTokenizer	Converts an input stream into a series of individual tokens
StringBufferInputStream	An input stream from a String object

Table E.4   Java.awt Package

Interfaces

LayoutManager	Methods for laying out containers
MenuContainer	Methods for menu-related containers

Classes

BorderLayout	A layout manager for arranging items in border formation
Button	A UI pushbutton
Canvas	A canvas for drawing and performing other graphics operations
CardLayout	A layout manager for HyperCard-like metaphors
Checkbox	A checkbox
CheckboxGroup	A group of exclusive checkboxes (radio buttons)
CheckboxMenuItem	A toggle menu item
Choice	A popup menu of choices
Color	An abstract representation of a color
Component	The abstract generic class for all UI components
Container	Abstract behaviour for a component that can hold other components or containers
Dialog	A window for brief interactions with users
Dimension	An object representing width and height
Event	An object representing events caused by the system or based on user input
FileDialog	A dialog for getting filenames from the local file system
FlowLayout	A layout manager that lays out objects from left to right in rows
Font	An abstract representation of a font
FontMetrics	Abstract class for holding information about a specific font's character shapes and height and width information
Frame	A top-level window with a title
Graphics	Abstract behaviour for representing a graphics context, and for drawing and painting shapes and objects
GridBagConstraints	Constraints for components laid out using GridBagLayout
GridBagLayout	A layout manager that aligns components horizontally and vertically based on their values from GridBagConstraints
GridLayout	A layout manager with rows and columns; elements are added to each cell in the grid
Image	An abstract representation of a bitmap image
Insets	Distances from the outer border of the window; used to layout components
Label	A text label for UI components
List	A scrolling list

(Continued)

Table E.4 (*Continued*)

MediaTracker	A way to keep track of the status of media objects being loaded over the Net
Menu	A menu, which can contain menu items and is a container on a menubar
Menubar	A menubar (container for menus)
MenuComponent	The abstract superclass of all menu elements
MenuItem	An individual menu item
Panel	A container that is displayed
Point	An object representing a point (x and y coordinates)
Polygon	An object representing a set of points
Rectangle	An object representing a rectangle (x and y coordinates for the top corner, plus width and height)
Scrollbar	A UI scrollbar object
TextArea	A multilane, scrollable, editable text field
TextComponent	The supeclass of all editable text components
TextField	A fixed-size editable text field
Toolkit	Abstract behaviour for binding the abstract AWT classes to a platform-specific toolkit implementation
Window	A top-level window, and the superclass of the Frame and Dialog classes

Table E.5   Java.awt.image Package

Interfaces

ImageConsumer	Methods for receiving image created by an ImageProducer
ImageObserver	Methods to track the loading and construction of an image
ImageProducer	Methods for producing image data received by an ImageConsumer

Classes

ColorModel	An abstract class for managing color information for images
CropImageFilter	A filter for cropping images to a particular size
DirectColorModel	A specific color model for managing and translating pixel color values
FilteredImageSource	An ImageProducer that takes an image and an ImageFilter object, and produces an image for an ImageConsumer
ImageFilter	A filter that takes image data from an ImageProducer, modifies it in some way, and hands it off to an ImageConsumer
IndexColorModel	A specific color model for managing and translating color values in a fixed-color map
MemoryImageSource	An image producer that gets its image from memory; used after constructing an image by hand
PixelGrabber	An ImageConsumer that retrieves a subset of the pixels in an image
RGBImageFilter	Abstract behavior for a filter that modifies the RGB values of pixels in RGB images

Table E.6   Java.applet Package

Interfaces

AppletContext	Methods to refer to applet's context
AppletStub	Methods to implement applet viewers
AudioClip	Methods to play audio files

Classes

Applet	The base applet class

Table E.7   Java.net Package

Interfaces

ContentHandler Factory	Methods for creating ContentHandler objects
SocketImplFactory	Methods for creating socket implementations (instance of the SocketImpl class)
URLStreamHandlerFactory	Methods for creating URLStreamHandler objects

Classes

ContentHandler	Abstract behaviour for reading data from a URL connection and constructing the appropriate local object, based on MIME types
DatagramPacket	A datagram packet (UDP)
DatagramSocket	A datagram socket
InetAddress	An object representation of an Internet host (host name, IP address)
ServerSocket	A sever-side socket
Socket	A socket
SocketImpl	An abstract class for specific socket implementations
URL	An object representation of a URl
URLConnection	Abstract behaviour for a socket that can handle various Web-based protocols (http, ftp, and so on)
URLEncoder	Turns strings into x-www-form-urlencoded format
URLStreamHandler	Abstract class for managing streams to object referenced by URLs

Appendix  **F**

Java Classes and Their Packages

This appendix lists the frequently used classes in alphabetical order and indicates in which package a given class is defined. It also lists the classes that extend them.

Class	Package	Subclasses
AbstractMethodError	java.lang	Nil
AppletContext	java.applet	Nil
AppletStub	java.applet	Nil
Applet	java.applet	Nil
ArithmeticException	java.lang	Nil
ArrayIndexOutofBoundsException	java.lang	Nil
ArrayStoreException	java.lang	Nil
AudioClip	java.applet	Nil
AWTError	java.awt	Nil
AWTException	java.awt	Nil
BitSet	java.util	Nil
Boolean	java.lang	Nil
BorderLayout	java.awt	Nil
BufferedInputStream	java.io	Nil
BufferedOutputStream	java.io	Nil

(Continued)

(*Continued*)

Class	Package	Subclasses
ButtonPeer	java.awt.peer	Nil
Button	java.awt	Nil
ByteArrayInputStream	java.io	Nil
ByteArrayOutputStream	java.io	Nil
CanvasPeer	java.awt.peer	Nil
Canvas	java.awt	Nil
CardLayout	java.awt	Nil
Character	java.lang	Nil
CheckboxGroup	java.awt	Nil
CheckboxMenuItemPeer	java.awt.peer	Nil
CheckboxMenuItem	java.awt	Nil
CheckboxPeer	java.awt.peer	Nil
Checkbox	java.awt	Nil
ChoicePeer	java.awt.peer	Nil
Choice	java.awt	Nil
ClassCastException	java.lang	Nil
ClassCircularityError	java.lang	Nil
ClassFormatError	java.lang	Nil
ClassLoader	java.lang	Nil
ClassNotFoundException	java.lang	Nil
Class	java.lang	Nil
Cloneable	java.lang	Nil
CloneNotSupportedException	java.lang	Nil
ColorModel	java.awt.image	DirectColorModel, IndexColorModel
Color	java.awt	Nil
Compiler	java.lang	Nil
ComponentPeer	java.awt.peer	ButtonPeer, CanvasPeer, CheckboxPeer, ChoicePeer ContainerPeer, LabelPeer, ListPeer, ScrollbarPeer, TextComponentPeer
Component	java.awt	Button, Canvas, Checkbox, Choice, Container, Lable, List, Scrollbar, TextComponent

(*Continued*)

(*Continued*)

Class	Package	Subclasses
ContainerPeer	`java.awt.peer`	PanelPeer, WindowPeer
Container	`java.awt`	Panel, Window
ContentHandlerFactory	`java.net`	Nil
ContentHandler	`java.net`	Nil
CropImageFilter	`java.awt.image`	Nil
DatagramPacket	`java.net`	Nil
DatagramSocket	`java.net`	Nil
DataInputStream	`java.io`	Nil
DataInput	`java.io`	Nil
DataOutputStream	`java.io`	Nil
DataOutput	`java.io`	Nil
Date	`java.util`	Nil
DialogPeer	`java.awt.peer`	FileDialogPeer
Dialog	`java.awt`	FileDialog
Dictionary	`java.util`	Hashtable
Dimension	`java.awt`	Nil
DirectColorModel	`java.awt.image`	Nil
Double	`java.lang`	Nil
EmptyStackException	`java.util`	Nil
Enumeration	`java.util`	Nil
EOFException	`java.io`	Nil
Error	`java.lang`	AWTError, LinkageError, ThreadDeath, VirtualMachineError
Event	`java.awt`	Nil
Exception	`java.lang`	AWTException, ClassNotFoundException, CloneNotSupportedException, IllegalAccessException, InstantiationException, InterruptedException, IOException, NoSuchMethodException RuntimeException
FileDescriptor	`java.io`	Nil
FileDialogPeer	`java.awt.peer`	Nil

(*Continued*)

(*Continued*)

Class	Package	Subclasses
FileDialog	java.awt	Nil
FileInputStream	java.io	Nil
FilenameFilter	java.io	Nil
FileNotFoundException	java.io	Nil
FileOutputStream	java.io	Nil
File	java.io	Nil
FilteredImageSource	java.awt.image	Nil
FilterInputStream	java.io	BufferedInputStream, DataInputStream, LineNumberInputStream, PushbackInputStream BufferedOutputStream, DataOutputStream, Print Stream
Float	java.io	Nil
FlowLayout	java.awt	Nil
FontMetrics	java.awt	Nil
Font	java.awt	Nil
FramePeer	java.awt.peer	Nil
Frame	java.awt	Nil
Graphics	java.awt	Nil
GridBagConstraints	java.awt	Nil
GridBagLayout	java.awt	Nil
GridLayout	java.awt	Nil
Hashtable	java.util	Properties
IllegalAccessError	java.lang	Nil
IllegalAccessException	java.lang	Nil
IllegalArgumentException	java.lang	IllegalThreadStateException, NumberFormatException
IllegalMonitorStateException	java.lang	Nil
IllegalThreadStateException	java.lang	Nil
ImageConsumer	java.awt.image	Nil
ImageFilter	java.awt.image	CropImageFilter, RGBImageFilter
ImageObserver	java.awt.image	Nil
ImageProducer	java.awt.image	Nil
Image	java.awt	Nil

(*Continued*)

(*Continued*)

Class	Package	Subclasses
IncompatibleClassChangeError	java.lang	AbstractMethodError, IllegalAccessError, InstantiationError, NoSuchFieldError, NoSuchMethodError
IndexColorModel	java.awt.image	Nil
IndexOutofBoundsException	java.lang	ArrayIndexOutOfBounds Exception, StringIndexOutOfBounds Exception
InetAddress	java.net	Nil
InputStream	java.io	ByteArrayInputStream, FileInputStream, FilterInputStream, PipedInputStream, SequenceInputStream, StringBufferInputStream
Insets	java.awt	Nil
InstantiationError	java.lang	Nil
InstantiationException	java.lang	Nil
Integer	java.lang	Nil
InternalErorr	java.lang	Nil
InterruptedException	java.lang	Nil
InterruptedIOException	java.io	NIl
IOException	java.io	EOFException, FileNotFoundException, InterruptedIOException, MalformedURLException, ProtocolException, SocketException, UnknownHostException, UnknownServiceException, UTFDataFormatException
LabelPeer	java.awt.peer	Nil
Label	java.awt	Nil
LayoutManager	java.awt	Nil

(*Continued*)

(*Continued*)

Class	Package	Subclasses
LineNumberInputStream	java.io	Nil
LinkageError	java.lang	ClassCircularityError ClassFormatError, IncompatibleClassChange Error, UnsatisfiedLinkError, VerifyError
ListPeer	java.awt.peer	Nil
ListPeer	java.awt	Nil
Long	java.lang	Nil
MalformedURLException	java.net	Nil
Math	java.lang	Nil
MediaTracker	java.awt	Nil
MemoryImageSource	java.awt.image	Nil
MenuBarPeer	java.awt.peer	Nil
MenuBar	java.awt	Nil
MenuComponentPeer	java.awt.peer	CheckboxMenuItemPeer, MenuPeer
MenuComponent	java.awt	MenuBar, MenuItem
MenuContainer	java.awt	Nil
MenuItemPeer	java.awt.peer	CheckboxMenuItemPeer, MenuPeer
MenuItem	java.awt	CheckboxMenuItem, Menu
MenuPeer	java.awt.peer	Nil
Menu	java.awt	Nil
NegativeArraySizeException	java.lang	Nil
NoClassDefFoundError	java.lang	Nil
NoSuchElementException	java.util	Nil
NoSuchFieldError	java.lang	Nil
NoSuchMethodError	java.lang	Nil
NoSuchMethodException	java.lang	Nil
NullPointerException	java.lang	Nil
NumberFormatException	java.lang	Nil
Number	java.lang	Double, Float, Integer, Long
Object	java.lang	BitSet, Boolean, BorderLayout, CardLayout, Character,

(*Continued*)

Class	Package	Subclasses
		CheckboxGroup, Class, ClassLoader, Color, ColorModel, Compiler, Component, ContentHandler, DatagramPacket, DatagramSocket, Date, Dictionary, Dimension, Event, File, FileDescriptor, FilteredImageSource, FlowLayout, Font, FontMetrics, Graphics, GridBagConstraints GridBagLayout, GridLayout, Image, ImageFilter, InetAddress, InputStream, Insets, Math, MediaTracker, MemoryImageSource, MenuComponent, Number, Observable, OutputStream, PixelGrabber, Point, Polygon, Process, Random, RandomAccessFile, Rectangle, Runtime, SecurityManager, ServerSocket, Socket, SocketImpl, StreamTokenizer, String, StringBuffer, StringTokenizer, System, Thread, ThreadGroup, Thorwable, Toolkit, URL, URLConnection, URLEncoder, URLStreamHandler, Vector
Observable	java.util	Nil
Observer	java.util	Nil
OutOfMemoryError	java.lang	Nil
OutputStream	java.io	ByteArrayOutputStream, FileOutputStream, FilterOutputStream, PipedOutputStream,
PanelPeer	java.awt.peer	Nil
Panel	java.awt	Applet

(*Continued*)

(*Continued*)

Class	Package	Subclasses
PipedInputStream	`java.io`	Nil
PipedOutputStream	`java.io`	Nil
PixelGrabber	`java.awt.image`	Nil
Point	`java.awt`	Nil
Polygon	`java.awt`	Nil
PrintStream	`java.io`	Nil
Process	`java.lang`	Nil
Properties	`java.util`	Nil
ProtocolException	`java.net`	Nil
PushbackInputStream	`java.io`	Nil
RandomAccessFile	`java.io`	Nil
Random	`java.util`	Nil
Rectangle	`jav.awt`	Nil
RGBImageFilter	`java.awt.image`	Nil
Runnable	`java.lang`	Nil
RuntimeException	`java.lang`	ArithmeticException, ArrayStoreException, ClassCastException, EmptyStackException, IllegalArgumentException, IllegalMonitorStateException, IndexOutOfBoundsException, NegativeArraySizeException, NoSuchElementException, NullPointerException, SecurityException
Runtime	`java.lang`	Nil
ScrollbarPeer	`java.awt.peer`	Nil
Scrollbar	`java.awt`	Nil
SecurityException	`java.lang`	Nil
SecurityManager	`java.lang`	Nil
SequenceInputStream	`java.io`	Nil
ServerSocket	`java.net`	Nil
SocketException	`java.net`	Nil
SocketImplFactory	`java.net`	Nil
SocketImplFactory	`java.net`	Nil

(*Continued*)

(*Continued*)

Class	Package	Subclasses
Socket	java.net	Nil
StackOverflowError	java.lang	Nil
Stack	java.util	Nil
StreamTokenizer	java.io	Nil
StringBufferInputStream	java.io	Nil
StringBuffer	java.lang	Nil
StringIndexOutOfBoundsException	java.lang	Nil
StringTokenizer	java.util	Nil
String	java.lang	Nil
System	java.lang	Nil
TextAreaPeer	java.awt.peer	Nil
TextArea	java.awt	Nil
TextComponentPeer	java.awt.peer	TextAreaPeer, TextFieldPeer
TextComponent	java.awt	TextArea, TextField
TextFieldPeer	java.awt.peer	Nil
TextField	java.awt	Nil
ThreadDeath	java.lang	Nil
ThreadGroup	java.lang	Nil
Thread	java.lang	Nil
Throwable	java.lang	Error, Exception
Toolkit	java.awt	Nil
UnknownError	java.lang	Nil
UnknownHostException	java.net	Nil
UnknownServiceException	java.net	Nil
UnsatisfiedLinkError	java.lang	Nil
URLConnection	java.net	Nil
URLEncoder	java.net	Nil
URLStreamHandlerFactory	java.net	Nil
URLStreamHandler	java.net	Nil
URL	java.net	Nil
UTFDataFormatException	java.io	Nil
Vector	java.util	Stack
VerifyError	java.lang	Nil
VirtualMachineError	java.lang	InternalError, OutOfMemoryError, StackOverflowError, UnknownError
WindowPeer	java.awt.peer	DialogPeer, FramePeer
Window	java.awt	Dialog, Frame

Appendix **G**

What's New in Java 1.1 and Java 2

G.1 Introduction

Java is the most important advance in the programming technology invented during the last decade of the 20th century. Java technology is still evolving and is likely to be the primary programming language of the next millennium.

Java technology has many facets that work together to get the job done. Java environment basically consists of the following three entities:

- The language itself
- A class library (Application Program Interface (API) packages)
- A set of development tools.

Sun Microsystems, the inventors of Java, calls these three entities put together as *Java Development Kit* (JDK). This means that the JDK contains everything we need for developing Java programs. The new versions of Java are released as JDK versions by Sun Microsystems. That is, version JDK x.y means version Java x.y and vice versa.

Since the release of the original version of Java (known as Java 1.0) in May 1995, Sun Microsystems has been regularly releasing updates (changes and enhancements) of Java systems. Java 1.1 was released in March 1997 and Java 1.2 in early 1998. Fortunately, most of the changes and enhancements are related to the API packages and tools and very little changes have been introduced in the language itself. In early 1999, the Java 1.2 was renamed as Java 2 by Sun Microsystems and therefore, JDK 1.2, Java 1.2, and Java 2 all refer to the same thing.

The core API packages that contain numerous classes and interfaces have grown from around 200 in version 1.0 to more than 1500 in version 2. Table G.1 summarizes the core API packages available in

Java 2 and their functions. The table shows not only the packages added during the stages 1.1 and 2 but also the number of classes and interfaces added to the various existing packages at these stages. These packages together contain more than 1500 classes and interface and define more than 13,000 methods. It is beyond the scope of this book to provide a complete description of all these classed and methods. (For more details, readers may refer to the JDk 1.2 documentation available in one of the Sun web sites or refer to the book *Java Developers Almanac 1998*, Patrick Chan, Addison Wesley). More statistics of Java packages are given in Appendix I.

Table G.1   API Packages Available in Java 2

Sl No.	Package	Stage First Added	Total Classes and Interfaces			Task/Function
			1.0	1.1	2	
1.	java.applet	1.0	4	4	4	Provides basic functionality needed to implement applets.
2.	java.awt	1.0	46	61	78	Provides the standard GUI controls as well as drawing, printing and other capabilities
3.	java.awt. accessability	2	–	–	13	Supports the use of assistive technologies for disabled users.
4.	java.awt.color	2	–	–	7	Supports the ability to work with different color models.
5.	java.awt.	1.1	–	6	6	Supports clipboard operations, for transferring data between applications.
6.	jawa.awt.dnd	2	–	–	17	Supports drag–and–drop operations.
7.	java.awt.dnd. peer	2	–	–	3	Provides capability to access platform–dependent drag–and–drop facilities.
8.	java.awt.event	1.1	–	30	33	Provides foundation for processing events fired by AWT components.
9.	java.awt.font	2	–	–	15	Provides support for advanced font capabilities.
10.	java.awt.geom	2	–	–	33	Supports standard geometrical objects and transformations, in 2D.
11.	java.awt.im	2	–	–	3	Supports the Input Method API for internationalization.
12.	java.awt.image	1.0	12	14	52	A Java 2D API package that supports image processing.
13.	java.awt.image. codec	2	–	–	6	Supports image compression.
14.	java.awt.image. renderable	2	–	–	7	Supports functions for producing rendering-independent images.
15.	java.awt.peer	1.0	22	27	26	Provides support for interfacing with the underlying window system.

(Continued)

Table G.1 (*Continued*)

Sl No.	Package	Stage First Added	Total Classes and Interfaces			Task/Function
			1.0	*1.1*	*2*	
16.	`java.awt.print`	2	–	–	12	A Java 2D API package that supports printing of text and graphics.
17.	`java.awt.swing`	2	–	–	169	Provides foundation for the swing API, for creating completely portable GUI.
18.	`java.awt.swing.` `border`	2	–	–	10	Implements borders and border styles, around a swing component.
19.	`java.awt.swing.event`	2	–	–	38	Implements Swing events and event listeners.
20.	`java.awt.swing.plaf`	2	–	–	40	Supports the use of the pluggable look-and-feel, capabilities.
21.	`java.awt.swing.plaf.` `basic`	2	–	–	107	Provides default look-and-feel of Swing components.
22.	`java.awt.swing.plaf.` `metal`	2	–	–	42	Provides "metal" look-and-feel of Swing components.
23.	`java.awt.swing.` `preview`	2	–	–	21	Contains classes whose API have not been finalized yet.
24.	`java.awt.swing.table`	2	–	–	13	Implements the Swing table component for managing tables.
25.	`java.awt.swing.text`	2	–	–	87	Implements text processing functions such as selection, editing, etc.
26.	`java.awt.swing.text.` `html`	2	–	–	39	Provides basic HTML editing capabilities.
27.	`java.awt.swing.text.` `rtf`	2	–	–	1	Provides the capability to edit Rich Text Format documents
28.	`java.awt.swing.tree`	2	–	–	11	Provides capability to construct and manage tree-type data structure.
29.	`java.awt.swing.undo`	2	–	–	9	Provides undo and redo capabilities in applications.
30.	`java.beans`	1.1	–	23	25	Provides the basic Java beans functionality.
31.	`java.beans.` `beancontext`	2	–	–	19	Supports the implementation of execution environment for beans.
32.	`java.io`	1.0	31	69	77	Performs a wide variety of input and output functions.
33.	`java.lang`	1.0	64	69	76	Provides support for implementing fundamental Java objects.
34.	`java.lang.ref`	2	–	–	6	Supports Reference Objects that are used to refer to other objects.

(Continued)

Table G.1 *(Continued)*

Sl No.	Package	Stage First Added	Total Classes and Interfaces			Task/Function
			1.0	1.1	2	
35.	java.lang.reflect	1.1	–	7	9	Provides capability to obtain reflective information about classes, and objects.
36.	java.math	1.1	–	2	2	Provides capability to perform arbitrary-precision arithmetic.
37.	java.net	1.0	19	26	32	Supports features for network programming.
38.	java.rmi	1.1	–	19	20	Provides capability to access objects on remote computers.
39.	java.rmi.activation	2	–	–	16	Supports persistent object reference and remote object activation.
40.	java.rmi.dgc	1.1	–	3	3	Supports functions for distributed garbage collection.
41.	java.rmi.registry	1.1	–	3	3	Supports distributed registry operations.
42.	java.rmi.server	1.1	–	23	24	Provides capabilities for supporting the server side of RMI.
43.	java.security	1.1	–	26	57	Provides basic foundation for the Security API.
44.	java.security.acl	1.1	–	8	8	Provides capability for implementing security access controls.
45.	java.security.cert	2	–	–	12	Provides support for parsing and managing digital certifications.
46.	java.security.interfaces	1.1	–	5	5	Supports implementation of the NIST digital signature of algorithm.
47.	java.security.spec	2	–	–	10	Provides specification for cryptographic keys
48.	java.sql	1.1	–	17	24	Provides support for the Java database connectivity.
49.	java.text	1.1	–	19	28	Provides support for internationalization of text and messages.
50.	java.util	1.0	14	26	49	Supports a variety of common programming needs.
51.	java.util.jar	2	–	–	8	Provides support for working with JAR (Java Archive) files.
52.	java.util.mime	2	–	–	3	Provides capability to work with MIME type objects.
53.	java.util.zip	1.1	–	17	17	Provides support for working with compressed files.
54.	org.omg.CORBA	2	–	–	104	Implements the foundation for supporting Java-CORBA integration.

(Continued)

Table G.1   (*Continued*)

Sl No.	Package	Stage First Added	Total Classes and Interfaces			Task/Function
			1.0	1.1	2	
55.	org.omg.CORBA. ContainedPackage	2	–	–	1	Describes a CORBA object in a CORBA container.
56.	org.omg.CORBA. ContainerPackage	2	–	–	1	Describes a CORBA container object.
57.	org.omg.CORBA. InterfaceDefPackage	2	–	–	1	Describes a CORBA interface definition.
58.	org.omg.CORBA. ORBPackage	2	–	–	1	Raises an exception when an invalid name is passed to an object request broker.
59.	org.omg.CORBA.	2	–	–	2	Signals exceptions related to type usage and constraints.
60.	org.omg.CORBA. portable	2	–	–	5	Supports vender-specific CORBA implementation.
61.	org.omg.CosNaming	2	–	–	22	Implements a tree-structured data type naming.
62.	org.omg.CosNaming. NamingContextPackage	2	–	–	18	Implements nodes within the tree-structured naming scheme.

 ## G.2   Changes in Java 1.1

As pointed out earlier, the updates include five kinds of changes:

1. Additions to the existing packages
2. Addition to new packages
3. Changes in the existing classes and members
4. Changes in the language itself
5. Changes in tools

Addition to the Existing Packages

Additions to the existing packages may include two things:

1. New classes in the existing packages
2. New members (fields, constructors, and methods) in the existing classes

As seen from Table G.1, new classes have been added to all the classes except **Applet** class. Similarly, a comparison of Tables I.2 and I.3 shows that new members have been added to many classes in almost all the existing packages. All these additions are aimed at enhancing the functionality of the existing API. Some important enhancements are listed as follows:

Abstract Windowing Toolkit (AWT) Enhancements   The additions have improved the functionality of AWT to make the large-scale GUI development more feasible. Java 1.1 supports delegation-based event handling, data transfer such as cut-copy-paste, desktop color schemes, printing, mouseless operation, faster scrolling, popup menus and much more. These improvements have made Java 1.1 faster than Java 1.0.

I/O Enhancements Java 1.1 has added character streams to the existing **java.io** package. These are like byte streams of Java 1.0 except that they operate on 16-bit Unicode characters rather than eight-bit bytes. Character streams make it easy to write programs that are independent of the user's culture and language and therefore easier to write "global programs". The process of writing a global program and ensuring that it can be used without change by anyone in the world is known as *internationalization*. In addition, two byte streams were added to support object serialization. Serialization lets us store objects and handle them with binary input/output streams.

Networking Enhancements The 1.1 release made several enhancements to the networking package, **java.net**. It supports selected BSD-style options in the base classes and provides facility for finer granularity in reporting and handling network errors.

Native Methods Interface Native methods are written in languages other than Java. The native methods interface from 1.0 has been completely rewritten and formalized. This interface is now known as the Java Native Interface (JNI). This provides capability for Java objects to access native methods.

Addition of New Packages

Java 1.1 has added the following new packages to provide new capabilities.

1. `java.awt.datatransfer`
2. `java.awt.event`
3. `java.beans`
4. `java.lang.reflect`
5. `java.math`
6. `java.rmi`
7. `java.rmi.dgc`
8. `java.rmi.registry`
9. `java.rmi.server`
10. `java.security`
11. `java.security.acl`
12. `java.security.interfaces`
13. `java.sql`
14. `java.text`
15. `java.util.zip`

Some major new capabilities are discussed as follows:

Security and Signed Applets Java 1.1 supports the developments of digitally signed Java applications. It provides capability for key management, certificate management and security access controls.

Java Archive Files Java Archive (JAR) files introduced in version 1.1 provide the capability for storing a number of files together by zipping them to shrink them, so the user can download many files at once. JAR files help us organize applets, applications, beans, and class libraries and support more efficient use of network resources.

JavaBeans Architecture The new JavaBeans architecture provides specifications that describe Java objects suitable for reuse. The JavaBeans API allows third-party software vendors to create and ship reusable components (known as Beans), such as text, spreadsheets, graphic widgets, etc., that can be used by non-programmers to build applications.

Math Package   The new package **java.math** added to Java 1.1 contains two classes, **BigInteger** and **BigDecimal**. They provide support for performing arithmetic and bit manipulation on arbitrary precision decimal and integer numbers, without causing overflow or loss of precision.

Remote Method Invocation (RMI)   RMI API, introduced in 1.1, provides capability to create distributed Java-to-Java applications. Java objects in a local computer can invoke the methods of objects on a remote computer. The concept of object serialization is used to pass objects as parameters and return values in the remote method invocations.

Reflection   Reflection means identification of fields, constructors and methods of loaded classes and objects and using this information at runtime. These capabilities are used by Java Beans, object inspection tools, debuggers, and other Java applications and applets.

Java Database Connectivity (JDBC)   JDBC capability is provided by the package **java.sql**. This provides a uniform access to a wide range of relational databases from Java.

Changes in the Existing Classes and Methods

Many classes and methods have undergone changes from 1.0 to 1.1. Changes may be:

1. New members in the existing classes
2. Deprecation of classes
3. Deprecation of methods
4. Removal of classes
5. Removal of methods
6. Modification of design of classes
7. Modification of definition of methods

A complete description of all these changes is beyond the scope of this appendix. A brief description of classes and methods that have been deprecated or removed is given in Appendix H.

Changes in Language Itself

Changes in language itself were very minor. Bytes and shorts are accommodated as wrapped numbers by adding new classes **Byte** and **Short**. The abstract class **Number** gets two new concrete methods **byteValue** and **shortValue**.

A new class **Void** has been added as an uninstantiable place holder.

Inner Classes   One important change to the Java 1.1 is the ability to define classes as members of other classes. Such classes are called *nested classes*. Inner classes are one type of nested classes.

Instance Initializers   Java 1.0 supported initialization of only static variables (also known as class variables). Example:

```
class TestClass
{
  static {
       -------
       -------          // Initialization code
       -------
     }
}
```

Java 1.1 permits initialization of instance variables as well. Example:

```
class TestClass
{
    {
        - - - - - - -
        - - - - - - -      //Initialization code
        - - - - - - -
    }
}
```

Array Initialization   Java 1.1 permits initialization of an array content in a **new** statement. For example, the following code creates an array of strings:

```
String [ ]      city =       new String [  ] {
                             "Madras"
                             "Delhi"
                             "Bombay" } ;
```

New Uses for Final   Java 1.1 allows us to declare the method parameters and local variables as final. However, a subclass can override a method and add or drop any final parameter modifiers. We can also deter initialization of a final variable, as long as we initialize it before it is used and assign a value to it exactly once.

G.3   Changes in Java 2

Java 2 is a major upgrade of the core API and adds a standard extension architecture. Again the changes may be classified as follows:

1. Additions to the existing packages (Enhancements)
2. Adding new packages (New capabilities)
3. Changes in the existing class and methods
4. Changes in the language
5. Changes in tools

Enhancements in Java 2

Capabilities of java has been considerably enhanced by adding new classes to the existing packages as well as new members to almost all the existing classes. A comparison of Tables 1.3 and 1.4 (see Appendix I) will reveal this.

Security Enhancement   Java 2 provides users with the capability to specify security policies simply by editing the security permissions stored in their policy text files. Unless a permission is explicitly specified to code, it cannot access the resource that is guarded by that permission.

Java Beans Enhancement   Java 2 provides facilities to create more sophisticated JavaBeans components and applications. It provides capability to incorporate with other Beans and to learn information about their execution environment.

RMI Enhancement Java 2 has significantly enhanced the RMI API. It supports remotely activated objects and object references that persist across multiple object activation.

JNI Enhancement Java 2 extends Java native Interface (JNI) to incorporate new features to provide capabilities for controlling the manner in which native methods interact with the Java Virtual Machine.

JDBC Enhancement Java 2 includes an improved version of JDBC–ODBC bridge driver and supports JDBC 2.0.

Audio Enhancement Java 2 contains a new, high-quality sound engine that provides support for audio in applications as well as applets. The sound engine also provides support for the Musical Interface Digital Interface (MIDI) in addition to other traditional sounds.

JAR Enhancement Java 2 JAR enhancements include improved tools for creating and updating JAR files and performing JAR I/O operations.

Reflection Enhancement Reflection support was introduced in 1.1. Java 2 adds additional capability to identify a field, method, or constructor as suppressing Java language access controls. This facilitates the better use of reflection with the improved Java 2 security model.

New Capabilities in Java 2

In addition to improving the existing capabilities of the API, Java 2 has also added a number of new capabilities to it. Perhaps, the single most new feature is the addition of Java Foundation Classes (JFC) to Java 2. The JFC includes the functionalities such as Swing, Java 2D, Drag-and-Drop and Accessibility. Besides integrating JFC, Java 2 provides a number of other new capabilities. The new packages added include the following:

```
 1. java.awt.accessibility     21. java.awt.swing.text.rtf
 2. java.awt.color             22. java.awt.swing.tree
 3. java.awt.dnd               23. java.awt.swing.undo
 4. java.awt.dnd.peer          24. java.beans.beancontext
 5. java.awt.font              25. java.lang.ref
 6. java.awt.geom              26. java.rmi.activation
 7. java.awt.im                27. java.security.cert
 8. java.awt.image.codec       28. java.security.spec
 9. java.awt.image.renderable  29. java.util.jar
10. java.awt.print             30. java.util.mime
11. java.awt.swing             31. org.omg.CORBA
12. java.awt.swing.border      32. org.omg.CORBA.ContainedPackage
13. java.awt.swing.event       33. org.omg.CORBA.ContainerPackage
14. java.awt.swing.plaf        34. org.omg.CORBA.InterfaceDefPackage
15. java.awt.swing.plaf.basic  35. org.omg.CORBA.ORBPackage
16. java.awt.swing.plaf.metal  36. org.omg.CORBA.TypeCodePackage
17. java.awt.swing.preview     37. org.omg.CORBA.portable
18. java.awt.swing.table       38. org.omg.CosNaming
19. java.awt.swing.text        39. org.omg.CosNaming.NamingContextPackage
20. java.awt.swing.text.html
```

Swing   Swing is the code word used by the JavaSoft team for the improved AWT. Swing implements a new set of GUI components with a "pluggable" look and feel. Swing is implemented completely in Java. Pluggable look and feel architecture allows us to design a single set of GUI components that can automatically have the look and feel of any OS platform.

Java 2D   The new Java 2D API includes a set of tools for dealing with two-dimensional drawings and images. These include provision for colorspaces, text, line art and printing.

Accessibility   Accessibility API provides support for the use of *assistive technologies*, such as screen magnifiers, speech recognition systems, and Braile terminals intended for use by disabled users.

Drag and Drop   Drag and Drop capability of Java 2 facilitates data transfer across Java and native applications, between Java applications, and within a single application.

Java IDL   Java IDL in Java 2 provides a set of tools for interfacing Java objects with CORBA (Common Object Request Broker Architecture) objects and for developing CORBA objects in Java. It also includes a Java ORB (Object Request Broker) and an ORB name server.

Collections   The Collections API provides an implementation-independent framework for working with collection of objects such as sets, maps, lists, and linked lists.

Package Version Identification   A new capability of Java 2 allows applets and applications to obtain version information about a particular Java package at runtime.

Reference Objects   Reference objects (introduced in version 2) stores references to other objects. This feature can be used to implement object-catching mechanisms.

Input Method API   The new Input Method API provides support for Java's internationalisation. This enables all text-editing components to receive foreign language text input through input methods. It currently supports Japanese, Chinese and Korean languages.

Language Changes

There are not major changes in language. Only three methods of **Thread** class, **stop( ), suspend( ),** and **resume( )** have been depreciated because of errors and inconsistencies caused by them. Instead of using the **stop( )** method, it is proposed that a thread may monitor the state of a shared variable and stop execution by returning from its **run( )** method. Similarly, a thread may suspend and resume its execution based on the value of shares variables (by monitoring interface events).

Tools Changes

Java 2 has improved the tools available in the earlier versions and also added new tools. The **javakey** tool of 1.1 has been replaced by the new **keytool** and **javasinger** tools. The Java 2 now includes the following tools:

- **keytool**   for maintaining a database of key pairs and digital certificates.
- **javasinger**   for signing JAR files and verifying the signatures of signed files.
- **policytool**   for creating and modifying the files that define security policy.
- **tnameserv**   for implementing CORBA Common Object Services (COS) Naming Service.
- **rmid**   for remote activation system daemon.

G.4 Performance Enhancements

The enhancements and new features added to Java 2 has considerably improved the performance of Java which has been a subject of criticism. Given below are some of the performance improvements achieved in Java 2.

- Improvements in multithreading performance
- Reduction in memory usage for string constants
- Faster memory allocation and garbage collection
- Improvements in the performance of the thread monitor methods
- Support of native libraries for some critical API classes
- Inclusion of just-in-time (JIT) compilers with Java 2

Appendix **H**

Deprecated Classes and Methods

H.1 Introduction

As a part of the effort to enhance the performance and capabilities of the Java language, Sun Microsystems has altered and eliminated many classes and methods during upgradations. The altered methods have been added as new methods and the older ones have been retained in order to maintain backward compatibility with older versions of Java. However, the older methods have been marked "deprecated".

A deprecated method means that it has lost its importance and likely to be phased out of future Java versions. Although programs that use deprecated methods will still compile and work, the compiler will generate warning messages. It is recommended that programs be modified to eliminate the use of any deprecated methods and classes due to two reasons.

1. Modified programs will retain compatibility with future releases of Java.
2. Many new methods provide better implementations and therefore make programs faster and more efficient.

H.2 Deprecated Classes and Methods of Version 1.0

A large number of classes and methods of version 1.0 have been declared deprecated. This appendix gives package-wise tables (Tables H.1 to H.4) that list class-wise methods that have been declared deprecated in Java 1.1. Tables also indicate alternative replacements. Table H.5 gives a list of version 1.0 classes that have been declared deprecated totally.

Table H.1   List of Deprecated 1.0 Methods in Java.lang

Classes	Methods	Replacement
Character	isJavaLetter (char) isJavaLetterOrDigit (char) isSpace (char)	isJavaIdentifierStart (char) isJavaIdentifierPart (char) isWhitespace (char)
ClassLoader	defineClass (byte [ ], int, int) toLocaleString ( ) toGMTString ( ) parse (String s)	defineClass (byte [ ], int,int) Use java.text. Format and its subclasses
Runtime	getLocalizedInputStream (InputStream in) getLocalizedOutputStream (OutputStream out)	BufferedReader (InputStream) InputStreamReader (InputStream) BufferedWriter (OutputStream) OutputStreamWriter (OutputStream) PrintWriter (OutputStream)
String	String (byte [ ], int, int, int) String (byte [ ], int) getBytes (int, int, byte [ ], int)	String (byte [ ], String) String (byte [ ], int, int, String) byte [ ] setbytes ( )
System	getenv (String)	String get property (String)

Table H.2   List of Deprecated 1.0 Methods in Java.util

Classes	Methods	Replacement
DateDate (int, int, int)	Date (int, int, int, int, int) Date (int, int, int, int, int, int) Date (String)	Create a java.util.GregorianCalendar object and use its getTime method to convert it to a Date
	UTC (int, int, int, int, int, int) getTimezoneOffset ( ) getYear ( ) setYear (int) getMonth ( ) setrMonth (int) getDate ( ) setDate (int) getDay ( ) getHours ( ) setHours (int) getMinutes ( ) setMinutes (int)	Create a java.util.GregorianCalendar object and use its setters and getters.

(Continued)

Table H.2 (*Continued*)

Classes	Methods	Replacement
	getSeconds ( )	
	setSeconds (int)	
	toLocaleString ( )	Use java.txt.Format and its classes
	toGMTString ( )	
	parse (String s)	

Table H.3 List of Deprecated 1.0 Methods in Java.io

Classes	Methods	Replacement
ByteArrayOutputStream	toString (int)	toString (String)
DataInputStream	String readLine ( )	BufferedReader.readLine ( )
StreamTokenizer	StreamTokenizer (InputStream)	StreamTokenizer (Reader)

Table H.4 List of Deprecated 1.0 Methods in Java.awt

Classes	Methods	Replacement
BorderLayout	addLayout Component (String, Component)	addLayoutComponent (Component, Object)
CardLayout	addLayoutComponent (String, Component)	addLayoutComponent (Component, Object)
CheckboxGroup	getCurrent ( )	getSelectedCheckbox ( )
	setCurrent (checkbox)	setSelectedCheckbox (Checkbox)
Choice	countItems ( )	getItemCount ( )
Component	getPeer ( )	None
	enable ( )	setEnabled (boolean)
	enable (boolean)	setEnabled (boolean)
	disable ( )	setEnabled (boolean)
	show ( )	setVisible (boolean)
	show (boolean)	setVisible (boolean)
	hide ( )	setVisible (boolean)
	location ( )	getLocation ( )
	move (int, int)	setLocation (int, int)
	size ( )	getSize ( )
	resize (int, int)	setSize (int, int)
	resize (Dimension)	setSize (Dimension)
	bounds ( )	getBounds ( )
	reshape (int, int, int, int)	setBounds (int, int, int, int,)
	preferredSize ( )	getPreferredSize ( )
	minimumSize ( )	getMinimumSize ( )

(*Continued*)

Table H.4   *(Continued)*

Classes	Methods	Replacement
	layout ( )	doLayout ( )
	inside (int, int)	contains (int, int)
	locate (int, int)	getComponentAt (int, int)
	deliverEvent (Event)	dispatchEvent (AWTEvent)
	postEvent (Event)	dispatchEvent (AWTEvent)
	handleEvent (Event)	processEvent (AWTEvent)
	mouseDown(Event, int, int)	processMouseEvent (MouseEvent)
	mouseDrag (Event, int, int)	processMouseMotion Event (MouseEvent)
	mouseUp (Event, int, int)	processMouseEvent (MouseEvent)
	mouseMove (Event, int, int)	processMouseMotionEvent (MouseEvent)
	mouseEnter (Event, int, int)	processMouseEvent (MouseEvent)
	mouseExit (Event, int, int)	processMouseEvent (MouseEvent)
	keyDown (Event, int)	processKeyEvent (KeyEvent)
	keyUp (Event, int)	processKeyEvent (KeyEvent)
	action (Event, Object)	Should register this component as Action Listener on component which fires action events
	lostFocus (Event, Object)	processFocusEvent (FocusEvent)
	nextFocus ( )	transferFocus ( )
Container	countComponents ( )	getComponentCount ( )
	insets ( )	getInsets ( )
	layout ( )	doLayout ( )
	preferredSize ( )	getPreferredSize ( )
	minimumSize ( )	getMinimumSize ( )
	deliverEvent (Event)	dispatchEvent (AWTEvent e)
	locate (int, int)	getComponentAt (int, int)
	nextFocus (Component)	transferFocus (Component)
Frame	setCursor (int)	Component.setCursor (Cursor)
	getCursorType ( )	Component.setCursor (Cursor) Component.getCursor ( )
Graphics	getClipRect ( )	getClipBounds ( )
ListcountItems ( )		getItemCount ( )
	clear ( )	removeAll ( )
	isSelected (int)	isIndexSelected (int)
	allowsMultipleSelections ( )	isMultipleMode ( )
	setMultipleSelections (boolean)	setMultipleMode (boolean)
	preferredSize (int)	getPreferredSize (int)

(Continued)

Table H.4 (*Continued*)

Classes	Methods	Replacement
	preferredSize ( )	getPreferredSize ( )
	minimumSize (int)	getMinimumSize (int)
	minimumSize ( )	getMinimumSize ( )
	delItems (int, int)	Not for public use in the future. This method is expected to be retained only as a package private method.
Menu countItems ( )		getItemCount ( )
MenuBar	countMenus ( )	getMenuCount ( )
MenuComponent	getPeer ( )	None
MenuItem	enable ( )	setEnabled (boolean)
	enable (boolean)	setEnabled (boolean)
	disable ( )	setEnabled (boolean)
Polygon	getBoundingBox ( )	getBounds ( )
	inside (int, int)	contains (int, int)
Rectangle	reshape (int, int, int, int)	setBounds (int, int, int, int)
	move (int, int)	setLocation (int, int)
	reSize (int, int)	setSize (int, int)
	inside (int, int)	contains (int, int)
Scrollbar	getVisible ( )	getVisibleAmount ( )
	setLineIncrement (int v)	setUnitIncrement (int)
	getLineIncrement ( )	getUnitIncrement ( )
	setPageIncrement (int v)	setBlockIncrement (int)
	getPageIncrement ( )	getBlockIncrement ( )
ScrollPane	layout ( )	doLayout ( )
TextArea	insertText (String, int)	insert (String, int)
	appendText (String)	append (String)
	replaceText (String, int, int)	replaceRange (String, int, int)
	preferredSize (int, int)	getPreferredSize (int, int)
	preferredSize ( )	getPreferredSize ( )
	minimumSize (int, int)	getMinimumSize (int, int)
	minimumSize ( )	getMinimumSize ( )
TextField	setEchoCharacter (char)	SetEchochar (char)
	preferredSize (int)	GetPreferredSize (int)
	preferredSize ( )	getPreferredSize ( )
	minimumSize (int)	GetMinimumSize (int)
	minimumSize ( )	GetMinimumSize ( )
Window	nextFocus (Component)	TransferFocus (Component)
	postEvent (Event)	DispatchEvent (AWTEvent)

	Table H.5	**List of Deprecated 1.0 Methods in Java.net**	

Classes	*Methods*	*Replacement*
Socket	Socket (String, int, boolean)	Use DatagramSocket's constructors
	Socket (inetAddress, int, boolean)	Use DatagramSocket's constructors

Table H.6	**List of Deprecated Classes**

Class	*Package*
EventListener	java.util
EventObject	java.util
LineNumberInputStream	java.io
PrintStream	java.io
Serializable	java.io
StringBufferInputStream	java.io

H.3 Deprecated Classes and Members of Version 1.1

Some of the classes and members of version 1.1 have been removed or declared deprecated in version 2. They are summarized in Tables H.7 and H.8.

	Table H.7	**Deprecated Members of Version 1.1**

Package	*Class*	*Members*
java.awt	Frame	CROSSHAIR_CURSOR
		DEFAULT_CURSOR
		E_RESIZE_CURSOR
		HAND_CURSOR
		MOVE_CURSOR
		N_RESIZE_CURSOR
		NE_RESIZE_CURSOR
		NW_RESIZE_CURSOR
		S_RESIZE_CURSOR
		SE_RESIZE_CURSOR
		SW_RESIZE_CURSOR
		TEXT_CURSOR
		W_RESIZE_CURSOR
		WAIT_CURSOR
java.awt.image	BufferedImage	getGraphics ( )
java.awt	List	addItem ( )
		delItem ( )

(Continued)

Table H.7   (*Continued*)

Package	Class	Members
java.awt.swing	AbstractButton	getLabel ( )
		setLabel ( )
java.io	ObjectInputStream	readLine ( )
java.lang	SecurityManager	classDepth ( )
		classLoaderDepth ( )
		getInCheck ( )
		inCheck ( )
		inClass ( )
		inClassLoader ( )
	Thread	resume ( )
		stop ( )
		suspend ( )
	ThreadGroup	resume ( )
		stop ( )
		suspend ( )
java.rmi.registry	RegistryHandler	registryImpl ( )
		registryStub ( )
java.security	Certificate	**Entire class**
	Identity	addCertificate ( )
		certificates ( )
		removeCertificate ( )
	Signature	getParameter ( )
		setParameter ( )
	SignatureSpi	engineGetParameter ( )
		engineSetParameter ( )
java.sql	Date	Date ( )
		getHours ( )
		getMinutes ( )
		getSeconds ( )
		setHours ( )
		setMinutes ( )
		setSeconds ( )
	DriverManager	getLogStream ( )
		setLogStream ( )
	PreparedStatement	setUnicodeStread ( )
	ResultSet	getUnicodeStream ( )
	Time	getDate ( )
		getDay ( )

(*Continued*)

Table H.7 (*Continued*)

Package	Class	Members
		getMonth ( )
		getYear ( )
		setDate ( )
		setMonth ( )
		setYear ( )
	TimeStamp	TimeStamp ( )

Table H.8 Removed Members of Version 1.1		
Package	*Class*	*Members*
java.awt.peer	ActiveEvent	dispatch ( )
java.net	URLConnection	fileNameMap
java.rmi	RMISecurityManager	checkAwtEventQueueAccess ( )
		checkCreateClassLoader ( )
		checkDelete ( )
		checkExec ( )
		checkExit ( )
		checkLink ( )
		checkListen ( )
		checkMemberAccess ( )
		checkMulticast ( )
		checkPrintJobAccess ( )
		checkPropertiesAccess ( )
		checkPropertyAccess ( )
		checkRead ( )
		checkSecurityAccess ( )
		checkSetFactory ( )
		checkSystemClipboardAccess ( )
		checkTopLevelWindow ( )
		checkWrite ( )
java.security	KeyPairGenerator	generateKeyPair ( )
		initialize ( )
	MessageDigest	engineDigest ( )
		engineReset ( )
		engineUpdate ( )
	Signature	enginegetParameter ( )
		engineInitSign ( )
		engineInitVerify ( )
		engineSetParameter ( )

(*Continued*)

Table H.8 (*Continued*)

Package	Class	Members
		engineSign ( )
		engineUpdate ( )
		engineVerify ( )
java.util	GregorianCalendar	after ( )
		before ( )
		equals ( )
	Vector	toString ( )

Since Java classes undergo continuous revision and modifications, the list of removed/deprecated methods and classes given here may not be entirely complete. It is only intended as a quick reference. For a latest list; the reader should consult the JDK documentation available in one of the Sun web sites.

We can obtain a complete list of deprecated methods in a program by using the **javac** compiler with the –*deprecation* option, when the compiler generates warning messages about usage of such methods.

Appendix **I**

Statistics of Java Packages

Table I.1   Growth of Java from 1.0 to 2

Java Version	Packages	Class and Interfaces				Members			
		Classes	Interfaces	Total		Fields	Constructor	Methods	Total
1.0	8	172	40	212		261	319	1545	2125
1.1	23	391	113	504		926	701	3851	5478
2	62	1287	305	1592		3107	2095	13635	18837

Table I.2   Contents of Java 1.0 Packages

Package	Classes	Interfaces	Total Members
java.applet	1	3	38
java.awt	44	2	740
java.awt.image	9	3	124
java.awt.peer	0	22	84
java.io	28	3	340
java.lang	62	2	505
java.net	16	3	148
java.util	12	2	146

Table I.3   Contents of Java 1.1 Packages

Package	Classes	Interfaces	Total Members
java.applet	1	3	39
java.awt	54	7	1317
java.awt.datatransfer	4	2	29
java.awt.event	19	11	304
java.awt.image	11	3	155
java.awt.peer	0	27	117
java.beans	17	6	147
java.io	61	8	645
java.lang	67	2	660
java.lang.reflect	6	1	98
java.math	2	0	86
java.net	22	4	254
java.rmi	18	1	68
java.rmi.dgc	2	1	10
java.rmi.registry	1	2	13
java.rmi.server	16	7	96
java.security	21	5	158
java.security.acl	3	5	30
java.security.interfaces	0	5	8
java.sql	9	8	423
java.text	18	1	315
java.util	23	3	355
java.util.zip	16	1	151

Table I.4   Contents of Java 2 Packages

Package	Classes	Interfaces	Total Members
java.applet	1	3	40
java.awt	64	14	1640
java.awt.accessibility	6	7	193
java.awt.color	7	0	179
java.awt.datatransfer	4	2	45
java.awt.dnd	13	4	134
java.awt.dnd.peer	0	3	19
java.awt.event	20	13	356
java.wt.font	13	2	353
java.awt.geom.	32	1	613
java.awt.im	2	1	27
java.awt.image	42	10	794
java.awt.image.codec	6	0	109
java.awt.image.renderable	4	3	94
java.awt.peer	0	26	116
java.awt.print	9	3	176

(Continued)

Table I.4 (*Continued*)

java.awt.swing	147	22	3256
java.awt.swing.border	9	1	131
java.awt.swing.event	19	19	167
java.awt.swing.plaf	39	1	135
java.awt.swing.plaf.basic	107	0	1788
java.awt.swing.plaf.metal	42	0	446
java.awt.swing.preview	20	1	257
java.awt.swing.table	9	4	266
java.awt.swing.text	66	21	961
java.awt.swing.text.html	39	0	100
java.awt.swing.text.rtf	1	0	7
java.awt.swing.tree	4	7	202
java.awt.swing.undo	7	2	97
java.beans	17	8	178
java.beans.beancontext	11	8	175
java.io	66	11	733
java.lang	72	4	802
java.lang.ref	6	0	21
java.lang.reflect	8	1	104
java.math	2	0	88
java.net	28	4	298
java.rmi	19	1	53
java.rmi.activation	12	4	68
java.rmi.dgc	2	1	10
java.rmi.registry	1	2	14
java.rmi.server	17	7	119
java.security	51	6	342
java.security.acl	3	5	30
java.security.cert	11	1	80
java.security.interfaces	0	5	8
java.security.spec	8	2	27
java.sql	10	18	649
java.text	20	4	352
java.util	38	13	717
java.util.jar	8	0	75
java.util.mime	3	0	29
java.util.zip	16	1	157
org.omg.CORBA	78	26	661
org.omg.CORBA.ContainedPackage	1	0	4
org.omg.CORBA.ContainerPackage	1	0	5
org.omg.CORBA.InterfaceDefPackage	1	0	10
org.omg.CORBA.ORBPackage	1	0	1
org.omg.CORBA.TypeCodePackage	2	0	2
org.omg.CORBA.portable	4	1	95
or.omg.CosNaming	20	2	138
org.omg.CosNaming.NamingContextPackage	18	0	91

Appendix **J**

S C J P Exam
Model Questions

This appendix provides a number of true/false, multiple-choice, and short-answer questions which are modeled on the Sun Certified Java Programmer (SCJP) examination conducted by Sun Microsystems, the creator of Java language. Readers must try to analyze and understand each question before attempting to answer it. They are also encouraged to verify the answers by actually testing the code snippets given. This would enable them not only to check their answers but also to enhance their understanding of Java concepts considerably.

Part A: True/False Questions

1. The name of a Java program file must match the name of the class with the extension .java
   A. True
   B. False

2. Two methods cannot have the same name in Java.
   A. True
   B. False

3. The modulus operator (%) can be used only with integer operands.
   A. True
   B. False

4. Declarations can appear anywhere in the body of a Java method.
   A. True
   B. False

5. All the bitwise operators have the same level of precedence in java.
   A. True
   B. False

6. When x is a positive number, the operations x > > 2 and x > > > 2 both produce the same result.
   A. True
   B. False

7. If a = 10 and b = 15, then the statement x = (a > b)? a : b;
   assigns the value 15 to x.
   A. True
   B. False

8. In evaluating a logical expression of type
   ```
   boolean expression1 && boolean expression2
   ```
   both the boolean expressions are not always evaluated.
   A. True
   B. False

9. In evaluating the expression (x = = y && a < b) the boolean expression x = = y is evaluated first and then a < b is evaluated.
   A. True
   B. False

10. The **default** case is always required in the switch selection structure.
    A. True
    B. False

11. The **break** statement is required in the default case of a switch selection structure.
    A. True
    B. False

12. The expression (x = = y && a < b) is true if ether x = = y is true or a < b is true.
    A. True
    B. False

13. A variable declared inside the **for** loop control cannot be referenced outside the loop.
    A. True
    B. False

14. Java always provides a default constructor to a class.
    A. True
    B. False

15. When present, **package** must be the first noncomment statement in the file.
    A. True
    B. False

16. The **import** statement is always the first noncomment statement in a Java program file.
    A. True
    B. False

17. Objects are passed to a method by use of call-by-reference.
    A. True
    B. False

18. It is perfectly legal to refer to any instance variable inside of a **static** method.
    A. True
    B. False

19. When we implement an interface method, it should be declared as **public**.
    A. True
    B. False

20. We can overload methods with differences only in their return type.
    A. True
    B. False

21. It is an error to have a method with the same signature in both the super class and its subclass
    A. True
    B. False

22. A constructor must always invoke its super class constructor in its first statement.
    A. True
    B. False

23. Subclasses of an abstract class that do not provide an implementation of an abstract method, are also abstract.
    A. True
    B. False

24. Any class may be inherited by another class in the same package.
    A. True
    B. False

25. Any method in a super class can be overridden in its subclass.
    A. True
    B. False

26. One of the features of Java is that an array can store many different types of values
    A. True
    B. False

27. An individual array element that is passed to a method and modified in that method will contain the modified value when the called method completes execution.
    A. True
    B. False

28. Members of a class specified as a **private** are accessible only to the methods of the class.
    A. True
    B. False

29. A method declared as **static** cannot access **non-static** class members.
    A. True
    B. False

30. A **static** class method can be invoked by simply using the name of the method alone.
    A. True
    B. False

31. It is an error, if a class with one or more **abstract** methods is not explicitly declared **abstract**.
    A. True
    B. False

32. It is perfectly legal to assign an object of a super class to a subclass reference without a cost.
    A. True
    B. False

33. It is perfectly legal to assign a subclass object to a super class reference.
    A. True
    B. False

34. Every method of a **final** class is implicitly **final**.
    A. True
    B. False

35. All methods in an **abstract** class must be declared **abstract**.
    A. True
    B. False

36. When the **String** objects are compared with = =, the result is true if the strings contain the same values.
    A. True
    B. False

37. A **String** object cannot be modified after it is created.
    A. True
    B. False

38. The length of a **String** object **s1** can be obtained using the expression **s1.length**.
    A. True
    B. False

39. A **catch** can have comma-separated multiple arguments.
    A. True
    B. False

40. It is an error to catch the same type of exception in two different **catch** blocks associated with a particular **try** block.
    A. True
    B. False

41. Throwing an **Exception** always causes program termination.
    A. True
    B. False

42. Every call to **wait** has a corresponding call to **notify** that will eventually end the waiting.
    A. True
    B. False

43. Declaring a method **synchronized** guarantees that the deadlock cannot occur.
    A. True
    B. False

44. The programmer must explicitly create the **System.in** and **System.out** objects.
    A. True
    B. False

45. If the file-position pointer points to a location in a sequential file other than the beginning, we must use the **seek** method to bring the pointer to the beginning, to read from the beginning of the file again.

A. True
B. False

46. To delete a file, we can use an instance of class **File**.
    A. True
    B. False

47. A panel cannot be added to another panel.
    A. True
    B. False

48. Frames and applets cannot be used together in the same program.
    A. True
    B. False

49. A **final** class may not have any **abstract** methods.
    A. True
    B. False

50. A class may be both **abstract** and **final**.
    A. True
    B. False

51. A thread wants to make a second thread ineligible for execution. To achieve this, the first thread can call the **yield( )** method on the second thread.
    A. True
    B. False

52. A thread can make a second thread ineligible for execution by calling the **suspend( )** method on the second thread.
    A. True
    B. False

53. A Java monitor must either extend **Thread** class or implement **Runnable** interface.
    A. True
    B. False

54. The **CheckboxGroup** class is a subclass of the **Component** class.
    A. True
    B. False

55. If a frame uses a Grid layout manager and does not contain any panels, then all the components within the frame are of the same width and height.
    A. True
    B. False

56. With a Border layout manager, the component at the centre gets all the space that is left over, after the components at North and South have been considered.
    A. True
    B. False

57. The CODE value in an <APPLET> tag must name a class file that is in the same directory as the calling HTML page.
    A. True
    B. False

58. If **getParameter( )** returns null, then assigning the return value to a variable of type **String** may cause an exception to be thrown.
    A. True
    B. False

59. It is possible to use the **File** class to list the contents of the current working directory.
    A. True
    B. False

60. **Reader** class has a method that can read and return floats and doubles.
    A. True
    B. False

Part B: Multiple-choice Questions

1. The range of values for the long type data is
   A. -2^{31} to $2^{31} - 1$
   B. -2^{64} to 2^{64}
   C. -2^{63} to $2^{63} - 1$
   D. -2^{32} to $2^{32} - 1$

2. Which of the following represent(s) of a hexadecimal number?
   A. 570
   B. (hex) 5
   C. 0X9F
   D. 0X5

3. Which of the following assignments are valid?
   A. float x = 123.4;
   B. long m = 023;
   C. int n = (int)false;
   D. double y = 0X756;

4. The default value of char type variable is
   A. '\u0020'
   B. '\u00ff'
   C. " "
   D. '\u0000'

5. What will be the result of the expression 13 & 25?
   A. 38
   B. 25
   C. 9
   D. 12

6. What will be result of the expression 9 | 9?
   A. 1
   B. 18
   C. 9
   D. None of the above

7. Which of the following are correct?
   A. int a = 16, a >> 2 = 4
   B. int b = –8, b >> 1 = –4
   C. int a = 16, a >>> 2 = 4
   D. int b = –8, b >>> 1 = –4
   E. All the above

8. What will be the values of x, m, and n after execution of the following statements?
   ```
   int x, m, n;
   m = 10;
   n = 15;
   x = ++m + n++;
   ```
   A. x = 25, m = 10, n = 15
   B. x = 27, m = 10, n = 15
   C. x = 26, m = 11, n = 16
   D. x = 27, m = 11, n = 16

9. If m and n are int type variables, what will be the result of the expression
   ```
   m % n
   ```
   when m = 5 and n = 2?
   A. 0
   B. 1
   C. 2
   D. None of the above

10. If m and n are int type variables, what will be the result of the expression
    ```
    m % n
    ```
    when m = –14 and n = –3?
    A. 4
    B. 2
    C. –2
    D. –4
    E. None of the above

11. Consider the following statements:
    ```
    int x = 10, y = 15;
    x = ( (x<y) ? (y+x) : (y–x) ;
    ```
    What will be the value of x after executing these statements?
    A. 10
    B. 25
    C. 15
    D. 5
    E. Error. Cannot be executed.

12. Which of the following operators are overloaded for String objects?
    A. –
    B. +
    C. +=
    D. &

E. <<
F. None of these

13. What is the result of the expression

    (1 & 2) + (3 | 4)

    in base ten.
    A. 1
    B. 2
    C. 8
    D. 7
    E. 3

14. Which of the following will produce a value of 22 if x = 22.9?
    A. ceil(x)
    B. round(x)
    C. rint(x)
    D. abs(x)
    E. floor(x)

15. Which of the following will produce a value of 10 if x = 9.7?
    A. floor(x)
    B. abs(x)
    C. rint(x)
    D. round(x)
    E. ceil(x)

16. Which of the following expressions are illegal?
    A. (10 | 5)
    B. (false && true)
    C. boolean x = (boolean)10;
    D. float y = 12.34;

17. Which of the following lines will not compile?
    1. byte b1 = 5, b2 = 3, b3;
    2. short s = 25;
    3. b2 = s;
    4. b3 = b1 * b2;
    A. Line 1 only
    B. Line 3 only
    C. Line 4 only
    D. Line 1 and Line 4 only
    E. Line 3 and Line 4 only

18. Which of the following are illegal loop constructs?
    A. while(int i > 0)
        {i- -; other statements;}
    B. for(int i = 10, int j = 0; i+j > 5; i = i–2, j++)
        {
              Body statements
        }

C. int i = 10;
    while(i)
    {
        Body statements
    }
D. int i = 1, sum = 0;
    do {loop statements}
    while(sum < 10 || i<5);

19. Consider the following code

```
if (number >= 0)
  if (number > 0)
  System.out.println ("Number is positive") :
else
  System.out.println ("Number is negative") :
```

What will be the output if number is equal to 0?
A. Number is negative
B. Number is positive
C. Both A and B
D. None of the above

20. Which of the following control expressions are valid for an if statement?
A. an integer expression
B. a boolean expression
C. either A or B
D. Neither A nor B

21. In the following code snippet, which lines of code contain error?
    1. int j = 0;
    2. while(j < 10) {
    3. j++;
    4. if(j = = 5) continue loop;
    5. System.out.println("j is" + j); }
A. Line 2
B. Line 3
C. Line 4
D. Line 5
E. None of the above

22. Consider the following code:

```
char c = 'a' :
switch (c)
{
  case 'a' :
  System.out.println ("A") :
  case 'b' :
  System.out.println ("B") :
  default:
  System.out.println ("C") :
}
```

For this code, which of the following statement is true?
A. output will be A
B. output will be A followed by B
C. output will be A, followed by B, and then followed by C
D. code is illegal and therefore will not compile

23. Consider the following class definition.
```
class Student extends String
{
}
```
What happens when we try to compile this class?
A. Will not compile because class body is not defined
B. Will not compile because the class is not declared **public**
C. Will not compile because String is **abstract**
D. Will not compile because String is **final**
E. Will compile successfully.

24. What is wrong in the following class definitions?
```
abstract class Print
{
   abstract show ( ) ;
}
class Display extends Print
{
}
```
A. Nothing is wrong
B. Wrong. Method **show( )** should have a return type
C. Wrong. Method **show( )** is not implemented in Display
D. Wrong. **Display** does not contain any members

25. What is the error in the following class definition?
```
abstract class XY
{
   abstract sum (int x, int y) { }
}
```
A. Class header is not defined properly
B. Constructor is not defined
C. Method is not defined properly
D. No error

26. Consider the following class definitions:
```
class maths
{
   Student student1;
}
class Student
{
   String name;
}
```

This code represents:

A. an 'is a' relationship
B. a 'has a' relationship
C. both
D. neither

27. Consider the following class definition:

```
class A extends B
{
    public A (int x) { }
    public A (int x, int y)
    {
        super (x, y) ;
    }
}
```

Which of the following are legal statements to construct A type objects?

A. A a = new A( );
B. A a = new A(4, 2, 7);
C. A a = new A(5, 6);
D. A a = new A(10);
E. A a = new A(Base(4, 5), 6);

28. Which of the following are overloading the method

```
int sum(int x, int y) { }
```

A. int sum(int x, int y, int z) { }
B. float sum(int x, int y) { }
C. int sum(float x, float y) { }
D. int sum(int a, int b) { }
E. float sum(int x, int y, float z) { }

29. What is the error in the following code?

```
class Test
{
    abstract void display ( ) ;
}
```

A. No error
B. Method **display( )** should be declared as **static**
C. **Test** class should be declared as **abstract**
D. **Test** class should be declared as **public**

30. Which of the following statements are true?

1. We cannot use abstract classes to instantiate objects directly.
2. The abstract methods of an abstract class must be defined in its subclass.
3. We cannot declare abstract constructors.
4. We may declare abstract static methods.

A. Line 1 only
B. Line 2 only
C. Line 1 and line 2 only

    D. Line 1, line 2 and line 3 only

    E. All are true

31. Which keyword can protect a class in a package from accessibility by the classes outside the package?

    A. private

    B. protected

    C. final

    D. don't use any keyword at all (make it default)

32. We would like to make a member of a class visible in all subclasses regardless of what package they are in. Which one of the following keywords would achieve this?

    A. private

    B. protected

    C. public

    D. private protected

33. The use of protected keyword to a member in a class will restrict its visibility as follows:

    A. Visible only in the class and its subclass in the same package.

    B. Visible only inside the same package.

    C. Visible in all classes in the same package and subclasses in other packages

    D. Visible only in the class where it is declared.

34. Which of the following are not keywords?

    A. NULL

    B. implements

    C. protected

    D. extended

    E. string

35. Which of the following are keywords?

    A. switch

    B. integer

    C. default

    D. boolean

    E. object

36. Which of the following keywords are used to control access to a class member?

    A. default

    B. abstract

    C. protected

    D. interface

    E. public

37. The keywords reserved but not used in the initial version of Java are:

    A. union

    B. const

    C. inner

    D. goto

    E. boolean

    F. synchronized

38. Consider the following code:

```
class ClassA
{
   public static void main (String args [ ] )
   {
      ClassB b = classB ( ) ;
   }
   ClassA (int x) { }
}
class ClassB extends ClassA
{
}
```

What will happen when we compile and run this code?
A. Compile and run successfully
B. Error. ClassA does not define a no-argument constructor
C. Error. ClassB does not define a no-argument constructor
D. Error. There is no code in the class ClassB
E. Error. There is no code in the constructor ClassA (int x)

39. A package is a collection of
A. classes
B. interfaces
C. editing tools
D. classes and interfaces

40. Which of the following statements are true?
A. An abstract class may not have any final methods.
B. A final class may not have any abstract methods.
C. An inner class may be declared with any accessibility keyword.
D. Transient variables must be static.

41. Which of the following defines a legal abstract class?
A. class Vehicle {
        abstract void display( ); }
B. abstract Vehicle {
        abstract void display( ); }
C. abstract class Vehicle {
        abstract void display( ); }
D. class abstract Vehicle {
        abstract void display( ); }
E. abstract class Vehicle {
        abstract void display( ); {
        System.out.println("Car"); }}

42. Package pl contains the following code:

```
package p1;
public class Student { Body of student }
class Test { Body of Test }
```

Now consider the following code:

```
import p1.*;
class Result
{
    Student s1;
    Test t1;
}
```

This code will not compile because
A. Class Result should be declared public.
B. Student class is not available.
C. Test class is not available.
D. Result body is not fully defined.

43. Consider the following code:

```
interface Area
{
    float compute (float x, float y) ;
}
class Room implements Area
{
    float compute (float x, float y)
    {
        return (x & y) ;
    }
}
```

What is wrong with the code?
A. Interface definition is incomplete
B. Method **compute( )** in interface **Area** should be declared public
C. Method **compute( )** in class **Room** should be declared public
D. All the above

44. The concept of multiple inheritance is implemented in Java by
A. extending two or more classes
B. extending one class and implementing one or more interfaces
C. implementing two or more interfaces
D. all the above

45. Which of the following statements are valid array declaration?
A. int number( );
B. float average[ ];
C. double[ ] marks;
D. counter int[ ];

46. Consider the following code

```
int number [ ] = new int [5] ;
```

After execution of this statement, which of the following are true?
A. number[0] is undefined
B. number[5] is undefined
C. number[4] is null
D. number[2] is 0
E. number.length( ) is 5

47. What will be the content of array variable table after executing the following code?

```
for (int i=0; i<3; i++)
    for (int j=0, j<3; j++)
        if (j == i) table [i] [j] = 1;
        else table [i] [j] = 0;
```

A.			B.			C.			D.		
0	0	0	1	0	0	0	0	1	1	0	0
0	0	0	1	1	0	0	1	0	0	1	0
0	0	0	1	1	1	1	0	0	0	0	1

48. Which of the following classes are available in the **java.lang** package?
A. Stack
B. Object
C. Math
D. Random
E. String
F. StringBuffer
G. Vector

49. Which of the following are the wrapper classes?
A. Random
B. Byte
C. Vector
D. Integer
E. Short
F. Double
G. String

50. Which of the following contain error?
A. int x[ ] = int[10];
B. int[ ] y = new int[5];
C. float d[ ] = {1, 2, 3};
D. x = y = new int [10];
E. int a[ ] = {1, 2}; int b[ ]; b = a;
F. int i = new int(10);

51. Which of the following methods belong to the **String** class?
A. length( )
B. compareTo( )
C. equals( )
D. substring( )

   E. All of them

   F. None of them

52. Given the code

```
String s1 = "yes";
String s2 = "yes";
String s3 = new String (s1) ;
```

   Which of the following would equate to **true**?

   A. s1 = = s2

   B. s1 = s2

   C. s3 = = s1

   D. s1.equals(s2)

   E. s3.equals(s1)

53. Suppose that s1 and s2 are two strings. Which of the statements or expressions are correct?

   A. String s3 = s1 + s2;

   B. String s3 = s1 − s2;

   C. s1 <= s2

   D. s1.compareTo(s2);

   E. int m = s1.length( );

54. Given the code

```
String s = new String ("abc") ;
```

   Which of the following calls are valid?

   A. s.trim( )

   B. s.replace('a', 'A')

   C. s.substring(3)

   D. s.toUpperCase( )

   E. s.setCharAt(1,'A')

   F. s.append("xyz")

55. The methods **wait( )** and **notify( )** are defined in

   A. java.lang.String

   B. java.lang.Runnable

   C. java.lang.Object

   D. java.lang.Thread

   E. java.lang.ThreadGroup

56. Which of the following statements are true?

   A. A Java monitor must either extend Thread or implement Runnable.

   B. The sleep( ) method should be enclosed in try ... catch block.

   C. The yield( ) method should be enclosed in try ... catch block.

   D. A thread can be temporarily suspended from running by using the wait( ) method.

   E. A suspended thread using suspend( ) method can be revived using the resume( ) method.

57. Given the following code:

```
class Base { int x = 10; }
class Derived extends Base
{ int x = 20; }
```

```
Base b = new Base ( ) :
Derived d = new Derived( ) ;
Base bd = new Derived( ) :
```

The statement

```
System.out.println (b.x + "  " + d.x + "  " + bd.x) :
```

will produce the output

A. 10 20 20

B. 10 20 10

C. 20 10 20

D. 20 20 10

58. Given the class definitions

```
class Base
{
    void display( )
    { System.out.println ("Base") ; }
}
class Derived extends Base
{
    void display ( )
    { System.out.println ("Derived") ; }
}
```

and objects

```
Base b = new Base( );
Derived d = new Derived( );
Base bd = new Derived( ):
```

then the print statements

```
System.out.print(b.display( ) + "  ");
System.out.print(d.display( ) + "  ");
System.out.print(bd.display( ) + "  ");
System.out.println( );
```

will display:

A. Base Base Derived

B. Base Derived Base

C. Base Derived Derived

D. Derived Derived Derived

59. When we invoke **repaint( )** for a Component, the AWT invokes the method:

A. draw( )

B. show( )

C. update( )

D. paint( )

60. What does the following line of code do?

```
TextField text = new TextFiled(10);
```

A. Creates text object that can hold 10 rows of text.

B. Creates text object that can hold 10 columns of text.

C. Creates the object text and initializes it with the value 10.

D. The code is illegal.

61. Which of the following applet tags is legal to embed an applet class named Test into a Web page?

    A. < applet

       class = Test width = 200 height = 100>

       < /applet>

    B. < applet>

       code = Test.class width = 200 height = 100>

       < /applet>

    C. < applet

       code = Test.class width = 200 height = 100

       < /applet>

    D. < applet

       param = Test.class width = 200 height = 100>

       < /applet>

    E. < applet

       code = Test.class width = 200 height = 100>

       < / applet>

62. Which of the following methods can be used to draw the outline of a square?

    A. fillRect( )

    B. drawLine( )

    C. drawRect( )

    D. drawString( )

    E. drawPolygon( )

63. Which of the following methods can be used to change the size of a component

    A. dimension( )

    B. setSize( )

    C. area( )

    D. size( )

    E. resize( )

64. Which of the following methods can be used to remove a component from the display?

    A. delete( )

    B. remove( )

    C. disappear( )

    D. hide( )

    E. move( )

65. The setBackground( ) method is part of the class

    A. Graphics

    B. Applet

    C. Component

    D. Container

    E. Object

66. When we implement the Runnable interface, we must define the method

    A. start( )

    B. init( )

    C. run( )

D. runnable( )

E. resume( )

F. main( )

67. Which of the following strings can be used as mode strings for creating a RandomAccessFile object?

A. " r "

B. " w "

C. " rw "

D. " wr "

E. " 0 "

68. What will be the output of the following program?

```
class Main1
{
  public static void main(String args [ ])
  {
    boolean b = true;
    System.out.println("XXX");
    return;
    System.out.println("YYY");
  }
}
```

A. XXX

B. YYY

C. XXX followed by YYY

D. Error. Won't compile

69. What will be output of the following program?

```
class Main2
{
  public static void main(String args[ ])
  {
    boolean b = true;
    System.out.println("XXX");
    if( !b ) return;
    System.out.println("YYY");
  }
}
```

A. XXX

B. YYY

C. XXX followed by YYY

D. Error. Won't compile

70. DataInput is

A. an abstract class defined in java.io.

B. a class we can use to read primitive data types.

C. an interface that defines methods to open files.

D. an interface that defines methods to read primitive data types.

71. Which of the following statements are *true*?
    A. Unicode characters are all 16 bits.
    B. UTF characters are all 24 bits.
    C. Reader class has methods that can read integers and floats.
    D. File class may be used to rename a file.
    E. DataOutputStream objects are used to write primitive data to a file.

72. Which are the valid ways to create DataInputStream streams?
    A. new DataInputStream( );
    B. new DataInputStream("in.dat", "r");
    C. new DataInputStream("in.dat")
    D. new DataInputStream(new File("in.dat"));
    E. new DataInputStream(new FileInputStream("in.dat");

73. Which exception is thrown by the read( ) method of InputStream class?
    A. Exception
    B. FileNotFoundException
    C. ReadException
    D. IOException
    E. None of the above

74. In the code below, what data types the variable x can have?
    ```
    byte b1 = 5;
    byte b2 = 10;
    x = b1 * b2;
    ```
    A. byte
    B. int
    C. short
    D. long
    E. float
    F. double

75. If you want to assign a value of 99 to the variable year, then which of the following lines can be used within an <applet> tag?
    A. number = getParameter(99)
    B. < number = 99 >
    C. < param = radius value = 99 >
    D. < param name = number value = 99 >
    E. < param number = 99 >

76. What is java_g used for?
    A. Using the jdb tool
    B. Executing a class with optimization turned off
    C. To provide information about deprecated methods
    D. None of the above

77. With javadoc, which of the following denotes a javadoc comment?
    A. //#
    B. /*
    C. /**
    D. //**

78. Given file is a File object, which of the following are legal statements to create a new file
    A. file.create( );
    B. FileOutputStream fos = new FileOutputStream(file);
    C. FileWriter out = new FileWriter(file);
    D. FileInputStream fis = new FileInputStream(file);
    E. RandomAccessFile raf = new RandomAccessFile(file);

79. Which javadoc tage is used to denote a comment for a method parameter?
    A. @method
    B. @parameter
    C. @argument
    D. @param
    E. @value

80. Which of the following command lines options generates documentation for all classes and methods?
    A. –protected
    B. –public
    C. –private
    D. –verbose
    E. –encoding

81. Given the declarations
    ```
    int x, m = 2000;
    short y;
    byte b1 = -40, b2;
    long n;
    ```
    which of the following assignment statements will evaluate correctly?
    A. x = m * b1;
    B. y = m * b1;
    C. n = m * 3L;
    D. x = m * 3L;

82. Given the declarations
    ```
    boolean b;
    short x1 = 100, x2 = 200, x3 = 300;
    ```
    Which of the following statements are evaluated to *true*?
    A. b = x1 * 2 = x2;
    B. b = x1 + x2 != 3 * x1;
    C. b = (x3 – 2*x2<0) || ((x3 = 400) <2**x2);
    D. b = (x3 – 21*x2>0) || (x3 = 400) 2*x2);

83. In which of the following code fragments, the variable x is evaluated to 8.
    A. int x = 32;'
       x = x >> 2;
    B. int x = 33;
       x = x >> 2;
    C. int x = 35;
       x = x >> 2;
    D. int x = 16;
       x = x >> 1;

84. Consider the following code snippet:

```
.....

.....
try {
int x = 0;
int y = 50/x;
System.out.println("Division by zero");
}
catch(ArithmeticException e) {
System.out.println("catch block");
}
.....

.....
```

What will be the output?
A. Error. Won't compile
B. Division by zero
C. Catch block
D. Division by zero
   Catch block

85. Which of the following represent legal flow control statements?
A. break;
B. break( );
C. continue outer;
D. continue(inner);
E. return;
F. exit( );

Part C: Short-answer Questions

1. What will be the output of the following code?
```
byte x = 64, y;
y = (byte) (x << 2);
System.out.println(y);
```

2. What will be the output of the following code:
```
byte b;
double d = 417.35;
b = (byte) d;
System.out.println(b);
```

3. Given the value of a variable, write a statement, without using if construct, which will produce the absolute value of the variable.

4. What is wrong with the following code?
```
switch(x)
{
   case 1:
   n1 = 10;
   n2 = 20;
```

```
       case 2:
       n3 = 30;
       break;
       n4 = 40;
     }
```

5. What will be the output of the following program code?

```
     int m = 100;
     int n = 300;
     while (++m < --n);
     System.out.println(m);
```

6. What does the following fragment display

```
     String s = "six:" + 3 + 3;
     System.out.println(s);
```

7. What is the output of the following code?

```
     String s;
     System.out.println("s = " + s);
```

8. What is the output of the following code?

```
     String s = new String( );
     System.out.println("s = " + s);
```

9. What is the problem with the following snippet?

```
     class Q9
     {
       public static void main(String args[ ])
       {
         int i = 5, j = 10;
         if ( (i<j) || (i=10) )
           System.out.println("OK");
         System.out.println("NOT OK");
       }
     }
```

10. What will be the output of the following code snippet?

```
     int x = 10;
     int y = 20;
     if ((x<y) || (x=5)>10)
       System.out.println(x);
     else
       System.out.println(y);
```

11. Show the output the following code:

```
     int a, b;
     a = 5;
     b = 10;
     if(a > 5)
         if(b > 5)
```

```
    {
      System.out.println("b is " + b);
    }
    else
      System.out.println("a is " + a);
```

12. State the output of the following code:

```
    int a = 10;
    int b = 5;
    if(a > b)
    {
      if(b > 5)
      System.out.println("b is " + b);
    }
    else
      System.out.println("a is" + a);
```

13. Give the output of the following code:

```
    int m = 100;
    while(true)
    {
      if(m < 10)
        break;
      m = m - 10;
    }
    Systm.out.println("m is " + m);
```

14. Give the output of the following code:

```
    int m = 100;
    while(true)
    {
      if(m < 10)
      continue;
      m = m - 10;
    }
    System.out.println("m is " + m);
```

15. Using a single line of code, complete the following class so that it returns x+y if the value of x is equal to y, otherwise returns 0:

```
    public class XY
    {
    public return int fun(int x, int y)
    {
      .......... (one line code her)
    }
    }
```

16. Given a package named **EDU.Student**, how would you import a class named **Test** contained in this package? Write one line statement.

17. Consider the following class definition:
    ```
    class Student
    {
      abstract double result( )
    }
    ```
    This code will not compile since a keyword is missing in the first line. What is the keyword?

18. Consider the following class file?
    ```
    import java.awt.*;
    import java.io.*;
    package studentBase;
    class Test
    {
      void display( )
      {
        System.out.println("RESULTS");
      }
    }
    ```
    Will it compile? YES or NO. Give reason, if No:

19. Consider the following code:
    ```
    class Product
    {
      public static void main(String args [ ])
      {
        int x = 10, y = 20;
        System.out.println(mul (x, y));
      }
      int mul(int a, int b)
      {
        return(a * b);
      }
    }
    ```
    Will it compile? YES or NO. Give reason, if No:

20. Given below are two files:

    File Employee.java

    ```
    package purchase;
    public class Employee
    {
      protected double age = 35.00;
    }
    ```

File Company.java

```
import purchase.Employee;
public class Company
{
  public static void main(String arg[ ])
  {
    Employee e = new Employee( );
    System.out.println("Age = " + e.age);
  }
}
```

Will the file Company.java compile? YES or NO. Give reason, if No.

21. Consider the following code:

```
class A
{
  void method(int x)
  { System.out.println("x = " + x); }
}
class B extends A
{
  void method(int y)
  { System.out.println("y = " + y); }
  void method(String s)
  { System.out.println("s = " + s); }
  public static void main(String args[ ])
  {
    A a1 = new A( );
    A a2 = new B( );
    a1.method(10);
    a2.method(20);
  }
}
```

What will be the output, when executed?

22. There are three classes that implement and **DataInput** and **DataOutput** interfaces. Two of them are **DataInputStream** and **DataOutputStream**. Which is the third one?

23. What output will the following program produce?

```
class Bits
{
  public static void main(String args[ ])
  {
    short s1 = 3;  // 0000 0011
    short s2 = 13; // 0000 1101
    s1 = (short) (s1 ^ s2);
    System.out.println("Result is " + s1);
  }
}
```

24. State the output of the following program:
```
class Condition
    {
        public static void main(String args[ ])
        {
            int x = 10;
            int y = 15;
            System.out.println((x>y)? 3.14 : 3));
        }
    }
```

25. Which of the classes in **java.io** package defines a method to delete a file?

26. Given a valid File object reference, we can create a new file using two classes defined in **java.io** package. One is **FileOutputStream** class. Which is the other one?

27. If raf is an instance of **RandomAccessFile**, how can we move the file pointer to the end of the file? Write the statement.

28. What will be the output of the following program when it is executed with the command line

    java Command Java is wonderful
```
class Command
    {
        public staitic void main(String args[ ])
        {
            for(int i = 1; i < args.length; i++)
            {
                System.out.print(args[i]);
                if( i != args.length )
                System.out.print(" ");
            }
            System.out.println(" ");
        }
    }
```

29. What will be the output of the following code snippet when combined with suitable declarations and run?
```
StringBuffer city = new StringBuffer("Madras");
StringBuffer string = new StringBuffer( );
string.append(new String(city));
string.insert(0, "Central ");
String.out.println(string);
```

30. Consider the following program code:
```
class Thread1 extends Thread
    {
        public void run( )
        {
            System.out.println("Begin");
            suspend( );
            resume( );
```

```
      System.out.println("End");
    }
  }
class ThreadTest
  {
    public static void main(String args[ ])
    {
      Thread1 T1 = new Thread1( );
      T1.start( );
    }
  }
```

On execution, what will be the output?

31. Consider the following application:

```
class Max
  {
    public static void main(String args[ ])
    {
      int max = 10;
      max(max, 20, 30);
      System.out.println(max);
    }
    static void max(int max, int x1, int x2)
    {
      if(x1 > x2)
      max = x1;
      else
      max = x2;
    }
  }
```

What value is printed out, when executed?

32. State the output of the following program:

```
class Recur
  {
    public static void main(String args[ ])
    {
      int Result = result(10);
      System.out.println("Result = " + Result);
    }
    static int result(int m)
    {
      if (m <= 2)
        return m;
      else
        return m + result(m-2);
    }
  }
```

33. Consider the class definition:

```
class Default
{
  public static void main(String args[ ])
  {
    int m;
    System.out.println("m is " + m);
  }
}
```

Will this code compile? YES or NO. Give reason, if No.

34. What is the output of the following program?

```
class Static
{
  static int m = 0;
  static int n = 0;
  public static void main(String args[ ])
  {
    int m = 10;
    int x = 20;
    {
      int n = 30;
      System.out.println("m + n = " + m + n);
    }
    x = m + n;
    System.out.println("x = " + x);
  }
}
```

35. Consider the following class definitions:

```
class Square
{
  private square( ) { }
  int area(int side)
  {
    return(side * side);
  }
}
class Constructor
{
  public static void main(String args[ ])
  {
    Square S1 = new Square( );
    int area = S1.area(10);
    System.out.println(area);
  }
}
```

Will the code above compile and run successfully. YES or NO. Give reason, if No.

36. Write a statement to draw a rounded rectangle with the following features:

    width = 200

    height = 100

    corner horizontal diameter = 20

    corner vertical diameter = 40

    Select a suitable upper-left corner of the rectangle.

37. Which line of the following HTML file contains an error?

    ```
    1.      < applet
    2.                      WIDTH = 400 HEIGHT = 200
    3.                      CODE = HelloJava.Class >
    4.      < param
    5.                      NAME = "string"
    6.                      VALUE = "Hello" >
    7.      </applet>
    ```

38. Give the output of the following program:

    ```java
    class MainString
    {
      public static void main(String args[ ])
      {
        StringBuffer s = new StringBuffer("String");
        if(s.length()>5) &&
                    (s.append("Buffer").equals("X")
                    ; // empty statement
        System.out.println(s);
      }
    }
    ```

39. What is the range of the value that can be assigned to a variable of type long?

40. Consider the following program:

    ```java
    class Number
    {
      int x;
      void store(Number num)
      {
        num.x++;
      }
    }
    class MainNumber
    {
      public static void main(String args[ ])
      {
        Number n = new Number( );
        n.x = 10;
        n.store(n);
        System.out.println(n.x);
      }
    }
    ```

    What is the output?

41. Given the code:

```java
class Continue
{
  public static void main(String args[ ])
  {
  int m = 0;
  loop1: for(int i=0; i<10; i++)
    loop2: for(int j=0;j<10;j++)
      loop3: for(int k=0;k<10;k++)
      {
        System.out.println(++m);
        if( (k%10) == 0)
          continue loop2;
      }
  }
}
```

What is the last value printed?

42. Can an abstract method by declared final? YES or NO. If NO, give reason.

43. Can an abstract method be declared static? YES or NO. If NO, give reason.

44. Consider the following **try ... catch** block:

```java
class TryCatch
{
  public static void main(String args[ ])
  {
    try
    {
      double x = 0.0;
      throw(new Exception("Thrown"));
      return;
    }
    catch(Exception e)
    {
      System.out.println("Exception caught");
      return;
    }
    finally
    {
      System.out.println("finally");
    }
  }
}
```

What will be the output?

45. Write a statement that would construct a 20 point bold Helvetica font.

ANSWERS

Part A: True/False Questions

1.	A	2.	B	3.	B	4.	A	5.	B
6.	A	7.	A	8.	A	9.	B	10.	B
11.	B	12.	B	13.	A	14.	B	15.	A
16.	B	17.	A	18.	B	19.	A	20.	B
21.	B	22.	B	23.	A	24.	B	25.	B
26.	B	27.	B	28.	A	29.	A	30.	B
31.	A	32.	B	33.	A	34.	A	35.	B
36.	B	37.	A	38.	B	39.	B	40.	A
41.	B	42.	A	43.	A	44.	B	45.	B
46.	A	47.	B	48.	B	49.	A	50.	B
51.	B	52.	A	53.	B	54.	B	55.	A
56.	B	57.	B	58.	B	59.	A	60.	B

Part B: Multiple-choice Questions

1.	C	2.	D & E	3.	B & D	4.	D	5.	C
6.	C	7.	A, B, & C	8.	C	9.	B	10.	C
11.	B	12.	B & C	13.	D	14.	C & E	15.	D & E
16.	C & B	17.	E	18.	A & C	19.	A	20.	B
21.	A	22.	B	23.	D	24.	C	25.	C
26.	B	27.	C & D	28.	A, C, & E	29.	C	30.	D
31.	D	32.	D	33.	C	34.	A, D & E	35.	A & C
36.	B, C & E	37.	B, C & D	38.	B	39.	D	40.	B & C
41.	C	42.	C	43.	C	44.	B & C	45.	B & C
46.	B, D & E	47.	D	48.	B, C, E & F	49.	B, D, E & F	50.	A, D, & F
51.	E	52.	A, D & E	53.	A, D, & E	54.	A, B, C & D	55.	C
56.	B, D & E	57.	B	58.	C	59.	C	60.	B
61.	E	62.	B, C & E	63.	B & E	64.	D	65.	C
66.	C	67.	A & C	68.	D	69.	C	70.	D
71.	A, D & E	72.	E	73.	D	74.	B, D, E & F	75.	D
76.	B	77.	C	78.	B, C & E	79.	D	80.	C
81.	A & C	82.	A & C	83.	A, B, C & D	84.	C	85.	A, C & E

Part C: Short answer Questions

1.	0	2.	161
3.	x = x < 0? −x :x;	4.	n = 40; is unreachable
5.	200	6.	six : 33
7.	null	8.	s =
9.	(i = 10) is the problem	10.	10
11.	a is 5	12.	No output
13.	m is 0	14.	No output; Infinite loop

15. retrun (x = = y)? x+y : 0;
16. import EDU.Student.Test;
17. abstract
18. No; The package definition must come first
19. No; The static method trying to invoke a non-static method
20. No; The field **age** in the Employee class should be public
21. x = 10; y = 20
22. RandomAccessFile class
23. Result is 14
24. Result = 3.0
25. File class
26. RandomAccessFile class
27. raf.seek(raf.length(( );
28. is wonderful
29. Central Madras
30. Begin
31. 10
32. 30
33. No
34. m + n = 40; x = 10
35. No
36. drawRoundRect(10,10,200,100,20,40);
37. Line 3
38. StringBuffer
39. -2^{63} to $2^{63} - 1$
40. 11
41. 100
42. No
43. No
44. Exception caught finally
45. new Font("Monospaced", Font.BOLD,20);

Appendix **K**

Points to Remember

K.1 General

1. It is important that the name of the file match the name of the class and the extension be **.java.**

2. All functions in Java must be members of some class.

3. Member functions are called methods in Java.

4. Creating two methods with the same name but different arguments is called method overloading.

5. Method overloading allows set of methods with very similar purpose to be given the same name.

6. When a method makes an unqualified reference to another member of the same class, there is an implicit reference to **this** object.

7. Java does not provide a default constructor if the class defines a constructor of its own.

8. When present, **package** must be the first noncomment statement in the file.

9. The **import** statement must follow the **package** statement but must also precede all other noncomment statements.

10. The full method or class name, including the package name, must be used when two imported packages contain a method or class with the same name.

11. Due to security reasons, it is not possible to perform file I/O operations from an applet.

12. When a simple type is passed to a method, it is done by use of call-by-value. Objects are passed by use of call-by-reference.

13. It is illegal to refer to any instance variables inside of a **static** method.

14. All command-line arguments are passed as strings. We must therefore convert numeric values to their original forms manually.

15. A class member declared as private will remain private to its class. It is not accessible by any code outside its class, including subclasses.

16. The star form of import statement may increase compile time. It will be good practice to explicitly name the classes that we want to use rather than importing whole packages.

17. Interfaces add most of the functionality that is required for many applications which would normally require the use of multiple inheritance in C++.

18. When we implement an interface method, it must be declared as **public**.

19. If a **finally** block is associated with a try, the **finally** will be executed upon conclusion of the **try**.

20. Java uses pointers (addresses) internally to store references to objects, and for elements of any array of objects. However, these pointers are not available for use by programmers.

21. We cannot overload methods with differences only in their return type.

22. When a method with the same signature occurs in both the super class and its subclass, the method in the subclass overrides the method in the super class.

23. Every constructor must invoke its super class constructor in its first statement. Otherwise, the default constructor of the super class will be called.

24. A class marked as **final** cannot be inherited.

25. A method marked **final** cannot be overridden.

26. Subclasses of an abstract class that do not provide an implementation of an abstract method, are also abstract.

 ## K.2 C/C++ Related

27. A Java string is not implemented as a null-terminated array of characters as it is in C and C++.

28. Most of the Java operators work much the same way as their C/C++ equivalents except for the addition of two new operators, >>> and ^.

29. The comparison operators in Java return a Boolean **true** or **false** but not the integer one or zero.

30. The modulo division may be applied to floating point values in Java. This is not permitted in C/C++.

31. The control variable declared in **for** loop is visible only within the scope of the loop. But in C/C++, it is visible even after the loop is exited.

32. Methods cannot be declared with an explicitly void argument list, as done in C++.

33. Java methods must be defined within the class. Separate definition is not supported.

34. Unlike C/C++, Java checks the range of every subscript and generates an error message when it is violated.

35. Java does not support the destructor function. Instead, it uses the **finalize** method to restore the memory.

36. Java does not support multiple inheritance.

37. C++ has no equivalent to the **finally** block of Java.

38. Java is more strictly typed than C/C++ languages. For example, in Java, we cannot assign a floating point value to an integer (without explicit type casting).

39. Unlike C/C++ which allow the size of an integer to vary based on the execution environment, Java data types have a strictly defined range and does not change with the environment.

40. Java does not support pointers.

41. Java supports labelled **break** and labelled continue statements.

42. **break** has been designed for use only when some sort of special situation occurs. It should not be used to provide the normal means by which a loop is terminated.

43. The use of **final** to a variable is similar to the use of **const** in C/C++.

44. Overridden methods in Java are similar to virtual functions in C++.

45. Java does not have a generalized console input method that parallels the **scanf** in C or **cin** in C++.

46. Integer types are always signed in Java. There are no unsigned qualifiers.

47. Java does not define escape codes for vertical tab and the bell character.

48. In Java multidimensional arrays are created as arrays of arrays. We can define variable size arrays of arrays.

Appendix **L**

Common Coding Errors

This appendix lists some coding errors that Java programmers are likely to make.

1. File name is not identical to the class name (in both spelling and case).
2. File not ending with **.Java** extension for a file containing the **main** method class (or applet's class definition).
3. Not ending a Java statement with a semicolon.
4. Providing spaces between the symbols of the operators = =, < =, > =, and !=.
5. Using operators < =, > =, and != as = <, = > and =!.
6. Using the operators = in the place of = =.
7. Using the keywords as identifiers.
8. Not properly matching the braces.
9. Placing a semicolon after the condition in an **if** statement or a **while** statement.
10. Using uppercase letters while writing a keyword.
11. Not initializing the variables properly.
12. Using floating point values in relational expressions.
13. Applying increment or decrement operator or an expression other than a simple variable.
14. Using commas instead of semicolons in a **for** header.
15. Placing a semicolon immediately after a **for** header.
16. Defining a method outside the braces of a class definition.
17. Not providing the return type in a method definition.

18. Not matching the type of the value returned by a method with its **return** type declared.
19. Placing a semicolon immediately after a method header.
20. Declaring a method parameter as a local variable inside the method.
21. Defining a method inside another method.
22. Attempting to assign a value to a **final** variable.
23. Using the same variable name in both the outer and inner blocks of a program.
24. Changing only return types for method overloading.
25. Referring to an element outside the array bounds.
26. Declaring a return type for a constructor method.
27. A class trying to access a **private** variable of another class.
28. Using **this** reference explicitly in a static method.
29. Trying to access an instance variable or an instance method inside a static method.
30. Assigning an object of a superclass to a subclass reference (without a cast).
31. Not using **super** method call as a first statement in the subclass constructor.
32. Attempting to instantiate an object of an **abstract** class.
33. Not declaring explicitly a class as **abstract** when it contains one or more **abstract** methods.
34. Using the instance variable **length** instead of method **length( )** to determine the length of a string.
35. Using the method **length( )** instead of the instance variable **length** to determine the size of an array.
36. Using string objects to access **StringBuffer** methods that are not members of the class **String**.
37. Attempting to access a character that is outside the bounds of a string.
38. Using a lower case f in **TextField**.
39. Trying to catch the same type of exception in two different **catch** blocks associated with a particular **try** block.
40. Placing **catch (Exception e)** before other **catch** blocks. This should be the last in the list of catch blocks.
41. Placing a **catch** that catches a superclass object *before* a **catch** that catches an object of its subclass.
42. Opening an existing file for output, when, in fact, the user wants to preserve the file.
43. Not opening a file before attempting to reference it in a program.
44. Using an incorrect stream object to refer to a file.

Appendix **M**

Glossary of Java Terms

abstract class	A class that cannot be instantiated directly. Abstract classes exist so that subclasses can inherit variables and methods from them.
access control	A way to restrict access to classes, variables and methods.
API	Application Programming Interface. The Java API contains classes a programmer can use to build applications and applets.
applet	A Java program that is embedded in an HTML document and runs in the context of a Java-capable browser.
appletviewer	A tool created by SUN to run applets without a browser.
argument	A value that is sent to a method when the method is called.
array	A list of values of the same type. All values in an array have a common name.
ASCII	A standard set of values for representing text characters.
assignment expression	Assigns a value to a variable.
attribute	A specifier for an HTML tag (for example, code is an attribute of the <APPLET> tag
AWT	The Abstract Windowing Toolkit, or group of classes for writing programs with graphical user interfaces.
baseclass	A class from which another class inherits functionality. In java, a baseclass is often called a superclass.

bit	The smallest piece of data a computer understands. A bit can represent only two values, 0 or 1.
bitmap	A graphical image that is usually stored in a file.
Boolean	A value that can be either true or false.
Boolean expression	A Boolean expression evaluates to either true or false.
branching	When an execution jumps forward or backward in the program.
browser	A program used for reading, displaying, and interacting with objects on the World Wide Web.
byte	In Java, the byte is a data type, which is eight bits long.
bytecode	The machine-independent output of the Java compiler and input to the Java interpreter.
canvas	A applet component that can display graphics and text.
casting	Converting one type of value to another.
character	A value used in text. For example, the letters A–the digits 0–0 (when not used as mathematical values), spaces, and even tabs and carriage returns are all characters.
class	A collection of variables and methods that an object can have, or a template for building objects.
.class file	A file containing machine-independent Java bytecodes. The Java compiler generates .class files for the interpreter to read.
class variable	A variable allocated once per class. Class variables have global class scope and belong to the entire class instead of an instance.
client	A program that relies on services provided by another program called a server.
code	An attribute of the HTML <APPLET> tag that specifies the class to be loaded.
codebase	An attribute of the HTML <APPLET> tag that specifies the location of the classes to load.
comparison operators	Operators like = = (equals) and > (greater than) that compare two expressions, giving a result of true or false.
compiler	A language translator. A program that transforms source code into another format without executing the program.
concatenate	Adding one text string to the end of another.
conditional branching	When a program jumps to a different part of a program based on a certain condition being met.
configurable applet	An applet that the user can customise by supplying different parameters when writing the applet's tag in an HTML document.
constant	A value that never changes throughout the life of a program.
constructor	A method that is used to create an instantiation of a class.

control variable	The variable that a program evaluates to determine whether or not to perform an action. Control variables are used in loops, switch statements, and other similar programming constructs.
data field	The data that is encapsulated in an object.
data type	The type of value represented by a constant, variable, or some other program object. Java data types include the integer types byte, short, int, and long; the floating-point types float and double; the character type char; and the Boolean type boolean.
deadlock	Deadlock occurs when two or more threads are waiting for resources that they can't get.
derived class	A class that inherits from a base class.
dialog box	A special pop-up window that can present important information to the user or that requests information from the user. A dialog box is an object of Java's Dialog class.
doctags	Special symbols used by the javadoc tool to document Java packages and methods.
double	In Java, the double is a data type, which is 62 bits in length.
dynamic linking	When functions called within a program are associated with the program at runtime rather than at compile time.
encapsulation	A way to contain data and methods in a class so that methods and variables may be added, changed, or deleted without requiring the code that uses the class to change.
exception	A signal that something has happened to stop normal execution of a program, usually an error.
exception handler	Code that responds to and attempts to recover from an exception.
expression	A line of program code that can be reduced to a value or that assigns a value.
extends	A keyword used to make one class a subclass of another, for example, class subclass extends superclass.
field	A data object encapsulated in a class.
final	A modifier that prevents subclass definition, makes variables constant, and prevents a subclass from overriding a method.
finalize	A method that is called when there are no further references to an object and it is no longer needed. This method releases resources and does any other necessary cleanup that Java does not handle during garbage collection.
float	In Java, the float is a data type, which is thirty-two bits long.
floating point	A value with both whole number (including zero) and fractional parts.
font	A set of characters of the same style.

frame window	A special pop-up window that can be displayed from an applet. A frame window is an object of Java's Frame class.
GIF	One type of data format for storing graphical images on disk.
GUI	Stands for Graphical User Interface. It is pronounced like "gooey".
high-level language	A computer language that isolates the programmer from the intricate details of programming a computer. Java is a high-level language.
HotJava	A Java-capable browser from Javasoft.
hspace	An attribute of the HTML <APPLET> tag that specifies the amount of horizontal space(to the left and right) between the applet and the text on the page.
HTML	Hypertext Markup Language, the language used to create Web pages.
identifier	A symbol that represents a program object.
index	The same as a subscript. Used to identify a specific array element.
infinite loop	A loop that cannot stop executing because its conditional expression can never be true.
inheritance	A property of object-oriented languages where a class inherits the methods and variables of more general classes.
initialise	Set the starting state of a program object. For example, you should initialise variables to a value before you attempt to use them in comparisons and other operations.
instance	A concrete representation of a class or object. A class can have many instances.
instance variable	A variable allocated once per instance of a class.
instantiate	To create a concrete object from a class "template". New objects are instantiated with new.
int	In Java, the int is a data type, which is 32 bits long.
integer	A whole-number value.
interface	A collection of methods and variables that other classes may implement. A class that implements an interface provides implementations for all the methods in the interface.
Internet	A huge world-spanning network of computers that can be used by anyone with a suitable connection.
Interpreter	A program that performs both language translation and program execution. java is the Java interpreter.
java	The program used to invoke the Java interpreter, which executes Java programs.

.java file	A file containing Java source code.
javac	A command for running the Java compiler.
javac_g	A command for running a non-optimized version of the Java compiler. The javac_g command can be used with debuggers, such as jdb.
Java-capable browser	A Web browser that can run Java applets. Also called a Java-enabled or Java-enhanced browser.
javadoc	A command that is used to generate API-style HTML documentation automatically.
javah	A command that can create C include files and stubs from a Java .class file. The resulting C files allow C code to access parameters passed from Java, return values to Java, and access Java class variables.
javah_g	A command that can create C include files and stubs with debug information from a Java .class file.
javap	A command that disassembles Java .class files.
JavaScript	A Java-based scripting language.
jdb	The Java debugger.
JDBC	A database access API from JavaSoft that allows developers to access databases with Java programs.
JDK	The Java Developers Kit.
literals	Values, such as a number or text string, that are written literally as part of program code. The opposite of a literal is a variable.
local applet	An applet that is stored on the local computer system, rather than somewhere else on the Internet.
logical expression	An expression that results in a value of true or false. (see Boolean expression)
logical operators	Operators like && (AND) and || (OR) that enable you to create logical expressions that yield true or false results.
long	In Java, the long is a data type which is 64 bits in length and can hold truly immense numbers.
loop	A program construct that enables a program to perform repetitive tasks.
method	A routine that belongs to a class.
modifier	A Java keyword that is applied to a method or variable declaration to control access, control execution, or provide additional information.
modular programming	Breaking a large program down into a number of functions, each of which performs a specific, well-defined task.

multidimensional array	An array that must be accessed using more than one subscript.
multiple inheritance	When a class simultaneously inherits methods and fields directly from more than one base class.
multitasking	Running more than one computer program concurrently (see multithread).
multithreaded	Having multiple threads of execution so that parts of a program can execute concurrently.
native methods	Methods that are declared in Java with the keyword native but are implemented in another language. Usually, native methods are written to do something that the Java API does not already do, to interact with a particular computer's hardware or operating system or to improve performance. Since native methods are not portable across platforms, applets cannot contain native methods.
nesting	When one program block is placed within another program block.
numerical expression	A combination of numbers, variables, or constants with operators.
Oak	The original name of the Java programming language.
object	An instantiation of a class.
object-oriented programming	A programming paradigm that treats program elements as objects that have data fields and functions that act on the data fields. The three main characteristics of OOP are encapsulation, inheritance, and the polymorphism.
one-dimensional array	An array that's set up like a list and requires only one subscript to identify a value contained in the array.
operator precedence	Determines the order in which mathematical operations are performed.
override	To replace a method inherited from a superclass.
package	A Java keyword used to assign the contents of a file to a package. Packages are Java's mechanism for grouping classes. Packages simplify reuse, and they are very useful for large projects.
parameter	A value that is passed to an applet or method. In the case of an applet, the parameters are defined in the HTML document, using the <PARAM> tag.
pass by reference	When an argument is passed into a method by passing a copy of the value. In this case, if you change the argument in the method, you also change the original.
pass by value	When an argument is passed into a method by passing a copy of the value. In this case, changing the copy doesn't affect the original value.
pixel	The smallest dot that can appear on the screen.
platform-neutral language	A programming language that can be used on any computer, regardless of the computer's operating system.

point	A unit of measurement of a font's height. One point is equal to 1/72 of an inch.
polymorphism	In object-oriented programming, this is the ability for a new object to implement the base functionality of a parent object in a new way.
protocol handler	A java routine that interprets a protocol, generally for a browser.
radio buttons	A group of checkboxes in which only one checkbox can be selected at a time.
remote applet	An applet that is stored on another computer and which must be downloaded to the local computer over the Internet.
Runnable interface	An interface that allows a class the ability to run in a distinct thread without being a subclass of Thread.
runtime exception	An exception thrown by the system in response to unexpected problem when a program is running. An example would be the exception generated when an applet attempts to perform a division by zero.
scope	Defines where a method or variable is visible. A variable defined in a method is visible only.
server	A computer system that supplies services to another computer called client.
short	In Java, the short is a data type which is sixteen bits in length.
single inheritance	When a class inherits methods and fields directly from only one baseclass.
spaghetti code	Program code that keeps jumping from one place to another in the program without any apparent organisation.
standalone application	In the context of the Java language, an pan that doesn't need to be embedded in an HTML document. The opposite of an applet.
Streams	Controlled flows of data from one source to another. Java supplies several classes to create and manage streams. Classes that handle input data are derived from class InputStream, and classes that handle output data are derived from class OutputStream.
structured programming	A style of programming in which the program code is divided into logically structured chunks of code.
stub	Part of the interface between Java code and a native method. A stub allows a native method to access Java parameters, access Java class variables, and return data to Java.
subclass	A class that inherits methods and variables from another class. The statement class SubClass extends SuperClass means that SubClass is a subclass of SuperClass.

subscript	A subscript is a number that identifies the element of an array in which a value is stored. A subscript is sometimes called an index.
superclass	A generalization of another class. X is a superclass of Y if Y inherits variables and methods from X.
symbolic constant	A word that represents a value in a program.
synchronized	A Java keyword that prevents more than one thread from executing inside a method at once.
tag	A command in an HTML document that identifies the type of document component.
thread	A single path of execution that is a subprocess of the main process. All applications have at least one thread, which represents the main program. An application can create additional threads to handle multiple tasks concurrently.
top-down programming	A style of programming that divides tasks up into general modules. At the top level of the program are only the general tasks, whereas, as we work out way deeper into the program code, the programming becomes more and more detailed.
two-dimensional array	An array that is set up much like a table, with a specific number of columns and rows.
type cast	Convert one type of value to another.
unconditional branching	When program execution jumps to a new part of the program regardless of any conditions.
unicode	A new set of standard values for representing the symbols used in text. The unicode character set is much larger than the ASCII character set and allows for foreign-language symbols.
unsigned	A value that can only be positive. This is the opposite of signed. Unsigned numbers are not used in Java programming.
URL	Stands for Uniform Resource Locator, which is an Internet address.
variable	A value that can change as often as necessary during the execution of a program. Variables are always represented by symbolic names.
virtual machine	An abstract, logical model of a computer used to execute Java bytecodes. A Java virtual machine has an instruction set, registers, a stack, a heap, and a method area.
VRML	Virtual Reality Modelling Language.
vspace	An attribute of the HTML <APPLET> tag that specifies the amount of vertical space above and below the applet and the text on the page.
Web browser	An application used to access the Internet's World Wide Web.
World Wide Web	The graphical part of the Internet.

Appendix **N**

Projects

I. The Calculator Application

Learning Objectives

The development process of the Calculator application will aid the students to:

- Create a simple Java console application
- Understand the object-oriented concepts of inheritance, polymorphism and data hiding
- Create application which request input from users, validate, process the input received and provide desired output
- Use features of java like type conversion, interfaces, inheriting interfaces, looping and branching, packages and I/O classes.

Understanding the Calculator Application

The Calculator application performs both basic and scientific operations. The application provides user an option to choose between the basic mode and scientific mode. Based on the option selected by the user, the application calls the corresponding class and the user can perform various mathematical operations provided in the class. There is a base class in the application which contains all the methods for calculation, basic as well as scientific. The application validates the user input also and provides appropriate messages when wrong input is given by the user.

Creating the Calculator Application

To create the Calculator application, 5 java files were created. First, an interface iCalc, with the file name "iCalc.java" is created. Then, we create the base class Calculate, with the file name "Calculate.java" which contains all the methods for calculation. After the base class, two classes, Calculator and ScientificCalculator, with the file names as "Calculator.java" and "ScientificCalculator.java" are created. These classes call the methods defined in the base class Calculate. Class Calculator contains an instance of Class Calculate, whereas Class ScientificCalculator inherits Class Calculate and then uses its methods. After creation of all the above classes, a main class UseCalculate is created, with the file name "UseCalculate.java" which provides creates instances of Class Calculator or Class ScientificCalculator, based on the option selected by user.

Creating the Java Files

The iCalc Interface (iCalc.java)

Interface iCalc provides the structure of methods which can be used in any calculator application. It contains the following two methods:

- doCalculation(): Declares a method for providing methods for calculation.
- getResult(): Declares a method for extracting the result of the calculation.

The Calculate Class (Calculate.java)

Class Calculate contains the business logic of the Calculator application. It contains the methods for calculation of various mathematical operations like addition, divide and tangent. Class Calculate uses interfaces by implementing Interface iCalc. The class contains following methods:

Method	Description
Calculate()	Default constructor for the class without any arguments.
Calculate(Double dblNum, char cOperator)	Constructor containing two arguments. This constructor is used for scientific calculations.
Calculate(int iFirstNum, char cOperator, int iSecondNum)	Constructor containing three arguments. This constructor is used for basic calculations.
doCalculation()	Calculates the result based on the numbers and operator inputted by the user. Overriding the doCalculation function.of iCalc interface.
getResult()	Prints the result of calculation. Overriding the getResult function.of iCalc interface.
checkSecondNum()	In case of division of two numbers, it checks for value 0 in the second number entered.
checkInt()	Checks if basic calculation is performed.
checkDouble()	Checks if scientific calculation is performed.

The Calculator Class (Calculator.java)

Class Calculator calculates basic operations, namely, addition, subtraction, multiplication and division of two numbers. The class provides option to user to enter first number to be calculated, then the operation to be performed and then, the second number to be used for calculation. The input is received using java class BufferedReader. Class calculator creates an object of Class Calculate, by calling its constructor by passing three arguments, First Number, Operator and Second Number. After the creation of object of Class Calculate, doCalculation() method is called followed by getResult() method, which presents the result of calculation to the user.

Class Calculator also uses a do-while loop to provide an option to the user perform multiple calculations, till the user does not indicate the end of processing by typing 'n'.

The ScientificCalculator Class (ScientificCalculator.java)

Class Calculator performs calculation of scientific operations, namely, sine, cosine, tangent and log of a number. The class provides option to user to enter the operation to be performed and the number to be calculated. The input is received using java class BufferedReader. Class ScientificCalculator inherits Class Calculate to use its methods. The class passes the user entered values to Class Calculate by calling its constructor having two arguments, Operator and the Number. The class calls doCalculation() method which is followed by getResult() method, which shows the result of calculation to the user.

Class ScientificCalculator also uses a do-while loop to provide an option to the user perform multiple calculations, till the user does not indicate the end of processing by typing 'n'.

The UseCalculator Class (UseCalculator.java)

Class Calculator provides two options to the user—Basic or Scientific. Based on the option entered by the user, the class creates an instance of Class Calculator for Basic operations or an instance of Class ScientificCalculator for scientific operations.

Class UseCalculator also uses a do-while loop to provide an option to the user perform multiple calculations, till the user does not indicate the end of processing by typing 'n'.

Generating the Class Files

Command for generating the class files:

```
javac <classname.java>
```

The steps for generating the class files for Calculator application are:

- Place all java files in a directory named as "Calculator".
- In the command prompt, go to the directory where the java files are stored for the Calculator application.
- Compile the following java files in the sequence given below using the command for compiling the java files:
  - iCalc.java
  - Calculate.java
  - Calculator.java
  - ScientificCalculator.java
  - UseCalculator.java

Working with the Calculator Application

The steps for working with the Calculator application are:

- In the command prompt, go to the parent directory of "Calculator" directory which contains the class files for Calculator application.
- Enter the following command to run the Calculator application:

    ```
    java Calculator.UseCalculator
    ```

- Enter 'b' (for Basic operations) or 's' (for scientific operations) depending on the operations to be performed.
- If 'b' is entered, the following input is to be entered by the user:
  - First Number
  - Operator
  - Second Number
- The result is shown on the command prompt based on the above values.
- Enter 'y' to continue or 'n' to discontinue using the application.
- If 's' is entered, the following input is to be entered by the user:
  - Operator
  - Number
- The result is shown on the command prompt based on the above values.
- Enter 'y' to continue or 'n' to discontinue using the application.

Code for the Calculator Application

iCalc.java

— Interface iCalc represents the basic methods for the Calculate class
— Creates Interface Structure
— Can be used for creating any class which would do any sort of calculations

---

```java
// Adds the Interface to the Package
package Calculator;
//Interface Definition
interface iCalc
{
    public void doCalculation();
    public void getResult();
}
```

Calculate.java

— Class Calculate has all methods for calculation as required by any Calculator classes
— Implements an interface iCalc

```java
// Adds the Class to the Package
package Calculator;
// Class Definition
class Calculate implements iCalc
{
    private char Operator;
    private int  iFNum, iSNum;
    private Double dblNumber=new Double(0);
    private Double dblResult=new Double(0);
    private int iResult=0;
    private boolean typeDouble=false;
    private boolean typeInt=false;
    // Defines a constructor for scientific calculations
    public Calculate()
    {}
    public Calculate(Double dblNum, char cOperator)
    {
        dblNumber=dblNum;
        Operator=cOperator;
        typeDouble=true;
    }
    // Defines a constructor for basic calculations
    public Calculate(int iFirstNum, char cOperator, int iSecondNum)
    {
        iFNum=iFirstNum;
        iSNum=iSecondNum;
        Operator=cOperator;
        typeInt=true;
    }
    // Calculates the Result based on the operator selected by the user
    public void doCalculation()
    {
        iResult=0;
        dblResult=0.0;
        switch (Operator)
        {
            case '+':
```

```
                checkInt();
                iResult = iFNum + iSNum;
                break;
case '-':
                checkInt();
                iResult = iFNum - iSNum;
                break;
case '*':
                checkInt();
                iResult = iFNum * iSNum;
                break;
case '/':
                checkInt();
                if(!checkSecondNum())
                {
                        iResult = iFNum / iSNum;
                        break;
                }
case 'S':
case 's':
                checkDouble();
                dblResult = Math.sin(dblNumber);
                break;
case 'C':
case 'c':
                checkDouble();
                dblResult = Math.cos(dblNumber);
                break;
case 'T':
case 't':
                checkDouble();
                dblResult = Math.tan(dblNumber);
                break;
case 'L':
case 'l':
                checkDouble();
                dblResult = Math.log(dblNumber);
                break;
default:
                iResult=0;
                dblResult=0.0;
                System.out.println("***Operation Not Available. Please
```

```
                           select any of the available options.***");
                    break;
        }
}

// Displays the result of calculation to the user
public void getResult()
{
    if(typeInt)
    {
        System.out.println("The result is: " + iResult);
    }
    else if(typeDouble)
    {
        System.out.println("The result is: " + dblResult);
    }
}

// Checks for zero
public boolean checkSecondNum()
{
    if(iSNum==0)
    {
        System.out.println("Zero Not allowed");
        System.exit(0);
        return true;
    }
    else
    {
        return false;
    }
}

public void checkInt()
{
    if(!typeInt)
    {
        iResult=0;
        System.out.println("***Operation Not Available. Please select any of
                           the available options.***");
        System.exit(0);
    }
}

public void checkDouble()
{
```

```
        if(!typeDouble)
        {
            dblResult=0.0;
            System.out.println("***Operation Not Available. Please select any of
                                the available options.***");
            System.exit(0);
        }
    }
}
```

Calculator.java

— Class Calculator Performs basic operations like Add, Substract, Multiply, Division for two numbers
— Uses class Calculate by creating its objects and then calling its methods

```java
// Adds the Class to the Package
package Calculator;
// Imports Required Packages
import java.io.*;
// Class Definition
class Calculator
{
    public void Calc() throws java.io.IOException
    {
        boolean next;
        do
        {
            Integer iFirstNumber=new Integer(0);
            Integer iSecondNumber=new Integer(0);
            BufferedReader buffer
            = new BufferedReader(new InputStreamReader(System.in));
            // Gets User Input
            System.out.println("Please enter First Number: ");
            System.out.flush();
            try
            {
                iFirstNumber=Integer.parseInt(buffer.readLine());
            }
            catch(NumberFormatException e)
            {
                System.out.println("***Please provide numeric values.***");
                System.exit(0);
            }
```

```java
        System.out.println("Please enter the Operation (Add : +, Minus : -,
                        Product : *, Divide : /):");
        System.out.flush();
        String option=buffer.readLine();
        System.out.println("Please enter Second Number: ");
        System.out.flush();
        try
        {
            iSecondNumber=Integer.parseInt(buffer.readLine(),10);
        }
        catch(NumberFormatException e)
        {
            System.out.println("***Please provide numeric values.***");
            System.exit(0);
        }
        if(option.length()==1)
        {
            // Creates Calculate Class Instance
            Calculate c= new
            Calculate(iFirstNumber,option.charAt(0),iSecondNumber);
            // Calls the class methods
            c.doCalculation();
            c.getResult();
        }
        else
        {
            System.out.println("***Operation Not Available. Please select
                        any of the available options.***");
        }
        // Checks if the user would like to compute again
        System.out.println("Would you like to calculate again (y/n)?");
        System.out.flush();
        char response=(char)buffer.read();
        if ((response=='y') || (response=='Y'))
        {
            next=false;
        }
        else
        {
            next=true;
        }
    }
    while (!next);
```

```
        }

}

```

ScientificCalculator.java

— Class ScientificCalculator Performs scientific calculations like Sine, Cosine, Tangent and Log of a number
— Inherits class Calculate
— Methods of Super class Calculate can be directly called by using the object of this Sub class ScientificCalculator

---

```java
// Adds the Class to the Package
package Calculator;
// Imports Required Packages
import java.io.*;
// Class Definition
class ScientificCalculator extends Calculate
{
    char Operator;
    Double dblNumber = new Double(0);
    ScientificCalculator(){}
    ScientificCalculator(double dblNumber,char Operator)
    {
        // Calls Super Class Constructor
        super(dblNumber,Operator);
        this.Operator=Operator;
        this.dblNumber=dblNumber;
    }
    public void Calc() throws java.io.IOException
    {
        boolean next;
        do
        {
            Double d=new Double(0);
            BufferedReader buffer
             = new BufferedReader(new InputStreamReader(System.in));
            // Gets User Input
            System.out.println("Please enter the Operation (Sine-s, Cosine-c,
                                Tangent-t, Log-l):");
            System.out.flush();
            String option=buffer.readLine();
```

```java
System.out.println("Please enter a Value: ");
System.out.flush();
try
{
    d=Double.valueOf(buffer.readLine());
}
catch(NumberFormatException e)
{
    System.out.println("***Please provide numeric values.***");
    System.exit(0);
}
if(option.length()==1)
{
    // Creates Class Instance
    ScientificCalculator sc=new ScientificCalculator(d,option.charAt(0));
    // Calls Super Class Methods
    sc.doCalculation();
    sc.getResult();
}
else
{
    System.out.println("***Operation Not Available. Please select
                        any of the available options.***");
}
// Checks if the user would like to compute again
System.out.println("Would you like to calculate again (y/n)?");
System.out.flush();
char aa=(char)buffer.read();
if ((aa=='y') || (aa=='Y'))
{
    next=false;
}
else
{
    next=true;
}
}
while (!next);
}
}
```

UseCalculator.java

— Class UseCalculator is the Main Class for the Calculator Application
— Provides options to the user: Basic or Scientific Calculator

```java
// Adds the Class to the Package
package Calculator;
// Imports Required Packages
import java.io.*;
// Class Definition
class UseCalculator
{
    public static void main(String[] args) throws java.io.IOException
    {
        BufferedReader buffer
        = new BufferedReader(new InputStreamReader(System.in));
        // Gets User Input
        System.out.println("Select the Calculator: Basic - B or Scientific - S.");
        System.out.flush();
        String option=buffer.readLine();
        if(option.length()==1)
        {
            if (option.equals("B") || option.equals("b"))
            {
                // Calls the Basic Calculator Application
                Calculator c=new Calculator();
                c.Calc();
            }
            else if(option.equals("S") || option.equals("s"))
            {
                // Calls the Scientific Calculator Application
                ScientificCalculator sc=new ScientificCalculator();
                sc.Calc();
            }
            else
            {
                System.out.println("***Please enter option 'B' or 'S'.***");
            }
        }
        else
        {
            System.out.println("***Please enter option 'B' or 'S'.***");
        }
    }
}
```

EXERCISES

1. Write the java code to calculate scientific operations like asin, atan and acos in the Calculator application.
2. Write the java code to use both, basic and scientific operations available in Class Calculate using multiple inheritance.

II. The FontAnimation Application

Learning Objectives

The development process of the FontAnimation application will help the students to:

- Create a simple Java based GUI application
- Understand the concept of applet programming
- Implement Graphics and multi-threading programming concepts.

Understanding the FontAnimation Application

The FontAnimation application presents the concepts of Applets, Graphics and multi-threading in java. The application creates an applet which draws a text and keeps on increasing its font size to a defined maximum limit and then reduces the font size back to the original size. The process is dynamic and continuous. The user is provided options to change the text and text color. Events and listeners have also been used in the application.

Creating the FontAnimation Application

Class FontAnimation uses Abstract Window Toolkit (AWT) controls to add textfields and buttons to provide options to users for dynamically changing the text and its color, while running the applet. To create the FontAnimation application, create a file named FontAnimation.java which inherits Applet and implements Listener ActionListener which listens to actions performed using JButton control.

Creating the Java File

The FontAnimation Class (FontAnimation.java)

Class FontAnimation inherits applet and uses thread programming to dynamically change the text size and its color. It contains the following methods:

- init(): init() Is a lifecycle method of applet and is used to initialize the applet object. Adds controls to the applet and registers the ActionListener for JButton control.

- actionPerformed(): Method of Listener ActionListener and is called on the click of JButton control. The method contains the code for getting the user input, namely, text and the text color properties and applying the user-entered values to the initial values. After updating the text, applet is painted again to show the changes made.
- paint(): Draws the text and sets its color and uses threads to continuously change the size of the text.

Generating the Class Files

The steps for generating the class file for FontAnimation application are:

- Place the FontAnimation.java file in the required directory.
- In the command prompt, go to the directory where the java file is stored.
- Compile the file using the command for compiling the java files:

```
javac FontAnimation.java
```

Creating the HTML File

To use an applet, an HTML file has to be created which will call the Java Applet. To add Class FontAnimation to FontAnimation.html file, HTML tag <APPLET> is used in which the code attribute will contain the value "FontAnimation.class".

Working with the FontAnimation Application

The steps for working with the FontAnimation application are:

- In the command prompt, go to the directory containing the class files for FontAnimation.
- Enter the following command to run the Calculator application:

```
appletviewer FontAnimation.html
```

- The applet will be displayed with the default text as "Hello" and color as "black".
- The user can change the text and Red, Green and Blue values for color of the text. On clicking button "Apply", the text changes according to the user entered values.
- During the running of the applet, the text size will continuously increase and decrease.

Code for the FontAnimation Application

FontAnimation.java

```
import java.applet.*;
import java.awt.*;
import java.awt.event.*;
public class FontAnimation extends Applet implements ActionListener
{
```

```java
TextField text=new TextField(20);
TextField red=new TextField(20);
TextField gr=new TextField(20);
TextField blue=new TextField(20);
Button b1=new Button("Apply");
String str="Hello";
int size=10;
Font f;
boolean inc=true;
int r,g,b;
Color fcolor;
public void init()
{
    add(new Label("Enter Text to animate here"));
    add(text);
    add(new Label("Enter value for Red Color here"));
    add(red);
    red.setText("0");
    add(new Label("Enter value for Green Color here"));
    add(gr);
    gr.setText("0");
    add(new Label("Enter value for Blue Color here"));
    add(blue);
    blue.setText("0");
    add(b1);
    b1.addActionListener(this);
}
public void actionPerformed(ActionEvent e)
{
    if(e.getSource()==b1)
    {
        str=text.getText();
        if(str=="")
                str="Hello";
        r=Integer.parseInt(red.getText());
        g=Integer.parseInt(gr.getText());
        b=Integer.parseInt(blue.getText());
        fcolor=new Color(r,g,b);
        repaint();
    }
}
public void paint(Graphics g)
{
```

```
        f=new Font("Arial",Font.BOLD,size);
        g.setFont(f);
        g.setColor(fcolor);
        g.drawString(str,50,200);
        try
        {
             Thread.sleep(500);
        }
        catch(Exception e)
        {
             System.out.println(e.getMessage());
        }
        if(inc==true)
        {
             size+=10;
             if(size==100)
                      inc=false;
        }
        else
        {
             size-=10;
             if(size==10)
                      inc=true;
        }
        repaint();
    }
}
```

FontAnimation.html

```
<html>
<head>
<title>Applet Demonstrating Applet and Thread Programming in Java</title>
</head>
<body>
       <APPLET CODE=FontAnimation.class
       WIDTH=400 HEIGHT=800>
       </APPLET>
</body>
</html>
```

EXERCISE

1. Write the java code to add other graphics controls to an applet like line, rectangle and others.

Bibliography

1. Aaron E.Walsh, *Foundations of Java Programming for the World Wide Web*, IDG Books Worldwide, 1996.
2. Anuff Ed, *The Java Sourcebook*, John Wiley & Sons, 1996.
3. Au, Edith and Dave Makower, *Java Programming Basics*, MIS Press, 1996.
4. Balagurusamy, E., *Object-Oriented Programming with C++,* Tata McGraw-Hill, 1995.
5. Balagurusamy, E., *Programming in ANSI C,* Tata McGraw-Hill, 1992.
6. Bartlett, Leslie and Simkin, *Java Programming Explorer,* Coriolis Group Books, 1996.
7. Boone, Barry, *Java Essentials for C and C++ Programmers,* Addison Wesley Developers Press, 1996.
8. Daconta, Michael C., *Java for C/C++ Programmers,* John Wiley & Sons, 1996.
9. Davis, Stephen R., *Learn Java Now,* Microsoft Press, 1996.
10. December, John, *Presenting Java,* Sams.net, 1995.
11. Flanagan, D, *Java in a Nutshell,* O'Reilly & Associates, 1996.
12. Holzner, Steven, *Java Workshop Programming,* M & T Books, 1996.
13. Lemay, Laura and Charles L.Perkins, *Teach Yourself Java in 21 Days,* Sams.net, 1996.
14. Naughton, Patrick and Herbet Schildt, *Java: The Complete Reference, Osborne McGraw-Hill,* 1996.
15. Naughton, Patrick, *The Java Handbook,* Osborne McGraw-Hill, 1996.
16. Newman, Alexander, et al., *Using Java,* Que Corporation, 1996.
17. Norton, Peter and William Stanek, *Guide to Java Programming,* Sams.net, 1996.
18. Perry, Paul J., *Creating Cool Web Applets with Java,* IDG Books, 1996.
19. Sams.net, *Java Unleased,* 1996.
20. Siyam, Karanjit S., *Inside Visual J++,* New Riders, 1996.
21. Stout, Rick, *The World Wide Web,* Complete Reference, Osborne McGraw-Hill, 1996.
22. Tyma, Paul M., Gabriel Torok and Troy Downing, *Java Primer Plus,* Waite Group Press, 1996.
23. Walnum, Clayton, *Java by Example,* Que Corporation, 1996.

Index